Schooling the Symbolic Animal

Schooling the Symbolic Animal

Social and Cultural Dimensions of Education

Edited by Bradley A. U. Levinson

with Kathyrn M. Borman, Margaret Eisenhart, Michèle Foster, Amy E. Fox, and Margaret Sutton

ROWMAN & LITTLEFIELD PUBLISHERS, INC.
Lanham • Boulder • New York • Oxford

For my teachers

ROWMAN & LITTLEFIELD PUBLISHERS, INC.

Published in the United States of America
by Rowman & Littlefield Publishers, Inc.
A wholly owned subsidary of The Rowman & Littlefield Publishing Group, Inc.
4501 Forbes Boulevard, Suite 200, Lanham, Maryland 20706
www.rowmanlittlefield.com

PO Box 317
Oxford
OX2 9RU, UK

British Library Cataloguing in Publication Information Available

Library of Congress Cataloging-in-Publication Data

Schooling the symbolic animal : social and cultural dimensions of education / edited by
Bradley A. U. Levinson
    p. cm.
    Includes bibliographical references and index.
    ISBN 0-7425-0119-1 (alk. paper)—ISBN 0-7425-0120-5 (pbk. : alk. paper)
      1. Education—Social aspects. 2. Educational anthropology. I. Title: Social
and cultural dimensions of education. II. Levinson, Bradley A., 1963–

LC191 .S267 2000
306.43—dc21   00-040286

Printed in the United States of America

♾™ The paper used in this publication meets the minimum requirements of
American National Standard for Information Sciences—Permanence of Paper
for Printed Library Materials, ANSI/NISO Z39.48-1992.

Pages 397–398 are an extension of this copyright page.

Contents

Acknowledgments

I would like to thank, first and foremost, my colleagues who agreed to serve as section editors for this volume: Kathryn M. Borman, Margaret Eisenhart, Michèle Foster, Amy E. Fox, and Margaret Sutton. I enjoyed working together with them to select the best articles, make abridgements where necessary, and craft short essays for the novice in the field.

Choosing the articles for this volume was an imposing task, and we are sure to have left out a number of very fine scholars and readings. Considerations of cost and accessibility required us to pass over otherwise excellent articles in the field. We wished to present an alternative and a complement to other volumes in the area: a reader rooted in anthropology, yet extending beyond the topically or theoretically delimited readers already available. A few articles have been written or revised especially for this book, but most were published originally in another book or professional journal. Most have never been reprinted outside that original context. Significant abridgements have been indicated with ellipses. Meanwhile, we have preserved the original, androcentric language of earlier pieces, jarring as this may be to contemporary eyes. Our thanks to the publishers who have given permission to reprint those articles here (see pages 397–398 for exact references to original articles).

We also wanted to present a book that beginning and advanced students alike could appreciate. To that end, I sent out a query to a number of scholars who teach courses in the social and cultural foundations of education, asking for their syllabi and preferred readings. The input of these scholars—some of whom eventually became section editors and essayists here—was crucial to the formulation of this book, and I would like to acknowledge their help here: Robert Arnove, Richard Blot, Donna Deyhle, Amy Stambach, Hugh Mehan, Douglas Foley, Kathryn Anderson-Levitt, Kathryn Borman, Joyce Canaan, Margaret Eisenhart, Thomas Shaw, James

Collins, and Dorothy Holland. With their help, and the good work of the section editors, we have tried to couple accessible and original scholarly readings with framing essays that situate the readings historically and conceptually, and point to further possibilities for deeper study.

For their suggestions and editorial help with my own introduction, I would also like to thank Richard Blot, Wendy Gaylord, E. Doyle Stevick, Debra Unger, and Teresa Winstead, not to mention the many students who have taken my courses in Anthropology of Education at Augustana College and Indiana University. Most of the articles in this reader have been field-tested in that course.

Many thanks must go to Dean Birkenkamp of Rowman & Littlefield for having the confidence to nurse this project through its tentative stages. His patience, vision, and support have been steadfast. A hearty thanks also to Dean's editorial assistants, Rebecca Hoogs and Matt Boullioun, for their fine work.

Introduction

Whither the Symbolic Animal? Society, Culture, and Education at the Millennium

Bradley A. U. Levinson

The question I pose here interrogates the evolution of humankind: How are we unfolding, and what form will our individual capacities and our global society eventually take? Education, of course, provides an important key to the answer, and the fields comprising the interpretive social sciences provide important intellectual resources for understanding and improving education. This reader presents some of the very best work produced by the interpretive social sciences on the *social* and *cultural foundations of education*. My aim is to provide teachers and students with the basic conceptual tools to understand a variety of sociocultural dynamics that shape the educational process in its many dimensions. Such sociocultural understanding is especially crucial for designing educational experiences—forging "tools for conviviality," in Ivan Illich's (1973) rich phrase—worthy of the multicultural societies of the present and future. Therefore, this book aims to compose one small part of the answer to the question: Whither the symbolic animal?

By referring to human beings as the "symbolic animal," I call attention to the evolutionary dimension of human existence, the broad historical development of human communication and reproduction. As animals, we share an important biological legacy and an equally important ecological fate with the rest of the organic world. The evolutionary design of our bodies provides the most basic parameters for how we can and ought to be educated. Yet along with our physical shape, deeply rooted patterns of social exchange and community life evolved with the species as well. Clever but physically defenseless, early humans required complex forms of social coordination and tool use to survive (Keesing 1976; Lewin 1989; Wenke 1980). Language and culture thus emerged as distinctive adaptive traits in early human social cooperation. Eventually, the human mind became part and parcel of this unique sociocultural adaptation—a way of perceiving and thinking that relies on manipulating *symbols* to interpret and thus communicate about the world (Geertz 1973; Bruner 1996).

1

Conventionally, a symbol is defined as any tangible thing (a tree, a cloth, even the sound wave constituting a spoken word) that stands for, or signifies, something else. Human beings are above all great symbol makers and manipulators. As Bruner puts it (1996, 164), any human culture "seems to be a shared network of communal 'standings for'." We are perhaps the only species to regularly use symbols to understand and act upon the world, and we are probably the only species to systematically *transmit* the rules of symbol use to succeeding generations. And of course, unlike most other animals, we cannot rely on instinct alone to survive in the world. We must learn, or *acquire* the way of creating and using symbols. That is indeed the heart of education.[1]

The process of education thus can be construed broadly as humanity's unique methods of *acquiring*, *transmitting*, and *producing* knowledge for interpreting and acting upon the world. In the broadest sense, education underlies every human group's ability to adapt to its environment. Effective education allows a group to continually adapt and thereby reproduce the conditions of its existence. Yet amidst this group imperative, individuals develop their own educational repertoire from the cultural resources at their disposal. Through their creative practice, both constrained and enabled by the structures of social life (Giddens 1979), individuals may alter the very pattern and substance of "*social reproduction*" (Bruner 1996; Corsaro 1997). In this sense, education is often a balancing act between group interests and individual concerns.

In recent years, with the political and ecological fate of humanity growing ever more precarious, the social reproduction of any particular group and the self-expression of any particular individual must now be pursued under a global horizon. We are necessarily interconnected across vast reaches of time and space, and our species now requires an education that cultivates a vibrant sense of this interconnectedness. It is clear as we cross into the new millennium that education will play a crucial role in the global transformation of consciousness and identity necessary to sustain the human endeavor on Earth. In order to achieve a proper balance with the natural environment, in order to develop sane and life-affirming uses for new technologies, and—perhaps most important—in order to create a global order respectful of human difference and nurturing of compassionate sensibilities, we need an education that reflects and accommodates the multifaceted cultural basis of human activity. In short, we must find new ways to nourish the symbolic animal.

Such nourishment necessarily goes hand in hand with continuous inquiry and investigation, for how can we feed an animal whose behavior we hardly understand? The various fields of interpretive social science (Rabinow and Sullivan 1987) are ideally suited to researching how and why humans act the way they do. We might distinguish this interpretive approach from a conception of social science that is oriented toward explaining and ultimately predicting human behavior. Such "positivist" or "empiricist" research usually follows the assumptions and methods of the natural sciences. For many decades now, most of the social sciences have been characterized by a split between those who conduct positivist research and those who take a more interpretive approach. Most of the authors whose work we present in this book belong to the interpretive branch of anthropology, though some were trained primarily as philosophers, sociologists, historians, psychologists, or linguists. What they share is a concern to understand education as a *situated human activity* embedded in the flow of everyday social life, and therefore necessarily intertwined with political, economic, and cultural dimensions of society. With few exceptions, they draw on sustained analysis of this human activity, typically through the anthropological research method of *participant-observation* and interviewing called *ethnography* (Spradley and McCurdy 1997; Wolcott 1999). Ethnography refers to the process of documenting the lifeways of a social group (the written product of this research is also called ethnography). In this type of research, ethnographers tend to immerse themselves in a community or institution for long periods of time. They participate in the life of that community or institution, attempting to interpret patterns of behavior and eventually to understand the "native's point of view" (Geertz 1983).

Anthropologists are perhaps uniquely qualified to study the symbolic animal. Some of you may have seen an anthropologist on television digging for fossil remains of the earliest humans, or reconstructing the temples of a great city long since fallen into ruins. What does this have to do with education, you may ask? Actually, few people know that most anthropologists study neither fossils nor ruins. Called social or cultural anthropologists, they study contemporary living societies and cultures. Yet in studying these societies, anthropologists never lose sight of the past or of the great diversity of societies still in existence. In other words, anthropology is inherently *historical* and *comparative*. The writings in this volume examine education as a historically and contextually specific process, in the United States and elsewhere; taken together, the authors compare education within and across societies and cultures. Moreover, in their studies of contemporary societies, most anthropologists have a great deal to say about educational processes, especially in the formation of cultural identity and social competence (Levinson 1999). Some of these societies have no formal schools, but their educational traditions are nevertheless rich and compelling. Margaret Mead, perhaps the most famous anthropologist of this century, studied how children grew up in South Pacific island societies like Samoa and Manau. In the 1920s and 1930s, schools were hardly a part of these children's lives, but Mead (1964) compared their education to that conducted in U.S. schools, families, and communities (see section I).

Great debates have raged in the social sciences over how to define "society" and "culture," and my aim is not to resolve those debates here. Indeed, a discussion about society and culture runs through many of the articles in this volume. Provisionally, I use the term "society" to refer to an assemblage of interrelated human beings, "an aggregate of people who recurrently interact with one another" (Keesing 1976, 143). A society exists when a collection of human beings has identifiable and recognizable links with one another, and interacts in patterned ways. In that sense, it is true, we can today speak of a "global society," since virtually all human beings are now interlinked through the flow of information and commerce. Still, we can analyti-cally distinguish between such a global society and various other levels of human interrelatedness, such as national society, regional society, urban society, and neigh-borhood society—even the societies composing institutions, such as schools, churches, and businesses.

Now, social scientists and ordinary citizens alike tend to use the term "culture" to refer to many of these same societal units: we talk casually about French cul-ture, New York culture, Catholic culture, even the culture of, say, IBM. Yet this is simply a more colloquial meaning that has developed in contemporary English us-age. In this book, I prefer to use "culture" in its ideational sense, referring broadly to shared values, beliefs, and codes—those "historically created designs for living" (Kluckhohn and Kelly 1945, quoted in Keesing 1976, 139). To speak of "culture" is thus to denote the *symbolic meanings* expressed through language, dress, and other means, by which people in a society attempt to communicate with and understand themselves, each other, and the world around them. Anthropologists and sociolo-gists have described culture in a number of different ways, including as publicly observable symbols (Geertz 1973), shared knowledge (Spradley and McCurdy 1997), or cognitive models (Holland and Quinn 1987). In one of my favorite formulations, sociologist Charles Lemert (1995, 174) calls culture the "code of practical instruc-tions whereby members are given permission to talk meaningfully about some things while ignoring others." Many social scientists now agree that culture is also a form of *practice* informed by symbolic knowledge stored in the brain; that is, culture is what people *do* in everyday life, informed by implicit and shared knowledge (Chaiklin and Lave 1996; Holland et al. 1998). Through practice, people both draw upon and produce symbolic meanings. There are several examples of such a prac-tice approach to culture sprinkled throughout this book.[2]

To sum up: With some risk to the nuances contained in the terms, you can think of "society" as a collection of interrelated persons; "culture" is the meaning system, the communicative "stuff" that enables those persons to make sense of one another. We each learn about how society works through culture, which is communicated through educational processes. The framing essays by Bradley A. U. Levinson and Margaret Eisenhart in the first and final sections explore discussions about society, culture, and education in greater depth.

One of the ongoing puzzles for interpretive social scientists concerns the degree of fit and overlap between different societies and their cultural meaning systems. Anthropologists are in large part responsible for the popular perception that the world is divided up into distinct "cultures." This is what Eric Wolf (1982) has called the "billiard ball" conception of the world, the image of separate and bounded units bouncing off one another—Japanese and Korean, Igbo and Yoruban, Latino and African American. Yet for some time now, anthropologists above all have recog-nized that culture should not be identified exclusively with discrete national or ethnic groups. Yes, it is of some value to identify the common meanings, the "Japa-nese culture," that people in Japanese society use to understand one another. Yet we might just as well identify the meanings that a middle-class Japanese department store manager shares with a middle-class Argentine department store manager. Would we say these two share a "culture"? As the world becomes increasingly complex, we must be careful not to assume that the members of a given "society" all have shared meanings. Some of their meanings may overlap, and others may not.[3] By the same token, those occupying similar occupational or status positions in widely separated societies—like Argentina and Japan—might in fact share a kind of cultural understanding.

Increasingly, anthropologists analyze the multiple and shifting identities of people, the ability of individuals to "organize" culture for themselves and carve out a unique stock of cultural knowledge (Eisenhart 1995; Wolcott 1991). *Microcultures* or subcultures formed by crosscutting interests and positions within conventionally defined cultures are important to understand (Hannerz 1992; 1996), as is the process by which identities and cultural meanings are constantly *produced*, rather than statically and uniformly transmitted (Holland et al. 1998; Levinson and Holland 1996).

Why is this book titled *Schooling the Symbolic Animal*, why do the authors refer to the present period of history as "modernity," and why do we still appear to foreground the modern *school* if we wish to encourage a broader view of education? After all, the school is typically an age-graded, hierarchical setting, an institution where "learners learn vicariously, in roles and environment defined as distinct from those in which the learning will eventually be applied" (Hansen 1990, 28; see also Yehudi Cohen, section II). Anthropology has the great advantage of studying societies that may preserve forms of social organization and communication characteristic of premodern human life (i.e., before approximately 1800). "Primitive" or "tribal" societies have always maintained complex and deliberate educational traditions, though usually not in separate institutions like those we call schools (Reagan 1996). In such societies, educational processes are typically a seamless part of everyday life. Yet since the beginnings of the modern period some two hundred years ago—a period characterized by the rise of capitalism, an extensive new division of labor, and the rapid development of new communication and transportation technologies—much of human learning has taken place increasingly within the confines of schools. Especially since the Second World War and the great wave of decolonization—in fact as part of the package of "development" that northern societies encouraged upon the former colonial world—schools have become the most dominant and pervasive institutional format for learning. Throughout the world, schools have come to form part of our common sense, the normal way of "growing up modern" (Fuller 1991; cf. Meyer et al. 1992).

Thus, I refer to the schooling of the symbolic animal as a historically emergent process. I want to understand what changes—what is lost and gained—and how best to make adjustments in the transition from some forms of education to others. Yet the schooling of the symbolic animal is not only a historical process located in the past. It continues to happen today, every day, in two specific senses. First, previously unschooled groups, with their own forms of education and notions of the "educated person" (Levinson and Holland 1996), are constantly joining the modern school under the aegis of the nation-state (see Laura Rival and Juliana Flinn, section II). Second, young children everywhere must move from the educational environment of their homes and communities into the rather alien context of the school (Skolnick 1976, 11; see also Foster's essay, section III). The goals of learning can undergo rather drastic changes across such contexts. Referring to contemporary schools in the United States, Frederick Erickson astutely summarizes the challenges of schooling the symbolic animal:

> Students in school, like other humans, learn constantly. When we say they are "not learning" what we mean is that they are not learning what school authorities, teachers, and administrators intend for them to learn as the result of intentional instruction. Learning what is deliberately taught can be seen as a form of political assent. Not learning can be seen as a form of political resistance. (1993, 6)

Notwithstanding the variety of educational practices in human societies past and present, the school in some form is probably here to stay, and we'd best understand its promises and perils. Some might suggest that late modernity—or what many now call "postmodernity"—presents the possibilities for moving beyond schools. With new information technologies and highly mobile economies, other organized learning practices may come to the fore. Yet wherever we end up, and whatever we do, we must not forget the embedded social wisdom of the tribal societies still with us. We have not "evolved" beyond them; they still provide us with important models for situating education practically and socially. Most of us have so habituated ourselves to equating school with "education" that only with some difficulty can we consider nonschool sites of learning properly educative. Still, our students often grow weary of the supposed educative fruits of schooling, and they pose their own worldly wise alternative: "I get a better education at my job or in the streets." "I have to leave school in order to get a real education." Such statements betray an acute awareness of the formality of institutional knowledge, of the persistent separation of schools from the vital "communities of practice" outside them (Lave and Wenger 1991). Our task as students, educators, and educational researchers is to boldly situate the knowledge generated in schools within broader streams of social practice and learning.

This book is organized into thematic sections, and the readings in each section were selected through consultation between myself and each of the introductory essayists, who contribute brief historical and conceptual sketches of the corresponding literature. In the first section, I explicate the development of the culture concept in anthropology and invite the reader to explore a range of work on some of the most basic and pressing questions in cultural foundations: What makes the symbolic animal symbolic, and how does culture get acquired, transmitted, and organized in social life? In what ways does culture constitute education?

From there, Margaret Sutton introduces us to important work that examines what happens when indigenous educational systems are incorporated into modern state systems, when locally oriented knowledge production suddenly faces the educational demands and distortions of a wider world. As Sutton points out, the lessons garnered from this experience can teach us a lot about the assumptions behind our own schooling practices in the United States.

Next, Michèle Foster undertakes a vital review of scholarship that examines the cultural and linguistic discontinuities between schools and the settings of everyday life in homes and communities. This body of work presents powerful insights about the cultural and political contexts of learning, and reminds us how much we need to know about our students to be able to teach them well.

Kathryn M. Borman, Amy E. Fox, and I introduce a sampling of articles that together explore how students and teachers participate in reproducing or challenging existing inequalities in stratified societies. Following on the critical articles of previous sections, these readings address more squarely the issues of power and the production of student culture in schools.

Margaret Eisenhart frames the final section of the reader on new directions and approaches in the study of culture and education. She invites us to consider the implications of the new media technologies and the increasingly diverse intertwining of race, class, and gender identities in education. Through a critique of the concept of culture and the methods designed for studying it, Eisenhart urges us to expand our conceptual frameworks for understanding educational processes.

Finally, Margaret Sutton and I conclude the volume with an afterword that highlights several readings from across the different sections to make recommendations for improving educational policy and practice.

I must note here the importance of the new scholarship on language and literacy to the development of this entire volume. The interpretive social sciences have undergone a virtual revolution since the "linguistic turn" of the 1960s, when structuralism and behaviorism—intellectual movements each in its own way hostile to the rich expressions of cultural-linguistic particularity—gave way to a renewed emphasis on the linguistic dimension of human culture and behavior. Educational research has shared in such emphasis, and this is amply reflected in the present volume. Initially, I had proposed a separate section for "perspectives on language and literacy in education," but eventually I decided to integrate such perspectives across each of the sections. The "new literacy studies" (Street 1993) have powerfully shown how people develop "multiple literacies" in specific contexts, and that such literacies can take many different forms and interrelate in different ways with dominant forms of speaking and writing. Likewise, work on the many contexts and modalities of linguistic representation and decoding (Silverstein and Urban 1996; Boyarin 1993) have advanced our understanding of educational processes. Most of the articles in this reader reflect the influence of the linguistic turn, but some of the readings that best represent these new perspectives include Keith H. Basso on

"Stalking with Stories" (section I), Shirley Brice Heath on "What No Bedtime Story Means" (section III), and Hugh Mehan on "Beneath the Skin and between the Ears: A Case Study in the Politics of Representation" (section IV).

By now the reader will have discovered that this is not a textbook in the conventional sense. The readings assembled here are meant to foster open inquiry, to initiate students and scholars alike into an ongoing conversation. They are not meant to provide final definitions or authoritative accounts. Moreover, most of these articles originally appeared in scholarly journals or volumes. Though the section editors and I have abridged some of them, none have been written especially for a textbook or trade book press. Therefore, the arguments are original, and rich in their complexity. We trust in students' and teachers' abilities to wrestle with the authors' words and meanings, and use them as a prompt for further discussion.

We also don't advise strict adherence to the order of the sections and articles assembled here. Though we have provided a conceptual framework and grouping, teachers should feel free to assign combinations of readings that best serve the interests of their students. The order of the thematic sections and the original dates of the readings might suggest a historical development of the field, but I must warn the reader not to hew too closely to this conception. I especially do not wish to present the work of the earlier sections as merely historical, or to imply they have been superseded by better and finer accounts. Rather, this work has been foundational in the best and broadest sense of that term, in providing programmatic insights and frameworks that inform and inspire subsequent research. Likewise, the final section on "new directions" does not undermine earlier work; rather, it builds upon and elaborates foundational work, updating and contextualizing it for the conditions educators presently face. Indeed, the astute reader will note that all of the sections overlap considerably. We have tried to group articles according to key areas of concern in both the historical and contemporary expressions of the field, but we have also tried to preserve something of the productive messiness of a field always in movement. Those wishing for a more conventional or critical "overview" of the field might turn to Judith Friedman Hansen (1979), George Spindler and Louise Spindler (1987; 1997), Murray Wax, Stanley Diamond, and Frederick Gearing (1971), or Bradley A. Levinson, Douglas Foley, and Dorothy Holland (1996).

In this fashion, we invite readers into the interpretive social sciences, to participate in an ongoing discussion about the sociocultural dimensions of education. Like the researchers themselves, readers can initiate their own inquiries into education, and then use such inquiries as a basis for deeper understanding. It is my hope that such understanding will serve as a prompt for committed and compassionate educational action. We can all work together in nourishing the symbolic animal.

NOTES

1. Recent studies of chimpanzees' use of symbols in the wild, as well as successful attempts to teach gorillas and chimpanzees elementary language use, have called into question our

species' exceptionality in this regard. Such developments, in turn, must make us question whether other animals "educate" one another by and through using symbols (see Salzman 1998). Regardless of whether or not we recognize the capacity for symbol use in other species, it seems clear that only humans rely so centrally on symbolic knowledge and communication in organizing their societies. This is a point that Clifford Geertz makes in a reading for section I.

2. See, for example, articles by Laura Rival in section II, and Hugh Mehan in section IV.

3. Feminist theorists have been especially perceptive in revealing the usually male-dominant perspectives glossed over as "shared culture" (Rosaldo and Lamphere 1974; Morgen 1990; Moore 1988; Ortner 1996). Subaltern, critical race, and Marxist-socialist theorists have also pointed to the ways in which the "shared meanings" of culture can serve as ideological cover, as *hegemonic* alibis, for the dominance of powerful groups in a society (Williams 1977; Nelson and Grossberg 1988; Gilroy 1987).

REFERENCES AND READINGS

Appadurai, Arjun. 1996. *Modernity at Large*. Minneapolis: University of Minnesota Press.

Blot, Richard, Julie Niehaus, and Robert Schmertzing, eds. 2000. *Critical Perspectives on Foundations of Anthropology of Education*. New York: Bergin and Garvey.

Borofsky, Robert. 1994. *Assessing Cultural Anthropology*. New York: McGraw-Hill.

Boyarin, Jonathan, ed. 1993. *The Ethnography of Reading*. Berkeley: University of California Press.

Bruner, Jerome. 1996. *The Culture of Education*. Cambridge, Mass.: Harvard University Press.

Calhoun, Craig. 1995. *Critical Social Theory*. London: Blackwell.

Chaiklin, Seth, and Jean Lave, eds. 1996. *Understanding Practice*. Cambridge: Cambridge University Press.

Corsaro, William. 1997. *The Sociology of Childhood*. Thousand Oaks, Calif.: Pine Forge Press.

Eisenhart, Margaret. 1995. The Fax, the Jazz Player, and the Self-Storyteller: How Do People Organize Culture? *Anthropology and Education Quarterly* 26 (1): 3–26.

Erickson, Frederick. 1993. Transformation and School Success: The Politics and Culture of Educational Achievement. In *Minority Education: Anthropological Perspectives*, edited by Evelyn Jacob and Cathie Jordan. Norwood, N.J.: Ablex.

Fuller, Bruce. 1991. *Growing-up Modern: The Western State Builds Third World Schools*. London: Routledge.

Geertz, Clifford. 1973. *The Interpretation of Cultures*. New York: Basic.

———. 1983. From the Native's Point of View: On the Nature of Anthropological Understanding. In *Local Knowledge*. New York: Basic.

Giddens, Anthony. 1979. *Central Problems in Social Theory*. Berkeley: University of California Press.

———. 1990. *The Consequences of Modernity*. Stanford, Calif.: Stanford University Press.

Gilroy, Paul. 1987. *There Ain't No Black in the Union Jack*. London: Routledge.

Gupta, Akhil, and James Ferguson, eds. 1997. *Culture, Power, Place*. Durham, N.C.: Duke University Press.

Hannerz, Ulf. 1992. *Cultural Complexity*. New York: Columbia University Press.

———. 1996. *Transnational Connections*. London: Routledge.

Hansen, Judith Friedman. 1990. Reprint. *Sociocultural Perspectives on Human Learning: Foundations of Educational Anthropology*. Prospect Heights, Ill.: Waveland. Original edition, Englewood Cliffs, N.J.: Prentice Hall, 1979.

Harris, Marvin. 1979. *Cultural Materialism*. New York: Harper.

Holland, Dorothy, and Naomi Quinn, eds. 1987. *Cultural Models in Language and Thought*. Cambridge: Cambridge University Press.

Holland, Dorothy, William Lachicotte, Debra Skinner, and Wanda C. Cain. 1998. *Identity and Agency in Cultural Worlds*. Cambridge, Mass.: Harvard University Press.

Illich, Ivan. 1973. *Tools for Conviviality*. New York: Harper.

Jacob, Evelyn, and Cathie Jordan, eds. 1993. *Minority Education: Anthropological Perspectives*. Norwood, N.J.: Ablex.

Keesing, Roger. 1976. *Cultural Anthropology: A Contemporary Perspective*. New York: Holt, Rinehart and Winston.

King, Anthony, ed. 1997. *Culture, Globalization, and the World-system*. Minneapolis: University of Minnesota Press.

Knauft, Bruce. 1997. *Genealogies for the Present in Cultural Anthropology*. New York: Routledge.

Lave, Jean, and Etienne Wenger. 1991. *Situated Learning: Legitimate Peripheral Participation*. Cambridge: Cambridge University Press.

Lemert, Charles. 1995. *Sociology after the Crisis*. Boulder, Colo.: Westview.

Levinson, Bradley A. U. 1999. Resituating the Place of Educational Discourse in Anthropology. *American Anthropologist* 101 (3): 594–604.

Levinson, Bradley A. U., and Dorothy Holland. 1996. The Cultural Production of the Educated Person: An Introduction. In *The Cultural Production of the Educated Person: Critical Ethnographies of Schooling and Local Practice*, edited by Bradley A. Levinson, Douglas Foley, and Dorothy Holland. Albany: SUNY Press.

Levinson, Bradley A., Douglas Foley, and Dorothy Holland, eds. 1996. *The Cultural Production of the Educated Person: Critical Ethnographies of Schooling and Local Practice*. Albany: SUNY Press.

Lewin, Roger. 1989. *Human Evolution: An Illustrated Introduction*. 2nd ed. London: Blackwell.

Marcus, George, and Michael Fischer. 1986. *Anthropology as Cultural Critique: An Experimental Moment in the Human Sciences*. Chicago: University of Chicago Press.

Mead, Margaret. 1964. Our Educational Emphases in Primitive Perspective. In *Anthropology: A Human Science. Selected Papers, 1939–1960*. Princeton, N.J.: D. Van Nostrand.

Meyer, John W., David H. Kamens, and Aaron Benauot. 1992. *School Knowledge for the Masses: World Models and National Primary Curricular Categories in the Twentieth Century*. Washington, D.C.: Falmer.

Moore, Henrietta. 1988. *Feminism and Anthropology*. Minneapolis: University of Minnesota Press.

Morgen, Sandra. 1990. *Gender and Anthropology*. Washington, D.C.: American Anthropological Association.

Nelson, Cary, and Lawrence Grossberg, eds. 1988. *Marxism and the Interpretation of Culture*. Urbana-Champaign: Illinois University Press.

Ortner, Sherry. 1996. *Making Gender*. Boston: Beacon.

Rabinow, P., and M. Sullivan, eds. 1987. *Interpretive Social Science*. Berkeley: University of California Press.

Reagan, Timothy. 1996. *Non-western Educational Traditions: Alternative Approaches to Educational Thought and Practice.* Mahwah, N.J.: Lawrence Erlbaum.

Rosaldo, Michelle Z., and Louise Lamphere, eds. 1974. *Woman, Culture, and Society.* · Stanford, Calif.: Stanford University Press.

Rosaldo, Renato. 1989. *Culture and Truth.* Boston: Beacon.

Salzman, Zdenek. 1998. *Language, Culture, and Society.* 2nd ed. Boulder, Colo.: Westview.

Silverstein, Michael, and Greg Urban, eds. 1996. *Natural Histories of Discourse.* Chicago: University of Chicago Press.

Skolnick, Arlene, ed. 1976. *Rethinking Childhood.* Boston: Little, Brown.

Spindler, George, ed. 1997. *Education and Cultural Process: Anthropological Approaches.* 3rd ed. Prospect Heights, Ill.: Waveland.

Spindler, George, and Louise Spindler, eds. 1987. *Interpretive Ethnography of Education: At Home and Abroad.* Hillsdale, N.J.: Lawrence Erlbaum.

Spradley, James, and David McCurdy. 1997. *Conformity and Conflict: Readings in Cultural Anthropology.* 8th ed. Boston: Little, Brown.

Street, Brian, ed. 1993. *Cross-cultural Approaches to Literacy.* Cambridge: Cambridge University Press.

Wax, Murray, Stanley Diamond, and Frederick Gearing, eds. 1971. *Anthropological Perspectives on Education.* New York: Basic.

Wenke, Robert J. 1980. *Patterns in Prehistory: Mankind's First Three Million Years.* Oxford: Oxford University Press.

Williams, Raymond. 1977. *Marxism and Literature.* Oxford: Oxford University Press.

Wolcott, Harry. 1991. Propriospect and the Acquisition of Culture. *Anthropology and Education Quarterly* 22 (3): 251–273.

———. 1999. *Ethnography: A Way of Seeing.* Thousand Oaks, Calif.: Sage.

Wolf, Eric. 1982. *Europe and the People without History.* Berkeley: University of California Press.

Section I

The Symbolic Animal
Foundations of Education in Cultural Transmission and Acquisition

The Symbolic Animal: Foundations of Education in Cultural Transmission and Acquisition

Bradley A. U. Levinson

In this section I present a number of key writings on the nature of education and culture. My aim is to illuminate how the very foundations of the educational process are rooted in the human penchant for making meaning out of experience and communicating that meaning to others. I hope to show that, in a very real sense, education *is* culture, that is, education involves the continual remaking of culture as human beings transmit and acquire the symbolic meanings that infuse social life.

Most of the readings in this section—from Emile Durkheim (originally written around the turn of the century), to Gregory Bateson and Clifford Geertz (written in the 1960s), and Keith H. Basso (written in the 1980s)—focus on the social scientific concern with the so-called conservative element in education. From their very origins as disciplines in the 1800s, anthropologists and sociologists wondered how human societies could reproduce themselves from one generation to the next without falling into disarray. What allowed a society to adapt to its environment while retaining some historical cohesion and continuity? How did a society "conserve" the essential features of its cultural and technological repertoire? Theories of education largely sought to address these questions, and emphasis was placed on the process of cultural transmission—the passing on of basic cultural knowledge across the generations (Spindler 1997). Processes of "teaching" were highlighted more than processes of "learning" (Wolcott 1982). It wasn't until later that scholars shifted their focus. By the 1960s the pendulum had swung to the other side, and scholars were mostly asking how education contributed to change. If cultural transmission occurred smoothly, how did societies challenge their own inertia? If education mainly served to mold the young into the cultural patterns of a society, how did innovation ever occur? Scholars began to emphasize the process of cultural acquisition, giving attention to how novice individuals learned the basic cultural knowledge of a society (Wolcott 1982; 1991), bringing their own distinctive interests and traits to the process. As we will see, this focus eventually broadened out into a conception of cultural production as a dynamic process of continuous cultural transmission, acquisition, and modification. In the process of "acquiring" elements of cultural knowledge transmitted through education, individuals could modify and extend the knowledge, in effect organizing knowledge for themselves (see Margaret Eisenhart, section IV), while producing and adding new knowledge to the common stock. As Judith Friedman Hansen (1979, 26) summarizes, "the transmission of knowledge is subject both to conservative forces and to tendencies toward continual redefinition."

From an interpretive perspective, the basic building blocks of education are the symbols that comprise cultural knowledge. Therefore, we begin with readings that address these terms head on. You will recall that in the introduction I defined a symbol as any tangible thing that stands for, or signifies something else. Typically, this definition is elaborated with some reference to the *arbitrary* quality of symbols. What this means is that symbols, as a human construct, have no intrinsic or natural relationship to that which they signify. The green, leafy object I see outside my office window may be called a "tree" in English, but in Spanish it's *árbol* and in German, *baum*. One could imagine a limitless variety of human sounds that might be conjured to refer to that same green, leafy thing. This is what is meant by the arbitrariness of symbols.[1]

I have already provided an anthropological definition of "culture" as shared symbolic knowledge, that is, the values and meanings that provide a framework of interaction between people. Yet in our more basic, everyday language, culture has acquired a number of different meanings and uses. Such uses can be placed into two broadly different categories. On the one hand, in a variety of contexts we may speak or hear about the "culture" of business, youth culture, or even the culture of terrorism. Such uses are oddly anthropological. Though not referring to an ethnic or national group, these phrases point to a realm of common symbolic meanings shared by the people of a given organization or social stratum. They grant that everyone *has* culture, regardless of how we might interpret or judge it. Yet on the other hand, we may also say that some people have more "culture" than others. Wouldn't we tend to remark that the professor of art is rather "cultured," while the gang member who dropped out of school and eschews the fine arts is "lacking culture"? This use of the term is rather different. It suggests that culture is a limited body of special knowledge and refined taste. Some people have more culture, and some people have less. Those who have more culture are thought to be more advanced, and education is supposed to promote this kind of advancement. Some countries incarnate this principle with a national Ministry of Culture, under which a Ministry of Education occasionally may be subsumed. So how and why did culture become such an important term in our discourse, and why should we consider it in the study of education? Is there some way to reconcile these very different uses and meanings of the term?

The term "culture" has a long and illustrious history.[2] It harks back to the Latin verb for cultivation, or the tending of crops and animals. We see its first English use in the fifteenth century, whence it quickly developed associations with European notions of progress and evolution in civilization. For hundreds of years, to have culture was to "cultivate" the higher qualities of civilization, to practice or appreciate the arts or sciences, to develop a refined language. Culture was something one could possess in varying degrees, something that could be developed through advanced schooling. In this earlier usage, perhaps epitomized by the British writer Matthew Arnold, culture became a benchmark for judging stages of evolutionary development. Much as Christian racial chauvinism had judged black slaves as lacking souls, the secular chauvinism of the eighteenth and nineteenth centuries judged so-called primitives as lacking culture.

Yet by the late eighteenth century, the German Romantic poets and philosophers were already giving *kultur* a new cast. The prolific Johann Gottfried von Herder, writing in ironic tones, bravely challenged the assumption that Europe constituted the most advanced point in a linear process of evolution:

> Men of all the quarters of the globe, who have perished over the ages: you have not lived solely to manure the earth with your ashes, so that at the end of time your posterity should be made happy by European culture. The very thought of a superior European culture is a blatant insult to the majesty of Nature. (Quoted in Williams, 1983, 89)

Herder was perhaps the first to speak of cultures, to propose the use of culture in the plural as a means of deflating European conceit. Gradually this new German usage made its way into English as well. By 1871, the British anthropologist Sir Edward Burnett Tylor would write a book called *Primitive Culture* (1871), one of anthropology's founding texts. In it, he discussed the customs and beliefs of tribal societies encountered by European explorers and missionaries. Tylor still adhered to strong notions of evolution, as evidenced by the use of the judgmental term "primitive." Yet by coupling the word "primitive" with "culture" he produced a title that would have been considered an oxymoron by most of his contemporaries. Tylor's text was a kind of bridge between existing European chauvinism and the broader vision proposed by Herder: Yes, the primitives had culture, but they were primitives, after all, with a debased form of culture.

It was not until the great German Jewish immigrant Franz Boas founded North American anthropology around the turn of the century that Herder's vision was fully validated. Boas insisted on the point of *cultural relativism*, the idea that cultural values and practices are specific to their social contexts, and cannot be judged by supposedly universal criteria. He also struggled against the growing movement for racial eugenics, and in 1911, Boas would write one of his great texts, *The Mind of Primitive Man*, to advance his thesis that there were no significant differences in the cognitive traits or abilities of so-called moderns and primitives. Eventually, the

Boasian view of culture came to dominate the field, and it came to permeate much of our everyday thinking as well. Most would now agree that all human beings acquire cultural competence in specific cultural milieus, and that there are many different kinds of cultures. Still, as we have seen, some of the earlier meanings of culture have remained with us.

The cultural anthropologist Clifford Geertz is probably best known for his writing on the ethnographic research process and the place of symbols in public life, but he also reflected on broad evolutionary questions about human behavior. In one of his earlier essays, Geertz drew on research in biological anthropology to argue for the centrality of culture to human adaptation. He liked to call culture a set of "control mechanisms—plans, recipes, rules, instructions—for the governing of behavior." Virtually every other animal, said Geertz, has such behavioral mechanisms genetically hardwired in the form of instinct. Only human beings rely upon—in the words of Geertz, "desperately depend" upon—cultural programs transmitted and learned socially. Without culture, Geertz memorably wrote, humans would be "unworkable monstrosities with very few useful instincts, fewer recognizable sentiments, and no intellect: mental basket cases." Through an evolutionary process Geertz describes here, we are genetically predisposed to operate with and through culture. According to Geertz, the "cultural programs" for human behavior can be found primarily in the public symbols circulating in social life. Each culture historically develops its own repertoire of significant symbols, its own framework for interpreting experience. Such symbols can be apprehended and interpreted only through long and intimate acquaintance—the kind of work cultural anthropologists do through ethnographic study, as if they were being "raised" in a society. Geertz ends the passage we've reprinted here by reaffirming the particularity of cultural learning and experience. If it is true that humans can only "complete themselves" through culture, they must do so necessarily through membership in *particular* primary cultures. This acquisition of a specific cultural competence, of the rules for using and interpreting particular sets of significant symbols, is the developmental journey incumbent upon all of us.

Emerging out of a rather different intellectual tradition, the great British literary theorist Raymond Williams reminds us that culture is always "ordinary." By this, he does not mean that it is never worthy of study or admiration. Rather, Williams wishes to debunk the defenders of "high culture," the heirs of Matthew Arnold, who persist to this day. Williams came from a working-class background, the son of Welsh farmers and railwaymen. Though he eventually acquired a Cambridge education and achieved renown through his writing on literature, he remained a socialist throughout his life. For this reason, Williams never reserved the term "culture" for the achievements of the cultivated classes, the supposedly refined manners of "the teashop." Rather, Williams emphasized the ordinariness of culture, the process, "both traditional and creative," by which every human society strove to create and impose meanings upon the world. Echoing Geertz, Williams insisted that all human beings, regardless of their social standing, operate through culture. From this, it followed for Williams that education, too, ought to be "ordinary." Again, he did not mean by this to minimize its stature or importance. Rather, Williams thought it objectionable that only certain students be deemed worthy of advanced study. If culture and education were ordinary, he argued, then a common British culture ought to be extended across all regions and social classes. Williams's concrete proposals regarding education stemmed from his own social class background, but his portrait of culture resonates with broader anthropological postulates.

Because the discipline of anthropology began through the study of so-called primitive peoples, anthropologists have been at pains to compare tribal lifeways with the social patterns of modern industrial and information societies. In this section, I present instances of such comparison. Margaret Mead's famous book on *Coming of Age in Samoa* (1928) is laced with implicit contrasts between Samoan patterns of childrearing and adolescent behavior, and the corresponding American patterns. Mead's editor even insisted she add a final section to the book, drawing together the insights and recommendations such comparison afforded. (Mead is justly famous, and justly controversial—see Freeman [1983]and Cote [1994]—for the carefree portrait of Samoan adolescent behavior she developed as a means of critiquing American educational and socialization practices.) Jules Henry's (1963) reflection on "education and the human condition" similarly sheds light on the apparent absurdity of U.S. classrooms by situating the behavior he observed there in a broader cultural and evolutionary context.

Mead's book, *Coming of Age in Samoa,* is considered by some as an important precursor to the field known as the anthropology of education. I have excerpted just a few pages from the book's second chapter, "The Education of the Samoan Child." Mead's observations of the way Samoan youths are socialized were fairly typical of anthropological work of the period, which portrayed daily routines in tribal societies. Yet Mead was distinctive in her preoccupation with the experience of the youth, and in her attempt to draw explicit conclusions from such experience for our socialization practices in the West. Her writing illustrates a number of important points in the foundations of education. For one thing, Mead shows how education can be conceived as part of a broader process of *enculturation*, the constant learning of cultural knowledge. She shows how different teaching modalities, different "pedagogies" if you will, can be used to transmit culture. Among the Samoans, such modalities differ by age and gender. They range from observation and imitation of skills like fishing and cooking, to adults' and siblings' "perpetual admonitions" about avoiding danger, to the chiefs' "badgering" of young men through "rivalry, precept, and example." With this depiction, Mead also effectively reminds us of the distinction between education and schooling. We moderns tend to think of education only as that which occurs in schools. In fact, education occurs all around us, all the time, in a variety of sites that may or may not include schools. Mead shows us how education is embedded in ongoing social relationships that are affectively charged. Such relationships provide a *context* for learning (cf. McDermott 1977). Finally, Mead's chapter was notable for the mention it made of the arrival of "government schools." In the 1920s, few Samoans had been to school, but this would soon change. Mead hints at the beginnings of a cultural clash between traditional forms of education and the imperatives of these "government schools." The Samoans' cultural routines would soon be disrupted by the imposition of an extraneous institution, directed by bureaucratic groups with different sets of interests and cultural meanings (see section II for further discussion of this).

Working in the rather more contemporary setting of the Cibecue Western Apache Indian reservation in Arizona, Keith H. Basso provides us with a startling account of how place names constitute some of the central cultural meanings of a society. Among the Cibecue Apache, most features of the landscape itself have been named. The surrounding environment thus acquires an intimate familiarity, and the names of the places are incorporated into the telling of stories, "historical tales," that carry moral weight in the community. Stories are told and place names recounted at different moments of everyday life. Sometimes the stories are told indirectly in order to send a poignant message to one of the listeners, to "shoot" them with an arrow, as they say. Referring to the surrounding places, these narratives are meant to educate youth about fundamental moral values in social life. Following the Apache, Basso calls this educational practice "stalking with stories." As he puts it, the Apache acknowledge the "power of oral narratives, especially historical tales, to promote beneficial change in people's attitudes toward their responsibilities as members of a moral community." Because the Apache have been oppressed by the whites' dominant political and educational institutions, they place a premium on maintaining a distinctive cultural identity. The stories are told to remind Apache of this identity, and to encourage their ongoing adherence to it. Stories thus constitute an important part of Apache education. Basso's depiction of this remarkable storytelling tradition reminds us that symbols do not merely "stand for" something else. Apache place names are key symbols that acquire meaning through their telling and retelling in a variety of contexts and stories.

By the time Jules Henry conducted his studies of U.S. public schools in the late 1950s, he had already undergone the traditional anthropological apprenticeship of fieldwork in a tribal society—specifically, in Argentina and Brazil. In the broad-ranging book he authored about U.S. culture and society, *Culture against Man* (1963), Henry sought to apply the insights garnered from such tribal societies to the educational practices of his own society (see also Henry 1960). Written at the height of the Cold War, the book was in many ways an angry critique of blind cultural indoctrination. The section I reprint here, "Education and the Human Condition," introduced a chapter on "American schoolrooms" that called U.S. educators to task for encouraging docility and conformity in their students while brainwashing them to hate the Soviet Union. Henry recognized, however, that in some sense this was the central paradox of all education systems—"we must conserve culture while changing it." In his terms, education had to be both "fettering and freeing." On the one hand, education as cultural learning is a "device for binding the intellect," an attempt to "prevent the truly creative intellect from getting out of hand." On the other hand, education might also be used to inspire innovation, creativity, and change. In these brief few pages, Henry presents us with a disquieting dilemma: How to reform an educational system for creative learning, for the "stimulation of young minds," while still honoring the perennial human need to conserve fundamental cultural values and ideals.

The great French scholar Emile Durkheim is commonly considered the founder of modern sociology. Writing at the turn of the century, he was especially preoccupied with the shift from agrarian-based societies to the modern urban industrialism of the West. Of course, educational processes would undergo major changes through this shift as well. In the passage we reprint here, Durkheim emphasizes how education functions to produce the kinds of persons deemed necessary by the predominant institutions in society. For Durkheim, society exists as an ongoing, organic collectivity, created historically, and the individual can only be educated within the parameters of this collective achievement. Like Henry, Durkheim emphasizes this "fettering" dimension of education, by which individual initiative is subordinated to the social will, and individual thought is only made possible by the prior accumulation of social wisdom. Durkheim asks, "How can the individual pretend to reconstruct, through his own private reflection, what is not a work of individual thought?" Yet in calling attention to the molding power of social norms, Durkheim still acknowledges the growing specialization of educational goals. With the increasing occupational and class differentiation of modern industrialism, "there are as many different kinds of education as there are different milieux in a given society." These milieux, or contexts, require "particular aptitudes and specialized knowledge, in which certain ideas, certain practices, certain modes of viewing things, prevail." Still, such specialized contexts could never be "sufficient unto themselves." An overarching education system would always be necessary to coordinate these specialized contexts and create "a degree of homogeneity; education perpetuates and reinforces this homogeneity by fixing in the child, from the beginning, the essential similarities that collective life demands." In this way, Durkheim provided a powerful rationale for the rise of state-controlled public education in this century.

Gregory Bateson, the anthropologist married to Margaret Mead for much of her career, developed his own original ideas about the cultural basis of human communication. Most of these ideas were brought together in his 1972 book, *Steps to an Ecology of Mind*, from which the short metalogue, "Why Do Frenchmen?" is taken. Bateson opened that book with a series of short reconstructed "metalogues," exploratory discussions between himself and his young daughter. The metalogue was an ingenious form that allowed Bateson to express sophisticated scientific principles through elementary question and response. In this one example, Bateson's daughter asks him why Frenchmen look so "silly and excited" when waving their arms in conversation. Bateson eventually gets us to see how this phrase, "silly and excited," may be an inaccurate assessment because it is lacking the cultural knowledge provided only by an insider's perspective. He reframes his daughter's question as, "What does one Frenchman tell another Frenchman by waving his arms?" Posing it this way, Bateson examines the symbolic meaning provided by human gesture. An important component of human culture consists in the mostly unconscious codes for kinesic communication, that is, how our cultural knowledge is "embodied" and expressed in bodily movement. As Bateson puts it, "The messages which we exchange in gestures are really not the same as any translation of those gestures into words." This metalogue enables us to see how education may involve far more than words, for cultural communication draws on a varied repertoire of symbolic resources, including the human body. In effect, the waving of arms becomes a symbol of emotion, engagement, respect, and the like. Both the speech and the gesturing are deeply encoded aspects of culture. Moreover, messages conveyed by one set of symbols (waving arms) may reinforce, alter, or even contradict the messages conveyed by others (words, clothing, and so on). Importantly, it is the *form* of the message, more than the content itself, that may provide the most important meaning. Bateson provides an intellectual grounding for later sociological work on the "hidden curriculum" of schooling—the messages that are communicated to students alongside the overt content matter of the classroom.

Our final selection, "Becoming a Marihuana User," comes from a 1960 book by the sociologist Howard Becker, called *Outsiders: Studies in the Sociology of Deviance.* Becker's intent was to show how persistent socially "deviant behavior" could develop out of a series of experiences with that behavior, rather than some underlying "deviant motivation," per se. While describing how a habitual marihuana user comes to appreciate this activity, Becker provides us with a powerful account of cultural learning. Through close ethnographic observation of a smoking subculture, Becker shows how the sensations of smoking themselves are neither inherently pleasant nor unpleasant. Rather, the novice smoker must learn the proper technique for smoking, must learn to perceive the effects of marihuana, and eventually must learn to enjoy the effects. In a sense, the more experienced smokers form a kind of community to "educate" the novice in the ways to use and enjoy marihuana. This portrayal of education may surprise us because we tend to view marihuana use as a noneducational, if not antieducational, behavior. Yet the process Becker describes has many similarities with the notion of "situated learning" in "communities of practice" developed much later by Jean Lave and her associates (Lave and Wenger 1991; Chaiklin and Lave, 1996). Though we may not agree with the goals or means of such learning, we should bear in mind that education always occurs in a specific context with its own social and cultural dimensions.

NOTES

1. In her article on "Symbolization and Value," Dorothy Lee (1959) delves even more deeply into this topic. Lee was an anthropologist writing in the 1940s and 1950s; she was well known for her work on American Indian systems of thought and belief. She drew on

this work to anticipate some of the more important findings of later cognitive and linguistic theorists. Questioning the notion that symbols had a completely arbitrary relation to the world they described, Lee highlighted the "acts" comprising a "system of symbolization, by means of which the individual punctuates, categorizes, shapes this physical reality, transforming it into the world of sensory perception and concept." In certain cultures, symbols do not merely "represent" something else; through the act of perception, they actually *become* that something else, in effect fusing their essences in a process called "consubstantiation." Lee drew on this insight to suggest that people are always adding their own meanings as they use and interpret symbols across different contexts. As she says, "the symbol . . . is a thing in process, containing and conveying the value that has become embodied in it." It is the context, or the situation, which ultimately provides the value of symbols. As one might say of education more broadly, true symbols "acquire valid existence and value only through participation in meaningful situations."

2. For most of the following discussion, I draw upon Raymond Williams's (1983) great work of cultural criticism, *Keywords*, especially pp. 87–93. Williams refers to "culture" as "one of the two or three most complicated words in the English language" (1983, 87).

REFERENCES AND READINGS

Chaiklin, Seth, and Jean Lave, eds. 1996. *Understanding Practice: Perspectives on Activity and Context*. Cambridge: Cambridge University Press.

Cote, James E. 1994. *Adolescent Storm and Stress: An Evaluation of the Mead-Freeman Controversy*. Hillsdale, N.J.: Lawrence Erlbaum.

Firth, Raymond. 1936. *We, the Tikopia*. London: Allen and Unwin.

Freeman, Derek. 1983. *Margaret Mead and Samoa: The Making and Unmaking of an Anthropological Myth*. Cambridge, Mass.: Harvard University Press.

Hallowell, A. Irving. 1955. *Culture and Experience*. New York: Schocken Books

Hansen, Judith Friedman. 1990. Reprint. *Sociocultural Perspectives on Human Learning: Foundations of Educational Anthropology*. Prospect Heights, Ill.: Waveland. Original edition, Englewood Cliffs, N.J.: Prentice Hall, 1979.

Henry, Jules. 1960. A Cross-cultural Outline of Education. *Current Anthropology* 1 (4): 267–305.

————. 1963. *Culture against Man*. New York: Random House.

Lave, Jean, and Etienne Wenger. 1991. *Situated Learning: Legitimate Peripheral Participation*. Cambridge: Cambridge University Press

Lee, Dorothy. 1959. Symbolization and Value. In *Freedom and Culture*. New York: Prentice Hall.

McDermott, R. P. 1977. Social Relations as Contexts for Learning in School. *Harvard Educational Review* 47 (2): 198–213.

Mead, Margaret. 1964. Our Educational Emphases in Primitive Perspective. In *Anthropology: A Human Science*. Princeton, N.J.: D. Van Nostrand. Originally published in *American Journal of Sociology* 48 (1943): 633–639.

Middleton, John, ed. 1970. *From Child to Adult: Studies in the Anthropology of Education*. Garden City, N.Y.: Natural History Press.

Moore, Alexander. 1973. *Life Cycles in Atchalán: The Diverse Careers of Certain Guatemalans*. New York: Teachers College Press.

Singleton, John, ed. 1998. *Learning in Likely Places: Varieties of Apprenticeship in Japan.* Cambridge: Cambridge University Press.

Spindler, George. 1997. The Transmission of Culture. In *Education and Cultural Process: Anthropological Approaches.* 3rd ed. Edited by George Spindler. Prospect Heights, Ill.: Waveland.

Williams, Raymond. 1983. *Keywords: A Vocabulary of Culture and Society.* Rev. ed. New York: Oxford University Press.

Wolcott, Harry. 1982. The Anthropology of Learning. *Anthropology and Education Quarterly* 13 (2): 83–108.

———. 1991. Propriospect and the Acquisition of Culture. *Anthropology and Education Quarterly* 22 (3): 251–273.

1

The Impact of the Concept of Culture on the Concept of Man

Clifford Geertz

. . . I want to propose two ideas. The first of these is that culture is best seen not as complexes of concrete behavior patterns—customs, usages, traditions, habit clusters—as has, by and large, been the case up to now, but as a set of control mechanisms—plans, recipes, rules, instructions (what computer engineers call "programs")—for the governing of behavior. The second idea is that man is precisely the animal most desperately dependent upon such extragenetic, outside-the-skin control mechanisms, such cultural programs, for ordering his behavior.

Neither of these ideas is entirely new, but a number of recent developments, both within anthropology and in other sciences (cybernetics, information theory, neurology, molecular genetics) have made them susceptible of more precise statement as well as lending them a degree of empirical support they did not previously have. And out of such reformulations of the concept of culture and of the role of culture in human life comes, in turn, a definition of man stressing not so much the empirical commonalities in his behavior, from place to place and time to time, but rather the mechanisms by whose agency the breadth and indeterminateness of his inherent capacities are reduced to the narrowness and specificity of his actual accomplishments. One of the most significant facts about us may finally be that we all begin with the natural equipment to live a thousand kinds of life but end in the end having lived only one.

The "control mechanism" view of culture begins with the assumption that human thought is basically both social and public—that its natural habitat is the house yard, the marketplace, and the town square. Thinking consists not of "happenings in the head" (though happenings there and elsewhere are necessary for it to occur) but of a traffic in what have been called, by G. H. Mead and others, significant symbols—words for the most part but also gestures, drawings, musical sounds, mechanical devices like clocks, or natural objects like jewels—anything, in fact, that is disengaged from its mere actuality and used to impose meaning upon experience. From the point of view of any particular individual, such symbols are largely given. He finds them already current in the community when he is born, and they remain, with some additions, subtractions, and partial alterations he may or may not have had a hand in, in circulation after he dies. While he lives he uses them, or some of them, sometimes deliberately and with care, most often spontaneously and with ease, but always with the same end in view: to put a construction upon the events through which he lives, to orient himself within "the ongoing course of experienced things," to adopt a vivid phrase of John Dewey's.

Man is so in need of such symbolic sources of illumination to find his bearings in the world because the nonsymbolic sort that are constitutionally ingrained in his body cast so diffused a light. The behavior patterns of lower animals are, at least to a much greater extent, given to them with their physical structure; genetic sources of information order their actions within much narrower ranges of variation, the narrower and more thoroughgoing the lower the animal. For man, what are innately given are extremely general response capacities, which, although they make possible far greater plasticity, complexity, and, on the scattered occasions when everything works as it should, effectiveness of behavior, leave it much less precisely regulated. This, then, is the second face of our argument: Undirected by culture patterns—organized systems of significant symbols—man's behavior would be virtually ungovernable, a mere chaos of pointless acts and exploding emotions, his experience virtually shapeless. Culture, the accumulated totality of such patterns, is not just an ornament of human existence but—the principal basis of its specificity—an essential condition for it.

Within anthropology some of the most telling evidence in support of such a position comes from recent advances in our understanding of what used to be called the descent of man: the emergence of Homo sapiens out of his general primate background. Of these advances three are of critical importance: (1) the discarding of a sequential view of the relations between the physical evolution and the cultural development of man in favor of an overlap or interactive view; (2) the discovery that the bulk of the biological changes that produced modern man out of his most immediate progenitors took place in the central nervous system and most especially in the brain; (3) the realization that man is, in physical terms, an incomplete, an unfinished, animal; that what sets him off most graphically from nonmen is less his sheer ability to learn (great as that is) than how much and what particular sorts of things he *has* to learn before he is able to function at all. Let me take each of these points in turn.

The traditional view of the relations between the biological and the cultural advance of man was that the former, the biological, was for all intents and purposes completed before the latter, the cultural, began. That is to say, it was again stratigraphic: Man's physical being evolved, through the usual mechanisms of genetic variation and natural selection, up to the point where his anatomical structure had arrived at more or less the status at which we find it today; then cultural development got under way. At some particular stage in his phylogenetic history, a marginal genetic change of some sort rendered him capable of producing and carrying culture, and thenceforth his form of adaptive response to environmental pressures was almost exclusively cultural rather than genetic. As he spread over the globe, he wore furs in cold climates and loin cloths (or nothing at all) in warm ones; he didn't alter his innate mode of response to environmental temperature. He made weapons to extend his inherited predatory powers and cooked foods to render a wider range of them digestible. Man became man, the story continues, when, having crossed some mental Rubicon, he became able to transmit "knowledge, belief, law, morals, custom" (to quote the items of Sir Edward Tylor's classical definition of culture) to his descendants and his neighbors through teaching and to acquire them from his ancestors and his neighbors through learning. After that magical moment, the advance of the hominids depended almost entirely on cultural accumulation, on the slow growth of conventional practices, rather than, as it had for ages past, on physical organic change.

The only trouble is that such a moment does not seem to have existed. By the most recent estimates the transition to the cultural mode of life took the genus *Homo* several million years to accomplish; and stretched out in such a manner, it involved not one or a handful of marginal genetic changes but a long, complex, and closely ordered sequence of them.

In the current view, the evolution of *Homo sapiens*—modern man—out of his immediate pre*sapiens* background got definitely under way nearly four million years ago with the appearance of the now famous Australopithecines—the so-called ape men of southern and eastern Africa—and culminated with the emergence of *sapiens* himself only some one to two or three hundred thousand years ago. Thus, as at least elemental forms of cultural, or if you wish protocultural, activity (simple toolmaking, hunting, and so on) seem to have been present among some of the Australopithecines, there was an overlap of, as I say, well over a million years between the beginning of culture and the appearance of man as we know him today. The precise dates—which are tentative and which further research may later alter in one direction or another—are not critical; what is critical is that there was an overlap and that it was a very extended one. The final phases (final to date, at any rate) of the phylogenetic history of man took place in the same grand geological era— the so-called Ice Age—as the initial phases of his cultural history. Men have birthdays, but man does not.

What this means is that culture, rather than being added on, so to speak, to a finished or virtually finished animal, was ingredient, and centrally ingredient, in the production of that animal itself. The slow, steady, almost glacial growth of culture through the Ice Age altered the balance of selection pressures for the evolving *Homo* in such a way as to play a major directive role in his evolution. The perfection of tools, the adoption of organized hunting and gathering practices, the beginnings of true family organization, the discovery of fire, and, most critically, though it is as yet extremely difficult to trace it out in any detail, the increasing

reliance upon systems of significant symbols (language, art, myth, ritual) for orientation, communication, and self-control all created for man a new environment to
which he was then obliged to adapt. As culture, step by infinitesimal step, accumulated and developed, a selective advantage was given to those individuals in the
population most able to take advantage of it—the effective hunter, the persistent
gatherer, the adept toolmaker, the resourceful leader—until what had been a small-
brained, protohuman *Australopithecus* became the large-brained fully human *Homo
sapiens*. Between the cultural pattern, the body, and the brain, a positive feedback
system was created in which each shaped the progress of the other, a system in which
the interaction among increasing tool use, the changing anatomy of the hand, and
the expanding representation of the thumb on the cortex is only one of the more
graphic examples. By submitting himself to governance by symbolically mediated
programs for producing artifacts, organizing social life, or expressing emotions, man
determined, if unwittingly, the culminating stages of his own biological destiny.
Quite literally, though quite inadvertently, he created himself.

Though, as I mentioned, there were a number of important changes in the gross
anatomy of genus *Homo* during this period of his crystallization—in skull shape,
dentition, thumb size, and so on—by far the most important and dramatic were
those that evidently took place in the central nervous system; for this was the period when the human brain, and most particularly the forebrain, ballooned into its
present top-heavy proportions. The technical problems are complicated and controversial here; but the main point is that though the Australopithecines had a torso
and arm configuration not drastically different from our own, and a pelvis and leg
formation at least well-launched toward our own, they had cranial capacities hardly
larger than those of the living apes—that is to say, about a third to a half of our
own. What sets true men off most distinctly from protomen is apparently not overall
bodily form but complexity of nervous organization. The overlap period of cultural
and biological change seems to have consisted in an intense concentration on neural
development and perhaps associated refinements of various behaviors—of the hands,
bipedal locomotion, and so on—for which the basic anatomical foundations—
mobile shoulders and wrists, a broadened ilium, and so on—had already been se-
curely laid. In itself, this is perhaps not altogether startling; but, combined with what
I have already said, it suggests some conclusions about what sort of animal man is
that are, I think, rather far not only from those of the eighteenth century but from
those of the anthropology of only ten or fifteen years ago.

Most bluntly, it suggests that there is no such thing as a human nature independent of culture. Men without culture would not be the clever savages of Golding's
Lord of the Flies thrown back upon the cruel wisdom of their animal instincts; nor
would they be the nature's noblemen of Enlightenment primitivism or even, as classical anthropological theory would imply, intrinsically talented apes who had somehow failed to find themselves. They would be unworkable monstrosities with very
few useful instincts, fewer recognizable sentiments, and no intellect: mental basket cases. As our central nervous system—and most particularly its crowning curse

and glory, the neocortex—grew up in great part in interaction with culture, it is incapable of directing our behavior or organizing our experience without the guidance provided by systems of significant symbols. What happened to us in the Ice Age is that we were obliged to abandon the regularity and precision of detailed genetic control over our conduct for the flexibility and adaptability of a more generalized, though of course no less real, genetic control over it. To supply the additional information necessary to be able to act, we were forced, in turn, to rely more and more heavily on cultural sources—the accumulated fund of significant symbols. Such symbols are thus not mere expressions, instrumentalities, or correlates of our biological, psychological, and social existence; they are prerequisites of it. Without men, no culture, certainly; but equally, and more significantly, without culture, no men.

We are, in sum, incomplete or unfinished animals who complete or finish ourselves through culture—and not through culture in general but through highly particular forms of it: Dobuan and Javanese, Hopi and Italian, upper-class and lower-class, academic and commercial. Man's great capacity for learning, his plasticity, has often been remarked, but what is even more critical is his extreme dependence upon a certain sort of learning: the attainment of concepts, the apprehension and application of specific systems of symbolic meaning. Beavers build dams, birds build nests, bees locate food, baboons organize social groups, and mice mate on the basis of forms of learning that rest predominantly on the instructions encoded in their genes and evoked by appropriate patterns of external stimuli: physical keys inserted into organic locks. But men build dams or shelters, locate food, organize their social groups, or find sexual partners under the guidance of instructions encoded in flow charts and blueprints, hunting lore, moral systems and aesthetic judgments: conceptual structures molding formless talents.

We live, as one writer has neatly put it, in an "information gap." Between what our body tells us and what we have to know in order to function, there is a vacuum we must fill ourselves, and we fill it with information (or misinformation) provided by our culture. The boundary between what is innately controlled and what is culturally controlled in human behavior is an ill-defined and wavering one. Some things are, for all intents and purposes, entirely controlled intrinsically: we need no more cultural guidance to learn how to breathe than a fish needs to learn how to swim. Others are almost certainly largely cultural; we do not attempt to explain on a genetic basis why some men put their trust in centralized planning and others in the free market, though it might be an amusing exercise. Almost all complex human behavior is, of course, the interactive, nonadditive outcome of the two. Our capacity to speak is surely innate; our capacity to speak English is surely cultural. Smiling at pleasing stimuli and frowning at unpleasing ones are surely in some degree genetically determined (even apes screw up their faces at noxious odors); but sardonic smiling and burlesque frowning are equally surely predominantly cultural, as is perhaps demonstrated by the Balinese definition of a madman as someone who, like an American, smiles when there is nothing to laugh at. Between the basic ground plans for our life that our genes lay down—the capacity to speak or to smile—and the precise behavior we in fact execute—speaking English in a certain tone of voice, smiling enigmatically in a delicate social situation—lies a complex set of significant symbols under whose direction we transform the first into the second, the ground plans into the activity.

Our ideas, our values, our acts, even our emotions, are, like our nervous system itself, cultural products—products manufactured, indeed, out of tendencies, capacities, and dispositions with which we were born, but manufactured nonetheless. Chartres is made of stone and glass. But it is not just stone and glass; it is a cathedral, and not only a cathedral, but a particular cathedral built at a particular time by certain members of a particular society. To understand what it means, to perceive it for what it is, you need to know rather more than the generic properties of stone and glass and rather more than what is common to all cathedrals. You need to understand also—and, in my opinion, most critically—the specific concepts of the relations among God, man, and architecture that, since they have governed its creation, it consequently embodies. It is no different with men: they, too, every last one of them, are cultural artifacts. . . .

2

Culture Is Ordinary

Raymond Williams

The bus stop was outside the cathedral. I had been looking at the Mappa Mundi, with its rivers out of Paradise, and at the chained library, where a party of clergymen had got in easily, but where I had waited an hour and cajoled a verger before I even saw the chains. Now, across the street, a cinema advertised the *Six-Five Special* and a cartoon version of *Gulliver's Travels*. The bus arrived, with a driver and a conductress deeply absorbed in each other. We went out of the city, over the old bridge, and on through the orchards and the green meadows and the fields red under the plough. Ahead were the Black Mountains, and we climbed among them, watching the steep fields end at the grey walls, beyond which the bracken and heather and whin had not yet been driven back. To the east, along the ridge, stood the line of grey Norman castles; to the west, the fortress wall of the mountains. Then, as we still climbed, the rock changed under us. Here, now, was limestone, and the line of the early iron workings along the scarp. The farming valleys, with their scattered white houses, fell away behind. Ahead of us were the narrower valleys: the steel-rolling mill, the gasworks, the grey terraces, the pitheads. The bus stopped, and the driver and conductress got out, still absorbed. They had done this journey so often, and seen all its stages. It is a journey, in fact, that in one form or another we have all made.

I was born and grew up halfway along that bus journey. Where I lived is still a farming valley, though the road through it is being widened and straightened, to carry the heavy lorries to the north. Not far away, my grandfather, and so back through the generations, worked as a farm labourer until he was turned out of his cottage and, in his fifties, became a roadman. His sons went at thirteen or fourteen on to the farms, his daughters into service. My father, his third son, left the farm at fifteen to be a boy porter on the railway, and later became a signalman, working in a box in this valley until he died. I went up the road to the village school, where a curtain divided the two classes—Second to eight or nine, First to fourteen. At eleven I went to the local grammar school, and later to Cambridge.

Culture is ordinary: that is where we must start. To grow up in that country was to see the shape of a culture, and its modes of change. I could stand on the mountains and look north to the farms and the cathedral, or south to the smoke and the flare of the blast furnace making a second sunset. To grow up in that family was to see the shaping of minds: the learning of new skills, the shifting of relationships, the emergence of different language and ideas. My grandfather, a big hard labourer, wept while he spoke, finely and excitedly, at the parish meeting, of being turned out of his cottage. My father, not long before he died, spoke quietly and happily of when he had started a trade-union branch and a Labour Party group in the village, and, without bitterness, of the 'kept men' of the new politics. I speak a different idiom, but I think of these same things.

Culture is ordinary: that is the first fact. Every human society has its own shape, its own purposes, its own meanings. Every human society expresses these, in institutions, and in arts and learning. The making of a society is the finding of common meanings and directions, and its growth is an active debate and amendment under the pressures of experience, contact, and discovery, writing themselves into the land. The growing society is there, yet it is also made and remade in every individual mind. The making of a mind is, first, the slow learning of shapes, purposes, and meanings, so that work, observation and communication are possible. Then, second, but equal in importance, is the testing of these in experience, the making of new observations, comparisons, and meanings. A culture has two aspects: the known meanings and directions, which its members are trained to; the new observations and meanings, which are offered and tested. These are the ordinary processes of human societies and human minds, and we see through them the nature of a culture: that it is always both traditional and creative; that it is both the most ordinary common meanings and the finest individual meanings. We use the word culture in these two senses: to mean a whole way of life—the common meanings; to mean the arts and learning—the special processes of discovery and creative effort. Some writers reserve the word for one or other of these senses; I insist on both, and on the significance of their conjunction. The questions I ask about our culture are questions about our general and common purposes, yet also questions about deep personal meanings. Culture is ordinary, in every society and in every mind.

Now there are two senses of culture—two colours attached to it—that I know about but refuse to learn. The first I discovered at Cambridge, in a teashop. I was not, by the way, oppressed by Cambridge. I was not cast down by old buildings, for I had come from a country with twenty centuries of history written visibly into the earth: I liked walking through a Tudor court, but it did not make me feel raw. I was not amazed by the existence of a place of learning; I had always known the cathedral, and the bookcases I now sit to work at in Oxford are of the same design as those in the chained library. Nor was learning, in my family, some strange eccentricity; I was not, on a scholarship in Cambridge, a new kind of animal up a brand-new ladder.

Learning was ordinary; we learned where we could. Always, from those scattered white houses, it had made sense to go out and become a scholar or a poet or a teacher. Yet few of us could be spared from the immediate work; a price had been set on this kind of learning, and it was more, much more, than we could individually pay. Now, when we could pay in common, it was a good, ordinary life.

I was not oppressed by the university, but the teashop, acting as if it were one of the older and more respectable departments, was a different matter. Here was culture, not in any sense I knew, but in a special sense: the outward and emphatically visible sign of a special kind of people, cultivated people. They were not, the great majority of them, particularly learned; they practised few arts; but they had it, and they showed you they had it. They are still there, I suppose, still showing it, though even they must be hearing rude noises from outside, from a few scholars and writers they call—how comforting a label is!—angry young men. As a matter of fact there is no need to be rude. It is simply that if that is culture, we don't want it; we have seen other people living.

But of course it is not culture, and those of my colleagues who, hating the teashop, make culture, on its account, a dirty word, are mistaken. If the people in the teashop go on insisting that culture is their trivial differences of behaviour, their trivial variations of speech habit, we cannot stop them, but we can ignore them. They are not that important, to take culture from where it belongs.

Yet, probably also disliking the teashop, there were writers I read then, who went into the same category in my mind. When I now read a book such as Clive Bell's *Civilisation*, I experience not so much disagreement as stupor. What kind of life can it be, I wonder, to produce this extraordinary fussiness, this extraordinary decision to call certain things culture and then separate them, as with a park wall, from ordinary people and ordinary work? At home we met and made music, listened to it, recited and listened to poems, valued fine language. I have heard better music and better poems since; there is the world to draw on. But I know, from the most ordinary experience, that the interest is there, the capacity is there. Of course, farther along that bus journey, the old social organization in which these things had their place has been broken. People have been driven and concentrated into new kinds of work, new kinds of relationship; work, by the way, which built the park walls, and the houses inside them, and which is now at last bringing, to the unanimous disgust of the teashop, clean and decent and furnished living to the people themselves. Culture is ordinary: through every change let us hold fast to that. . . .

I give myself three wishes, one for each of the swans I have just been watching on the lake. I ask for things that are part of the ethos of our working-class movement. I ask that we may be strong and human enough to realize them. And I ask, naturally, in my own fields of interest.

I wish, first, that we should recognize that education is ordinary: that it is, before everything else, the process of giving to the ordinary members of society its full common meanings, and the skills that will enable them to amend these meanings, in the light of their personal and common experience. If we start from that, we can get rid of the remaining restrictions, and make the necessary changes. I do not mean only money restrictions, though these, of course, are ridiculous and must go. I mean also restrictions in the mind: the insistence, for example, that there is a hard maximum number—a fraction of the population as a whole—capable of really profiting by a university education, or a grammar school education, or by any full course of liberal studies. We are told that this is not a question of what we might personally prefer, but of the hard cold facts of human intelligence, as shown by biology and psychology. But let us be frank about this: are biology and psychology different in the USA and USSR (each committed to expansion, and not to any class rigidities), where much larger numbers, much larger fractions, pass through comparable stages of education? Or were the English merely behind in the queue for intelligence? I believe, myself, that our educational system, with its golden fractions, is too like our social system—a top layer of leaders, a middle layer of supervisors, a large bottom layer of operatives—to be coincidence. I cannot accept that education is a training for jobs, or for making useful citizens (that is, fitting into this system). It is a society's confirmation of its common meanings, and of the human skills for their amendment. Jobs follow from this confirmation: the purpose, and then the working skill. We are moving into an economy where we shall need many more highly trained specialists. For this precise reason, I ask for a common education that will give our society its cohesion, and prevent it disintegrating into a series of specialist departments, the nation become a firm.

But I do not mean only the reorganization of entry into particular kinds of education, though I welcome and watch the experiments in this. I mean also the rethinking of content, which is even more important. I have the honour to work for an organization through which, quite practically, working men amended the English university curriculum. It is now as it was then: the defect is not what is in, but what is out. It will be a test of our cultural seriousness whether we can, in the coming generation, redesign our syllabuses to a point of full human relevance and control. I should like to see a group working on this, and offering its conclusions. For we need not fear change; oldness may or may not be relevant. I come from an old place; if a man tells me that his family came over with the Normans, I say 'Yes, how interesting; and are you liking it here?' Oldness is relative, and many 'immemorial' English traditions were invented, just like that, in the nineteenth century. What that vital century did for its own needs, we can do for ours; we can make, in our turn, a true twentieth-century syllabus. And by this I do not mean simply more technology; I mean a full liberal education for everyone in our society, and then full specialist training to earn our living in terms of what we want to make of our lives. Our specialisms will be finer if they have grown from a common culture, rather than being a distinction from it. And we must at all costs avoid the polarization of our culture, of which there are growing signs. High literacy is expanding, in direct relation to exceptional educational opportunities, and the gap between this and common literacy may widen, to the great damage of both, and with great consequent tension. We must emphasize not the ladder but the common highway, for every man's ignorance diminishes me, and every man's skill is a common gain of breath.

My second wish is complementary: for more and more active public provision for the arts and for adult learning. We now spend £20,000,000 annually on all our libraries, museums, galleries, orchestras, on the Arts Council, and on all forms of adult education. At the same time we spend £365,000,000 annually on advertising. When these figures are reversed, we can claim some sense of proportion and value. And until they are reversed, let there be no sermons from the Establishment about materialism: this is their way of life, let them look at it. (But there is no shame in them: for years, with their own children away at school, they have lectured working-class mothers on the virtues of family life; this is a similar case.)

I ask for increased provision on three conditions. It is not to be a disguised way of keeping up consumption, but a thing done for its own sake. A minister in the last Labour government said that we didn't want any geniuses in the film industry; he wanted, presumably, just to keep the turnstiles clicking. The short answer to this is that we don't want any Wardour Street thinkers in the leadership of the Labour Party. We want leaders of a society, not repair-workers on this kind of cultural economy.

The second condition is that while we must obviously preserve and extend the great national institutions, we must do something to reverse the concentration of this part of our culture. We should welcome, encourage and foster the tendencies to regional recreation that are showing themselves; for culture is ordinary, you should not have to go to London to find it.

The third condition is controversial. We should not seek to extend a ready-made culture to the benighted masses. We should accept, frankly, that if we extend our culture we shall change it: some that is offered will be rejected, other parts will be radically criticized. And this is as it should be, for our arts, now, are in no condition to go down to eternity unchallenged. There is much fine work; there is also shoddy work, and work based on values that will find no acceptance if they ever come out into the full light of England. To take our arts to new audiences is to be quite certain that in many respects those arts will be changed. I, for one, do not fear this. I would not expect the working people of England to support works which, after proper and patient preparation, they could not accept. The real growth will be slow and uneven, but state provision, frankly, should be a growth in this direction, and not a means of diverting public money to the preservation of a fixed and finished partial culture. At the same time, if we understand cultural growth, we shall know that it is a continual offering for common acceptance; that we should not, therefore, try to determine in advance what should be offered, but clear the channels and let all the offerings be made, taking care to give the difficult full space, the original full time, so that it is a real growth, and not just a wider confirmation of old rules. . . .

3

The Education of the Samoan Child

Margaret Mead

. . . By the time a child is six or seven she [can] be trusted with the care of a younger child. And she also develops a number of simple techniques. She learns to weave firm square balls from palm leaves, to make pin-wheels of palm leaves or frangi-pani blossoms, to climb a cocoanut tree by walking up the trunk on flexible little feet, to break open a cocoanut with one firm well-directed blow of a knife as long as she is tall, to play a number of group games and sing the songs which go with them, to tidy the house by picking up the litter on the stony floor, to bring water from the sea, to spread out the copra to dry and to help gather it in when rain threat-ens, to roll the pandanus leaves for weaving, to go to a neighbouring house and bring back a lighted fagot for the chief's pipe or the cook-house fire, and to exercise tact in begging slight favours from relatives.

But in the case of the little girls all of these tasks are merely supplementary to the main business of baby-tending. Very small boys also have some care of the younger children, but at eight or nine years of age they are usually relieved of it. Whatever rough edges have not been smoothed off by this responsibility for younger children are worn off by their contact with older boys. For little boys are admitted to interesting and important activities only so long as their behaviour is circum-spect and helpful. Where small girls are brusquely pushed aside, small boys will be patiently tolerated and they become adept at making themselves useful. The four or five little boys who all wish to assist at the important business of helping a grown youth lasso reef eels, organise themselves into a highly efficient working team; one boy holds the bait, another holds an extra lasso, others poke eagerly about in holes in the reef looking for prey, while still another tucks the captured eels into his *lavalava*. The small girls, burdened with heavy babies or the care of little staggerers who are too small to adventure on the reef, discouraged by the hostility of the small boys and the scorn of the older ones, have little opportunity for learning the more

36

adventurous forms of work and play. So while the little boys first undergo the chastening effects of baby-tending and then have many opportunities to learn effective co-operation under the supervision of older boys, the girls' education is less comprehensive. They have a high standard of individual responsibility but the community provides them with no lessons in co-operation with one another. This is particularly apparent in the activities of young people; the boys organise quickly; the girls waste hours in bickering, innocent of any technique for quick and efficient co-operation.

And as the woman who goes fishing can only get away by turning the babies over to the little girls of the household, the little girls cannot accompany their aunts and mothers. So they learn even the simple processes of reef fishing much later than do the boys. They are kept at the baby-tending, errand-running stage until they are old enough and robust enough to work on the plantations and carry foodstuffs down to the village.

A girl is given these more strenuous tasks near the age of puberty, but it is purely a question of her physical size and ability to take responsibility, rather than of her physical maturity. Before this time she has occasionally accompanied the older members of the family to the plantations if they were willing to take the babies along also. But once there, while her brothers and cousins are collecting cocoanuts and roving happily about in the bush, she has again to chase and shepherd and pacify the ubiquitous babies.

As soon as the girls are strong enough to carry heavy loads, it pays the family to shift the responsibility for the little children to the younger girls and the adolescent girls are released from baby-tending. It may be said with some justice that the worst period of their lives is over. Never again will they be so incessantly at the beck and call of their elders, never again so tyrannised over by two-year-old tyrants. All the irritating, detailed routine of housekeeping, which in our civilisation is accused of warping the souls and souring the tempers of grown women, is here performed by children under fourteen years of age. A fire or a pipe to be kindled, a call for a drink, a lamp to be lit, the baby's cry, the errand of the capricious adult— these haunt them from morning until night. With the introduction of several months a year of government schools these children are being taken out of their homes for most of the day. This brings about a complete disorganisation of the native households which have no precedents for a manner of life where mothers have to stay at home and take care of their children and adults have to perform small routine tasks and run errands.

Before their release from baby-tending the little girls have a very limited knowledge of any of the more complicated techniques. Some of them can do the simpler work in preparing food for cooking, such as skinning bananas, grating cocoanuts, or scraping taro. A few of them can weave the simple carrying basket. But now they must learn to weave all their own baskets for carrying supplies; learn to select taro leaves of the right age for cooking, to dig only mature taro. In the cook-house they learn to make *palusami*, to grate the cocoanut meat, season it with hot stones, mix it with sea water and strain out the husks, pour this milky mixture into a properly made little container of taro leaves from which the aromatic stem has been scorched off, wrap these in a breadfruit leaf and fasten the stem tightly to make a durable cooking jacket. They must learn to lace a large fish into a palm leaf, or roll a bundle of small fish in a breadfruit leaf; to select the right kind of leaves for stuffing a pig, to judge when the food in the oven of small heated stones is thoroughly baked. Theoretically the bulk of the cooking is done by the boys and where a girl has to do the heavier work, it is a matter for comment: "Poor Losa, there are no boys in her house and always she must make the oven." But the girls always help and often do a great part of the work.

Once they are regarded as individuals who can devote a long period of time to some consecutive activity, girls are sent on long fishing expeditions. They learn to weave fish baskets, to gather and arrange the bundles of fagots used in torch-light fishing, to tickle a devil fish until it comes out of its hole and climbs obediently upon the waiting stick, appropriately dubbed a "come hither stick"; to string the great rose-coloured jelly-fish, *lole,* a name which Samoan children give to candy also, on a long string of hibiscus bark, tipped with a palm leaf rib for a needle; to know good fish from bad fish, fish that are in season from fish which are dangerous at some particular time of the year; and never to take two octopuses, found paired on a rock, lest bad luck come upon the witless fisher.

Before this time their knowledge of plants and trees is mainly a play one, the pandanus provides them with seeds for necklaces, the palm tree with leaves to weave balls; the banana tree gives leaves for umbrellas and half a leaf to shred into a stringy "choker"; cocoanut shells cut in half, with cinet strings attached, make a species of stilt; the blossoms of the *Pua* tree can be sewed into beautiful necklaces. Now they must learn to recognise these trees and plants for more serious purposes; they must learn when the pandanus leaves are ready for the cutting and how to cut the long leaves with one sure quick stroke; they must distinguish between the three kinds of pandanus used for different grades of mats. The pretty orange seeds which made such attractive and also edible necklaces must now be gathered as paint brushes for ornamenting bark cloth. Banana leaves are gathered to protect the woven platters, to wrap up puddings for the oven, to bank the steaming oven full of food. Banana bark must be stripped at just the right point to yield the even, pliant, black strips, needed to ornament mats and baskets. Bananas themselves must be distinguished as to those which are ripe for burying, or the golden curved banana ready for eating, or bananas ready to be sun-dried for making fruit-cake rolls. Hibiscus bark can no longer be torn off at random to give a raffia-like string for a handful of shells; long journeys must be made inland to select bark of the right quality for use in weaving.

In the house the girl's principal task is to learn to weave. She has to master several different techniques. First, she learns to weave palm branches where the central rib of the leaf serves as a rim to her basket or an edge to her mat and where the leaflets are already arranged for weaving. From palm leaves she first learns to weave a carrying basket, made of half a leaf, by plaiting the leaflets together and curving the rib into a rim. Then she learns to weave the Venetian blinds which hang between the house posts, by laying one-half leaf upon another and plaiting the leaflets together. More difficult are the floor mats, woven of four great palm leaves, and the food platters with their intricate designs. There are also fans to make, simple two-strand weaves which she learns to make quite well, more elaborate twined ones which are the prerogative of older and more skilled weavers. Usually some older woman in the household trains a girl to weave and sees to it that she makes at least one of each kind of article, but she is only called upon to produce in quantity the simpler things, like the Venetian blinds. From the pandanus she learns to weave the common floor mats, one or two types of the more elaborate bed mats, and then, when she is thirteen or fourteen, she begins her first fine mat. The fine mat represents the high point of Samoan weaving virtuosity. Woven of the finest quality of pandanus which has been soaked and baked and scraped to a golden whiteness and paper-like thinness, of strands a sixteenth of an inch in width, these mats take a year or two years to weave and are as soft and pliable as linen. They form the unit of value, and must always be included in the dowry of the bride. Girls seldom finish a fine mat until they are nineteen or twenty, but the mat has been started, and, wrapped up in a coarser one, it rests among the rafters, a testimony to the girl's industry and manual skill. She learns the rudiments of bark cloth making; she can select and cut the paper mulberry wands, peel off the bark, beat it after it has been scraped by more expert hands. The patterning of the cloth with a pattern board or by free hand drawing is left for the more experienced adult.

Throughout this more or less systematic period of education, the girls maintain a very nice balance between a reputation for the necessary minimum of knowledge and a virtuosity which would make too heavy demands. A girl's chances of marriage are badly damaged if it gets about the village that she is lazy and inept in domestic tasks. But after these first stages have been completed the girl marks time technically for three or four years. She does the routine weaving, especially of the Venetian blinds and carrying baskets. She helps with the plantation work and the cooking, she weaves a very little on her fine mat. But she thrusts virtuosity away from her as she thrusts away every other sort of responsibility with the invariable comment, "Laititi a'u" ("I am but young"). All of her interest is expended on clandestine sex adventures, and she is content to do routine tasks as, to a certain extent, her brother is also.

But the seventeen-year-old boy is not left passively to his own devices. He has learned the rudiments of fishing, he can take a dug-out canoe over the reef safely, or manage the stern paddle in a bonito boat. He can plant taro or transplant cocoanut, husk cocoanuts on a stake and cut the meat out with one deft quick turn of the knife. Now at seventeen or eighteen he is thrust into the *Aumaga*, the society of the young men and the older men without titles, the group that is called, not in euphuism but in sober fact, "the strength of the village." Here he is badgered into efficiency by rivalry, precept and example. The older chiefs who supervise the activities of the *Aumaga* gaze equally sternly upon any backslidings and upon any undue precocity. The prestige of his group is ever being called into account by the *Aumaga* of the neighbouring villages. His fellows ridicule and persecute the boy who fails to appear when any group activity is on foot, whether work for the village on the plantations, or fishing, or cooking for the chiefs, or play in the form of a ceremonial call upon some visiting maiden. Furthermore, the youth is given much more stimulus to learn and also a greater variety of occupations are open to him. There is no specialisation among women, except in medicine and mid-wifery, both the prerogatives of very old women who teach their arts to their middle-aged daughters and nieces. The only other vocation is that of the wife of an official orator, and no girl will prepare herself for this one type of marriage which demands special knowledge, for she has no guarantee that she will marry a man of this class. . . .

4

Stalking with Stories

Keith H. Basso

This chapter focuses on a small set of spoken texts in which members of the Western Apache community of Cibecue express claims about themselves, their language, and the lands on which they live. The statements that interest me, which could be supplemented by a large number of others, are the following.

> The land is always stalking people. The land makes people live right. The land looks after us. The land looks after people. (Annie Peaches, age 77, 1978)

> We used to survive only off the land. Now it's no longer that way. Now we live only with money, so we need jobs. But the land still looks after us. We know the names of the places where everything happened. So we stay away from badness. (Nick Thompson, age 64, 1980)

> I think of that mountain called Tséé Ligai Dah Sidilé (White Rocks Lie Above In A Compact Cluster) as if it were my maternal grandmother. I recall stories of how it once was at that mountain. The stories told to me were like arrows. Elsewhere, hearing that mountain's name, I see it. Its name is like a picture. Stories go to work on you like arrows. Stories make you live right. Stories make you replace yourself. (Benson Lewis, age 64, 1979)

> One time I went to L.A., training for mechanic. It was no good, sure no good. I start drinking, hang around bars all the time. I start getting into trouble with my wife, fight sometimes with her. It was bad. I forget about this country here around Cibecue. I forget all the names and stories. I don't hear them in my mind anymore. I forget how to live right, forget how to be strong. (Wilson Lavender, age 52, 1975)

Whenever Apaches describe the land—or, as happens more frequently, whenever they tell stories about incidents that have occurred at specific points upon it—they take steps to constitute it in relation to themselves. Which is simply to observe that in acts of speech, mundane and otherwise, Apaches fashion images and understandings of the land that are accepted as credible accounts of what it actually is, why it is significant, and how it impinges on the daily lives of men and women. In short, portions of a world view are constructed and made available, and a Western Apache version of the landscape is deepened, amplified, and tacitly affirmed. With words, a massive physical presence is fashioned into a meaningful human universe.

This universe of meanings comprises the cultural context in which the Western Apache texts presented earlier acquire their validity and appropriateness. Consequently, if we are to understand the claims set forth in these statements, portions of that context must be explored and made explicit. We must proceed, in other words, by relating our texts to other aspects of Western Apache thought—in effect, to other texts and other claims—and continue doing this, more and more comprehensively, until finally it is possible to confront the texts directly and expose the major premises on which they rest. As we shall see, most of these premises are grounded in an unformalized native model of Western Apache storytelling which holds that oral narratives have the power to establish enduring bonds between individuals and features of the natural landscape, and that as a direct consequence of such bonds, persons who have acted improperly will be moved to reflect critically on their misconduct and resolve to improve it. A native model of how stories work to shape Apaches' conceptions of the landscape, it is also a model of how stories work to shape Apaches' conceptions of themselves. Ultimately, it is a model of how two symbolic resources—language and the land—are manipulated by Apaches to promote compliance with standards for acceptable social behavior and the moral values that support them.

Should it appear, then, that these Western Apache texts lack either substance or complexity, we shall see that in fact both qualities are present in ample measure. And should the aim of interpreting such modestly worded documents seem unduly narrow, or my strategy for trying to accomplish it too tightly bound up with an examination of linguistic and ethnographic particulars, it will become evident soon enough that wider and more general issues are very much involved. Of these, I shall suggest, none is more pressing or conspicuous than the reluctance of cultural ecologists to deal openly and in close detail with the symbolic attributes of human environments and the effects of environmental constructions on patterns of social action.

But I am getting ahead of myself. The problem now is how to get started, and for advice on that matter I turn here, as I actually did in Cibecue a number of years ago, to a gifted and unusual man. Teacher and consultant, serious thinker and salacious joker alike, he has so strongly influenced the content and organization of this essay that he has become, with his permission, a part of it himself—and so, too, of the interpretation it presents.

"LEARN THE NAMES"

Nick Thompson is, by his own admission, an old man. It is possible, he told me once, that he was born in 1918. Beneath snow-white hair cut short, his face is round and compact, his features small and sharply molded. His large, black, and very bright eyes move quickly, and when he smiles he acquires an expression that is at once mischievous and intimidating. I have known him for more than twenty years, and he has instructed me often on matters pertaining to Western Apache language and culture. A man who delights in play, he has also teased me unmercifully, concocted humorous stories about me that are thoroughly apocryphal, and embarrassed me before large numbers of incredulous Apaches by inquiring publicly into the most intimate details of my private life. Described by many people in Cibecue as a true Slim Coyote (Ma' Ts'ósé), Nick Thompson is outspoken, incorrigible, and unabashed. He is also generous, thoughtful, and highly intelligent. I value his friendship immensely.

As I bring my Jeep to a halt on the road beside the old man's camp, I hear Nick complaining loudly to his wife about the changing character of life in Cibecue and its regrettable effects on younger members of the community. I have heard these complaints before and I know they are deeply felt. But still, on this sunny morning in June 1980, it is hard to suppress a smile, for the image Nick presents, a striking example of what can be achieved with sartorial bricolage, is hardly what one would expect of a staunch tribal conservative. Crippled since childhood and partially paralyzed by a recent stroke, the old man is seated in the shade of a cottonwood tree a few yards from the modest wooden cabin where he lives with his wife and two small grandchildren. He is smoking a Salem cigarette and studying with undisguised approval the shoes on his feet—a new pair of bright blue Nike running shoes trimmed in incandescent orange. He is also wearing a pair of faded green trousers, a battered brown cowboy hat, and a white T-shirt with "Disneyland" printed in bold red letters across the front. Within easy reach of his chair, resting on the base of an up-ended washtub, is a copy of the *National Enquirer*, a mug of hot coffee, and an open box of chocolate-covered doughnuts. If Nick Thompson is an opponent of social change, it is certainly not evident from his appearance. But appearances can be deceiving, and Nick, who is an accomplished singer and a medicine man of substantial reputation, would be the first to point this out.

The old man greets me with his eyes. Nothing is said for a minute or two, but then we begin to talk, exchanging bits of local news until enough time has passed for me to politely announce the purpose of my visit. I explain that I am puzzled by certain statements Apaches have made about the country surrounding Cibecue and I am eager to know how to interpret them. To my surprise, Nick does not ask what I have been told or by whom. He responds instead by swinging his arm out in a wide arc. "Learn the names," he says. "Learn the names of all these places." Unprepared for such a firm and unequivocal suggestion (it sounds to me like nothing less than an order), I retreat into silence. "Start with the names," the old man continues. "I will teach you like before. Come back tomorrow morning." Nodding in agreement, I thank Nick for his willingness to help and tell him what I will be able to pay him. He says the wage is fair.

A few minutes later, as I stand to take my leave, Nick's face breaks suddenly into a broad smile and his eyes begin to dance. I know that look well and brace myself for the farewell joke that almost always accompanies it. The old man wastes no time. He says I look lonely. He urges me to have prolonged and abundant sex with very old women. He says it prevents nosebleeds. He says that someday I can write a book about it. Flustered and at a loss for words, I smile weakly and shake my head. Delighted with this reaction, Nick laughs heartily and reaches for his coffee and a chocolate-covered doughnut.

I return to the old man's camp the following day and start to learn Western Apache place-names. My lessons which are interrupted by mapping trips with more mobile Apache consultants, continue for the next ten weeks. In late August, shortly before I must leave Cibecue, Nick asks to see the maps. He is not impressed. "White men need paper maps," he observes. "We have maps in our minds."

"ALL THESE PLACES HAVE STORIES"

When I return to Cibecue in the spring of 1981, Nick Thompson is recovering from a bad case of the flu. He is weak, despondent, and uncomfortable. We speak very little and make no mention of place-names. His wife is worried about him and so am I. Within a week, however, Nick's eldest son comes to my camp with a message: I am to visit his father and bring with me two packs of Salem cigarettes and a dozen chocolate-covered doughnuts. This is good news.

When I arrive at the old man's camp, he is sitting under the cottonwood tree by his house. A blanket is draped across his knees and he is wearing a heavy plaid jacket and a red vinyl cap with white fur-lined earflaps. There is color in his cheeks and the sparkle is back in his eyes. Shortly after we start to converse, and apropos of nothing I can discern, Nick announces that in 1931 he had sexual intercourse eight times in one night. He wants to know if I have ever been so fortunate. His wife, who has brought us each a cup of coffee, hears this remark and tells him he is a crazy old man. Nick laughs loudly. Plainly, he is feeling better.

Eventually, I ask Nick if he is ready to resume our work together. "Yes," he says, "but no more on names." What then? "Stories," is his reply. "All these places have stories. We shoot each other with them, like arrows. Come back tomorrow morning." Puzzled once again, but suspecting that the old man has a plan he wants to follow, I tell him I will return. We then discuss Nick's wages. He insists that I pay him more than I did the year before as it is necessary to keep up with inflation. I agree and we settle on a larger sum. Then comes the predictable farewell joke: a fine piece of nonsense in which Nick, speaking English and imitating certain mannerisms he has come to associate with Anglo physicians, diagnoses my badly sunburned nose as an advanced case of venereal disease. This time it is Nick's wife who laughs loudest.

The next day Nick begins to instruct me on aspects of Western Apache storytelling. Consulting on a regular basis with other Apaches from Cibecue as well, I pursue this topic throughout the summer.

HISTORICAL TALES

If place-names appear frequently in ordinary forms of Western Apache discourse, their use is equally conspicuous in oral narratives. It is there, in conjunction with stories Apaches tell, that we can move closer to an interpretation of native claims about the symbolic importance of geographical features and the personalized relationships that individuals may have with them. Historical tales (*'ágodzaahí* or *'ágodzaahí nagoldi'é*; literally, 'to tell of that which has happened') recount events that took place 'long ago' (*doo' ániiná*) when the Western Apache people, having emerged from below the surface of the earth, were developing their own distinctive ways and customs. Most historical tales describe incidents that occurred prior to the coming of whitemen, but some of these stories are set in post-reservation times, which began for the Western Apache in 1872. Like myths, historical tales are intended to edify, but their main purpose is to criticize social delinquents (or, as the Apaches say, to "shoot" them), thereby impressing these individuals with the undesirability of improper behavior and alerting them to the punitive consequences of further misconduct. Not uncommonly, however, narratives in gossip are also used to ridicule and malign the character of their subjects.

Nowhere do place-names serve more important communicative functions than in the context of historical tales. As if to accentuate this fact, stories of the *'ágodzaahí* genre are stylistically quite simple. Historical tales can usually be delivered in less than five minutes. Western Apache storytellers point out that this is both fitting and effective, because *'ágodzaahí* stories, like the arrows they are commonly said to represent, work best when they move swiftly. Finally, and most significantly of all, historical tales are distinguished from all other forms of Apache narrative by an opening and closing line that identifies with a place-name where the events in the narrative occurred. These lines frame the narrative, mark it unmistakably as belonging to the *'ágodzaahí* genre, and evoke a particular physical setting in which listeners can imaginatively situate everything that happens. It is hardly surprising, then, that while Apache storytellers agree that historical tales are "about" the events recounted in the tales, they also emphasize that the tales are "about" the sites at which the events took place.

If the style of Western Apache historical tales is relatively unremarkable, their content is just the opposite. Without exception, and usually in very graphic terms, historical tales focus on persons who suffer misfortune as the consequence of actions that violate Apache standards for acceptable social behavior. More specifically, 'ágodzaahí stories tell of persons who have acted unthinkingly and impulsively in open disregard for 'Apache custom' (ndee bi 'at'ee') and who pay for their transgressions by being humiliated, ostracized, or killed. Stories of the 'ágodzaahí variety are morality tales pure and simple, and when viewed as such by the Apaches—as compact commentaries on what should be avoided so as to deal successfully and effectively with other people—they are highly informative. For what these narratives assert—tacitly, perhaps, but with dozens of compelling examples—is that immoral behavior is irrevocably a community affair and that persons who behave badly will be punished sooner or later. Thus, just as 'ágodzaahí stories are "about" historical events and their geographical locations, they are also "about" the system of rules and values according to which Apaches expect each other to organize and regulate their lives. In an even more fundamental sense, then, historical tales are "about" what it means to be a Western Apache, or, to make the point less dramatically, what it is that being an Apache should normally and properly entail.

To see how this is so, let us consider the texts of two historical tales and examine the manner in which they have been interpreted by their Apache narrators.

> It happened at T'iis Cho Naasikaadé (Big Cottonwood Trees Stand Here And There).
> Long ago, the Pimas and Apaches were fighting. The Pimas were carrying long clubs made from mesquite wood; they were also heavy and hard. Before dawn the Pimas arrived at Cibecue and attacked the Apaches there. The Pimas attacked while the Apaches were still asleep. The Pimas killed the Apaches with their clubs. An old woman woke up. She heard the Apaches crying out. The old woman thought it was her son-in-law because he often picked on her daughter. The old woman cried out: "You pick on my child a lot. You should act pleasantly toward her." Because the old woman cried out, the Pimas learned where she was. The Pimas came running to the old woman's camp and killed her with their clubs. A young girl ran away from there and hid beneath some bushes. She alone survived.
> It happened at Big Cottonwood Trees Stand Here And There.

Narrated by Annie Peaches, this historical tale deals with the harmful consequences that may come to persons who overstep traditional role boundaries. During the first year of marriage it is customary for young Apache couples to live in the camp of the bride's parents. At this time, the bride's mother may request that her son-in-law perform various tasks and she may also instruct and criticize him. Later, however, when the couple establishes a separate residence, the bride's mother forfeits this right and may properly interfere in her son-in-law's affairs only at the request of her daughter. Mrs. Peaches explains that women who do not abide by this arrangement imply that their sons-in-law are immature and irresponsible, which is a source of acute embarrassment for the young men and their wives. Thus, even when meddling might seem to serve a useful purpose, it should be scrupulously avoided. The woman on whom this story centers failed to remember this and was instantly killed.

It happened at Tséé Chiizh Dah Sidilé (Coarse-Textured Rocks Lie Above In A Compact Cluster).

Long ago, a man became sexually attracted to his stepdaughter. He was living below Coarse-Textured Rocks Lie Above In A Compact Cluster with his stepdaughter and her mother. Waiting until no one else was present, and sitting alone with her, he started to molest her. The girl's maternal uncle happened to come by and he killed the man with a rock. The man's skull was cracked open. It was raining. The girl's maternal uncle dragged the man's body up above to Coarse-Textured Rocks Lie Above In A Compact Cluster and placed it there in a storage pit. The girl's mother came home and was told by her daughter of all that had happened. The people who owned the storage pit removed the man's body and put it somewhere else. The people never had a wake for the dead man's body.

It happened at Coarse-Textured Rocks Lie Above In A Compact Cluster.

Narrated by Benson Lewis, this historical tale deals with the crime of incest, for sexual contact with stepchildren is considered by Western Apaches to be an incestuous act. According to Mr. Lewis, the key line in the story is the penultimate one in which he observes, "The people never had a wake for the dead man's body." We may assume, Lewis says, that because the dead man's camp was located near the storage pit in which his body was placed, the people who owned the pit were also his relatives. This makes the neglect with which his corpse was treated all the more profound, since kinspeople are bound by the strongest of obligations to care for each other when they die. That the dead man's relatives chose to dispense with customary mortuary ritual shows with devastating clarity that they wished to disown him completely.

So far my remarks on what Western Apache historical tales are "about" have centered on features of textual content. This is a familiar strategy and certainly a necessary one, but it is also incomplete. In addition to everything else—places, events, moral standards, conceptions of cultural identity—every historical tale is also "about" the person at whom it is directed. This is because the telling of a historical tale is almost always prompted by an individual's having committed one or more social offenses to which the act of narration, together with the tale itself, is intended as a critical and remedial response. Thus, on occasions when 'ágodzaahí stories are actually told—by real Apache storytellers, in real interpersonal contexts, to real social offenders—these narratives are understood to be accompanied by an unstated message from the storyteller that may be phrased something like this: "I know that you have acted in a way similar or analogous to the way in which someone acted in the story I am telling you. If you continue to act in this way, something similar or analogous to what has happened to the character in the story might also happen to you." This metacommunicative message is just as important as any conveyed by the text of the storyteller's tale. For Apaches contend that if the message is taken to heart by the person at whom the tale is aimed—and if, in conjunction with lessons drawn from the tale itself, he or she resolves to improve his or her behavior—a lasting bond will have been created between that individual and the site or sites at which events in the tale took place. The cultural premises that inform this powerful idea will be made explicit presently; but first, in order to understand more clearly what the idea involves, let us examine the circumstances that led to the telling of a historical tale at Cibecue and see how this narrative affected the person for whom it was told.

In early June 1977, a seventeen-year-old Apache woman attended a girls' puberty ceremonial at Cibecue with her hair rolled up in a set of pink plastic curlers. She had returned home two days before from a boarding school in Utah where this sort of ornamentation was considered fashionable by her peers. Something so mundane would have gone unnoticed by others were it not for the fact that Western Apache women of all ages are expected to appear at puberty ceremonials with their hair worn loose. This is one of several ways that women have of showing respect for the ceremonial and also, by implication, for the people who have staged it. The practice of presenting oneself with free-flowing hair is also understood to contribute to the ceremonial's effectiveness, for Apaches hold that the ritual's most basic objectives, which are to invest the pubescent girl with qualities necessary for life as an adult, cannot be achieved unless standard forms of respect are faithfully observed. On this occasion at Cibecue, everyone was following custom except the young woman who arrived wearing curlers. She soon became an object of attention and quiet expressions of disapproval, but no one spoke to her about the cylindrical objects in her hair.

Two weeks later, the same young woman made a large stack of tortillas and brought them to the camp of her maternal grandmother, a widow in her mid-sixties who had organized a small party to celebrate the birthday of her eldest grandson. Eighteen people were on hand, myself included, and all of us were treated to hot coffee and a dinner of boiled beef and potatoes. When the meal was over, casual conversation began to flow, and the young woman seated herself on the ground next to her younger sister. And then—quietly, deftly, and quite without warning—her grandmother narrated a version of the historical tale about the forgetful Apache policeman who behaved too much like a whiteman. Shortly after the story was finished, the young woman stood up, turned away wordlessly, and walked off in the direction of her home. Uncertain of what had happened, I asked her grandmother why she had departed. Had the young woman suddenly become ill? "No," her grandmother replied. "I shot her with an arrow."

Approximately two years after this incident occurred, I found myself in the company of the young woman with the taste for distinctive hairstyles. She had purchased a large carton of groceries at the trading post at Cibecue, and when I offered to drive her home with them she accepted. I inquired on the way if she remembered the time that her grandmother had told us the story about the forgetful policeman. She said she did and then went on, speaking in English, to describe her reactions to it. "I think maybe my grandmother was getting after me, but then I think maybe not, maybe she's working on somebody else. Then I think back on that dance and I know it's me for sure. I sure don't like how she's talking about me, so I quit looking like that. I threw those curlers away." In order to reach the young woman's camp, we had to pass within a few hundred yards of Men Stand Above Here And There, the place where the man had lived who was arrested for rustling in the story. I pointed it out to my companion. She said nothing for several moments. Then she smiled and spoke softly in her own language: "I know that place. It stalks me every day."

The comments of this Western Apache woman on her experience as the target of a historical tale are instructive in several respects. To begin with, her statement enables us to imagine something of the sizable psychological impact that historical tales may have on the persons to whom they are presented. Then, too, we can see how 'ágodzaahí stories may produce quick and palpable effects on the behavior of such individuals, causing them to modify their social conduct in quite specific ways. Last, and most revealing of all, the young woman's remarks provide a clear illustration of what Apaches have in mind when they assert that historical tales may establish highly meaningful relationships between individuals and features of the natural landscape.

To appreciate fully the significance of these relationships, as well as their influence on the lives of Western Apache people, we must explore more thoroughly the manner in which the relationships are conceptualized. This can be accomplished through a closer examination of Apache ideas about the activity of storytelling and the acknowledged power of oral narratives, especially historical tales, to promote beneficial changes in people's attitudes toward their responsibilities as members of a moral community. These ideas, which combine to form a native model of how oral narratives work to achieve their intended effects, are expressed in terms of a single dominant metaphor. By now it should come as no surprise to learn that the metaphor draws heavily on the imagery of hunting.

STALKING WITH STORIES

Nick Thompson is tired. We have been talking about hunting with stories for two days now and the old man has not had an easy time of it. At one point, bored and annoyed with my queries, he told me that I reminded him of a horsefly buzzing around his head. Later, however, when he was satisfied that I could follow at least the outline of his thoughts, he recorded on tape a lengthy statement which he said contained everything he wanted me to know. Here is Nick Thompson's statement:

> This is what we know about our stories. They go to work on your mind and make you think about your life. Maybe you've not been acting right. Maybe you've been stingy. Maybe you've been chasing after women. Maybe you've been trying to act like a whiteman. People don't *like* it! So someone goes hunting for you—maybe your grandmother, your grandfather, your uncle. It doesn't matter. Anyone can do it.
>
> So someone stalks you and tells a story about what happened long ago. It doesn't matter if other people are around—you're going to know he's aiming that story at you. All of a sudden it *hits* you! It's like an arrow, they say. Sometimes it just bounces off—

it's too soft and you don't think about anything. But when it's strong it goes in deep and starts working on your mind right away. No one says anything to you, only that story is all, but now you know that people have been watching you and talking about you. They don't like how you've been acting. So you have to think about your life.

Then you feel weak, real weak, like you are sick. You don't want to eat or talk to anyone. That story is working on you now. You keep thinking about it. That story is changing you now, making you want to live right. That story is making you want to replace yourself. You think only of what you did that was wrong and you don't like it. So you want to live better. After a while, you don't like to think of what you did wrong. So you try to forget that story. You try to pull that arrow out. You think it won't hurt anymore because now you want to live right.

It's hard to keep on living right. Many things jump up at you and block your way. But you won't forget that story. You're going to see the place where it happened, maybe every day if it's nearby and close to Cibecue. If you don't see it, you're going to hear its name and see it in your mind. It doesn't matter if you get old—that place will keep on stalking you like the one who shot you with the story. Maybe that person will die. Even so, that place will keep on stalking you. It's like that person is still alive.

Even if we go far away from here to some big city, places around here keep stalking us. If you live wrong, you will hear the names and see the places in your mind. They keep on stalking you, even if you go across oceans. The names of all these places are good. They make you remember how to live right, so you want to replace yourself again.

A WESTERN APACHE HUNTING METAPHOR

Nick Thompson's model of Western Apache storytelling is a compelling construction. To be sure, it is the formulation of one Apache only; but it is fully explicit and amply detailed, and I have been able to corroborate almost every aspect of it with other Apaches from Cibecue. This is not to imply that all Apache people interpret their hunting metaphor for storytelling in exactly the same fashion. On the contrary, one of the properties of any successful metaphor is that it can be refined and enlarged in different ways. Thus, some Apaches assert that historical tales, like arrows, leave wounds—mental and emotional wounds—and that the process of "replacing oneself" is properly understood as a form of healing. Other Apache consultants stress that place-names, rather than the sites to which the names refer, are what individuals are unable to forget after historical tales have done their work. But differences and elaborations of this kind only demonstrate the scope and flexibility of the hunting metaphor and do nothing to alter its basic contours or to diminish its considerable force. Neither does such variation reduce in any way the utility of the metaphor as an effective instrument of Western Apache thought.

Although I cannot claim to understand the full range of meanings that the hunting model for storytelling has for Western Apache people, the general premises on which the model rests seem clear to me. Historical tales have the capacity to thrust socially delinquent persons into periods of intense critical self-examination from which (ideally, at least) they emerge chastened, repentant, and determined to "live right." Simultaneously, people who have been "shot" with stories experience a form of anguish—shame, guilt, perhaps only pervasive chagrin—that moves them to alter aspects of their behavior so as to conform more closely to community expectations. In short, historical tales have the power to change people's ideas about themselves: to force them to admit to social failings, to dwell seriously on the significance of these lapses, and to resolve, it is hoped once and for all, not to repeat them. As Nick Thompson says, historical tales "make you think about your life."

After stories and storytellers have served this beneficial purpose, features of the physical landscape take over and perpetuate it. Mountains and arroyos step in symbolically for grandmothers and uncles. Just as the latter have "stalked" delinquent individuals in the past, so, too, particular locations continue to stalk them in the present. Such surveillance is essential, Apaches maintain, because "living right" requires constant care and attention, and there is always a possibility that old stories and their initial impact, like old arrows and their wounds, will fade and disappear. In other words, there is always a chance that persons who have "replaced themselves" once—or twice, or three times—will relax their guard against "badness" and slip back into undesirable forms of social conduct. Consequently, Apaches explain, individuals need to be continuously reminded of why they were "shot" in the first place and how they reacted to it at the time. Geographical sites, together with the crisp mental pictures of them presented by their names, serve admirably in this capacity, inviting people to recall their earlier failings and encouraging them to resolve, once again, to avoid them in the future. Grandmothers and uncles must perish, but the landscape endures, and for this the Apache people are grateful. "The land," Nick Thompson observes, "looks after us. The land keeps badness away."

Losing the land is something the Western Apaches can ill afford to do, for geographical features have served the people for centuries as indispensable mnemonic pegs on which to hang the moral teachings of their history.

It is also apparent that such locations, charged as they are with personal and social significance, work in important ways to shape the images that Apaches have—or should have—of themselves. Speaking to people like Nick Thompson, Annie Peaches, and Benson Lewis, one forms the impression that Apaches view the landscape as a repository of distilled wisdom, a stern but benevolent keeper of tradition, an ever-vigilant ally in the efforts of individuals and whole communities to maintain a set of standards for social living that is uniquely and distinctly their own. In the world that the Western Apaches have constituted for themselves, features of the landscape have become symbols of and for this way of living, the symbols of a culture and the enduring moral character of its people.

We may assume that this relationship with the land has been pervasive throughout Western Apache history, but in today's climate of social change, its importance for Apache people may well be deepening. Communities such as Cibecue, formerly isolated and very much turned inward, were opened up by paved roads less than twenty-five years ago, and the consequences of improved access and freer travel—including greatly increased contact with Anglo-Americans—have been pronounced.

Younger Apaches, who today complain frequently about the tedium of village life, have started to develop new tastes and ambitions, and some of them are eager to explore the outside world. Older members of the community understand this desire and do little to try to stifle it, but they are concerned that as younger people learn more and more of the "whiteman's way" they will also lose sight of portions of their own. Let the pink plastic curlers at the girls' puberty ceremonial stand as one case in point. What can be done to guard against this unsettling possibility? Perhaps, in the long run, nothing. But for now, and probably for some time to come, the landscape is doing a respectable job. It is there, "stalking" people all the time, and to the extent that it remains not merely a physical presence but an omnipresent moral force, young Apaches are not likely to forget that the "whiteman's way" belongs to a different world.

"GOODNESS IS ALL AROUND"

 The news sweeps through Cibecue like brush fire: Nick Thompson must have purchased a wheelchair because he was seen this morning *racing* in one, against his four-year-old grandson. The little boy, shrieking with glee and running as fast as he could, won the contest, but the old man finished close behind. Nick's wife was horrified and his oldest daughter yelled twice to him to stop. But he kept on going, wheeling himself along with his one good arm and paying no attention whatsoever. That old man will do anything! He doesn't care at all what people think! And what if he *crashed!*

Nick Thompson has no intention of crashing. Seated now in his familiar place beneath the cottonwood tree near his house, he says that racing his wheelchair is perfectly safe. He says he plans to do it again; he has already challenged his six-year-old granddaughter. He says he is tired of the women in his camp telling him what to do. He is also tired of not being able to move around freely, which is why he bought the wheelchair in the first place, and people should understand this and stop making such a fuss. And besides, the old man observes, the wheelchair has good brakes. That's what he likes best—getting up speed and jamming on the brakes.

The summer of 1981 is almost gone, and soon I must leave Cibecue. I have walked to Nick's camp to tell him good-bye. This is never easy for me, and we spend most of the time talking about other things. Eventually, I move to thank him for his generosity, his patience, and the things he has taught me. Nick responds by pointing with his lips to a low ridge that runs behind his home in an easterly direction away from Cibecue Creek. "That is a good place," he says. "These are all good places. Goodness is all around."

The old man pauses. Then he reaches beneath the seat of his chair and produces a blue and white cap which he places, slightly askew, on his head. The embossed emblem in front, which is in the shape of a car, reads "Ford Racing Team." We both begin to laugh . . . and laugh and laugh.

5

Education and the Human Condition

Jules Henry

LEARNING TO LEARN

The paradox of the human condition is expressed more in education than elsewhere in human culture, because learning to learn has been and continues to be *Homo sapiens'* most formidable evolutionary task. Although it is true that mammals, as compared to birds and fishes, have to learn so much that it is difficult to say by the time we get to chimpanzees what behavior is inborn and what is learned, the learning task has become so enormous for man that today learning—education—along with survival, constitutes a major preoccupation. In all the fighting over education we are simply saying that we are not yet satisfied—after about a million years of struggling to become human—that we have mastered the fundamental human task, learning. It must also be clear that we will never quite learn how to learn, for since *Homo sapiens* is self-changing, and since the *more* culture changes the *faster* it changes, man's methods and rate of learning will never quite keep pace with his need to learn. This is the heart of the problem of "cultural lag," for each fundamental scientific discovery presents man with an incalculable number of problems which he cannot foresee. Who, for example, would have anticipated that the discoveries of Einstein would have presented us with the social problems of the nuclear age, or that information theory would have produced unemployment and displacement in world markets?

FETTERING AND FREEING

Another learning problem inherent in the human condition is the fact that we must conserve culture while changing it; that we must always be *more* sure of surviving than of adapting—*as we see it.* Whenever a new idea appears our first concern as *animals* must be that it does not kill us; then, and only then, can we look at it from other points of view. While it is true that we are often mistaken, either because we become enchanted with certain modes of thought or because we cannot anticipate their consequences, this tendency to look first at survival has resulted in fettering the capacity to learn new things. In general, primitive people solved this problem simply by walling their children off from new possibilities by educational methods that, largely through fear (including ridicule, beating, and mutilation [sic]) so narrowed the perceptual sphere that other than traditional ways of viewing the world became unthinkable. Thus throughout history the cultural pattern has been a device for binding the intellect. Today, when we think we wish to free the mind so it will soar, we are still, nevertheless, bound by the ancient paradox, for we must hold our culture together through clinging to old ideas lest, in adopting new ones, we literally cease to exist.

In searching the literature on the educational practices of other civilizations I have found nothing that better expresses the need to teach and to fetter than the following, from an account by a traveler along the Niger River in Africa in the fourteenth century:

> their zeal for learning the Koran by heart [is so great that] they put their children in chains if they show any backwardness in memorizing it, and they are not set free until they have it by heart. I visited the *qadi* in his house on the day of the festival. His children were chained up, so I said to him, "Will you not let them loose?" He replied, "I shall not do so until they learn the Koran by heart."[1]

Perhaps the closest material parallel we have to this from our our cultural tradition is the stocks in which ordinary English upper-class children were forced to stand in the eighteenth century while they pored over their lessons at home. The fettering of the mind while we "set the spirit free" or the fettering of the spirit as we free the mind is an abiding paradox of "civilization" in its more refined dimensions. It is obvious that chimpanzees are incapable of this paradox. It is this capacity to pass from the jungles of the animal world into the jungle of paradox of the human condition that, more than anything else, marks off human from animal learning. It is this jungle that confronts the child in his early days at school, and that seals his destiny—if it has not previously been determined by poverty—as an eager mind or as a faceless learner.

Since education is always against some things and for others, it bears the burden of the cultural obsessions. While the Old Testament extols without cease the glory of the One God, it speaks with equal emphasis against the gods of the Philistines; while the children of the Dakota Indians learned loyalty to their own tribe, they learned to hate the Crow; and while our children are taught to love our American democracy, they are taught contempt for totalitarian regimes. It thus comes about that most educational systems are imbued with anxiety and hostility, that they are against as many things as they are for. Because, therefore, so much anxiety inheres in any human educational system—anxiety that it may free when it should fetter; anxiety that it may fetter when it should free; anxiety that it may teach sympathy when it should teach anger; anxiety that it may disarm where it should arm—our contemporary education system is constantly under attack. When, in anxiety about the present state of our world, we turn upon the schools with even more venom that we turn on our government, we are "right" in the sense that it is in the schools that the basic binding and freeing processes that will "save" us will be established. But being "right" derives not so much from the faults of our schools but from the fact that the schools are the central conserving force of the culture. The Great Fear thus turns our hostility unerringly in the direction of the focus of survival and change, in the direction of education.

CREATIVITY AND ABSURDITY

The function of education has never been to free the mind and the spirit of man, but to bind them; and to the end that the mind and spirit of his children should never escape *Homo sapiens* has employed praise, ridicule, admonition, accusation, mutilation, and even torture to chain them to the culture pattern. Throughout most of his historic course *Homo sapiens* has wanted from his children acquiescence, not originality. It is natural that this should be so, for where every man is unique there is no society, and where there is no society there can be no man. Contemporary American educators think they want creative children, yet it is an open question as to what they expect these children to create. And certainly the classrooms— from kindergarten to graduate school—in which they expect it to happen are not crucibles of creative activity and thought. It stands to reason that were young people truly creative the culture would fall apart, for originality, by definition, is different from what is given, and what is given is the culture itself. From the endless, pathetic, "creative hours" of kindergarten to the most abstruse problem in sociology and anthropology, the function of education is to prevent the truly creative intellect from getting out of hand. Only in the exact and the biological sciences do we permit unlimited freedom, for we have (but only since the Renaissance, since Galileo and Bruno underwent the Inquisition) found a way—or *thought* we had found a way—to bind the explosive powers of science in the containing vessel of the social system.

American classrooms, like educational institutions anywhere, express the values, preoccupations and fears found in the culture as a whole. School has no choice; it must train the children to fit the culture as it is. School can give training in skills; it cannot teach creativity. All the American school can conceivably do is nurture creativity when it appears. And who has the eyes to see it? Since the creativity that is conserved and encouraged will always be that which seems to do the most for the culture, which seems at the moment to do the most for the obsessions and the brutal preoccupations and anxieties from which we all suffer, schools nowadays encourage the child with gifts in mathematics and the exact sciences. But the child who has the intellectual strength to see through social shams is of no consequence to the educational system.

Creative intellect is mysterious, devious, and irritating. An intellectually creative child may fail, for example, in social studies, simply because he cannot understand the stupidities he is taught to believe as "fact." He may even end up agreeing with his teachers that he is "stupid" in social studies. Learning social studies is, to no small extent, whether in elementary school or the university, learning to be stupid. Most of us accomplish this task before we enter high school. But the child with a socially creative imagination will not be encouraged to play among new social systems, values, and relationships; nor is there much likelihood of it, if for no other reason than that the social studies teachers will perceive such a child as a poor student. Furthermore, such a child will simply be unable to fathom the absurdities that seem transparent *truth* to the teacher. What idiot believes in the "law of supply and demand," for example? But the children who do tend to *become* idiots, and learning to be an idiot is part of growing up! Or, as Camus put it, learning to be *absurd*. Thus the child who finds it impossible to learn to think the absurd the truth, who finds it difficult to accept absurdity as a way of life, the intellectually creative child whose mind makes him flounder like a poor fish in the net of absurdities flung around him in school, usually comes to think himself stupid.

The schools have therefore never been places for the stimulation of young minds. If all through school the young were provoked to question the Ten Commandments, the sanctity of revealed religion, the foundations of patriotism, the profit motive, the two-party system, monogamy, the laws of incest, and so on, we would have more creativity than we could handle. In teaching our children to accept fundamentals of social relationships and religious beliefs without question we follow the ancient highways of the human race, which extend backward into the dawn of the species, and indefinitely into the future. There must therefore be more of the caveman than of the spaceman about our teachers.

NOTE

1. Ibn Battuta, *Travels in Asia and Africa*, London: Broadway House, Carter Lane, 1957, p. 330. (Translated and selected by H. A. R. Gibb, from the original written in 1325–54.)

6

The Nature of Education

Emile Durkheim

. . . Education has varied infinitely in time and place. In the cities of Greece and Rome, education trained the individual to subordinate himself blindly to the collectivity, to become the creature of society. Today, it tries to make of the individual an autonomous personality. In Athens, they sought to form cultivated souls, informed, subtle, full of measure and harmony, capable of enjoying beauty and the joys of pure speculation; in Rome, they wanted above all for children to become men of action, devoted to military glory, indifferent to letters and the arts. In the Middle Ages, education was above all Christian; in the Renaissance, it assumes a more lay and literary character; today science tends to assume the place in education formerly occupied by the arts. Can it be said, then, that the fact is not the ideal; that if education has varied, it is because men have mistaken what it should be? But if Roman education had been infused with an individualism comparable to ours, the Roman city would not have been able to maintain itself; Latin civilization would not have developed, nor, furthermore, our modern civilization, which is in part descended from it. The Christian societies of the Middle Ages would not have been able to survive if they had given to free inquiry the place that we give it today. There are, then, ineluctable necessities which it is impossible to disregard. Of what use is it to imagine a kind of education that would be fatal for the society that put it into practice?

This assumption, so doubtful, in itself rests on a more general mistake. If one begins by asking, thus, what an ideal education must be, abstracted from conditions of time and place, it is to admit implicitly that a system of education has no reality in itself. One does not see in education a collection of practices and institutions that have been organized slowly in the course of time, which are comparable with all the other social institutions and which express them, and which, therefore, can no more be changed at will than the structure of the society itself. But it seems that this would be a pure system of *a priori* concepts; under this heading it appears to be a logical construct. One imagines that men of each age organize it voluntarily to realize a determined end; that, if this organization is not everywhere the same, it is because mistakes have been made concerning either the end that it is to pursue or the means of attaining it. From this point of view, educational systems of the past appear as so many errors, total or partial. No attention need be paid to them, therefore; we do not have to associate ourselves with the faulty observation or logic of our predecessors; but we can and must pose the question without concerning ourselves with solutions that have been given, that is to say, leaving aside everything that has been, we have only to ask ourselves what should be. The lessons of history can, moreover, serve to prevent us from repeating the errors that have been committed.

In fact, however, each society, considered at a given stage of development, has a system of education which exercises an irresistible influence on individuals. It is idle to think that we can rear our children as we wish. There are customs to which we are bound to conform; if we flout them too severely, they take their vengeance on our children. The children, when they are adults, are unable to live with their peers, with whom they are not in accord. Whether they had been raised in accordance with ideas that were either obsolete or premature does not matter; in the one case as in the other, they are not of their time and, therefore, they are outside the conditions of normal life. There is, then, in each period, a prevailing type of education from which we cannot deviate without encountering that lively resistance which restrains the fancies of dissent.

Now, it is not we as individuals who have created the customs and ideas that determine this type. They are the product of a common life, and they express its needs. They are, moreover, in large part the work of preceding generations. The entire human past has contributed to the formation of this totality of maxims that guide education today; our entire history has left its traces in it, and even the history of the peoples who have come before. It is thus that the higher organisms carry in themselves the reflection of the whole biological evolution of which they are the end product. Historical investigation of the formation and development of systems of education reveals that they depend upon religion, political organization, the degree of development of science, the state of industry, etc. If they are considered apart from all these historic causes, they become incomprehensible. Thus, how can the individual pretend to reconstruct, through his own private reflection, what is not a work of individual thought? He is not confronted with a *tabula rasa* on which he can write what he wants, but with existing realities which he cannot create, or destroy, or transform, at will. He can act on them only to the extent that he has learned to understand them, to know their nature and the conditions on which they depend; and he can understand them only if he studies them, only if he starts by observing them, as the physicist observes inanimate matter and the biologist, living bodies.

Besides, how else to proceed? When one wants to determine by dialectics alone what education should be, it is necessary to begin by asking what objectives it must have. But what is it that allows us to say that education has certain ends rather than others? We do not know *a priori* what is the function of respiration or of circulation in a living being. By what right would we be more well informed concerning the educational function? It will be said in reply that from all the evidence, its object is the training of children. But this is posing the problem in slightly different terms; it does not resolve it. It would be necessary to say of what this training consists, what its direction is, what human needs it satisfies. Now, one can answer these questions only by beginning with observation of what it has consisted of, what needs it has satisfied in the past. Thus, it appears that to establish the preliminary notion of education, to determine what is so called, historical observation is indispensable.

DEFINITION OF EDUCATION

To define education we must, then, consider educational systems, present and past, put them together, and abstract the characteristics which are common to them. These characteristics will constitute the definition that we seek.

We have already determined, along the way, two elements. In order that there be education, there must be a generation of adults and one of youth, in interaction, and an influence exercised by the first on the second. It remains for us to define the nature of this influence.

There is, so to speak, no society in which the system of education does not present a twofold aspect: it is at the same time one and manifold.

It is manifold. Indeed, in one sense, it can be said that there are as many different kinds of education as there are different milieux in a given society. Is such a society formed of castes? Education varies from one caste to another; that of the patricians was not that of the plebeians; that of the Brahman was not that of the Sudra. Similarly, in the Middle Ages, what a difference between the culture that the young page received, instructed in all the arts of chivalry, and that of the villein, who learned in his parish school a smattering of arithmetic, song and grammar! Even today, do we not see education vary with social class, or even with locality? That of the city is not that of the country, that of the middle class is not that of the worker. Would one say that this organization is not morally justifiable, that one can see in it only a survival destined to disappear? This proposition is easy to defend. It is evident that the education of our children should not depend upon the chance of their having been born here or there, of some parents rather than others. But even though the moral conscience of our time would have received, on this point, the satisfaction that it expects, education would not, for all that, become more uniform. Even though the career of each child would, in large part, no longer be predetermined by a blind heredity, occupational specialization would not fail to

result in a great pedagogical diversity. Each occupation, indeed, constitutes a milieu *sui generis* which requires particular aptitudes and specialized knowledge, in
which certain ideas, certain practices, certain modes of viewing things, prevail; and
as the child must be prepared for the function that he will be called upon to fulfill,
education, beyond a certain age, can no longer remain the same for all those to
whom it applies. That is why we see it, in all civilized countries, tending more and
more to become diversified and specialized; and this specialization becomes more
advanced daily. The heterogeneity which is thus created does not rest, as does that
which we were just discussing, on unjust inequalities; but it is not less. To find an
absolutely homogeneous and egalitarian education, it would be necessary to go back
to prehistoric societies, in the structure of which there is no differentiation; and
yet these kinds of societies represent hardly more than one logical stage in the history of humanity.

But, whatever may be the importance of these special educations, they are not
all of education. It may even be said that they are not sufficient unto themselves;
everywhere that one observes them, they vary from one another only beyond a
certain point, up to which they are not differentiated. They all rest upon a common base. There is no people among whom there is not a certain number of ideas,
sentiments and practices which education must inculcate in all children indiscrimi-
nately, to whatever social category they belong. Even in a society which is divided
into closed castes, there is always a religion common to all, and, consequently, the
principles of the religious culture, which is, then, fundamental, are the same
throughout the population. If each caste, each family, has its special gods, there are
general divinities that are recognized by everyone and which all children learn to
worship. And as these divinities symbolize and personify certain sentiments, certain ways of conceiving the world and life, one cannot be initiated into their cult
without acquiring, at the same time, all sorts of thought patterns which go beyond
the sphere of the purely religious life. Similarly, in the Middle Ages, serfs, villeins,
burgers and nobles received, equally, a common Christian education. If it is thus
in societies where intellectual and moral diversity reach this degree of contrast, with
how much more reason is it so among more advanced peoples where classes, while
remaining distinct, are, however, separated by a less profound cleavage! Where these
common elements of all education are not expressed in the form of religious symbols, they do not, however, cease to exist. In the course of our history, there has
been established a whole set of ideas on human nature, on the respective importance of our different faculties, on right and duty, on society, on the individual, on
progress, on science, on art, etc., which are the very basis of our national spirit; all
education, that of the rich as well as that of the poor, that which leads to professional careers as well as that which prepares for industrial functions, has as its object to fix them in our minds.

From these facts it follows that each society sets up a certain ideal of man, of
what he should be, as much from the intellectual point of view as the physical and
moral; that this ideal is, to a degree, the same for all the citizens; that beyond a

certain point it becomes differentiated according to the particular milieux that every society contains in its structure. It is this ideal, at the same time one and various, that is the focus of education. Its function, then, is to arouse in the child: (1) a certain number of physical and mental states that the society to which he belongs considers should not be lacking in any of its members; (2) certain physical and mental states that the particular social group (caste, class, family, profession) considers, equally, ought to be found among all those who make it up. Thus, it is society as a whole and each particular social milieu that determine the ideal that education realizes. Society can survive only if there exists among its members a sufficient degree of homogeneity; education perpetuates and reinforces this homogeneity by fixing in the child, from the beginning, the essential similarities that collective life demands. But on the other hand, without a certain diversity all cooperation would be impossible; education assures the persistence of this necessary diversity by being itself diversified and specialized. If the society has reached a degree of development such that the old divisions into castes and classes can no longer be maintained, it will prescribe an education more uniform at its base. If at the same time there is more division of labor, it will arouse among children, on the underlying basic set of common ideas and sentiments, a richer diversity of occupational aptitudes. If it lives in a state of war with the surrounding societies, it tries to shape people according to a strongly nationalistic model; if international competition takes a more peaceful form, the type that it tries to realize is more general and more humanistic. Education is, then, only the means by which society prepares, within the children, the essential conditions of its very existence. We shall see later how the individual himself has an interest in submitting to these requirements.

We come, then, to the following formula: *Education is the influence exercised by adult generations on those that are not yet ready for social life. Its object is to arouse and to develop in the child a certain number of physical, intellectual and moral states which are demanded of him by both the political society as a whole and the special milieu for which he is specifically destined.*

7

Why Do Frenchmen?

Gregory Bateson

Daughter: Daddy, why do Frenchmen wave their arms about?

Father: What do you mean?

D: I mean when they talk. Why do they wave their arms and all that?

F: Well—why do you smile? Or why do you stamp your foot sometimes?

D: But that's not the same thing, Daddy. I don't wave my arms about like a French-man does. I don't believe they can stop doing it, Daddy. Can they?

F: I don't know—they might find it hard to stop. . . . Can you stop smiling?

D: But Daddy, I don't smile all the time. It's hard to stop when I feel like smiling. But I don't feel like it *all* the time. And then I stop.

F: That's true—but then a Frenchman doesn't wave his arms in the same way all the time. Sometimes he waves them in one way and sometimes in another—and some-times, I think, he stops waving them.

F: What do you think? I mean, what does it make you think when a Frenchman waves his arms?

D: I think it looks silly, Daddy. But I don't suppose it looks like that to another French-man. They cannot all look silly to each other. Because if they did, they would stop it. Wouldn't they?

F: Perhaps—but that is not a very simple question. What else do they make you think?

D: Well—they look all excited . . .

F: All right—"silly" and "excited."

D: But are they really as excited as they look? If I were as excited as that, I would want to dance or sing or hit somebody on the nose . . . but they just go on waving their arms. They can't be really excited.

F: Well—are they really as silly as they look to you? And anyhow, why do you some-times want to dance and sing and punch somebody on the nose?

D: Oh. Sometimes I just feel like that.

F: Perhaps a Frenchman just feels "like that" when he waves his arms about.

D: But he couldn't feel like that *all* the time, Daddy, he just couldn't.

F: You mean—the Frenchman surely does not feel when he waves his arms exactly as you would feel if you waved yours. And surely you are right.

D: But, then, how *does* he feel?

F: Well—let us suppose you are talking to a Frenchman and he is waving his arms about, and then in the middle of the conversation, after something that you have said, he suddenly stops waving his arms, and just talks. What would you think then? That he had just stopped being silly and excited?

D: No . . . I'd be frightened. I'd think I had said something that hurt his feelings and perhaps he might be really angry.

F: Yes—and you might be right.

D: All right—so they stop waving their arms when they start being angry.

F: Wait a minute. The question, after all, is what does one Frenchman tell another Frenchman by waving his arms? And we have part of an answer—he tells him something about how he feels about the other guy. He tells him he is not seriously angry—that he is willing and able to be what you call "silly."

D: But—no—that's not sensible. He cannot do all that work so that *later* he will be able to tell the other guy that he *is* angry by just keeping his own arms still. How does he know that he is going to be angry later on?

F: He doesn't know. But, just in case . . .

D: No, Daddy, it doesn't make sense. I don't smile so as to be able to tell you I am angry by not smiling later on.

F: Yes—I think that that *is* part of the reason for smiling. And there are lots of people who smile in order to tell you that they are *not* angry—when they really are.

D: But that's different, Daddy. That's a sort of telling lies with one's face. Like playing poker.

F: Yes.

F: Now where are we? You don't think it sensible for Frenchmen to work so hard to tell each other that they are not angry or hurt. But after all what is most conversation about? I mean, among Americans?

D: But, Daddy, it's about all sorts of things—baseball and ice cream and gardens and games. And people talk about other people and about themselves and about what they got for Christmas.

F: Yes, yes—but who listens? I mean—all right, so they talk about baseball and gardens. But are they exchanging information? And, if so, *what* information?

D: Sure—when you come in from fishing, and I ask you "did you catch anything?" and you say "nothing," I didn't *know* that you wouldn't catch anything till you told me.

F: Hmm.

F: All right—so you mention my fishing—a matter about which I am sensitive—and then there is a gap, a silence in the conversation—and that silence tells you that I don't like cracks about how many fish I didn't catch. It's just like the Frenchman who stops waving his arms about when he is hurt.

D: I'm sorry, Daddy, but you did say . . .

F: No—wait a minute—let's not get confused by being sorry—I shall go out fishing again tomorrow and I shall still know that I am unlikely to catch a fish . . .

D: But, Daddy, you said all conversation is only telling other people that you are not angry with them . . .

F: Did I? No—not *all* conversation, but much of it. Sometimes if both people are willing to listen carefully, it is possible to do more than exchange greetings and good wishes. Even to do more than exchange information. The two people may even find out something which neither of them knew before.

F: Anyhow, most conversations are only about whether people are angry or something. They are busy telling each other that they are friendly—which is sometimes a lie. After all, what happens when they cannot think of anything to say? They all feel uncomfortable.

D: But wouldn't that be information, Daddy? I mean—information that they are not cross?

F: Surely, yes. But it's a different sort of information from "the cat is on the mat."

D: Daddy, why cannot people just *say* "I am not cross at you" and let it go at that?

F: Ah, now we are getting to the real problem. The point is that the messages which we exchange in gestures are really not the same as any translation of those gestures into words.

D: I don't understand.

F: I mean—that no amount of telling somebody in mere words that one is or is not angry is the same as what one might tell them by gesture or tone of voice.

D: But, Daddy, you cannot have words without some tone of voice, can you? Even if somebody uses as little tone as he can, the other people will hear that he is holding himself back—and that will be a sort of tone, won't it?

F: Yes—I suppose so. After all that's what I said just now about gestures—that the Frenchman can say something special by *stopping* his gestures.

F: But then, what do I mean by saying that "mere words" can never convey the same message as gestures—if there are no "mere words"?

D: Well, the words might be written.

F: No—that won't let me out of the difficulty. Because written words still have some sort of rhythm and they still have overtones. The point is that *no* mere words exist. There are *only* words with either gesture or tone of voice or something of the sort. But, of course, gestures without words are common enough.

D: Daddy, when they teach us French at school, why don't they teach us to wave our hands?

F: I don't know. I'm sure I don't know. That is probably one of the reasons why people find learning languages so difficult.

F: Anyway, it is all nonsense. I mean, the notion that language is made of words is all nonsense—and when I said that gestures could not be translated into "mere words," I was talking nonsense, because there is no such thing as "mere words." And all the syntax and grammar and all that stuff is nonsense. It's all based on the idea that "mere" words exist—and there are none.

D: But, Daddy . . .

F: I tell you—we have to start all over again from the beginning and assume that language is first and foremost a system of gestures. Animals after all have *only* gestures and tones of voice—and words were invented later. Much later. And after that they invented schoolmasters.

D: Daddy?

F: Yes.

D: Would it be a good thing if people gave up words and went back to only using gestures?

F: Hmm. I don't know. Of course we would not be able to have any conversations like this. We could only bark, or mew, and wave our arms about, and laugh and grunt and weep. But it might be fun—it would make life a sort of ballet—with dancers making their own music.

NOTE

This metalogue is reprinted from *Impulse 1951*, an annual of contemporary dance, by permission of Impulse Publications, Inc. It has also appeared in *ETC.: A Review of General Semantics*, Vol. X, 1953.

8

Becoming a Marihuana User

Howard Becker

LEARNING THE TECHNIQUE

The novice does not ordinarily get high the first time he smokes marihuana, and several attempts are usually necessary to induce this state. One explanation of this may be that the drug is not smoked "properly," that is, in a way that insures sufficient dosage to produce real symptoms of intoxication. Most users agree that it cannot be smoked like tobacco if one is to get high:

> Take in a lot of air, you know, and . . . I don't know how to describe it, you don't smoke it like a cigarette, you draw in a lot of air and get it deep down in your system and then keep it there. Keep it there as long as you can.

Without the use of some such technique[1] the drug will produce no effects, and the user will be unable to get high:

> The trouble with people like that [who are not able to get high] is that they're just not smoking it right, that's all there is to it. Either they're not holding it down long enough, or they're getting too much air and not enough smoke, or the other way around or something like that. A lot of people just don't smoke it right, so naturally nothing's gonna happen.

If nothing happens, it is manifestly impossible for the user to develop a conception of the drug as an object which can be used for pleasure, and use will therefore not continue. The first step in the sequence of events that must occur if the person is to become a user is that he must learn to use the proper smoking technique so that his use of the drug will produce effects in terms of which his conception of it can change.

66

Such a change is, as might be expected, a result of the individual's participation in groups in which marihuana is used. In them the individual learns the proper way to smoke the drug. This may occur through direct teaching:

> I was smoking like I did an ordinary cigarette. He said, "No, don't do it like that." He said, "Suck it, you know, draw in and hold it in your lungs till you . . . for a period of time."
> I said, "Is there any limit of time to hold it?"
> He said, "No, just till you feel that you want to let it out, let it out." So I did that three or four times.

Many new users are ashamed to admit ignorance and, pretending to know already, must learn through the more indirect means of observation and imitation:

> I came on like I had turned on [smoked marihuana] many times before, you know. I didn't want to seem like a punk to this cat. See, like I didn't know the first thing about it—how to smoke it, or what was going to happen, or what. I just watched him like a hawk—I didn't take my eyes off him for a second, because I wanted to do everything just as he did it. I watched how be held it, how he smoked it, and everything. Then when he gave it to me I just came on cool, as though I knew exactly what the score was. I held it like he did and took a poke just the way he did.

No one I interviewed continued marihuana use for pleasure without learning a technique that supplied sufficient dosage for the effects of the drug to appear. Only when this was learned was it possible for a conception of the drug as an object which could be used for pleasure to emerge. Without such a conception marihuana use was considered meaningless and did not continue.

LEARNING TO PERCEIVE THE EFFECTS

Even after he learns the proper smoking technique, the new user may not get high and thus not form a conception of the drug as something which can be used for pleasure. A remark made by a user suggested the reason for this difficulty in getting high and pointed to the next necessary step on the road to being a user:

> As a matter of fact, I've seen a guy who was high out of his mind and didn't know it. [How can that be, man?]
> Well, it's pretty strange, I'll grant you that, but I've seen it. This guy got on with me, claiming that he'd never got high, one of those guys, and he got completely stoned. And he kept insisting that he wasn't high. So I had to prove to him that he was.

What does this mean? It suggests that being high consists of two elements: the presence of symptoms caused by marihuana use and the recognition of these symptoms and their connection by the user with his use of the drug. It is not enough, that is, that the effects be present; alone, they do not automatically provide the experience of being high. The user must be able to point them out to himself and consciously connect them with having smoked marihuana before he can have this experience. Otherwise, no matter what actual effects are produced, he considers that the drug has had no effect on him: "I figured it either had no effect on me or other people were exaggerating its effect on them, you know. I thought it was probably psychological, see." Such persons believe the whole thing is an illusion and that the wish to be high leads the user to deceive himself into believing that something is happening when, in fact, nothing is. They do not continue marihuana use, feeling that "it does nothing" for them.

Typically, however, the novice has faith (developed from his observation of users who do get high) that the drug actually will produce some new experience and continues to experiment with it until it does. His failure to get high worries him, and he is likely to ask more experienced users or provoke comments from them about it. In such conversations he is made aware of specific details of his experience which he may not have noticed or may have noticed but failed to identify as symptoms of being high:

I didn't get high the first time . . . I don't think I held it in long enough. I probably let it out, you know, you're a little afraid. The second time I wasn't sure, and he [smoking companion] told me, like I asked him for some of the symptoms or something, how would I know, you know. . . . So he told me to sit on a stool. I sat on—I think I sat on a bar stool—and he said, "Let your feet hang," and then when I got down my feet were real cold, you know.

And I started feeling it, you know. That was the first time. And then about a week after that, sometime pretty close to it, I really got on. That was the first time I got on a big laughing kick, you know. Then I really knew I was on.

One symptom of being high is an intense hunger. In the next case the novice becomes aware of this and gets high for the first time:

They were just laughing the hell out of me because like I was eating so much. I just scoffed [ate] so much food, and they were just laughing at me, you know. Sometimes I'd be looking at them, you know, wondering why they're laughing, you know, not knowing what I was doing. [Well, did they tell you why they were laughing eventually?] Yeah, yeah, I come back, "Hey, man, what's happening?" Like, you know, like I'd ask, "What's happening?" and all of a sudden I feel weird, you know. "Man, you're on, you know. You're on pot [high on marihuana]." I said, "No, am I?" Like I don't know what's happening.

The learning may occur in more indirect ways:

I heard little remarks that were made by other people. Somebody said, "My legs are rubbery," and I can't remember all the remarks that were made because I was very attentively listening for all these cues for what I was supposed to feel like.

The novice, then, eager to have this feeling, picks up from other users some concrete referents of the term "high" and applies these notions to his own experience. The new concepts make it possible for him to locate these symptoms among his own sensations and to point out to himself a "something different" in his experience that he connects with drug use. It is only when he can do this that he is high. In the next case, the contrast between two successive experiences of a user makes clear the crucial importance of the awareness of the symptoms in being high and re-emphasizes the important role of interaction with other users in acquiring the concepts that make this awareness possible:

[Did you get high the first time you turned on?] Yeah, sure. Although, come to think of it, I guess I really didn't. I mean, like that first time it was more or less of a mild drunk. I was happy, I guess, you know what I mean. But I didn't really know I was high, you know what I mean. It was only after the second time I got high that I realized I was high the first time. Then I knew that something different was happening.

[How did you know that?] How did I know? If what happened to me that night would of happened to you, you would've known, believe me. We played the first tune for almost two hours—one tune! Imagine, man! We got on the stand and played this one tune, we started at nine o'clock. When we got finished I looked at my watch, it's a quarter to eleven. Almost two hours on one tune. And it didn't seem like anything.

I mean, you know, it does that to you. It's like you have much more time or something. Anyway, when I saw that, man, it was too much. I knew I must really be high or something if anything like that could happen. See, and then they explained to me that that's what it did to you, you had a different sense of time and everything. So I realized that that's what it was. I knew then. Like the first time, I probably felt that way, you know, but I didn't know what's happening.

It is only when the novice becomes able to get high in this sense that he will continue to use marihuana for pleasure. In every case in which use continued, the user had acquired the necessary concepts with which to express to himself the fact that he was experiencing new sensations caused by the drug. That is, for use to continue, it is necessary not only to use the drug so as to produce effects but also to learn to perceive these effects when they occur. In this way marihuana acquires meaning for the user as an object which can be used for pleasure.

With increasing experience the user develops a greater appreciation of the drug's effects; he continues to learn to get high. He examines succeeding experiences closely, looking for new effects, making sure the old ones are still there. Out of this there grows a stable set of categories for experiencing the drug's effects whose presence enables the user to get high with ease.

Users, as they acquire this set of categories, become connoisseurs. Like experts in fine wines, they can specify where a particular plant was grown and what time of year it was harvested. Although it is usually not possible to know whether these attributions are correct, it is true that they distinguish between batches of marihuana, not only according to strength, but also with respect to the different kinds of symptoms produced.

The ability to perceive the drug's effects must be maintained if use is to continue; if it is lost, marihuana use ceases. Two kinds of evidence support this statement. First, people who become heavy users of alcohol, barbiturates, or opiates do not continue to smoke marihuana, largely because they lose the ability to distinguish between its effects and those of the other drugs.[2] They no longer know whether the marihuana gets them high. Second, in those few cases in which an individual uses marihuana in such quantities that he is always high, he is apt to feel the drug has no effect on him, since the essential element of a noticeable difference between feeling high and feeling normal is missing. In such a situation, use is likely to be given up completely, but temporarily, in order that the user may once again be able to perceive the difference.

LEARNING TO ENJOY THE EFFECTS

One more step is necessary if the user who has now learned to get high is to continue use. He must learn to enjoy the effects he has just learned to experience. Marihuana-produced sensations are not automatically or necessarily pleasurable. The taste for such an experience is a socially acquired one, not different in kind from acquired tastes for oysters or dry martinis. The user feels dizzy, thirsty; his scalp tingles; he misjudges time and distances. Are these things pleasurable? He isn't sure. If he is to continue marihuana use, he must decide that they are. Otherwise, getting high, while a real enough experience, will be an unpleasant one he would rather avoid.

The effects of the drug, when first perceived, may be physically unpleasant or at least ambiguous:

> It started taking effect, and I didn't know what was happening, you know, what it was, and I was very sick. I walked around the room, walking around the room trying to get off, you know; it just scared me at first, you know. I wasn't used to that kind of feeling.

In addition, the novice's naive interpretation of what is happening to him may further confuse and frighten him, particularly if he decides, as many do, that he is going insane:

> I felt I was insane, you know. Everything people done to me just wigged me. I couldn't hold a conversation, and my mind would be wandering, and I was always thinking, oh, I don't know, weird things, like hearing music different. . . . I get the feeling that I can't talk to anyone. I'll goof completely.

Given these typically frightening and unpleasant first experiences, the beginner will not continue use unless he learns to redefine the sensations as pleasurable:

It was offered to me, and I tried it. I'll tell you one thing. I never did enjoy it at all. I mean it was just nothing that I could enjoy. [Well, did you get high when you turned on?] Oh, yeah, I got definite feelings from it. But I didn't enjoy them. I mean I got plenty of reactions, but they were mostly reactions of fear. [You were frightened?] Yes. I didn't enjoy it. I couldn't seem to relax with it, you know. If you can't relax with a thing, you can't enjoy it, I don't think.

In other cases the first experiences were also definitely unpleasant, but the person did become a marihuana user. This occurred, however, only after a later experience enabled him to redefine the sensations as pleasurable:

[This man's first experience was extremely unpleasant, involving distortion of spatial relationships and sounds, violent thirst, and panic produced by these symptoms.] After the first time I didn't turn on for about, I'd say, ten months to a year. . . . It wasn't a moral thing; it was because I'd gotten so frightened, bein' so high. An' I didn't want to go through that again, I mean, my reaction was, "Well, if this is what they call bein' high, I don't dig [like] it.". . . So I didn't turn on for a year almost, accounta that. . . .

Well, my friends started, an' consequently I started again. But I didn't have any more, I didn't have that same initial reaction, after I started turning on again.

[In interaction with his friends he became able to find pleasure in the effects of the drug and eventually became a regular user.]

In no case will use continue without a redefinition of the effects as enjoyable.

This redefinition occurs, typically, in interaction with more experienced users who, in a number of ways, teach the novice to find pleasure in this experience which is at first so frightening.[3] They may reassure him as to the temporary character of the unpleasant sensations and minimize their seriousness, at the same time calling attention to the more enjoyable aspects. An experienced user describes how he handles newcomers to marihuana use:

Well, they get pretty high sometimes. The average person isn't ready for that, and it is a little frightening to them sometimes. I mean, they've been high on lush [alcohol], and they get higher that way than they've ever been before, and they don't know what's happening to them. Because they think they're going to keep going up, up, up till they lose their minds or begin doing weird things or something. You have to like reassure them, explain to them that they're not really flipping or anything, that they're gonna be all right. You have to just talk them out of being afraid. Keep talking to them, reassuring, telling them it's all right. And come on with your own story, you know: "The same thing happened to me. You'll get to like that after awhile." Keep coming on like that; pretty soon you talk them out of being scared. And besides they see you doing it and nothing horrible is happening to you, so that gives them more confidence.

The more experienced user may also teach the novice to regulate the amount he smokes more carefully, so as to avoid any severely uncomfortable symptoms while retaining the pleasant ones. Finally, he teaches the new user that he can "get to like it after awhile." He teaches him to regard those ambiguous experiences formerly defined as unpleasant as enjoyable. The older user in the following incident is a person whose tastes have shifted in this way, and his remarks have the effect of helping others to make a similar redefinition:

> A new user had her first experience of the effects of marihuana and became frightened and hysterical. She "felt like she was half in and half out of the room" and experienced a number of alarming physical symptoms. One of the more experienced users present said, "She's dragged because she's high like that. I'd give anything to get that high myself. I haven't been that high in years."

In short, what was once frightening and distasteful becomes, after a taste for it is built up, pleasant, desired, and sought after. Enjoyment is introduced by the favorable definition of the experience that one acquires from others. Without this, use will not continue, for marihuana will not be for the user an object he can use for pleasure.

In addition to being a necessary step in becoming a user, this represents an important condition for continued use. It is quite common for experienced users suddenly to have an unpleasant or frightening experience, which they cannot define as pleasurable, either because they have used a larger amount of marihuana than usual or because the marihuana they have used turns out to be of a higher quality than they expected. The user has sensations which go beyond any conception he has of what being high is and is in much the same situation as the novice, uncomfortable and frightened. He may blame it on an overdose and simply be more careful in the future. But he may make this the occasion for a rethinking of his attitude toward the drug and decide that it no longer can give him pleasure. When this occurs and is not followed by a redefinition of the drug as capable of producing pleasure, use will cease.

The likelihood of such a redefinition occurring depends on the degree of the individual's participation with other users. Where this participation is intensive, the individual is quickly talked out of his feeling against marihuana use. In the next case, on the other hand, the experience was very disturbing, and the aftermath of the incident cut the person's participation with other users to almost zero. Use stopped for three years and began again only when a combination of circumstances, important among which was a resumption of ties with users, made possible a redefinition of the nature of the drug:

> It was too much, like I only made about four pokes, and I couldn't even get it out of my mouth, I was so high, and I got real flipped. In the basement, you know, I just couldn't stay in there anymore. My heart was pounding real hard, you know, and I was going out of my mind; I thought I was losing my mind completely. So I cut out of this basement, and this other guy, he's out of his mind, told me, "Don't, don't leave me, man. Stay here." And I couldn't.

I walked outside, and it was five below zero, and I thought I was dying, and I had my coat open; I was sweating, I was perspiring. My whole insides were all . . . , and I walked about two blocks away, and I fainted behind a bush. I don't know how long I laid there. I woke up, and I was feeling the worst, I can't describe it at all, so I made it to a bowling alley, man, and I was trying to act normal, I was trying to shoot pool, you know, trying to act real normal, and I couldn't lay and I couldn't stand up and I couldn't sit down, and I went up and laid down where some guys that spot pins lay down, and that didn't help me, and I went down to a doctor's office. I was going to go in there and tell the doctor to put me out of my misery . . . because my heart was pounding so hard, you know. . . . So then all week end I started flipping, seeing things there and going through hell, you know, all kinds of abnormal things. . . . I just quit for a long time then.

[He went to a doctor who defined the symptoms for him as those of a nervous breakdown caused by "nerves" and "worries." Although he was no longer using marihuana, he had some recurrences of the symptoms which led him to suspect that "it was all his nerves."] So I just stopped worrying, you know; so it was about thirty-six months later I started making it again. I'd just take a few pokes, you know. [He first resumed use in the company of the same user-friend with whom he had been involved in the original incident.]

A person, then, cannot begin to use marihuana for pleasure, or continue its use for pleasure, unless he learns to define its effects as enjoyable, unless it becomes and remains an object he conceives of as capable of producing pleasure.

In summary, an individual will be able to use marihuana for pleasure only when he goes through a process of learning to conceive of it as an object which can be used in this way. No one becomes a user without (1) learning to smoke the drug in a way which will produce real effects; (2) learning to recognize the effects and connect them with drug use (learning, in other words, to get high); and (3) learning to enjoy the sensations he perceives. In the course of this process he develops a disposition or motivation to use marihuana which was not and could not have been present when he began use, for it involves and depends on conceptions of the drug which could only grow out of the kind of actual experience detailed above. On completion of this process he is willing and able to use marihuana for pleasure.

He has learned, in short, to answer "Yes" to the question: "Is it fun?" The direction his further use of the drug takes depends on his being able to continue to answer "Yes" to this question and, in addition, on his being able to answer "Yes" to other questions which arise as he becomes aware of the implications of the fact that society disapproves of the practice: "Is it expedient?" "Is it moral?" Once he has acquired the ability to get enjoyment by using the drug, use will continue to be possible for him. Considerations of morality and expediency, occasioned by the reactions of society, may interfere and inhibit use, but use continues to be a possibility in terms of his conception of the drug. The act becomes impossible only when the ability to enjoy the experience of being high is lost, through a change in the user's conception of the drug occasioned by certain kinds of experience with it.

NOTES

1. A pharmacologist notes that this ritual is in fact an extremely efficient way of getting the drug into the blood stream. See R. P. Walton, *Marihuana: America's New Drug Problem* (Philadelphia: J. B. Lippincott, 1938), p. 48.

2. "Smokers have repeatedly stated that the consumption of whiskey while smoking negates the potency of the drug. They find it very difficult to get 'high' while drinking whiskey and because of that smokers will not drink while using the 'weed.'" (New York City Mayor's Committee on Marihuana, *The Marihuana Problem in the City of New York* (Lancaster, Penn.: The Jacques Cattell Press, 1944), p. 13.)

3. Sol Charen and Luis Perelman. "Personality Studies of Marihuana Addicts." *American Journal of Psychiatry* CII (March 1946), 674–82.

Section II

Culture, Modernization, and Formal Education

Culture, Modernization, and Formal Education

Margaret Sutton

No matter where in the world you travel today—to a remote hillside, a teeming metropolis, or the middle of a desert or a forest—wherever there is a community there is likely to be a school for local children. And no matter what the state of its physical structure—whether built of wood, wattle, or cement, and one small room or three stories high—you will know that it is a school by the organization of groups of children directed by adults in didactic activities. At the end of the twentieth century, there are nearly as many children enrolled in primary schools around the world as there are primary school age children. This represents an enormous increase from 1960, when only around 60 percent were enrolled in the schools of the so-called developing countries (UNESCO 1970; 1998).

The worldwide institutionalization of children in schools may rank among the most profound forces of global cultural change of the twentieth century. Yet this extraordinary transformation of the processes of cultural transmission and reproduction has, until quite recently, received little systematic attention from ethnographers. Juliana Flinn's chapter in this section, on schooling in the South Pacific, is among the exceptions. As her article demonstrates, the study of schooling and cultural change outside the United States has much to offer students of U.S. education.

Although anthropological studies are relatively few, the disciplines of sociology, economics, and political science have undertaken extensive discussions of schooling and cultural change in the Third World. In the 1960s and 1970s, "modernization theory" insisted that the adoption of "modern" attitudes and values was essential to economic growth and democratic political development. Such attitudes and values—including a belief in the efficacy of science and positive value placed on punctuality and technical knowledge—were thought to be provided by schools (Lerner 1958; Inkeles 1974). From the perspective of modernization theory, the

77

main barrier to economic development lay in the old-fashioned beliefs of non-Western people and cultures. This view has been strongly challenged by studies demonstrating that successful economic development in the West has resulted from systematic exploitation of people and natural resources in the Third World (see Cardoso and Faletto 1979; Frank 1981). More recently, world systems literature, which looks at the global spread of government systems and other forms of social organization, has focused on schools as a central institution in all countries. World systems theorists have argued that public schooling everywhere promotes similar values, such as citizenship and loyalty to nation states (Arnove 1980; Boli, Ramirez, and Meyer 1985). Yet these studies, while illuminating of macrosocial processes, have rarely recognized the complexities of schooling and culture as they play out in the daily lives of people around the world. As Laura Rival points out in the opening of her chapter, "Formal Schooling and the Production of Modern Citizens in the Ecuadorian Amazon," both modernization and world systems studies contain an implicit bias against analyzing how "traditional" societies themselves may shape and define the practices and meanings of formal schooling. Rival rejects the assumptions of these perspectives and, indeed, all four readings included in this section challenge simplistic notions of "modernity" and "traditionalism" as standard cultural forms.

There is no doubt that the expansion of formal schooling has had a profound impact upon societies into which it has been newly introduced. At the same time, anthropologists have continuously questioned the view that the expansion of schooling has simply made people and societies of the Third World more like those of the West. As Caroline Bledsoe observes in this section, Western scholarship "can be oblivious to remarkable transformations of meaning that Western practices undergo when transplanted to new contexts." Scattered though they have been, ethnographic studies of schooling have repeatedly challenged the belief that schools inexorably and predictably change local cultures. Even among the ethnographies of schooling in the Third World written during the heyday of modernization theory (see Shaeffer 1979; Colletta 1980), there is a consistent recognition that schools are not necessarily or entirely "modern." For example, schools may or may not operate, like factories, on the basis of standardized procedures and strict time periods; learning may or may not be considered an individual accomplishment, for which individuals are impartially rewarded. Both of these are thought to be central tenets of "modern" schooling. Rather, anthropologists have recognized that local societies insinuate local meanings and practices into the institution of schooling. More recent work, such as Amy Stambach's (1996) analysis of agricultural education in northern Tanzania, elaborates the ways in which existing beliefs and values of local cultures shape how children and parents think about the purpose of schooling.

The selection from Yehudi Cohen's classic article on education and socialization shows that, in fact, a broad continuum of teaching/learning arrangements is possible across time and place. Cohen distinguishes between the socialization of children by relatives or kin, and formal education carried out by a special category of people—teachers—designated to impart the same information to all. All societies support arrangements for socialization and recruitment of children into cultural norms and practices (see the introduction to this book). Cohen's chapter, however, looks more closely at the *mechanisms* for transmitting knowledge, values, and practices, rather than at their content. He points out that the deep meaning of cultural knowledge shifts according to who is conveying it and through what relationships to the child. What Cohen suggests are differences in degree, but not in kind, between what is learned and how it is learned by, say, children in New York City and children in the mountains of the Hindu Kush. This places Cohen's work squarely within the great anthropological tradition of emphasizing cross-cultural universals, that is, the fundamental similarities of human ways of life.

Schools always mean more and different things to a society than simply the transmission of knowledge. The mere introduction of a school into a community where no school existed before transforms the physical and social landscape. Rival shows this well in her discussion of formal schooling in the Ecuadorian Amazon. When a school is opened in a forest community, that community is literally put onto the map of Ecuador. The school demands a physical space with cleared land around it, making it stand out from the local environment—and creating a different form of behavior for all who enter that space, whether students or not. And, like the "hidden curriculum" of U.S. schooling (see deMarrais and LeCompte 1999), schools in the Amazon teach unintended lessons. In particular, the schools teach that to be modern is to possess not only a certain set of attitudes or skills, but also a certain set of material goods. Because children spend the major part of their day in the school, away from older members of the community, they do not have an opportunity to learn traditional knowledge and skills for creating food and shelter. The curriculum does not convey any of these skills, but rather a vision of urban, middle-class life. As a result of the curriculum and practices of schooling, Rival argues, forest children in Ecuador become *de-skilled* in relation to their immediate environment. At the same time, the knowledge acquired in schools may have little relevance to the local environment and economy. As Maurice Bloch argues for the similar case of the Zafimaniry people in Madagascar, the basic literacy conveyed by the schools becomes increasingly irrelevant as children grow older (Bloch 1993).

But the impact of schools on cultures does not move only in one direction. Flinn's chapter in this volume, "Transmitting Traditional Values in New Schools: Elementary Education of Pulap Atoll," nicely illustrates a case of reciprocal influences between schooling and local culture. With secondary school attendance now the norm among Micronesians as a whole, it is increasingly common for young Pulapese to leave their island after the eighth grade in order to attend high schools. Formal schooling is also, in Pulap as around the world, the key to future employment. These observations support the contentions of modernization theory, that the expansion of schooling redefines economic roles. At the same time, though, Flinn shows that patterns of social interaction, dress, and learning that are endogenous to Pulapese culture have been taken up within the classrooms of the schools of Pulap. Like classroom-based studies of Native American and Inuit communities (see Lipka 1991;

Paradise 1994), Flinn's chapter illuminates the profound variations in pedagogy that can be encompassed by the singular institution of formal schooling.

Bledsoe's chapter, "The Cultural Transformation of Western Education in Sierra Leone," further elaborates on the relationship of teachers to students and to subject matter, showing how local structures of authority relationships, like patterns of adult/child interaction, can transform the meanings of school-based learning. As Bledsoe demonstrates, the Mende people of Sierra Leone do not consider a child's success in school to rest solely on her abilities and efforts. Rather, the "blessings" of the teacher are required in order to attain the high examination marks that will enable passage up into higher levels of schooling. The need for a teacher's blessing can, in turn, provide a rationale for teachers to demand personal labor from students. These beliefs differ from fundamental assumptions and values underlying Western schooling. The institution of Western schooling carries with it assumptions about the nature, purpose, and meaning of knowledge, assumptions linked to the elaboration of specialized forms of science and scholarship in the academies of nineteenth-century Europe and North America. One of these assumptions is that knowledge is available equally to those who attend school so that talent and individual effort on the part of the student will determine how much learning is attained. Such beliefs are central to the notion of education as a foundation for meritocracy, the belief that individuals will be economically and socially rewarded for their attainments, not for the social status into which they are born. However, rather than maintaining an ideal of social neutrality towards their pupils, Mende teachers reinforce the personalized relations that Cohen, in the earlier article, associates with socialization.

The norm of social neutrality is also violated by gender differences in educational participation and experience, with girls around the world participating in schooling at a lower rate than boys. The basic economic reason, which is well documented among the poor of many and diverse societies, is the so-called opportunity cost of girls' schooling (Kelly and Elliott 1982; Floro and Wolf 1990; King and Hill 1993; Sutton 1998). Simply put, in rural and impoverished urban households around the world, girls' labor is more important to the domestic economy than is boys' labor. From a surprisingly early age—eight, ten, or twelve—girls provide a great deal of the childcare, food and fuel gathering, and meal preparation that keep a household running. As a result, girl children are less likely to enter, and even less to stay in school than are boys.

Although the basic economic limits to girls' schooling are well known, attention to local cultural practices and beliefs is extremely important for understanding how schooling provides different meanings and opportunities for girls and boys in specific societies. Within the literature on education and development, local culture is frequently treated as a "barrier" to girls' schooling, a source of gender-restrictive norms and values that make parents unwilling to promote and support education for their daughters. Recent ethnographic insights into increased girls' schooling, however, suggest a very different picture. With expanded supplies of schools and teachers and the growth of modern communication, the schooling experience is becoming as "normal" to girlhood as it is to boyhood. It has now become more important for those concerned with women's equality to look into the meaning of schooling for girls, than to endlessly reiterate the existence of economic and ideological barriers to their participation (see Biraimah 1982; Luttrell 1996; Skinner and Holland 1996).

The small but growing number of ethnographic studies on girls' schooling experiences have illustrated, as do the articles in this section, the dynamic exchange of meaning between local cultures and global institutions such as formal schooling. Around the world, curriculum analysis has shown that textbooks and formal curricula portray men and women in stereotyped roles. Concern is growing, for example, among groups like the Forum for African Women Educators (based in Nairobi, Kenya), that girls in Africa, like those in the United States, are not being encouraged to excel in math and sciences, fields that provide the foundations for entry into high-prestige professions.

In a similar vein, studies around the world illustrate how persistent ethnic and class divisions are reproduced through schooling. In a now-famous ethnographic study of working-class boys in a British high school, Paul Willis (1981) shows that as they near adulthood, these young men develop a belief that they should and must be part of the working class, rather than breaking into a different social status. Even relatively "invisible" minorities, such as the Burakumin of Japan (whose names and appearance cannot be distinguished from "majority group" Japanese), are among the less powerful groups in most societies that leave school at a greater disadvantage than they began, in comparison to more powerful groups. Somehow—and to the great frustration of educators everywhere—the institution of schooling does *not* appear to be "leveling the playing field" between social haves and have-nots. Close-up views of teaching practices, curriculum content, and school achievement in other countries can be highly illuminating for understanding how inequalities are reproduced in U.S. classrooms. Perhaps of most value to U.S. educators, however, is the deepened insight into our own education system that is provided by anthropological studies of education elsewhere. It can be easier, at first, to see how inequalities operate in other societies than in our own. With the wisdom so gained, it is possible to look at our own educational practices, and their relationship to society as a whole, with new and critical eyes.

REFERENCES AND READINGS

Arnove, R. F. 1980. Comparative Education and World System Analysis. *Comparative Education Review* 24 (1): 48–62.

Biraimah, K. C. 1982. The Impact of Western Schools on Girls' Expectations: A Togolese Case. In *Women's Education in the Third World: Comparative Perspectives*, edited by G. P. Kelly and C. M. Elliott. Albany: SUNY Press.

Bloch, M. 1993. The Uses of Schooling and Literacy in a Zafimaniry Village. In *Cross-cultural Approaches to Literacy*, edited by B. Street. Cambridge: Cambridge University Press.

Boli, J., Ramirez, F. O., and Meyer, J. W. 1985. Explaining the Origins and Expansion of Mass Education. *Comparative Education Review* 29:145–170.

Cardoso, F. H., and Faletto, E. 1979. *Dependency and Development in Latin America.* Berkeley: University of California Press.

Colletta, N. J. 1980. *American Schools for the Natives of Ponape: A Study of Education and Culture Change in Micronesia.* Honolulu: University Press of Hawaii.

deMarrais, K. B., and LeCompte, M. D. 1999. *The Way Schools Work: A Sociological Analysis of Education.* New York: Longman.

Floro, M., and Wolf, J. M. 1990. *The Economic and Social Impacts of Girls' Primary Education in Developing Countries.* Washington, D.C.: USAID.

Frank, A. G. 1981. *Crisis in the Third World.* New York: Holmes and Meier.

Hoben, A. 1982. Anthropologists and Development. *Annual Review of Anthropology* 11:349–375.

Inkeles, A. 1974. *Becoming Modern: Individual Change in Six Developing Countries.* Cambridge, Mass.: Harvard University Press.

Kelly, G. P., and Elliott, C. M., eds. 1982. *Women's Education in the Third World: Comparative Perspectives.* Albany: SUNY Press.

King, E. M., and Hill, M. A., eds. 1993. *Women's Education in Developing Countries: Barriers, Benefits, and Policies.* Baltimore, Md., and London: The Johns Hopkins University Press.

Lerner, D. 1958. *The Passing of Traditional Society: Modernizing the Middle East.* Glencoe, Ill.: Free Press.

Lipka, J. 1991. Towards a Culturally Based Pedagogy. *Anthropology and Education Quarterly* 22 (3): 203–223.

Luttrell, W. 1996. Becoming Somebody in and against School: Toward a Psychocultural Theory of Gender and Self-making. In *The Cultural Production of the Educated Person*, edited by B. A. Levinson, D. S. Foley, and D. C. Holland. Albany: SUNY Press.

Paradise, R. 1994. Interactional Style and Nonverbal Meaning: Mazahua Children Learning How to Be Separate-but-together. *Anthropology and Education Quarterly* 25 (2): 156–172.

Shaeffer, S. F. 1979. Schooling in a Developing Society: A Case Study of Indonesian Primary Education. Ph.D. dissertation. Stanford University.

Skinner, D., and Holland, D. 1996. Schools and the Cultural Production of the Educated Person in a Nepalese Hill Community. In *The Cultural Production of the Educated Person*, edited by B. A. Levinson, D. S. Foley, and D. C. Holland. Albany: SUNY Press.

Spindler, G. D., ed. 1987. *Education and Cultural Process: Anthropological Approaches.* Prospect Heights, Ill.: Waveland.

Stambach, A. 1996. "Seeded" in the Market Economy: Schooling and Social Transformations on Mount Kilimanjaro. *Anthropology and Education Quarterly* 27 (4): 545–567.

Sutton, M. 1998. Girls' Educational Access and Attainment. In *Women in the Third World: An Encyclopedia of Contemporary Issues*, edited by N. P. Stromquist. New York and London: Garland.

UNESCO. 1970. *World Education Indicators.* Paris: UNESCO.

———. 1998. *World Education Indicators.* Paris: UNESCO.

Willis, P. 1981. *Learning to Labour: How Working Class Kids Get Working Class Jobs.* New York: Columbia University Press.

9

The Shaping of Men's Minds: Adaptations to Imperatives of Culture

Yehudi A. Cohen

INTRODUCTION

One of the earliest and most significant of anthropology's discoveries was that culture is a particular way of shaping the mind. More than being a series of habits and patches of exotic customs, of ways of earning a livelihood, or of being clothed and adorned, anthropologists learned that the essence of a culture is to be sought in the material and intellectual symbols to which people respond in their social relations and in meeting their basic necessities. Indeed, many anthropologists are agreed that in their daily lives people in all societies respond to cultural symbols rather than to objective reality. Close on the heels of this insight was the awareness that the symbolizations of cultural life do not have their roots in race or any other aspect of biology but are learned as the result of systematic and consistent experiences to which the individual is exposed in the course of growing up.

With this also came another significant realization that has served as one of the cornerstones of modern anthropology, namely, that one way of conceptualizing a culture is as a self-perpetuating system. Thus, an important group of anthropologists asserted that one of the most important tasks in the study of culture is to seek an understanding of the means by which social systems shape the minds of their members in order to assure the perpetuation of their cultures.

During the 1940s, these concepts were given an added dimension as a result of Hallowell's investigations (1955) of the psychological components of acculturation among the Ojibwa, in which he found that the adoption of formal features of Euro-American culture, especially of material items, did not necessarily involve the reshaping of modes of mind; instead, he found that traditional patterns of cognition, motivation, and emotional functioning can often covary with the radios, guns, clothing, and money of their conquerors.

With growing attention by anthropologists generally to the concepts emerging from the study of biological evolution, and the timely resurgence of interest in the processes underlying the evolution of social organization, the conviction has been strengthened among anthropologists that it is the population, rather than the individual, that is the adaptive unit.

Adaptation refers to the relationship maintained by a group to its environment. The adaptive mechanisms that develop in a population to facilitate its survival are not only to be found in its technology and in its economic, political, and legal organizations but also in patterns of cognition, motivation, and impulse control. Whether we are dealing with technology, formal institutions, or psychological processes, patterns of institutional organization must be seen as aspects of adaptation by a population to highly specific environmental pressures.

I am going to deal in this paper with a limited aspect of the ways in which society shapes the individual's mind. Specifically, I am going to distinguish between *socialization* and *education*, and examine their relationships to each other. My contention is that the proportion assumed by one vis-à-vis the other is an adaptation to certain imperatives in the sociocultural environment, especially its structure of social relations. In terms of the principal focus of this paper, the modes of upbringing in a society—the means by which the mind is shaped—are to be regarded as mechanisms that are designed to create the kind of person who is going to be able to meet the imperatives of the culture in which he is going to participate as a mature adult, especially in respect to the maintenance of effective social relations. The notion that modes of shaping the mind must be understood within the total sociocultural context in which they develop is expressed in the following programmatic statement. If we substitute the phrase "any social system" for "the kibbutz" in this statement, it has universal or cross-cultural applicability:

> Education of the children cannot be for educational purposes as such. . . . Rather it must be intrinsically tied to the major objectives of the kibbutz and to prepare the children for the kibbutz way of life. . . . The kibbutz is a complicated economic, social and political organism and all educational efforts must be directed to prepare the children to accept the institution and to serve its aims. [Golan, quoted in Stern 1965, p. 118]

I am going to concentrate on the imperatives of social relations because I want to stress that the individual in society confronts a complex set of realities that are foreordained, over which he has little (if any) control, and that are the products of his society's history. I emphasize this because of the proclivity among many behavioral scientists to disregard the principle that men must adapt to the realities in which they find themselves. I also emphasize this in order to make explicit the idea that programs that advocate changes in modes of socialization and education must be congruent with the cultural realities for which individuals are being prepared.

By definition, the concept of culture includes change. Social systems not only prepare their succeeding generations to maintain their ways of life but they also seek to prepare their members for new conditions of life, for new modes of acquiring a livelihood, and for new political realities when these undergo change. In the discussion that follows, I am going to speak of cultures as if they were stable systems, but this will be done only for heuristic purposes and for the sake of parsimony; one of my basic premises is that when a culture changes, there must be congruent changes in the manners of shaping the minds.

SOCIALIZATION AND EDUCATION

My point of departure is that *socialization* and *education* are two fundamentally different processes in the shaping of mind. They are found in all societies, albeit in different proportions. Although socialization and education are aspects of growing up in all social systems, their quantitative roles in preparing individuals for participation in adult cultural life vary from one society to another. This variation is an adaptive response to—or a function of—different cultural imperatives.

By the socialization of children I mean the activities that are devoted to the inculcation and elicitation of basic motivational and cognitive patterns through ongoing and spontaneous interaction with parents, siblings, kinsmen, and other members of the community. These activities are geared toward the creation of attitudes, values, control of impulses, cognitive orientations, and the like, in the course of daily and routine activities, both within and outside the household. Education is the inculcation of standardized and stereotyped knowledge, skills, values, and attitudes by means of standardized and stereotyped procedures. Such procedures and content exist in all cultures, ranging from the repetitive recitation of lore, myth, and etiquette by grandparents to grandchildren around open fires in crude shelters to the stereotyped instruction of large groups of children and adolescents (and sometimes adults) by non-kinsmen, using electronic media of communication, in elaborate and permanent buildings.

Socialization consists of such daily events in the life of a child as a parent expostulating "No!" when the child does something undesirable, or receiving a reward after having done something well. The interaction between the parent and child might be predictable—as when a child tortures a cat or a younger sibling—but it is not stereotyped and standardized in the sense that the interaction occurs at regular times, in predictable ways, and at set places.

I hypothesize that the quantitative role played by socialization in the development of the individual is in direct proportion to the extent to which the network of kin relations coincides with the network of personal relations. Correlatively, education tends to increase proportionately with the degree to which the network of kin relations fails to coincide with the network of personal relations.

Education does not take place only in schools, although, as will be seen, such institutions play an important role in the shaping of mind. Education—in the sense of formal, stereotypic, predictable learning experiences—takes place in even the most primitive societies. One example of this is Hart's description (1963, p. 410) of puberty rites among the Tiwi; the implications of this passage for other societies in which there are initiation ceremonies are readily apparent.

> Among the Tiwi of North Australia, one can see the traumatic nature of the initiation period in very clear form, and part of the trauma lies in the sudden switch of personnel with whom the youth has to associate. A boy reaches thirteen or fourteen or so, and the physiological signs of puberty begin to appear. Nothing happens, possibly for many months. Then suddenly one day, toward evening when the people are gathering around their campfires for the main meal of the day after coming in from their day's hunting and food-gathering, a group of three or four heavily armed and taciturn strangers suddenly appear in camp. In full war regalia they walk in silence to the camp of the boy and say curtly to the household: "We have come for So-and-So!" Immediately pandemonium breaks loose. The mother and the rest of the older women begin to howl and wail. The father rushes for his spears. The boy, himself panic-stricken, tries to hide, the younger children begin to cry, and the household dogs begin to bark. It is all terribly similar to the reaction which is provoked by the arrival of the police at an American home to pick up a juvenile delinquent. This similarity extends to the behavior of the neighbors. These carefully abstain from identifying with either the strangers or the stricken household. They watch curiously the goings-on but make no move that can be identified as supporting either side. This is particularly notable in view of the fact that the strangers are strangers to all of them too, that is, they are from outside the encampment, or outside the band, who, under any other circumstances, would be greeted by a shower of spears. But not under these circumstances.

In terms of the hypotheses to be explored in this paper, I would like to take exception to one statement in the foregoing paragraph and, at the same time, add another dimension to the difference between education and socialization. I do not think that the comparison between the Tiwi experience just described and the American family's reaction to a visit by the police is apt—even though the overt behavior might be similar—because of its implications for the individual. In American society, having one's child picked up by the police as a delinquent is—at least in some circles—considered to be an unusual, if not an idiosyncratic, experience. It sets one off as being different from most other people. But the staged performance among the Tiwi has quite different consequences: it establishes a bond of common experience with others.

One of the pitfalls in many applications of psychological theories to the phenomena of culture is the prevailing implicit assumption that the formative experiences of early life have their effects—in the manner of information inputs—only at the times at which they occur. Without gainsaying the determinative effects of early life experiences for the shaping of personality, what is often overlooked is that adults frequently think back to their experiences in growing up, and that remembrances of things past themselves have their effects. All adults look back from time to time on their childhood and adolescent experiences in the privacies of their minds and—whether they are aware of it or not—they distinguish between those experiences that were shared with all peers and those that were unique or idiosyncratic. The latter are important in contributing to a sense of personal identity—the sense of being unique—while the shared experiences contribute immeasurably to identification with other members of the group. When an adult thinks back to the experiences of his childhood and later stages of development, each formative event also contains, explicitly or implicitly, a recollection of whether he alone had a particular experience or whether it was one that all people like him had gone through. In addition to its other consequences, an experience that is recalled as unique is an important contributor to the sense of exclusiveness that each person must maintain. An experience that is recalled as one that had been undergone by others—a vision quest, group circumcision, marriage, learning how to hunt or cultivate, a doctoral oral examination, and the like—is an important psychological contributor to the feeling of "I am like all the others." This, too, is necessary for social life, and can be generated by socializational or educational experiences.

I suggest that the experience described by Hart for the Tiwi makes its mark three times, each with its own effects on the mind. The first occurs when a prepubertal child observes this happening to an older sibling or neighbor. His terror must be profound. The second occurs when it happens to him. Painful as the event must be when he is called for, he must somehow recall having seen this happen to others, and it certainly contributes to his sense of being a Tiwi, in addition to its other repercussions for him. The third time that the incident leaves its mark is when he is an adult, when he observes its occurrence in the lives of future adult Tiwi. This observation must strengthen his bond with the others in the group, knowing that he had undergone the experience and that it is now part of the lives of others: it is part of becoming and being a Tiwi. As will be discussed more fully, the preponderance of such shared institutionally stereotypic experiences in the course of growing up, vis-à-vis more idiosyncratic experiences, contributes to the sense of sameness with others, and is an adaptive response to the pressures of certain of social systems.

Another example of stereotypicality and standardization of instruction that can be designated as education is provided by George Spindler (1963, p. 389) from the Menomini:

> Grandparents still tell children "bedtime stories," and the adults in the group remember when their grandparents told them stories. "Grandmaw told us kids a story every night before we went to sleep. First thing next morning she would ask us what the story was about. If we couldn't tell her, she would tell the same story again the next night. She would do that until we could tell her what the story was about." What Grandmaw was looking for was the moral point of the story, "that we shouldn't offend anybody's feelings," or "not to envy what someone else has got."

I am not trying to establish a taxonomy on the basis of which one particular behavior or another with respect to children can be designated as an example of socialization or education. Instead, my concern is with the proportion of the two to each other—and their institutional contexts—in the total experience of growing up and in being prepared for participation in the culture. The balance struck between the two in the shaping of mind, and their placement in different institutional settings, is in itself a formative experience; the proportions that are maintained in this regard are preparations for different styles of life.

Socialization

Socialization—the inculcation of basic psychological patterns through spontaneous interaction with parents, siblings, and others—is the predominant mode of the shaping of mind in social systems in which kinship is the primary principle in the organization of economic, political, and other social relations. One of the salient features of kinship as a standard for the organization of social relations is its emphasis on *particularistic* criteria in recruitment and in the evaluation of behavior. This is best expressed in the fundamental paradigmatic dictum that your brother is your brother, and you must get along and cooperate with him, regardless of how you feel about him. Such a value is often given religious and ritual validation in many societies in which kinship is the principal articulator in the organization of social relations, as in the rule that brothers may not sacrifice together when they are in a state of enmity. Expectations for performance, bases of reciprocity, access to the desiderata of the culture, and the like, are phrased in terms of who a person is instead of *what* he has accomplished. The particularistic values of kinship prescribe that solidarity and anchorage—what I have referred to elsewhere as "sociological interdependence" (Cohen 1964)—are to be sought within narrowly defined sociological limits often within the boundaries of the corporate kin group or the community. An excellent example of particularism in social life is provided by Wilson for the Nyakyusa (1959, p. 201): "In [traditional Nyakyusa] thought moral obligations are limited to kinsmen and neighbors: they do not extend beyond the chiefdom except to those relatives who may live beyond its bounds."

The predominance of socialization—vis-à-vis education—in the shaping of mind is thoroughly congruent with an emphasis in the social structure on particularism. If it is correct to characterize a culture as, *inter alia*, a self-perpetuating system, it is necessary to acknowledge explicitly that the enculturation of the future members of the society is one of the most important institutional activities of the group. Since one of the features of a social system is the achievement and maintenance of consistency in the values and criteria of its principal institutions, there is usually also an attempt to achieve and maintain consistency between the group's methods in shaping the mind and its other institutional activities.

The family is almost always the primary locus of socialization, and relationships within it are governed by particularistic considerations. . . . In family-socialization, the child learns behaviors and feelings that are appropriate to *his* family, *his* parents, *his* siblings, and the like, in addition to expressive patterns that are appropriate to general social life. Of course, children become aware at very early ages that there are other families and that there are variations among these families with respect to customary and permissible conduct. But when family-socialization predominates as the context in which the mind is shaped, children also learn very early that it is the norms of their own and closely related families to which they must respond. Where the family is the principal institutional vehicle for the transmission of culture, the embodiment of familial values serves as a prototype for an adult style of life in which the individual is expected to respond in terms of particularistic criteria—behavior that is appropriate to *his* kin group, *his* age set, *his* cult, *his* sex, and the like.

In no society, however, is the shaping of children's minds confined exclusively to the family. Another important locus of socialization is the network of kinsmen outside the household, and kinsmen are often assigned responsibility for the imposition of particular disciplines and the transmission of particular skills and knowledge to each other's children. The socialization of children by extrahousehold kinsmen is also intimately tied to a particularistic orientation in the culture as a whole, and kinsmen are responsible for a significant portion of the upbringing of each other's children in societies in which the network of kin relations coincides with the network of personal relations.

Peer Groups and Socialization

Another important locus of socialization—which, although it is found in all societies, has not received the systematic attention it warrants—is the peer group. Although the peer group is an important feature of the individual's growth in all societies, there seem to be very important—if not fundamental—differences in the relationship of the peer group to adult institutions, depending on the general orientation of social relations in the culture. Peer groups are particularistically oriented but, at the same time, are almost always prototypes of adult structuralizations of social relations, at least in part, and are important vehicles for the transmission of adult patterns of authority and cooperation. It appears that in societies in which the network of kin relations greatly coincides with social relations, parents play an important role in overseeing and controlling the content or nature of peer-group activities. On the other hand, it appears that in societies in which the network of kin relations does not coincide with social relations, parents are not directly involved in the behavior and activities of their children in relation to peers; instead, they seem to focus their control on the children's choice of friends.

This can be illustrated by reference to two different cultures. Among the Gusii [of Kenya], where kinship plays an important role in economic, political, and other spheres of activity, parents are directly involved in the behavior of their children within the peer group. In contemporary American society, where kinship is not supposed to be a factor affecting either the recruitment of children into systems of training for adult positions or in the evaluation of performance, parents do not seem to control the activities of the peer group directly; instead, their influence appears to be confined to choice of friends

In societies such as Gusii, which is ethnically homogeneous, children learn the idiom and values of kinship—and its significance in the organization of social relations—from their earliest days. The choice of friends in the formulation of peer groups does not present much of a problem in societies such as these because group memberships and affiliations are largely predetermined. On the other hand, in a heterogeneous society, contemporary United States for example, group memberships and affiliations are not foreordained, at least ideally. Hence, one of the principal concerns of parents is to teach their children the criteria by which their peers are to be selected. This is not to say that parents in American society do not influence the nature of social relations within their children's peer groups; they do, but by indirection. I suggest that it makes a great deal of difference whether parents explicitly control social relations within the peer group—as among the Gusii—or whether they do so indirectly, as in contemporary American society. This is a matter for further research, but it must be viewed within the context of the organization of social relations within the culture at large.

An illuminating description of the relationships of childhood peer groups to the adult generation is provided by LeVine and LeVine for the Gusii of Kenya. Noting that the structure of peer groups is often determined by economic considerations, such as whether families have cattle that have to be herded (1963, p. 170), they observe that

> at home and in the pastures, older children dominate younger ones. To some extent this is promulgated by parents, many of whom said they felt it important for one child to be in charge of the others and tell them what to do, and who select the oldest in the group of children for the position of leadership. . . . Since the parents may hold the appointed leader accountable for misdemeanors by and harm befalling the younger children, he is highly motivated to keep them in line and boss them around, though he is not permitted to punish them. In herding groups consisting of children from several homesteads, the oldest dominates the others, ordering them about, occasionally beating them, taking whatever articles they own. . . . Parents consider such behavior natural and even proper, but they do not accept the idea of the group or its leader dominating a boy so as to make him ignore or violate his parents' wishes. In fact, parents do not entirely recognize the existence of children's groups beyond those of siblings, and they try to maintain direct control over their children regardless of the amount of peer activity. [LeVine and LeVine 1963, p. 171]

Now to compare the foregoing accounts from the Gusii with material from a village in contemporary New England. From the descriptions of Gusii peer-group relationships, it can be gathered that parents are very concerned with the structure of relations within the group. In the New England community, called Orchard Town by Fischer and Fischer (1963), one gathers that parents are primarily concerned with the choices of friends made by their children, and little with the structure of relationships within the group.

> Although the parents try to give the play groups considerable autonomy, they do continue to exercise some influence, mostly indirect, on their elementary school child's choice of playmates. Mothers sometimes make critical remarks to their child about undesired playmates and also show differential hospitality to neighbors' children according to their suitability as playmates from the point of view of morals and manners. [Fischer and Fischer 1963, p. 994]

The role played by the peer group in the shaping of the individual's mind for participation in the culture represents one of the major gaps in our knowledge of how culture is transmitted and perpetuated. Nor, aside from a few brief ethnographic descriptions, do we have systematic comparative information about the role played by the peer group in cultural change. More important, however, peer groups are not only the province of children; they are also the concerns of adults who, it can be hypothesized, make certain that these networks are maintained in a culturally approved manner in the interest of the transmission and perpetuation of the culture.

Techniques of Socialization

There are also important variations in the techniques by which children are taught to respond to expectations in their performances. It is not necessary to belabor the point that children in all societies are disciplined and rewarded, and that children are subjected to pressures for conformity in all societies.

In societies where socialization plays a greater role in the shaping of the child's mind than does education, the techniques of the former are generally designed to elicit conformity to *small-group* pressures. Many students of patterns of child upbringing (see, for example, Pettit 1946) have stressed the important role of guilt and ridicule in the systems of socialization—and the general eschewal of corporal punishment—in many primitive societies. Many anthropologists and others have quoted parents' assertions that corporal punishment is "cruel" and that they "love" their children too much to punish them physically.

We have several excellent studies of social systems in which the elicitation of guilt is an important technique in gaining conformity in children. (Although many authors have sought to distinguish guilt and shame, I assume that there is little difference between them, or that they are at least correlative.) Among the best of these are DeVos' analysis of Japanese patterns (1960) and Dorothy Eggan's of the Hopi (1956). What emerges consistently from these studies is that a heavy reliance on the elicitation of guilt is a systematic means of training people to respond to the pressures for conformity from a small and solidary group. Eggan made this clear for the Hopi (1956, pp. 361–362):

For through the great strength of the emotional orientations conveyed within the kin-ship framework and the interwoven religious beliefs, young Hopi learned their world from dedicated teachers whose emotions were involved in teaching what they believed intensely, and this in turn engaged the children's emotions in learning. These experi-ences early and increasingly made explicit in a very personal way the values implicit in the distinction between a good heart and a bad heart. For public opinion, if intensely felt and openly expressed in a closely knit and mutually dependent group . . . can be more effective potential punishment than the electric chair. It is perhaps easier to die quickly than to live in loneliness in a small community in the face of contempt from one's fellows, and particularly from one's clan from whence . . . comes most of one's physical and emotional security. Small wonder that the children who experience this constant pressure to conform to clan dictates and needs, and at the same time this constant reinforcement of clan solidarity against outsiders, are reluctant as adults to stray too far from the clan's protective familiarity or to defy its wishes.

A Hopi wondering whether he is of "bad heart" is experiencing the guilt that is attuned to the imperatives of life in a Hopi clan. It is an effective orientation of mind to the social realities of the clan world.

There was, therefore, a constant probing of one's own heart, well illustrated by the anguished cry of a Hopi friend, "Dorothy, did my son die as the old folks said because my heart was not right? Do you believe this way, that if parents do not keep good hearts children will die?" And there was a constant examination of one's neighbors' hearts. "Movensie, it is those _____ clan people who ruined this ceremony! They have bad hearts and they quarrel too much. That bad wind came up and now we will get no rain." Conversation among the Hopi is rarely censored, and the children heard both of these women's remarks, feeling, you may be sure, the absolute belief which these "teachers" had in the danger which a bad heart carries for everyone in the group. [Eggan 1956, p. 361]

Training for sensitivity to group pressures for conformity by means of eliciting guilt does not take place in a vacuum; instead, it always takes place in the con-crete interactions between the child and highly specific individuals who are charged by the social system with the responsibility of producing the guilt, of manipulating it, and of teaching the instrumental responses by which it can be assuaged. Usu-ally, it is the mother who is most often responsible for this training, and the rea-sons for this are understandable. The mother is generally the most highly affectively charged individual in a growing child's life, and he often spends more time with her than with any other person.

But what is important in this connection is not only that the mother is the cen-tral object of the child's guilt, but that she performs this role as the representative of the group. This is abundantly illustrated in DeVos' analysis of the deep under-current of guilt as the psychological fulcrum in traditional Japanese socialization. Guilt toward the mother in this situation is specifically related to the child's fail-ure to meet expectations that are phrased in terms of the individual's duties and obligations in respect to the family and extended kin grouping. The overt phrase-ology of the consequences of transgressions, as taught in Japanese socialization—laziness and other nonproductive behavior—is that they "injure" the parents. But the thrust of the argument is not lost on the child, who also sees and hears his par-ents themselves responding consistently to the pressures of the kin group and com-munity. Furthermore, the systematic use of guilt as a means for eliciting conformity during childhood and adulthood must also be seen as an integral aspect of the par-ticularistic orientation of a social system. It is in terms of the consequences for a specific solidary grouping—family, lineage, community, and the like—that an in-dividual in such societies must weigh his actions. Guilt can become an object of humor and a primary concern of psychotherapeutic systems when its elicitation is inappropriate to—and incongruent with—the imperatives of a social system in which the principal (or at least growing) emphasis is on *universalistic* values and criteria.

The systematic development of sensitivity to ridicule and the loss of esteem by the group is another technique of socialization that is intimately tied to an orien-tation to particularistic values and to life in relatively self-contained and solidary groups. It is not the ridicule of everyone to which an individual is taught to respond in many primitive and peasant societies but rather to the threats of loss of esteem of the specific group in which he is expected to find his social and emotional an-chorage. Ridicule is only effective when an individual's self-value is equated with the worth placed on him by the group with which he is expected to identify, and within which he expects to function. It is an extremely potent means of assuring conformity when the solidary, limited, and circumscribed group constitutes the individual's universe wherein he seeks to secure a place. Ridicule is a rejection—or at least a threat of it—by the universe as it is subjectively experienced; the nar-rower the social stage on which the individual can maneuver during his life, the more effective is ridicule as a device of control.

The individual must learn the idiom and nuances of ridicule if it is to be an ef-fective weapon in the hands of the group; hence, the sensitivity to ridicule and threats of loss of esteem must be established early in his life. It might be self-evident that pressures to conformity are ineffective if people have not been sensitized to them, but the point has to be made explicit if we are to untangle the skein of a culture and its mechanisms of self-perpetuation.

It is in contrast with guilt and ridicule that corporal punishment can be under-stood as a technique of socialization. Corporal punishment is rare as a standard means of socialization in primitive and peasant societies because of its personal-ized quality. It is an activity that takes place in a dyadic context; its goal is to elicit conformist response to the demands of a particular individual who is exercising—or who is capable of exercising—force. The impact of corporal punishment is not only physical; it is also social and emotional. Specifically, the emphasis in corporal punishment is on person-to-person relationships at the expense of an emphasis to group pressures to conformity. One of the socioemotional messages conveyed in the relatively regular reliance on corporal punishment—as, for example, in Alor (DuBois 1944, p.137) or in a highland peasant Jamaican community (Cohen 1958)—is that if one can avoid detection by the punishing agent he can "get away with it." By contrast, one of the lessons taught in societies in which great reliance is placed on guilt and ridicule—and these are generally groups in which the individual is constantly exposed to group surveillance—is that the group is always present, even if it is only one other person who symbolizes the group, and that it is almost impossible to escape detection.

As an important technique of socialization, corporal punishment is eminently suited for preparation to participate in a social system of atomized relationships, but it is incompatible with preparation to participate in a solidary system with firmly bounded social relationships. But the close correspondence between corporal punishment in socialization and atomized relationships among adults does not rest exclusively on the fact that corporal punishment generally takes place in the context of a dyadic relationship. Corporal punishment in childhood arouses intense emotions in children, and evidence provided from animal experimentations suggests that this mode of socialization is effective in heightening and strengthening the emotional bond between child and parent; as I have tried to show elsewhere (1964) such intense relationships are established at the expense of wider extrafamiliar identifications.

Socialization and Traditionalism

Finally, socialization—vis-à-vis education—is oriented to traditionalism. As is well known, there tends to be a direct relationship between levels of sociotechnological development and the rate of cultural change. Without going into the reasons that the rate of change of a society is locked into its culture—and must be seen as an aspect of the culture—the fact also remains that every society maintains a highly specific attitude toward change; this is part of its value system, and it must be inculcated as part of the process of the shaping of mind. I hypothesize that in those societies in which the rate of change is slow and in which change is disvalued, socialization will predominate in the upbringing of the members of the group. I am not suggesting that socialization is in any way a source of a slow rate of change or that it is responsible for negative values associated with change. If a causal relationship is in order, I would hypothesize the converse, that a slow rate of change is a sociocultural feature that can underlie the predominance of socialization in the transmission of culture.

One of the most outstanding characteristics of socialization—especially within the family—is the high affective change that is associated with almost everything that is learned within that context. The reason for this is that the content of learning, especially in children, is often inseparable from the identity of their teachers. Furthermore, this is an important aspect of particularism in general—*who* states a proposition is directly relevant to its value.

Because agents of socialization (as distinct from agents of education) are so highly charged emotionally, the patterns of behavior that they inculcate—socially acceptable norms, the organization of social relationships, modes of belief and of thought, and the like—are equally charged. What is important with respect to the maintenance of traditionalism and resistance to change is that the relinquishment of such patterns can often arouse—unconsciously, to be sure—anticipations of loss of love and primary security, whereas the retention of traditional modes can elicit equally deep and subtle connotations of approval, reward, and a sense of belonging. This is not to imply that a predominance of socialization in the total experience of maturation will lead to a complete rejection of change; adults are usually oriented to reality and do adapt when the conditions in which they find themselves require change. But what is important is that the requirements for change do elicit different degrees of resistance and personal turmoil in different societies. The reliance on agents and techniques of socialization for the transmission of culture is an adaptive mechanism in many societies whose rate of change is slow and who, therefore, maintain negative values in connection with change.

This relationship between traditionalism and a predominant reliance on socialization—in which, to reiterate, the latter is the dependent variable—is illustrated by "the early learning hypothesis," explored by Bruner (1956) on the basis of material from the Mandan-Hidatsa. Bruner suggested that what is learned early in life is resistant to change while that which is learned later in life is most susceptible to change. In a discussion of Bruner's analysis, I added to his hypothesis the suggestion (Cohen 1961, p. 112) that what is learned inside the family is most resistant to change and that which is learned outside the family is most susceptible to change.

This discussion of the relationship between traditionalism and socialization would be incomplete, however, without pointing, at least, in passing, to another very important variable. In social systems in which change is disvalued, the individual more or less tends to grow up, live out his life, and die among the same people. In such environments, as noted, there tends to be little chance of escaping the scrutiny of affectively charged people for long. These relatively stable groupings of people are those with whom some of the most fundamental patterns of behavior were learned in childhood. The shame, guilt, need for approval, desire for belongingness, and the like, which are learned during the earliest years of psychological vulnerability are always the strongest; and the patterns of behavior that they underlie also tend to remain the strongest when the associations with those in whose midst such patterns were acquired are retained.

Also, in most of these societies, the family is a unit of both production and consumption and it involves the most inalienable ties. In addition to its symbolization of solidarity, such a family also carries with it the sociological imprints and emotional associations with one's parents, grandparents, and the traditions that they represent. In such social systems, people behave traditionally and tend not to follow their own inclinations because, in part, of the scrutiny of those with whom they have been in lifelong association and who are the symbolic reminders of the emotions associated with things their parents and other affectively charged persons had taught them (Cohen 1961, pp. 106–111). Thus, the experiences of childhood not only often underlie adult modes of behavior, but it is also important to recognize that the institutional structures in which adults participate underlie the means by which the culture is transmitted, as in the balance struck between socialization and education.

Education

Education—the inculcation of standardized knowledge and skills by standardized and stereotyped means—is the predominant mode of shaping the mind in social systems in which nonkinship and *universalistic* considerations are of primary significance in the organization of economic, political, and other social relations. Although, as noted, education is found in all societies, it begins to assume a predominant role in the course of history when it is institutionalized in schools. Considered as techniques of society for molding the individual to serve the aims of the social system, socialization and education are in competition. Coleman has noted this in his introduction to *Education and Political Development* (1965, p. 22) when he referred to "the wide gap between the modern and traditional sectors of the developing countries." "Yet," he observes, "it is the very existence of this gap which . . . elevates the formal educational system to a more determinative role in the political socialization process, and diminishes, if it does not extinguish, the role of the family, the prime socializer." While the latter assertion in this statement is somewhat overdrawn, it does point clearly to the proportionate relationship between socialization and education. The family is not faced with extinction; like all other social institutions, it is merely changing adaptively to meet new sociocultural pressures.

Every social system tends to insist that its members be quite blind, especially with respect to history (compare Henry's discussion in section I). Every culture requires that the people participating in it see the institutions of their society as unique, as outgrowths of present and immediate needs, and as expressions of its genius. Were this otherwise, most social systems would find it more difficult than they do to win loyalty and allegiance. Hence, most people in society tend to approach an understanding of the institutions by which they live in a manner akin to the proverbial blind man who is trying to describe an elephant. We thus observe many people— behavioral scientists among them—variously suggesting that our contemporary educational institutions are designed to cope with the demands of an industrially oriented technology; a mechanism for transmitting knowledge gained by our contemporaries and by other societies at different times in history; an institutional complex devoted to the life of the mind; a means of transmitting political values; an instrument for eliminating social inequality; a key to utopia, in which Everyman will be "creative" and self-expressive; and the like.

However, when we remove our historical blinders and look at educational institutions from their beginnings in human history, and at our own systems of education as outgrowths or products of history, we must conclude that they are all—and none—of these. Instead, we are compelled to look at these institutions as changing adaptations to changing sociocultural environments. As private citizens taking personal stands, we might not like what we see—there are, after all, some advantages to blindness—but a social system is more than, and different from, the sum of personal stands and likes or dislikes in the polity. Few institutions in history have been changed by conscious and deliberate means, except through violent revolution. Furthermore, no educational system in history—or at least any of which we know—has been consciously and deliberately transformed without first heaving over the entire social system to which it is an adaptation. Our task here is to understand the elephant rather than to write a manifesto for or about one of his hind legs. How and why did formal educational systems first develop, and what do today's institutions of learning have in common with the first schools?

If we examine the historical emergence of schools in the context of stages of cultural development, rather than chronologically, their first recorded appearance seems to have occurred during the stage represented by some West African societies, such as the Kpelle, in the form of the so-called "bush" schools (see Gibbs 1965; Watkins 1943). "The Kpelle have an incipient class system that distinguishes three classes" (Gibbs 1965, p. 214). While kinship does play an important role in the organization of social relations among them, it is secondary to tribal fraternities and other secret societies. These, too, are embodiments of particularistic orientations, although somewhat less so than kin-group organizations, like the lineage.

> Kpelle culture has two conflicting dominant themes. The first is a stress on personal autonomy and the individual achievement of status. Eligibility for high rank such as chieftaincy is not ascribed primarily on the basis of birth as a member of a particular lineage or clan as it is in many middle-range African societies. Rather, it is achieved on the basis of individual effort. A Kpelle may climb ahead of his fellows through the possession of certain obtainable skills Most important is the ability to work hard, that is, to farm well, and to manage his economic resources skillfully. . . . The counterweight to the theme of individual achievement is the stress on conformity and regulation as exemplified in the tribal societies. Through the initiation ["bush"] schools they assure the continuity of basic Kpelle values and by the application of combined ritual and secular sanctions, they ensure adherence to those values. This means that individual Kpelle are guided by the same expectations in the competition for power. They play by the same rules and for the same stakes, which means that no one goes too far in the means he uses to acquire position. If he does, the sanctions are forceful and effective. Through its officials, the Poro [tribal fraternity, secret society] regulates the speed with which a man with a following may acquire formal political or Poro office. [Gibbs 1965, pp. 229–230]

In terms of the hypotheses being explored in this paper, the "bush" schools of the Kpelle and other West African societies constitute an intriguing problem. On the one hand, these cultures exhibit many of the characteristics of societies in which socialization predominates over education. Until adolescence, the household is the principal context in which the individual matures (Gibbs 1965, pp. 207–210). On the other hand—and, at first blush, somewhat anomalously—they have a system of schools for initiates; this schooling, however, is not compulsory, and nowadays the person who does not attend does not suffer any severe social disabilities (Gibbs 1965, pp. 221–223). In some of these West African societies, attendance at these schools during early adolescence lasts several years.

How can we reconcile the presence of schools in a social system with the fact that kinship and secret societies—matrixes that inevitably subserve particularistic values and orientations—play such important roles in the organization of its economic, political, and other spheres of social relations? One of the keys to this paradox is the fact that after each group has completed its period of instruction, the buildings of its school are abandoned or destroyed; in either event, they may not be used again for any other group or for any other purpose. Moreover, Gibbs informs me (in a personal communication) that his recent investigations among the Kpelle indicate that there is a minimum of formal and standardized instruction in Kpelle "bush" schools.

The retention of the school structures after each age grade has "graduated" and the adoption of a curriculum and standardized instruction would be incompatible with the total institutional structures and value systems of these societies. If they were not repetitively demolished or abandoned and were allowed to be used again, the schools would soon come to be used more extensively, at earlier ages, and as a much more integral vehicle for the transmission of the culture. They would thus replace the household and other primary local groups as the principal mold for the shaping of the individual. If a standardized curriculum and formal and stereotyped instruction were introduced, the *particularistically* oriented sector of the culture's value system—household, kin group, secret society—would be subverted because, as will be illustrated, such means of instruction are designed to serve *universalistic* values. The recurrent demolition or abandonment of these "schools" and the eschewal of standardized instruction represent an avoidance of a pattern of upbringing that is incompatible with the rest of the social system.

Schools and States

The development of schools—the institutionalized predominance of education over socialization in the shaping of men's minds—is a characteristic feature of state societies. Not all state societies develop schools, but the important point is that schools do not emerge historically prior to the creation of states. By a state society is meant here a society in which "a single person, by whatsoever name he may be distinguished, is entrusted with the execution of the laws, the management of the revenue, and the command of the army" (Gibbon I, p. 52).

The essence of education—vis-à-vis socialization—is that one of its principal emphases is on universalistic values, criteria, and standards of performance. It is in these terms that, from the point of view of the total social system, education competes with socialization. The thrust of learning acquired in a context of socialization is the identity of the teacher—*who* states a proposition is the relevant consideration. The impact of learning in a context of education is that "*who* states a proposition is as such irrelevant to the question of its . . . value" (Parsons 1954, p. 42); instead, the relevant consideration in education is *what* is being taught and learned, regardless of who teaches it. One of the underlying premises of a system of education—whether it is conducted on an individual basis or in schools—is that teachers can be changed daily, or that the child can go from one teacher to another, without altering the content of what is being learned.

It is the universalistic orientation that is inherent in education that makes it eminently suitable as a predominant mode of shaping the mind to prepare people to serve the aims of a state society. Two outstanding characteristics of a state society that are relevant to our present consideration serve the growth of universalistic values in the society as a whole. First, one of the goals of a state is to subvert local—especially kin—sources of solidarity, loyalty, and authority.

A second major task confronted by a state in the legitimation of its authority is that it must establish an ideology—if not a reality—of uniformity among its polity. While there are many ways by which states accomplish this, one is the attempt to inculcate a universalistic or uniform and standardized set of symbols to which all the members of the society can be trained to respond uniformly. Such symbol-systems must be implanted early if they are to be effective. The implantation of standardized responses to the symbol-system of the state can appear in many guises, but their goals are the same—to contribute to the establishment of conformity to the aims and imperatives of a state system. Whether the means to this end take the form of uniform dress for schoolchildren (or even for their teachers), standardized sacred books and paraphernalia or fetishes, flags, pictures of culture heroes or rulers that students face throughout the school day, and the like, the object is to present all future participants in the society with uniform ideological symbols. The goal is to make these symbols integral parts of shaped minds, so that responses to them in adulthood will be uniform when the state bureaucracy feels that it needs to use them to gain acquiescence or mass participation in an activity of the society.

It is essential to bear in mind that schools are an important part of the political bureaucracies in those state societies in which there are schools. It goes without saying that each part of a state bureaucracy has its own relevant and specialized tasks: the collection of taxes, control of religious organization, management of economic activities, administration of law, leadership of the military, and the like. Similarly, the educational part of a state's bureaucracy has its relevant and specialized tasks, to implant politically meaningful and legitimating symbols and to elicit approved and appropriate responses to those symbols as one means among many for the maintenance of order and uniformity of response throughout the polity. If we are to understand educational institutions in terms of their provenance, we must remember that schools were not established originally to foster the life of the mind or the spirit of free inquiry. That they have in a few cases become devoted to such pursuits is another matter, and they are exceptional. But every organization and bureaucracy is self-serving; this is no less true of a state system than any other. Every state organization constantly looks to the sectors of its bureaucracy to make certain that its interests are being served. To expect that a state will allow its schools to serve aims other than those of the national political structure is to expect that a state will not behave like a state.

To take some examples from contemporary societies, we can ask, of what relevance is a daily oath of allegiance to a flag—and the flag itself, which the child faces throughout the learning period—to the acquisition of knowledge and skills? Of what relevance is the ubiquitous portrait of Washington, Mao, or Lenin to the teaching of grammar and the use of a slide rule in an American, Chinese, or Soviet classroom? Of what relevance is a cross in a religiously sponsored school to the learning of geography, history, literature, and the like? The relevance is this: As part of the state bureaucracy, schools are generally maintained under the sponsorship of the state organization that controls and supports them in one way or other. Just as courts are part of the state bureaucracy and display the material symbols of the state organization of which they are a part, so do schools. The relevance is also this: Learning is a rewarding experience for most children. Hence—as every variety of behavioristic psychology has demonstrated repeatedly—it is hardly a startling insight to suggest that, whether anyone is consciously aware of it or not, the child comes to associate everything he learns with the state's symbols that face or envelop him while he is learning. These symbols become as much a part of his mind as the alphabet and the concept of zero. School is not only the place to learn arithmetic; it is also the place to learn zealotry.

The fostering of universalistic values and criteria is one of the goals of a state organization, as, for example, in the ideal that all citizens are subject to the same laws, regardless of origin and affiliation. Schools serve the same ends. Thus, for example, it is not mere coincidence that schools and courts are currently among the major battlegrounds between the universalistic orientations of the central American government and the regional or community particularism of many sectors of the American South. The histories of colonialized societies also repeat this pattern with recurrent regularity.

How does education contribute to the predominance of a universalistic orientation; that is, why do social systems in which the balance of values and the criteria for performance are weighted on the side of universalism favor a reliance on education, vis-à-vis socialization, in the shaping of the minds of polities? Whether a curriculum is devoted to catechetical instruction, skills (like learning the multiplication tables), executing "proper" penmanship, learning the dates of wars and treaties (in which one's own society somehow always manages to emerge as wronged or righteous, or both), the names of rivers, mountains, cities, or ports, such learning is wholly independent of family background, ethnic or religious affiliation, regional membership, or any other nexus that is a natural breeding ground for particularistic orientations. While I do not intend to suggest that there is no difference between learning a catechism and the other subjects mentioned, the essence of education is that there is only one correct answer to a problem or to a question. The essence of a universalistic orientation is that there is only one correct way of behaving within the society as a whole—no matter where one goes within its borders—and that there is only one standard of loyalty to the state. The bane of university professors who demand that the student-products of secondary schools think for themselves instead of performing by rote is the fruit of a successful state system rather than of the ideology of any particular system of schooling.

It is in these terms that an educational system without regular and recurrent examinations is difficult to imagine. (I am speaking here principally of what are called in our society elementary and secondary schools, in which the overwhelming majority of the population are educated. One consequence that can be anticipated from mass college education is an even heavier reliance on procedures such as examinations.) The manifest or rational purpose served by examinations is, of course, to determine the degree to which material has been learned. However, a latent purpose is also served by examinations, namely, the application of universalistic criteria for the evaluation of performance: there is only one correct answer to a question, and everyone is evaluated by the same criteria. I suggest that this is the more important of the two in terms of the preparation of the individual for later participation in a social system in which universalism is the predominant orientation.

The techniques of education, especially in rote and standardized learning and in the use of examinations, explicitly deny and conflict with the conveyance of particularistic values and criteria. Individual differences in personality, or family, kin, and community backgrounds and traditions count for little, if anything, in the procedures of education. Instead, what is emphasized is uniformity.

Techniques of Education

There are several facets to the uniformity which is the inevitable by-product of education. Most readily apparent is the demand for standardization in performance. In this connection, one of the most important factors is the child's awareness that he is learning precisely the same things as all his peers throughout the realm, and that he must give the same responses. He does not know what the authority for this is and whence it derives, but that is one of the points of it all: he is expected to acquire the realization, which is not necessarily conscious, that such authority exists. He is not trained to conceptualize that authority as localized in a nexus of named lineal ancestors or collateral kinsmen.

Nor is he expected to associate that authority with a particular teacher of unique personality, whose attributes he might adopt for his own. Children tend to identify with those people who meet their needs, including those who teach them. Identification is an important source of particularistic values, and a society whose predominant orientation is to universalistic values must make certain that lasting emotional identifications do not become part of the mind that is being shaped for participation in that culture. Thus, an important aspect of the educational systems of societies that are primarily universalistic in their value orientations is that when these orientations become increasingly pervasive in the institutional structure there is a parallel tendency to thwart or interfere with the identifications of children with their teachers. One of the ways by which this is accomplished is by having children taught by a variety and succession of teachers. Whether a child's teachers change annually or several times a day, one of the consequences is to break into or seriously weaken any tendency to identify with a particular teacher. Such identifications during the formative years are dangerous to a social system whose principal reliance is on universalistic values and criteria. In the social system of the future, hints of which are already upon us, this danger will have been obviated even more by mechanical or electronic instruction on a mass scale.

Another very important facet of the uniformity that is instilled through education as a technique in the shaping of men's minds is the allocation of standardized rewards and punishments for standardized performance. There are no surprises for the student who excels above all others in his grade—unless he is fortunate enough to experience surprise in knowledge itself. He knows in advance—and such knowledge is as important to an educational system as the multiplication table and the chronology of wars and culture heroes—which mass-produced medals he will receive, and which accolades, monetary awards, conscription status, occupations, and the like, will be his due as a result of universalistically evaluated performances. What needs to be stressed in this connection is that this is not an expression of an "educational policy." It is, instead, the policy of a state system that seeks to maintain its authority and control through the establishment of homogeneity throughout its polity. One of the means to this end is the inculcation of reflexes of mind by which the individual is brought to expect automatic standard consequences for standard performance.

It is necessary to reiterate at this point that no society achieves these goals overnight. The dominance of universalistic values and criteria is a gradual process of accretion at the expense of particularism; the latter is displayed slowly and, in the experiences of many individuals in the society, painfully. Similarly, the development of techniques of education in the service of these goals is also a gradual process, and must be understood as an aspect of history, not unlike parallel developments in the legal sphere of social organization or in patterns of recruitment to the state bureaucracy. An excellent illustration of this is provided in Dore's *Education in Tokugawa Japan* (1965), which, unfortunately, stands alone as an analysis of the development of an educational system in tandem with a nascent state organization.

Education, Stratification, and Change

It would he misleading to convey the impression that educational systems, especially in state societies, are designed to prepare people only for universalistic values and criteria for performance. All educational systems are discriminatory to some extent, whether by sex, social class, caste, ethnic or religious membership, or the like. These differentials in education are not only unequal distributions of privilege with respect to education but they are also preparations for differences in access to participation in the political apparatus. Educational differentials not only perpetuate systems of social stratification but are also affirmations of the relative political statuses of the groups making up a social system. Such institutionalized inequalities continue to serve as seedbeds of particularistic values, but they are also in conflict with a state's rational ideology that seeks to establish homogeneity. One of the consequences of the elimination of social enclaves or ghettos, and the like, is to remove the sociological bases of particularistic values in the society. Uniform mass education is an important means to this end.

Hence, it is necessary to understand that education *per se* is not a vehicle of mobility in a system of social stratification. Whether we speak of the emancipation of women in primitive and peasant societies, of the access to higher status by commoners in modern emergent states, or of the mobility of ethnic groups in the United States, and although education almost invariably plays a role in these events, access to the educational system is always one aspect of the lowering of barriers generally. In these terms, the opening of schools to groups who had previously been barred from them is a by-product—not a cause—of social mobility.

I have suggested that the predominance of socialization in the shaping of the mind is oriented to traditionalism. In similar vein, I hypothesize that as the rate of change in a society accelerates, and as positive valuation of social change increases, commensurately greater emphasis is placed on education in preparing people to serve the aims of society's institutions. Just as a correlate of socialization is the affective charge of learned patterns, one of the consequences—if not a goal—of education is the relative "neutrality" or "secularization" of acquired knowledge. One of the ways by which this is accomplished is by impeding the development of strong emotional identifications between student and teacher; another, and closely related, is the reliance on nonkinsmen as agents of education.

An increasing reliance on education is adaptive to a rapid rate of change and to a high valuation of change because it contributes to the development of a habit of mind by which the individual evaluates an item of information in terms of its utility instead of the particular individuals or settings in association with whom it was learned. It not only contributes to an amenability to new knowledge but also to new social responses to changing conditions. Education, especially when it predominates over socialization, contributes to the establishment of a particular attitude toward change.

CONCLUSION

The study of educational institutions has been one of the stepchildren of social science, and has often been left by default to the educationists. The consequences are analagous to child neglect, abandonment, and abuse. What I have tried to show in this paper is that educational institutions—and others involved in the self-perpetuation of culture through the shaping of man's mind—warrant, and are amenable to, the same modes of analysis that have been developed by anthropologists for the study of kinship and marriage, legal and political institutions, economic activities, and religion and social stratification.

I am not seeking to idealize education. There are many standards which, when applied to the fruits of educational systems, cast a pall on one's hopes for the future of man. But that is sentimentalism, which is inappropriate to standards of universalism. I have, however, tried to place some aspects of education in a historical perspective in order to try to understand whence we have come—so that we might perhaps better appreciate where we are and get some hints into where we might be headed. While I do not think of education as the panacea to the ills of mankind, I have tried to convey the idea that, no matter what its other by-products, it has contributed much to an amelioration of the human situation. It has not done this alone; it has, as a matter of fact, committed some of its own horrors, about which we are sometimes too silent in our classrooms. But with other sociocultural developments of which it is an integral part, the predominance of education over socialization has contributed somewhat to the ability of a few people to realize their personal potentials—people who, in previous stages of cultural development, were charged with heresy, sorcery, or unconscionable deviance, and sentenced either to the stake or to bland compliance. That most educated people have substituted the gray flannel suit for the gray flannel loincloth is not entirely the fault of the educational institutions of society.

In stressing what seem to be the principal goals of education, I have also tried to convey the hypothesis that educational institutions were never designed—and thus cannot really be criticized for failing—to convert people to the intellectual life. That a few individuals have managed to develop a commitment to the life of the mind despite the ends and means of educational institutions sheds light only on man's evolutionary capacity, and on little else. Thus, when I say that education contributes to the establishment of a particular attitude toward change, I do not wish to sound like a commencement orator and suggest that it establishes these attitudes in the minds of all, or even most, who pass through its portals. It contributes to the establishment of these attitudes in the culture, which is very different than the sum of its carriers. While twentieth-century educated man often sounds like a socialized medieval peasant when faced with the inevitability of adaptive social change, the important fact is that many of these adaptive changes do take place nevertheless. Although he may sound like a medieval peasant, the important thing is that he behaves like one less and less. With a few relatively insignificant exceptions, he watches witch hunts on his television screen but does not ordinarily seek to lead them. He might personally empathize with the residents of Watts, California, and Cicero, Illinois, but education has played a role, albeit a small one, in the fact that the world is no longer all Watts and Cicero.

Thus, what I have also tried to say in this paper is that any social development—such as the unfolding of the potentials of educational institutions—never occurs rapidly. Nor are the consequences of educational experiences, such as attitudes toward change, ever established in a vacuum and without the support of other social institutions. I am not suggesting the eschewal of a critical stance with respect to educational institutions; but to demand that they be changed immediately, or to insist on new educational philosophies as though they were coffee in a vending machine, is to espouse an extreme anti-intellectualism that is grounded in the same assumptions as are found in the thinking of the manufacturer who has programmed his dies to produce little artifacts on demand or at monotonously regular intervals.

I have also tried to make a methodological point in this paper. This is that if we wish to measure the successes and failures of educational institutions—and it should be noted that most critics of school systems have been quite cavalier about making explicit the criteria by which they attribute success and failure in this regard—we do not focus on individuals but, rather, on generations. The danger in surveying individuals is that one can almost invariably find what he is looking for if he is skilled in designing survey instruments; is it any wonder that so many survey-tested hypotheses seem to be borne out? In order to understand the consequences—as well as the content—of education, it is necessary to compare generations or historical periods in the cycles of a society's development. Did education have the same effects on people who completed their schooling in 1867 or 1937 as on those who finished theirs in 1967? Why were schools different 30 or 100 years ago? If they have retained anything from these earlier periods, why did they do so? Attitudes and institutions do change, often without the awareness of the members of the society. If we confine our time spans to a single day, or even to five years, we necessarily have to conclude that nothing has changed. If, however, we adopt a historical perspective, we might emerge with a much more balanced picture.

I have tried to illustrate the hypothesis that the means adopted by different societies to shape the minds of their growing members are mechanisms of adaptation to the sociocultural environment. Historical analysis is essential to the study of adaptation generally; it is also indispensable to an understanding of educational institutions in particular. Without such understanding it is impossible to take sensible action.

NOTE

I want to thank James L. Gibbs, Jr., for his very helpful comments about this paper and for sharing with me some of his unpublished observations on the Kpelle of Liberia. I alone am responsible for errors and misinterpretations in this paper.

REFERENCES

Bruner, Edward M. 1956. Cultural transmission and cultural change. *Southwestern Journal of Anthropology* 12:191–199.

Cohen, Yehudi A. 1958. Character formation and social structure in a Jamaican community. *Psychiatry* 18:275–296.

———. 1961. *Social structure and personality: a casebook.* New York: Holt, Rinehart & Winston, Inc.

———. 1964. *The transition from childhood to adolescence: cross-cultural studies of initiation ceremonies, legal systems, and incest taboos.* Chicago: Aldine Publishing Company.

Coleman, James S. 1965. *Education and political development.* Princeton, New Jersey: Princeton University Press.

DeVos, George. 1960. The relation of guilt toward parents to achievement and arranged marriage among the Japanese. *Psychiatry* 23:287–301.

Diamond, Stanley. 1951. *Dahomey: a proto-state in West Africa.* Doctoral dissertation, Columbia University, University Microfilms, No. 2808. Ann Arbor, Michigan.

Dore, R. P. 1965. *Education in Tokugawa Japan.* Berkeley and Los Angeles: University of California Press.

DuBois, Cora. 1944. *The people of Alor: a socio-psychological study of an East Indian island.* Minneapolis: University of Minnesota Press.

Edgerton, Robert B. 1965. "Cultural" vs. "ecological" factors in the expression of values, attitudes, and personality characteristics. *American Anthropologist* 67:442–447.

Eggan, Dorothy. 1956. Instruction and affect in Hopi cultural continuity. *Southwestern Journal of Anthropology* 12:347–370.

Engels, Frederick. 1942. *The origin of the family, private property, and the state.* New York: International Publishers.

Fischer, John L., and Ann Fischer. 1963. The New Englanders of Orchard Town, USA. In *Six cultures: studies of child rearing,* edited by Beatrice B. Whiting. New York and London: John Wiley and Sons, Inc.

Gibbon, Edward. n.d. *The decline and fall of the Roman empire.* Modern Library edition. New York: Random House, Inc.

Gibbs, James L., Jr. 1965. The Kpelle of Liberia. In *Peoples of Africa,* edited by James L. Gibbs, Jr. New York: Holt, Rinehart and Winston, Inc.

Goldschmidt, Walter. 1965. Theory and strategy in the study of cultural adaptability. *American Anthropologist* 67:402–408.

Hallowell, A. I. 1955. *Culture and experience* [selected papers]. Philadelphia: University of Pennsylvania Press.

Hart, C. W. M. 1963. Contrasts between prepubertal and postpubertal education. In *Education and culture,* edited by George D. Spindler. New York: Holt, Rinehart and Winston, Inc.

LeVine, Robert A., and Barbara B. LeVine. 1963. Nyansongo: a Gusii community in Kenya. In *Six cultures: studies of child rearing,* edited by Beatrice B. Whiting. New York and London: John Wiley and Sons, Inc.

Mead, Margaret. 1939. *From the South Seas.* New York: William Morrow and Company, Inc.

Parsons, Talcott. 1954. *Essays in sociological theory* (revised edition). New York: The Free Press.

————. 1964. *Social structure and personality*. New York: The Free Press.

Pettit, George A. 1946. *Primitive education in North America*. University of California Publications in American Archaeology and Ethnology 63:1–182.

Sapir, Edward. 1949. *Selected writings of Edward Sapir*, edited by David Mandelbaum. Berkeley and Los Angeles: University of California Press.

Scott, J. P. 1962. Critical periods in behavioral development. *Science* 138:949–958.

Spencer, Herbert. 1891. *The principles of sociology*, II. New York: D. Appleton Company.

Spindler, George D. 1955. *Sociocultural and psychological processes in Menomini acculturation*. University of California Publications in Culture and Society 5.

————. 1963. Personality, sociocultural system, and education among the Menomini. In *Education and culture*, edited by George D. Spindler. New York: Holt, Rinehart and Winston, Inc.

Spindler, Louise S. 1962. *Menomini women and culture change*. Memoir 91, American Anthropological Association.

Stern, Boris. 1965. *The kibbutz that was*. Washington, D.C.: Public Affairs Press.

Watkins, Mark Hanna. 1943. The West African "bush" school. *American Journal of Sociology* 48:666–675.

Wilson, Monica. 1959. *Communal rituals of the Nyakyusa*. London: Oxford University Press.

————. 1963. *Good company: a study of Nyakyusa age-villages*. Boston: The Beacon Press.

10

Formal Schooling and the Production of Modern Citizens in the Ecuadorian Amazon

Laura Rival

To look at formal schooling in non-Western contexts is a necessary part of arguing that cultural transmission, far from being a straight-forward process, involves resistance, and that schools, aimed at producing homogeneity, may give rise to heterogeneity. State education in less-developed countries has often been presented as the main mechanism to bring about "economic growth" and achieve "modernization" (Anderson and Bawman 1965; Harbinson and Myers 1964; Rogers and Shoemaker 1971). In the 1950s and 1960s, it was believed that national education systems in the Third World were to provide skilled laborers and modern citizens free of divisive ethnic allegiances, ignorance, and backward religious beliefs. If these ideas have come under strong criticism, along with the unfounded and Eurocentric contentions of modernization theory, the effects of state schooling in the non-West have yet to be properly researched and analyzed.

This chapter deals with the introduction of formal schooling among the Huaorani,[1] a small group of Amazonian hunters-and-gatherers.[2] It shows that state schools, sought for their promotion of social cohesion and their promise of free access to manufactured goods, do not come without a whole range of constraints and obligations which, even when actively resisted, have an impact on Huaorani society and culture. By contrasting models of socialization, cultural settings, and processes of cultural acquisition in forest settlements and school villages, this chapter attempts to elucidate the unforeseen and contested institutional effects of formal schooling, and explore the ways in which such effects hinder the reproduction of Huaorani cultural practices. It ends with a discussion of how formal schooling, a major site of cultural production in contemporary societies, creates the conditions for dominant identities to undermine the continuity of minority identities. These conditions are resisted to a certain extent by local actors, but once the school institution has transformed local social relations, pre-school identities can no longer exist.

FROM "GOD WEALTH" TO SCHOOL RICHES

The Huaorani inhabit the heart of the Ecuadorian Amazon, between the Napo and Curaray rivers. Before their "pacification" by an evangelical mission, the Summer Institute of Linguistics (SIL), in the early 1960s, they lived in highly dispersed and transient collective dwellings located on hilltops away from rivers. Traditional longhouses of approximately 10 to 35 members were typically composed of an older couple (often a man married to one, two, or three sisters), their daughters (with, when married, their husbands and children), and their unmarried sons. Each of these self-sufficient and dispersed residential units formed strong alliances with two or three other ones, while avoiding contact with all others. Allied houses formed in this way regional groups within which most marriages took place.

The SIL "pacification" campaign—arguably one of the most infamous missionary stories in Amazonia—followed the death of five North American missionaries in 1956 (Rival 1992; Stoll 1982; Wallis 1971). The SIL missionaries who, from the mid-1960s to the mid-1970s, prompted the Huaorani to relocate on their mission-base, have progressively introduced new garden crops, shotguns, dogs, and Western medicine, as well as the intensive use of air transport and radio contacts. They have strongly advocated monogamy, sexual modesty, and praying, while vehemently discouraging feasts, chants, and dancing. Relocated sometimes hundreds of kilometers away from their traditional lands, long-feuding bands have had no choice but to coexist and intermarry. If the "mixing" of traditionally antagonistic groups and the high number of monogamous marriages between former enemies has put an end to warfare, it has also severely undermined the long-established boundaries between endogamous groups. Yet the SIL did more than trigger changes in traditional alliances, subsistence activities, and residence patterns. It habituated converted Huaorani to a sedentary existence in communities under the guidance of powerful outsiders who, through their ability to "attract" large flows of free manufactured goods, were able to secure social unity and stability.

The advance of oil prospecting and the SIL missionary work have resulted in the concentration of 80 percent of the population on less than 10 percent of the traditional Huaorani territory—formerly called the Protectorate.[3] The Huaorani number 1,250 today—they were no more than 600 twelve years ago—and 55 percent of the present-day population are under 16. The creation of primary schools in the Huaorani territory has furthered the concentration of people in a few villages, adding to the dramatic character of their demographic growth.

The Huaorani have not endured the exploitation suffered by many other Amazonian Indian groups: their native language has never been suppressed (nor was

Spanish forced on them), and they were exempted from the alienation of religious boarding schools. All this is due in large part to the fact that all the SIL has wanted is to translate the Bible into their language, and to design a literacy program (aimed at *both* adults and children) in order to give them the opportunity to read "God's words"[4] for themselves. However, a number of state schools have been established in their territory over the last decade, and teachers now act as "powerful outsiders." The Ecuadorian Ministry of Education appoints and pays the teachers, but most other costs (school buildings, radios, uniforms, textbooks, teaching aids, and so forth) are privately financed by oil companies and the North American evangelical missions which have replaced the SIL. According to my 1990 census, eight communities—out of seventeen—had a school. In 1990, approximately 500 school age children—that is, children between the ages of 6 and 15—were enrolled. The first elementary school was created in December 1973 on the northern edge of the Protectorate. Only in this village are there today parents who were themselves schooled and who thus can share the experience of formal education with their children. All the teachers are trained and qualified, but only three of them have some competence in speaking Huaorani.

Until recently, successive Ecuadorian governments have promoted state education in order to enhance economic growth, give unity to the young Ecuadorian nation-state, and modernize its citizens' views and ways. But today, with the slow recognition that the national society is multilingual and pluricultural, there is more political will to adopt a national project of official bilingualism in the country. Moreover, bilingual education has been actively promoted by the Ecuadorian Indianist movement. Given the current situation of intense interethnic contact, most Indian leaders think that the Indian cultural heritage will not resist the influences of the dominant culture if kept in its oral forms. They firmly believe that Amerindian cultural identities depend on the continuous use of the native languages in writing and at school, and that state education can play a major role in the maintenance of Indian cultural identities.

The Huaorani's responses to these developments have been mixed and varied. Huaorani settlements are very isolated and transient—often only accessible by helicopter. Among the Huaorani 95 percent are monolingual in their own language, and not one is fully fluent in Spanish. Some communities refuse state education altogether. Others have received a teacher, only to decide within a few months against the schooling of their children—a decision at times resulting in a community split. Villages which have accepted a school are further divided between those who, allied with the evangelical missions, have opted for the Spanish national curriculum, and those who, aligned with the CONFENIAE (Confederation of the Indian Nationalities of Amazonian Ecuador), have chosen a program of bilingual education. These choices, however, reflect more intratribal dynamics, enduring enmities between regional factions, and patterns of political alliances with powerful outsiders, than real convictions.

Three main reasons seem to have pushed local groups to accept state schools and a sedentary existence. First of all, and as I hinted earlier, the "mixed" communities created by the SIL cannot be maintained without the centripetal force exercised by outsiders such as teachers, who alone can lower tensions and smooth animosities between old factions. Secondly, outside leaders are sources of "natural abundance," that is, of goods and foodstuffs created outside the living community. Thirdly, it is realized that the centuries-long isolation can no longer be maintained. Willing or unwilling, the Huaorani are now part of the national society, and some are eager to become modern citizens. The school provides the public and secure arena they need to rehearse modern demeanors.

LEARNING TO BE MODERN CITIZENS

It is the quest for a modern identity that informs learning activities in school villages. My aim here is to explain the local meaning of "learning to be modern." I also show that schools introduce a new type of spatiotemporal organization, de-skill children in relation to their indigenous knowledge, alter the forest environment, and modify traditional social relationships.

The schools found in Huaorani land, like any other school in rural Latin America, or, indeed, in any part of the world,[5] are conceived as models of modern culture. With their concrete floors, plank walls, and corrugated iron roofs, they are the only "modern" buildings in the village, and house all that is "modern" and "foreign." The school village, clustered around the schoolhouse and the airstrip, is linked to the provincial capital by modern systems of communication and transport—contact-radios and airplanes. The schoolhouse is usually flanked, on one side, by an experimental plantation in which children—and their parents—learn to cultivate new tropical plants and cash crops (such as coffee, sugar cane, and coconut trees). On the other side, a school canteen is equipped with the modern cooking and serving implements necessary for the preparation of "proper" meals and modern eating. The rural development projects (for instance, the introduction of water mains, showers, and toilets), promoted by teachers as part of their professional duties, are inspired by the same ideology of modernism. Finally, teachers promote the deforestation of vast areas around the school village, both for pragmatic and cultural reasons. On the pragmatic side, they argue that large open areas facilitate aircraft landings and take-offs. On the cultural side, they regard deforestation as necessary for their ideal of a modern built environment clearly marked off from the forest, the domain of savagery.

People are also, if not primarily, the targets of modernization. This is why the Ecuadorian government, despite its limited budget, regards the education of a "deprived" and "backward" population such as the Huaorani as a priority. Convinced by the teachers that Huaorani children do not do well in school because of their deprivation from proper food, hygiene, and medical attention, government officials have ordered the allocation—through special aid programs of medicine, clothes, soap, toothbrushes, toothpaste, and food considered nutritious (rice, powdered milk, porridge, and sugar) to all school villages. In addition to these free goods, villagers can usually buy from teachers the consumer goods they need to become "educated and modern citizens."

There exists a striking consensus between the teachers and the Huaorani communities on one point: to be educated is to be modern, and to be modern means to consume imported, manufactured goods. For the teachers, the very low rates of proficient literacy and numeracy among the Huaorani, even after the completion of six years of primary education, are not caused by curriculum deficiencies, but due to a lack of modern socialization. Formal education, however good the program, they argue, will not be effective if Huaorani children have not acquired the discipline and concentration that mental work demands, that is, if they have not become "modern" and "civilized." To teach Huaorani children the general cognitive skills of reading, writing, and counting requires not only their disembedding from the context of daily life—as is the case in all forms of schooling—but, more specifically, from the context of the forest and the longhouse. As there is no routine context for literacy or math activity in Huaorani social life, what the cognitive development of Huaorani students calls for is not the de-contextualization of reading, writing, or counting for general application, but the *creation of a new context*, of a new social and cultural environment. This is why the teachers feel obliged to attend to the children's deficient *habitus* first, and dedicate a large part of the teaching time to reforming their diet, hygiene, and general behavior. This they achieve primarily through promoting the consumption of the right food (such as powdered milk and oat flakes), of the right medicine and toiletry (for example, antibiotics and toothpaste), and of the right gear (a school uniform, sportwear, notebooks, pens, and so forth).

Schoolchildren, therefore, learn to be modern by memorizing textbook lessons on hygiene, executing school commands such as, "Brush your teeth before entering the classroom!" and, above all, by *imitating* the teachers. Much informal teaching—and active learning—goes on in the school compound before, during, and after normal school hours. It is when off-duty (when getting ready in the mornings or when relaxing in the evenings) that teachers become involuntary masters, eagerly modelled by unwanted apprentices—youths, schoolchildren, or passing villagers. The teachers' ways of waking up and dressing, washing, cooking and eating, playing the guitar, conversing, reading, and listening to the radio, are scrutinized and endlessly commented upon (as are the activities and behaviors of tourists who, incidentally, when in need of shelter, are invariably lodged in the schoolhouse).

For Huaorani parents and children, in sum, competent literacy and numeracy are correlated with the acquisition of a new lifestyle, inscribed in the way one dresses, eats, and behaves. To learn new skills is to learn a new identity so one becomes at once educated, modern, and "civilized." Parents believe that children having access to school uniforms, bookcases, school dinners, and toothpaste will eventually learn how to write, read, and count. After having completed their primary education, youths still hang around the school, showing off (perhaps with a hint of nostalgia?) their decisive way of crossing the airstrip while looking straight ahead and holding a pen and a notebook—the characteristic manner of literates. Villagers of all ages (except perhaps the oldest ones, for whom clothing is an unbearable nuisance, and the waiststring the only proper decorum) carefully avoid the schoolhouse if not wearing bright and clean clothes, even if this implies long detours. And no one approaches the school compound without first combing one's hair and washing off the mud from one's legs and feet. These are just some of the behavioral changes observed in the public sphere that the school creates. Other aspects, such as restrained bodily postures, verbal exchanges across age-sets and genders, and socializing through sports could also be analyzed at length to show that to opt for "modernism" and "civilization" is to choose the development of a public life around the school compound. These behavioral changes would show further that if the change of collective identity is primarily effectuated through performance (not through the adoption of a new worldview), then the performance of modern identity also calls for the use of specific consumer goods.

I have discussed elsewhere the way in which the school, the modern center of the village, creates a new type of community (Rival 1992). Here I simply summarize the main points of my analysis in order to show how time and space are restructured, social relations modified, and Huaorani social habits relegated to the intimacy of family homes. We have seen that Huaorani settlements are impermanent locales that barely disturb the forest cover. Over time, they leave an imprint on the landscape, not in the form of buildings, but of enduring palm groves, the materialization of the feasting activities of past generations and of the continuity of endogamous groups (Rival 1993). Given the substantial amount of capital and labor represented by schoolhouses, villages, by contrast, are conceived as permanent sites of human occupation. As people invest an increasing amount of time and energy in equipping and maintaining them, they feel less inclined to simply abandon them, even when forest resources have become depleted and soils infertile.

As I have tried to show, the most direct consequences following from infrastructural deployment are sedentarization and higher population density. At the infrastructural level, a school cannot function unless there are enough children to attend classes regularly. The government will create the first teaching position in a school village only when there are at least 24 school-age children. It will not open a second post for less than 56 school-age children. In other words, a minimum of 150–170 villagers (i.e., a population equivalent to eight longhouses) are required for a school to function.

Not only does the school, a state institution, promote the continuous growth of the Huaorani villages, but it also increases their integration within the nation-state. As soon as the state grants a school to a village, it appears on the map of Ecuador, and the Huaorani villagers, now formally recognized as Ecuadorian citizens, especially in their parental capacity, are faced with new obligations and administrative formalities. They must vote, get birth and marriage certificates, and own identity cards.

Another direct consequence of schooling is the remaking of the social space, with the creation of a public sphere, and the introduction of a new division of labor based on the redefinition of production. These developments bring two new social categories into being: "children" and "parents." "Children" are those who go to school and become dependent consumers. "Parents" are those who produce food and do not go to school. To the deep resentment of villagers, far from being a "natural" source of free and abundant manufactured goods making sharing possible on a larger scale, the school imposes and constrains more than it enables. One has to live, socialize, and work with "others"—that is, former enemies—for, given the fast rate of decay and jungle growth, school buildings, lavatories, airstrips, and sports fields need constant maintenance and repair. Worse, teachers and schoolchildren must be fed every day. This implies giving up hunting and gathering, taking up agriculture, and running into debt by purchasing imported foodstuff from the teachers' stores.

Wealth, in Huaorani thought, must be created outside the living community.[6] Villagers, aware of the fact that schooling and the removal of children from subsistence activities lead to the creation of social divisions, are constantly searching for new sources of "free food," and resist the intensification of agriculture. They have no difficulty in accepting new sources of wealth, as long as no additional labor is involved. But in the end, parents become responsible for the village's agricultural production,[7] and children ("those who work mentally") become dependent consumers. This new social division of labor, explicitly presented as rational and progressive, is reinforced in the teachings dedicated to changing the conceptions of work, production, and gender. Children are taught, for example, that agriculture, the creation of abundance and welfare through hard labor, represents an evolutionary stage superior to that of hunting and that if their parents intensify horticultural production, food will be more nutritious and varied.

Schools, with their strong pro-agriculture advocacy, remove children from their natural environment and *de-skill* them with regard to forest knowledge. School children spend considerably less time in the forest than their nonsedentary counterparts, and when they go, it is during school holidays with their parents and other adults. In school most days, they tend to stay indoors when back home, helping with the washing or cooking. As the village environment (with its large grassy spaces, its compounds, and its dispersed plantations) differs substantially from the forest environment, and as the children have little exposure to the latter, their knowledge of the primary rainforest and its resources is undermined. From the survey I conducted with fifth- and sixth-graders in two school villages, it appeared that only 40 percent of the children knew how to climb trees (the majority of nonclimbers being girls); 80 percent of the boys had hunted with a blowpipe[8] (and only one girl), and none had prepared curare poison; 35 percent had hunted with a shotgun (and no girls); 5 percent of the girls had made a hammock on their own, but none had ever made a clay pot. Only two children had seen stone axes, and no one seemed to know that armbands were woven on simple looms in the past. These figures clearly indicate a high degree of de-skillment for traditional productive activities. I conducted another survey in the oldest school village to test the children's relative knowledge of plant and animal classification. The results suggest that both schooled and nonschooled children can name the same amount of species, but that only nonschooled children successfully associate names and wild specimens collected from the forest. Although too tentative to be taken as a firm indication, this test signals a loss of cultural knowledge affecting practical skills more than categories.

In the built environment of school villages, the forest has become marginal in people's practical activities, and in their *imaginary* as well. It is very rare to hear someone chant in a school village. Of course, youths who own "ghetto blasters" record and listen to the chants of elders, particularly of those who do not live in their communities. But they do not chant themselves, except—occasionally—during drinking ceremonies. Schoolchildren, despite the school lessons they have sometimes received in Huaorani cultural knowledge, do not chant either.

In conclusion, the school introduces new ways of interacting with the environment, new habits, and new experiences.[9] It is through the reform of ordinary practices, particularly those centered around the body and the domestic space, that social practices are reorganized and social identities reshaped. It is also through routine activities such as wearing a school uniform, brushing one's teeth before entering the classroom, or eating with a knife and a fork that new values and beliefs are acquired as normal and commonsensical ideas.

BECOMING A HUAORANI IN THE FOREST AND IN THE LONGHOUSE

My aim in this chapter is to show that Huaorani people consider learning[10] an integral part of growing. Children, who progressively become full members of the longhouse through their increased participation in ongoing social activities, learn to be Huaorani *experientially* by getting forest food and sharing it, by helping out in the making of blowguns, pots, or hammocks, and by chanting with longhouse co-residents.

Toddlers are encouraged to like being on their own, detached from the caregiver's body and exploring their surroundings. The basis of Huaorani pedagogy (and, more generally, of Huaorani social life) is that action should result from the exact correspondence between feeling (*huë*) and desire or will (*â*). This is why adults never order children around; they do not command, coerce, or exercise any kind of physical or moral pressure, but simply suggest and ask, without getting annoyed when the answer is, "No, I won't do it, I don't feel like doing it now" (*ba amopa*). The belief that harmonious social life should be based on the full respect of personal expression and free choice to act corresponds to the fear that actions performed under constraint result in social harm. This is why children, who grow in uxorilocal longhouses where bodily attitudes are extremely relaxed and the needs of individuals fully respected, are, by any standard, very independent and self-sufficient. As adults do not have a sense of hierarchical superiority, and are not overprotective (see Rival 1992, chapters 5–6), relations between what a non-Huaorani would call "adults" and "children" are totally devoid of authority.

Walking, talking, and eating meat are seen as three simultaneous acquisitions which mark the beginning of personal autonomy and which can be stimulated by the application of certain plants (for a full description, see Rival 1993:639–641). Only when they can walk on their own do toddlers start wearing the distinctive Huaorani cotton string around the waist. From field observations, I formed the impression that grownups attach far more importance to the first steps walked than to the first words uttered. Moreover, whereas I witnessed real excitement at a child's first attempts to sing, I never noticed any special reaction in response to a child's first efforts to speak. Older children, however, spend a lot of time with toddlers, making them repeat words and name body parts or objects. In any case, the child's activity that really arouses the pride of grown-ups is food sharing, the real measure of independence. Nothing is more cheering for a Huaorani parent than a three-year-old's decision to join a food gathering expedition. The young child, whose steps on the path are carefully guided away from thorns and crawling insects, is praised for carrying his/her own *oto* (a basket made of a single palm leaf hurriedly woven on the way), and bringing it back to the longhouse filled with forest food to "give away," that is, to share with co-residents. Food procurement is an essential area of learning for children who are "old enough to go on their own" (*piquèna bate opate gocamba*). Parents do not *teach* but encourage children to grow, mature, and participate in productive activities. And it is by participating more fully in the social relations of sharing that children learn subsistence skills, while increasing their knowledge of plants and animals.

If food procurement is the part of the process of culture-learning that takes children to the forest and makes them know about the natural world, the skilled practices of craft-making and chanting—two inseparable activities—are important means of entering the social world of the longhouse. Although Huaorani material culture is minimal, there are a few elaborate artifacts, such as the blowpipe. These objects are difficult to make, and like almost everywhere else in the world, their manufacture involves learning by observing masters and by doing. In other words, it involves apprenticeship in the sense defined by Lave (1977, 1990, 1993) and Lave and Wenger (1991). From a very young age, Huaorani children are given raw materials to hold, feel, and touch, while people around them weave, carve, or make pots. If they seek more participation, they are entrusted with the simplest phases of the productive process. For example, a boy[11] willing to help in the making of a blowpipe starts by sanding the surface of a nearly completed one. While he learns to make more difficult parts, he receives a small blowpipe for hunting practice. In this fashion, he acquires simultaneously the art of making and the art of using the full-size blowpipe, a gradual process through which he not only reaches technical competence, but also achieves personal style (Huaorani craftsmen "sign" their works with individual decorative designs). He also, and perhaps more fundamentally, becomes a grown man, ready for marriage and fatherhood.

People usually chant—several hours a day when at home, either resting in their hammocks or busy with some home-based activity. Chanting while making tools and artifacts can therefore be seen as the combination of "vocal artistry" and "technical artistry" (Ingold 1993:463), that is, the concurrent performance of mental and manual activities through which skilled practices and symbolic knowledge are simultaneously learned. In the combined action of chanting and making objects, of knowing and practicing, individuals not only communicate their feelings to co-residents, but also share with them their personal interpretations of Huaorani symbolism. It is within the communal life of the longhouse, and amidst practical activities, that children acquire the knowledge of myths, histories of warfare, and family sagas, while also learning the poetic imagery depicting significant aspects of their environment. This leads me to suggest that chanting and craft-making are two inseparable aspects of the same social activity, embedded in the social relations that characterize the longhouse. As acquired by children through participation, this cultural knowledge combines technical enskillment and many idiosyncratic versions of the ways in which Huaorani come to experience the world. By gradually becoming performers of practical skills, and learning the associated chants, attitudes, and values, children simultaneously acquire and reproduce Huaorani culture.

Their identity, therefore, is entirely bound to their learning experiences, which are in turn influenced by the structuring features of the social environment. They learn and acquire their identity in the longhouse and in the forest through performance, in much the same way as children who live in school villages acquire their modern identity through their participation—that is, their active engagement—in the process of decontextualized knowing. Hunting, gathering, chanting, and making artifacts are cultural and context-specific activities. They are sustained through specific practices, the use of particular objects, the consumption of special food, and the mastery of certain bodily techniques. Moreover, these activities produce and reproduce particular dispositions and cultural norms, most of which have to do with the concepts of personal autonomy and the collective sharing of natural abundance.

We have seen that the modern identity acquired through state schooling is entirely antithetical to such dispositions and cultural norms. Are these dispositions and norms used, then, to resist the undermining effects of school education? An example will illustrate how school modernity is enthusiastically adopted, but in a way that subverts its cultural dichotomies (that is, modern versus traditional, school versus home).

Villagers are actively defending their free and equal access to large quantities of manufactured goods. They want these goods which enable them to act modern. But they do not want to pay or work for them, nor do they want to economize, save, or make scarce commodities last. In the teachers' words, "they do not want to learn the value of things." In Ecuadorian cities, each school has its own uniform.[12] School uniforms are a sign of progress, development, and national pride. However, not many rural schools have one. Clothes wear out too quickly in the humid tropical lowlands, and Indian families are generally too poor. But Huaorani children do have a school uniform, offered by a North American evangelical mission, in exchange for reciting biblical verses twice a year. Teachers attach great importance to the proper use of these uniforms, and stress that they must be handled with care. Children are constantly reminded that they must not wear their uniform outside of school time. Those who come to school without their uniform on, or with a dirty one, are sent back home for the day. However, far from being deterred by these warnings, many children wear their uniforms all the time, and even sleep in them. In some villages, the population was astute enough to get school uniforms supplied in sufficient quantity for each villager to receive his or her own. In a village I visited while the school was closed for the holidays, virtually every one, old and young, male and female, parents and children, was wearing a school uniform. Through field observations and informal conversations, I soon realized that children refused to confine their modern identity to school time, and that parents wished to feel modern, even if they had passed the age of schooling.

Huaorani villagers, who wish to be modern *on their own terms*, seek a collective identity which does not fragment them into differentiated sociocultural categories. By wearing school uniforms *uniformly*, they are in fact perverting the system of differences built into formal education. Their prime concern is to defend their egalitarian social relations in whatever cultural context. This may hardly qualify as resistance, but it is a way of producing cultured persons, while rejecting the hierarchy of knowledge and sociability that comes with becoming school educated. Their way of wearing school uniforms is not determined by their decision to challenge school culture. Rather, it is a form of local appropriation, a semiconscious attempt to control the terms of modern behavior in practice. But the day-to-day wearing of school uniforms in villages (they are never worn in the forest) nevertheless recreates the conditions of its establishment. A school village is a very different environment from a longhouse in the forest.

THE POWER TO DE-SKILL

This chapter has discussed the introduction of formal schooling among a population of Amazonian hunter-gatherers. It has been argued that state schools are modernizing institutions which have the power to transform indigenous lifeways—whatever the adopted curriculum. The school institution creates a community around itself which calls for the restructuration of Huaorani social relations, subsistence activities and, more generally, mode of existence and identity. It is not so much that social life is now determined by new—modernist—cultural trends, but that new activities, through which a different type of knowledge gets distributed across minds, bodies and cultural settings, impede the practice and the development of typically Huaorani activities.

The impact of state education on Huaorani social life is, as we have seen, largely due to the infrastructural requirements of the school institution. Fixed standards corresponding to a model of what the school institution should offer, and to what an ideal learning situation is, determine the ways in which primary schools operate in Huaorani land. Like all institutions, formal schooling is the historical product of specific social relations and cultural norms. It is therefore possible to find, embedded in the apparently neutral infrastructure, a cultural model of what knowledge is, and how it should be acquired. Knowledge, which can only be acquired in isolation from everyday activities, demands discipline, obedience, and respect for the teachers' authority. Formal schooling, moreover, requires particular family relations. The social roles of parents and children must exist—or must be created—for schooling to occur. In addition, and the case under discussion fully illustrates this point, literacy and numeracy, the basics of school knowledge, are not dissociable from wider modes of cultural expression—here, from "modernization." Moreover, children learn more than literacy and numeracy skills; they learn to be members of a modern community, the school village and, beyond it, the national society. For the Huaorani, then, the educated person is above all a modern person, the product of a distinctive form of sociability, the end-result of particular acts of performance and consumption.

By comparing two sites of cultural (re)production, the school village and the longhouse in the forest, I have tried to show that culture is not primarily acquired through the internalization of norms and values, or the transmission of factual information and abstract skills, but through interactive learning. In the two learning settings I have examined, learning activities and the sociocultural order are dialectically constituted. The disparity between what schoolchildren in villages and children raised in longhouses in the forest know about their culture is best explained as resulting from the differences between the two social environments in which learning activities take place. As Lave (1988:14) so rightly states, "knowledge-in-practice, constituted in the settings of practice, is the locus of the most powerful knowledgeability of people in the lived-in world." Both in her work on craft apprenticeship among Vai and Gola tailors in Liberia (1977, 1982, 1990) and her investigation of everyday arithmetic practices (1984, 1988), Lave has demonstrated that culture is the acquisition of particular skills through active learning and repeated practice, as well as the reproduction of *ways of being in the world*.

Lave (1988:188–90) argues that knowledge is not isolated from experience and context, that social life is formed of continuing practices, and that, consequently, continuity results from social habits and routines. As she says so well, "Everyday practice is a more powerful source of socialization than intentional pedagogy" (Lave 1988:14). This implies that cultural continuity requires the continuity of community practices. In the case under study, the two "communities of practice" (Lave and Wenger 1991) are the school village and the longhouse in the forest, where continuity, the product of routinization (rather than of the internalization of transmitted facts, norms or values), is more likely than structural change.[13] However, as I have tried to demonstrate, these two communities of practice are incompatible. In school villages, Huaorani people can be seen to engage practically, actively and consciously in new social processes, which, given the relational nature of the self, the (partly) physical nature of cognitive processes, and the social construction of bodily experiences, undermine their Huaoraniness.

NOTES

Fieldwork among the Huaorani was generously supported by the Wenner Gren Foundation for Anthropological Research, with additional funding from the Linnean Society of London. The work on which this article is based was originally presented at the Conference on Hunter-Gatherer Societies (CHAGS 7) in Moscow, Russia, in August 1993. It has subsequently been read in various departmental seminars. I would like to thank the participants for their suggestions, especially Harvey Feit, Megan Biesele, and Jean Briggs. I am very grateful to Maurice Bloch, Dorothy Holland, and Aurolyn Luykx, who commented on an early draft, and to Bradley Levinson and Doug Foley for their helpful editorial comments.

1. I spent eighteen months working with schooled and nonschooled children. I lived both in school villages and in settlements with no school. The following observations and analyses are based on the data I recorded between January 1989 and June 1990.

2. I have argued elsewhere (Rival 1993) that Huaorani gardening is exceptional. Manioc and plantain are cultivated incipiently and sporadically for the preparation of ceremonial drinks, while daily subsistence is traditionally secured through hunting and gathering.

3. Two percent of the population is still uncontacted and lives in hiding.

4. By 1981, 20 percent of the population in the Protectorate could read the SIL translation of the Gospel according to St Mark (Rival 1992:15). That the SIL has not created a new dialect of Huaorani remains to be proven. I suspect that their linguistic analyses, which are shaped by the priorities and constraints of biblical translations, do not pay enough attention to everyday speech. Rather, they prioritize and formalize narrative styles, and standardize linguistic expressions which do not arise from the Huaorani cultural environment, but from the needs of Bible translation. For instance, a large number of figurative phrases and metaphors have been created in order to fill the semantic and cultural gaps between Huaorani and the biblical texts in Huaorani. Moreover, for the SIL, vernacular literacy is a definite sign of *salvation*, a notion which includes not only the idea of Christianization, but also of progress and modernization, and which, thus, comes close to meaning *civilization*. In any case, this is how the Huaorani themselves express it, when they say that the SIL has "civilized" them. See Rival (1992:323–348) for a fuller account.

5. The constraints which govern schools and limit learning have concerned educationalists for many years. Illich's (1973) *Deschooling Society* remains one of the most radical, provocative, and insightful essays on this subject, particularly for the Latin American context.

6. Forest resources represent the bounty created by the everyday activities linked to consumption of past generations. I have argued elsewhere (Rival 1992, chapter 4) that Huaorani social relations are based on consumption rather than production, and that their sharing economy relates to a fundamental belief in "natural abundance," that is, the exogenous creation of wealth. In the same way as the trees associated with their forefathers continuously provide for the living and secure their subsistence (Rival 1993), foreign organizations such as the SIL, the oil companies prospecting on Huaorani land, and now schools, are expected to behave like giving agencies and meet people's modern needs, *without asking anything in return.* The Huaorani have adjusted to demographic growth and increased population density by tapping new sources of food. Former enemies in mixed communities are willing to share with each other as long as sharing neither creates obligations, nor requires the management of scarce resources.

7. Parents are classified as *agricultores* (farmers) on school social category for registers. "Hunter-gatherers" is an unacceptable social category for people who send their children to school.

8. One should not be too impressed by the high rate of boys having used blowpipes. They use them as toys around the house (monkeys and birds are rare in the vicinity of sedentary villages), which, while giving them good practice, does not amount to the same skill as actual hunting.

9. It also creates new political discourses and competing ideologies about cultural identity and modernity. The evangelical missionaries now working with the Huaorani are highly critical of the SIL's attempt to translate the Bible in Huaorani. They are totally opposed to bilingual education, which they equate to "communism." They support financially state schools which implement the national curriculum in Spanish and teach religion—in Spanish as well.

10. To my knowledge, there is no Huaorani term to translate the idea of learning. In answer to my questions about children engaged in the making of a pot, a fishing net, or darts, my informants would simply say: "he is busy making darts, she is busy weaving a net . . ." Interestingly, SIL missionaries have used the word *iñe* (to listen) to translate the Western concept of learning. This term is indeed appropriate for the learning of the Bible, which takes place in the Church, when Christians assemble to listen to *Huegongui apene*, God's stories or teachings.

11. The same can be said of girls, who traditionally made clay pots. Clay pots, which have been replaced two decades ago by traded metallic pots, are no longer made. Today, girls and women are almost exclusively responsible for the making of hammocks, an activity which was not gender-specific in the past.

12. In addition to their normal school uniform, children have a second uniform for official ceremonies, parades, and the raising of the flag, which takes place every Monday.

13. A conclusion also reached by Giddens (1979:216), for whom routinization is an essential part of the concept of structuration.

REFERENCES

Anderson, Charles A., and M. J. Bawman. 1965. *Education and Economic Development.* London: Frank Cass.

Giddens, Anthony. 1979. *Central Problems in Social Theory.* London: Mcmillan.

Harbinson, Frank, and C. Myers. 1964. *Education, Manpower and Economic Growth.* New York: McGraw-Hill.

Illich, Ivan. 1973 [1971]. *Deschooling Society.* UK: Harmondsworth, Penguin.

Ingold, Tim. 1993. Epilogue. In *Tools, Language and Cognition in Human Evolution.* K. R. Gibson and T. Ingold, eds. Pp. 449–472. Cambridge: Cambridge University Press.

Lave, Jean. 1977. Cognitive Consequences of Traditional Apprenticeship Training in West Africa. *Anthropology and Education Quarterly* 8(3):177–80.

———. 1982. A Comparative Approach to Educational Reforms and Learning Processes. *Anthropology and Education Quarterly* 13(2):181–187.

———. 1988. *Cognition in Practice.* Cambridge: Cambridge University Press.

———. 1990. The Culture of Acquisition and the Practice of Understanding. In *Cultural Psychology: Essays on Comparative Human Development.* J. W. Stigler, R. Shweder, and G. Herdt, eds. Cambridge: Cambridge University Press.

———. 1993. The Practice of Learning. In *Understanding Practice: Perspectives on Activity and Context.* S. Chaiklin and J. Leve, eds. Pp. 3–32. Cambridge: Cambridge University Press.

Lave, Jean, M. Murtaugh, and O. de la Rocha. 1984. The Dialectic of Arithmetic in Grocery Shopping. In *Everyday Cognition: Its Development in Social Context.* B. Rogoff and J. Lave, eds. Cambridge, MA: Harvard University Press.

Lave, Jean, and E. Wenger. 1991. *Situated Learning: Legitimate Peripheral Participation.* Cambridge: Cambridge University Press.

Rival, Laura. 1992. *Social Transformations and the Impact of Schooling on the Huaorani of Amazonian Ecuador.* Ph.D. dissertation. University of London.

———. 1993. The Growth of Family Trees: Understanding Huaorani Perceptions of the Forest. *Man* 28(4):635–52.

Rogers, Edwin, and F. Shoemaker. 1971. *Communication of Innovations: A Cross-Cultural Approach.* New York: Free Press.

Stoll, David. 1982. *Fishers of Men or Founders of Empire? The Wycliffe Bible Translators in Latin America.* London: Zed Press.

Wallis, Elizabeth. 1971. *Aucas Down River.* New York: Harper & Row.

11

Transmitting Traditional Values in New Schools: Elementary Education of Pulap Atoll

Juliana Flinn

Micronesians want their young people trained both to contend with the modern world and to respect and practice traditional ways. Emphasis on one or the other has shifted over time—not so much because of Micronesian desires but because of policies held by foreign administrations. Especially since the 1960s, however, both Americans and Micronesians have viewed education as the key to development. Micronesians see formal schooling as the avenue to prestigious jobs, although they realize these jobs are increasingly scarce. Yet the desired development has not materialized. Most employment is with the government, although the service sector provides a few other jobs, thus exacerbating the problem of an economy heavily dependent on foreign funds.

With schooling the passport to a prestigious government job, education has fostered the growth of a new elite, an educated and fairly young group residing in urbanizing port towns. Members of this elite earn substantially more than many in the private sector, and certainly much more than their kin who fish and garden. Education also provides another avenue to prestige, a nontraditional path accessible at a far younger age than in the past, when specialists such as navigators and canoe builders acquired considerable prestige. Thus, schooling precipitates and reinforces transformations in traditional culture.

Despite the desire for success in the modern context, educators in Micronesia at the same time want formal schooling to transmit a Micronesian heritage. Thus, the administration encourages bilingual and bicultural education, and a few curriculum materials have been developed to teach history and legends. These may have a certain value in educating children about their language and culture, but formal schooling takes place in a manner and context quite different from indigenous learning. To the extent that Micronesians have control over their schools and they teach in the classrooms, values and patterns of behavior are transmitted in more indirect

123

ways than curriculum materials. Thus, Western schooling introduced to Micronesia can be transformed by local cultures.

These issues have come to the fore since the United States took over adminis-tration of Micronesia after World War II and implemented a formal educational system modeled on the American one. Elementary education was the primary fo-cus during the 1950s. Changes in U.S. policy in the 1960s promoted secondary education, and then in the middle of the 1970s, this "education explosion" (Hezel 1978) reached the level of college education, with many high school graduates leav-ing for college in the United States. The number of students enrolled in high school and the number leaving to attend college began to drop in the late 1970s (Hezel n.d.), but Micronesians still view education as essential to obtaining prestigious employment.

For the people of Pulap, an atoll to the west of Chuuk Lagoon in Chuuk State (formerly Truk),[1] seeking these opportunities means leaving home. The atoll economy remains primarily a subsistence one based on horticulture and fishing, and young people looking for paid employment must pursue at least a high school edu-cation in Chuuk Lagoon. An elementary school on Pulap provides for the first eight grades, but at each successive level of education, Pulap students move farther away from their own sociocultural setting. Secondary education is provided first at Weipat Junior High School on Ulul in the Namonuito Atoll north of Pulap and then at Chuuk High School on the island of Moen in Chuuk Lagoon.[2] Many go on to col-lege, either in Chuuk, Belau, Guam or the United States.

Many foreign American elements can easily be detected at the elementary school, but here at least the students live at home, most of the teachers were born and raised on Pulap, their own dialect is the medium of instruction, and—probably most im-portant—expectations of behavior and values are largely consistent with other as-pects of life on the island. More educated Pulapese, although interested in jobs in the port town and membership in the elite, are nonetheless in the forefront of ef-forts to retain Pulapese cultural values. Despite all the changes resulting from edu-cation in Chuuk and the intrusive foreign elements, especially beyond elementary education, the new educational system transmits some aspects of Pulapese culture. Though Western schooling transforms Pulap culture, Pulap culture transforms Western schooling.

FORMAL SCHOOLING IN CHUUK

Protestant American missionaries introduced the first formal Western education in Chuuk, in the 1880s, with a clear intention of transforming religion and other tra-ditional customs. Missionary teachers treated education as a vehicle to Christian-ize local natives and advocated literacy so that Chuukese could read the Bible. Set up in Chuuk Lagoon and atolls to the southeast, these mission schools operated far from Pulap. No Pulap students attended, although missionaries later briefly held classes on Pulap.

During the Spanish and German administrations, missionaries provided the only formal education, since neither government established its own schools. The Japanese, who took over in 1914, allowed mission schools to continue but also established their own system of public schools, one that emphasized Japanese culture. Rather than incorporating indigenous elements, the government introduced a Japanese system, complete with Japanese teachers, language, and texts, intending Chuuk to become an integral and loyal part of the Japanese empire. A few Pulapese, who recognized the value of learning Japanese, sent a handful of young men to school. No girls attended.

During World War II the Japanese closed their schools. Soon after the war, however, the United States Navy—responsible for administering the area—opened a school to teach English and train elementary school teachers. When recruiting their first students, the Navy preferred those who had attended the Japanese schools, including a few Pulapese.

Guided by American democratic ideals and faith in universal education, the Navy wanted to establish a system of elementary schools providing six years of education for all children, including girls (Kiste 1985:8; Singleton 1974:79). Although the Navy sponsored the system, local communities controlled many aspects of their own schools. The administration even sought consent of local magistrates before assigning new teachers to their schools (Nagao and Nakayama 1969). Indigenous teachers staffed the schools as much as possible, local communities provided the buildings, and schools in the outer islands operated largely on their own.

In addition to the elementary schools, the military government established a public secondary school in 1946 on Moen and staffed it with American teachers. It soon became Truk Intermediate School, with grades seven to nine, and continued as such until 1962. Because the intermediate school was too small to handle all the elementary school graduates, an entrance exam was administered to limit the number of students who could attend. Even fewer young people continued their education at Pacific Islands Central School (PICS), the only public high school in the entire Trust Territory until 1962. Thus, selective secondary education contrasted with universal elementary education.

In 1962, the United States budget calling for Trust Territory appropriations more than doubled, precipitating a fundamental change in the educational system. Education received a far heavier emphasis than before, with a goal of providing 12 years of free and universal education in Micronesia (Pearse and Bezanson 1970:29; Smith 1968:75). Secondary education lost its exclusiveness. More facilities, materials, and American teachers appeared in Trust Territory schools. Materials designed specifically for Micronesians entered the classrooms, and new methods of teaching English as a second language promoted the use of English.[3]

Education was to be the key to Micronesia's development. In fact, some saw education as a means of irrevocably binding Micronesia to the United States in a dependent relationship (Gale 1979; Nevin 1977). Education would induce rapid sociocultural change, and with American teachers, curricula, and language, Micronesians presumably would view education as the means to advancement and prestige (Gale 1979:121). The intent was to develop social, political, and economic ties through rapid development such that Micronesia would establish a permanent political affiliation with the United States. This heavy emphasis on education had other consequences.

> The rapid growth of an education industry had at least three important ramifications for the political structure of the Trust Territory. First, it led to a sustained, intimate contact with foreigners surpassing that previously experienced. Second, it was the major element in the growth of the Trust Territory bureaucracy and payroll. Third, it acted as a centralizing force that resulted in a diminution of local power and encouraged urbanization. [Gale 1979:123]

The Education Department is even now the largest employer (Hezel n.d.). Certainly on Pulap, elementary school teaching provides the only full-time employment, according the teachers considerable prestige.

Concurrent with these policy changes, local communities lost much of their control over elementary schools, and the administration began to take on more responsibility for teacher salaries (Nagao and Nakayama 1969). Consequently, the administration acquired the right to assign teachers without consulting community magistrates. The curriculum lost much of its island orientation, with an influx of American teachers contributing to the shift.[4]

In 1962, the High Commissioner transformed secondary education by replacing the single interdistrict school, PICS, with separate district high schools, including Truk High School on Moen.[5] Academically oriented secondary education was to be available for all young people rather than remain the privilege of a select few.

For Chuuk as a whole, secondary school enrollment increased when Truk High School opened and again when academic junior high schools opened in 1970. But for Pulapese, the establishment of vocational post-elementary schools, the forerunners of the academic junior high schools, marked the beginning of increased enrollments. Students from Pulap attended the post-elementary school Weipat on Ulul, in the Namonuito Atoll to the north. Before this time, only one Pulap boy had gone to PICS on Moen, and only one had graduated from Truk High School. Once Weipat opened, however, the situation changed. Although most Pulap students failed the high school entrance test, they were able to attend the post-elementary Weipat. A number of them went on to Truk High School and graduated in the early 1970s. Part of the explanation for the increase in graduates, however, lies in the fact that these first students were born from 1949 to 1951, when the birth rate increased sharply on the atoll. More Pulapese began graduating from high school partly because Weipat provided an alternative for those who failed the test, but also because, in sheer numbers, there were more of them.

Not only did more Pulap students in general pursue post-elementary education after Weipat opened, but Pulap girls also began to leave the island for post-elementary education.[6] This practice, as well as the American insistence on coeducational schooling, eventually persuaded the islanders to accept post-elementary education for females. Moreover, because Ulul is both geographically and cultur-ally closer to Pulap, adults felt less anxious about girls attending Weipat on Ulul than Truk Intermediate on Moen.

Pursuit of a secondary education has become the norm for all Pulap young people who can pass the entrance test. Since the opening of the school on Ulul, only a handful of Pulap's elementary school graduates have failed to pursue further school-ing. In general, students do not go on to secondary school if they fail the entrance test, become seriously ill, or, in the case of girls, marry. Then, once in secondary school, students tend to remain unless compelled to leave because of low grades, illness, or marriage.

The earliest postsecondary education during the American administration con-sisted of medical and vocational training (Singleton 1974:81–82), but young people soon began attending college. During the 1950s and 1960s the College of Guam was the popular choice. Furthermore, because the Trust Territory scholarships were awarded by merit to only a few students (Hezel 1978:26), those who attended col-lege represented the most intellectually able of the high school graduates.

In the early 1970s, more graduates continued with postsecondary education, and a higher percentage began attending the University of Hawai'i and mainland schools instead of Guam. Part of the explanation for the increase lies in the establishment of postsecondary schools within the Trust Territory. Another reason, however, is that Micronesians began to receive federal grants for education as low-income and minority students. Furthermore, many small U.S. colleges eagerly accepted Micronesians because their minority group status made the schools eligible for fed-eral funds (Hezel 1978:28). More students in sheer numbers, a higher percentage of students, and—since obtaining money was no longer based on merit—a far less select group of high school graduates began to attend college.

Although the first student from Pulap to attend a mainland school did not leave until 1974, since then almost every Pulap high school graduate has at least consid-ered attending college. Even if they return without a degree, simply having gone abroad and come back with tales of adventure provides them with prestige. At least until recently, most have simply assumed that appropriate jobs would be available, despite the fact that the government positions most of them expect are fast drying up (Hezel 1982:110–111).

SCHOOLING ON PULAP

The educational system in Chuuk substantially influences both long- and short-term mobility among Pulapese. A large number of Pulapese are away attending school, and most intend to look for employment on Moen once they finish. The begin-ning and end of the school year also produce the most marked change in resident population on Pulap, because most secondary school students come home for the summer and most elementary school teachers leave for education courses held in

Chuuk Lagoon. Even a few college students manage to return for visits during the summer months.

For the first eight grades, however, children can attend school on their own island, with their own local teachers, thus providing some cultural continuity. Even though the United States has set up a system of formal education based on American models emphasizing competitive individualism, Pulap elementary school teachers nonetheless conduct certain aspects of the class in accordance with their own beliefs about how children learn and their own notions of ideal character traits. These include humility, respectfulness, modesty, cooperation, and sharing.

The elementary school on Pulap is centrally located in the settlement area near the church and municipal buildings, all considered joint community structures and symbols of island unity.[7] And the school affects daily life in the whole community, not just the lives of students. Most noticeably, school occupies children for a good portion of the day, leaving them unavailable for subsistence activities. Students share school meals and food supplies with other family members. Furthermore, a two-way radio is housed in a classroom, and one of the teachers has been trained in its use and maintenance. Assuming the radio is in operation, the weekly education net is a major source of information from Moen for the entire island. Finally, one of the major island feasts celebrates eighth grade graduation—today's version of former puberty rites.

Like other Chuuk elementary schools, the one on Pulap has eight grades. Enrollment during the 1979–80 school year was 122 students, with a staff of six teachers, four Title I teacher aides, one principal, and two cooks funded through the federal Hot Lunch Program.[8] One teacher and two aides were women.

These school jobs are the only full-time paid positions available on the islet, providing teachers with money and prestige unavailable to others on Pulap. In the past, this sort of respect and prestige accrued to elders. Now it is the young who are able to attain such positions; their education provides a new status, a new opportunity. These are prized jobs because they enable young people both to have an income and to live in their own community. They gain additional prestige from their ability to be generous. For example, the teachers all go to Moen during the summer for courses, and their income assists in the support of all Pulap migrants on Moen. They are also expected to share the income with relatives, but this sharing and generosity is highly valued and provides prestige to the teachers. In fact, they acquire more prestige at their age than do any others.

Among the staff at the elementary school, all but two were born and raised on Pulap. The other two, sent to teach before enough Pulapese were qualified, soon married Pulap women. Today they are members of the Pulap community, raising families on the island. Having local teachers and being isolated from Chuuk Lagoon allow the school to conform to a certain extent with island values and attitudes, despite the extent to which the school is modeled on the American system.

To begin with a minor example, the school calendar is an American one of 180 days running from September to early June, with American holidays such as Thanksgiving and Presidents' Day. Yet classes are canceled for any number of reasons: the arrival of a ship, heavy rain, a death on the island, a religious holiday, practice for interisland athletic games, or a community activity that requires all the men, such as building a canoe house. These are activities that in general disrupt the normal daily routine of other aspects of life on the island. Students do not make up the days they miss.

Some materials teachers develop in the absence of books reflect their own experiences and understanding. In a fourth-grade science class, for instance, one teacher taught a unit on "living things." (These two words were in English, but the teacher conducted the rest of the lesson in the vernacular.) Rather than dividing up the realm, as an American might, into the three regions of land, air, and water, the teacher presented four regions that harbor living things. Consistent with their seafaring way of life, his regions consisted of air, land, fresh water, and salt water.

Even though islanders recognize the school as an intrusive institution, teachers and students both attend school dressed essentially as they are for other island activities, with older boys and men in loincloths, girls and women in lavalavas. Females make some concessions: women teachers usually add a shirt; and younger girls who otherwise would be naked wear lavalavas to school. Boys, however, tend to come to school naked until about the fifth grade. This traditional style of dress is an important symbol of Pulapese cultural identity, even—or perhaps especially— among the educated elite who spend most of their time in Chuuk Lagoon.

The female teachers and any of the schoolgirls who have reached puberty observe customary patterns of deference toward classificatory brothers who have also reached puberty. This behavior involves, in part, an obligation to *yoppworo* (stoop) in their presence. So older girls commonly enter the room on their knees, and female teachers often have to write on the blackboard while sitting on a chair or kneeling on the floor. This deference Pulap women show their brothers is another important aspect of Pulapese cultural identity and provides continuity with their own cultural tradition.

The medium of instruction in the classroom is the Pulap language, although the two non-Pulap teachers use their own dialects. Literacy is established, however, not in Pulapese, but in the dialect of Chuuk Lagoon, the lingua franca for all of Chuuk State and a dialect related to others in the area. English is taught as a second language from the earliest grades, but literacy is first encouraged in Chuukese.

English or Chuukese words crop up in a number of classroom contexts, especially when no appropriate Pulap term exists. The terms "paragraph" and "capital" are examples. In other cases, Pulap terms do exist, but English or Chuukese words are substituted in the classroom. In math classes, for instance, English numbers and the Chuukese word *kapach* (add) replace Pulap terms. Foreign expressions fit the classroom setting, but Pulap words predominate in contexts more closely connected with a home setting.

Although the educational system ostensibly derives from an American model, and the context is one the islanders recognize as a foreign, nontraditional one, many aspects nonetheless continue to transmit Pulapese culture rather than prepare them for American-style schooling. For example, the atmosphere at the school is very lax and permissive to an American observer. The appearance of the school itself indicates apparent negligence. Many of the windows have been boarded up because of vandalism, and paper and other debris litter the school yard and classrooms. The cupboards and shelves of the classrooms are in disarray, copra often lies drying in one room, and clothes hang on a line in another.

The bells marking the periods ring at haphazard times—resulting in periods of irregular and unpredictable length and a recess that lasts two or three times the designated length—and are not strictly heeded. Virtually everyone returns home for recess, and the bell usually has to be rung a second time to summon students and teachers back to school. And then minutes elapse before a class begins: students take time to arrive, grab chairs, and arrange them around the teacher; and teachers look through their materials. Teachers do not simply stop their lessons when the bell rings for the next period. They first finish whatever they had planned, even if it means the next class has to stand and wait. And when students have classwork or tests, they leave when they finish without waiting for a bell.

The classrooms look and sound chaotic. When I first walked in, I knew the place was a school in session only because I had been told so. Small children typically wander in the rooms, glance through books, pause to sit with students, talk with teachers and students, and bring food to teachers. A student or a teacher often holds a younger sibling or other child, or sits combing a toddler's hair. A teacher may babysit while teaching, occasionally wandering out to check on the child. A woman may nurse an infant while lecturing. Students roam around on their lunch break or while running errands for a teacher. Dogs enter and fight with each other. Teachers themselves sometimes talk with other students in the room or doorway, and call out to anyone meandering in with unidentified objects. Students talk freely, and when the teacher asks a question, the whole class calls out answers. They create even more commotion when asked to write, as they try to locate paper and pencils, a process that often involves consulting students in other classes.

Much of the seemingly chaotic behavior is consistent with other aspects of life on Pulap. No one follows a clock or is concerned with tardiness, and no island event scheduled for a particular time ever begins at that time. And people do not immediately jump when a bell rings for other activities such as church events and island meetings. Small children are neither regularly excluded from island community activities nor are they considered distractions.

Students in the lower grades pay little attention to the teachers. Instead, they tend to sing, talk among themselves, or look at other materials in the room. Among the older children, the situation improves. Part of the explanation for the change lies in the entrance exam for Weipat Junior High School, which the older students are anxious to pass to continue in school with their classmates. Furthermore, the names of those who pass are announced over the radio from Chuuk Lagoon during the summer, and both students and parents are acutely embarrassed if they fail.

Another reason for this behavior, however, lies in Pulap attitudes about how children learn. Pulapese believe that school is so new and strange to younger children that it takes time for them to understand, and if they do not listen to a teacher, it is simply because they do not understand him yet. Pulapese do not believe in coercing children, but feel that if teachers continue explaining, students will eventually learn. Children supposedly obey when they understand verbal instructions. Consequently, teachers show enormous patience with them. When giving instructions for classwork, for instance, teachers repeat them as many times as asked. Twenty students may ask the same question, but a teacher answers the last as patiently and as completely as the first. And the pace is often very slow. In one class, for instance, a teacher spent four days on the same five spelling words.

These attitudes about children are not unique to Pulap, but seem to be widespread among culturally related islands. Lutz (1985) has provided detailed accounts, analyzing beliefs about how children learn among the people of Ifaluk, an atoll west of Pulap. Ifaluk islanders believe that socially acceptable behavior, obedience, and learning depend on listening and understanding (Lutz 1985:61). It is not simply that children have the ability to obey and cooperate once they can understand verbal instructions; understanding in and of itself prompts obedience. Island belief also contends that this understanding is not possible before the age of six—about the time Pulapese children begin school. Before that age, children are not believed capable of distinguishing between right and wrong and therefore are not liable for their behavior. Obedience on the part of children is nonetheless desirable and encouraged, but adults tolerate disobedience because it presumably derives from a lack of understanding, not willful deliberation.

Spoken language is the key variable; an understanding of language leads to compliance. Lutz (1985:50) points out that this belief derives from general attitudes about the power of language to influence behavior. She provides an example of the speeches of chiefs, which commonly involve admonishing the community and lecturing to people concerning socially acceptable behavior. Similarly, on Pulap, women manage to obtain compliance from their older brothers and parents by repeated requests. These islanders do not deny or ignore the importance of observation and imitation for learning, but they certainly stress the key role of language. Furthermore, since obedience and learning are believed to depend on language, physical punishment is unimportant and is not found at the elementary school.

Children are not excluded from many adult activities, including conversations, in part because as children mature they are considered capable of gradual understanding. And accustoming children to people and attitudes is another way they learn and become receptive and compliant. People, activities, and attitudes that children become used to are those they supposedly feel positively about and embrace. Positive feelings lead to compliance and learning. Lutz points out that parents believe in lecturing their children quite early about correct behavior, even before the age when understanding is believed possible, so that children can become accustomed to the procedure.

Furthermore, the focus is not on the self and individual needs but on others. Becoming accustomed to kin and feeling positively toward others relate to an emphasis on cooperation and sharing, on group needs and concerns. Classroom behavior reflects these attitudes. In particular, teachers encourage cooperation and conformity rather than competition or individualism. They rarely single students out for either good or bad behavior, and they do not encourage students to compete with one another or ostentatiously display their skills or knowledge. Pulapese value *mehonohon*, "humility," and discourage *lamalam tekiyah*, "lofty thought," or "arrogance." When a teacher asks a question, the class as an indiscriminate body tries to answer. Children call out possible answers, and the teacher simply waits until he hears a correct one. Then he acknowledges the answer and not the student. A teacher rarely singles out a particular student to say "That's wrong!" or even "That's right!" Either one would embarrass a student. Such comments would provide individualized attention and would imply that the child is competing with others. Even when a teacher decides to call on particular students, rather than the class as a whole, and he hears a wrong answer, he will usually just go on to ask another student without commenting on the mistake. When a teacher is displeased or angry, again, he rarely directs his comments to a particular student but scolds the whole class in the manner of someone at an island meeting haranguing the entire community. In both cases, particular individuals are usually in mind, but are not named or addressed personally.

Teachers openly allow students to help one another: when one student is at the blackboard, others call out suggestions if he or she falters. Students also tend to assist one another with classwork such as math problems and spelling words. Teachers maintain that cheating on tests is very common; most seem to expect it, since in other activities children are encouraged to cooperate and help one another. Although some teachers make token attempts to curtail the practice, such as asking students to put their materials under the chairs, they fail to maintain a vigil to ensure that students do not peek at a neighbor's paper.

Teachers are also very fond of choral responses and drills initiated by the same cue ("uuhuuh") that marks the beginning of other activities, like the chant that accompanies the hauling of a canoe to a canoe house. The Tate Oral English series adopted by the Trust Territory makes use of choral responses, but this method is common in other areas as well, such as oral group reading and recitation of math paradigms. In addition to choral drills, teachers also lecture to classes, lectures typically delivered as though the teachers were telling a legend or gossiping about a recent island event.

Cooperation and sharing, with an orientation to the group rather than the individual, are highly valued patterns of behavior. Many writers commenting on related Micronesian cultures stress the importance of these values for islanders. Lutz describes how they are reflected even in the choice of pronouns: "we," "us," "ours" commonly occur where an American would choose the first-person singular (Lutz 1985:44). In other words, people should not think of their personal needs but of others, and should orient themselves toward joint, cooperative goals.

The value placed on modest, unassuming behavior, as opposed to arrogance, is consistent with this group orientation. If a person focuses on group, not individual concerns, she will also not make much of her special abilities, brag, or place herself above others as somehow special. Even generosity and sharing should emphasize the individual as a part of the group rather than as an individual giving to others; ideally something that is shared is not something originally "mine" that becomes "yours," but is something that is "ours" (Lutz 1985:45). Modesty as a positive value and arrogance as a negative one appear to be widespread in Chuuk (e.g., Caughey 1977:26; Gladwin and Sarason 1953:155, 289; Goodenough 1951:143; Swartz 1965:24–25; Tolerton and Rauch 1949:187).

ASSERTING TRADITION IN THE MIDST OF CHANGE

Schooling in Chuuk has undeniably resulted in change, with new jobs, goals, attitudes and social problems. Not only is education necessary for a number of jobs, but the system itself is also the single largest employer in Chuuk. Education presents young people with opportunities and roles unavailable, or at least extremely scarce, in earlier generations. It exposes them to new ideas and attitudes and, after eighth grade, takes them away from home for nine months at a time. The change and lack of continuity with the past are clearest at the levels of secondary and postsecondary education, especially since most students have to leave home at that point, and more of an emphasis is laid on individualism and competition.

At the elementary school, however, many Pulapese values, attitudes, and standards of behavior are transmitted along with the new ideas and aspirations. Here is where Pulapese have most control over their educational system: teachers are local, the school is far from the central administration, and students attend school in their own community. Thus, both deliberately and accidentally, Pulapese transform the introduced Western schooling to a form more consistent with their own culture.

This does not mean the teaching strategies are inherently good ones, however, or that they prepare students for later, American-style schooling, especially college. Elementary education does seem to adequately prepare them for secondary school; their performance is comparable to that of many others, and some even excel. Yet none of the public schooling truly prepares them for college. None truly follows an American model or encourages the critical thinking and individualism valued in United States education. It may, however, contribute to a maintenance of cultural identity and pride.

Although later schooling deviates much more from Pulapese values, educated young people are promoting retention of Pulap customs, even as they seek new opportunities. Those acquiring degrees are the most likely to become members of Chuuk's emerging elite because they are better able to acquire the government jobs and earn a good salary. This is an alternative to traditional routes to prestige that is available to relatively young people. At the same time, these educated Pulapese are in the forefront of attempts to preserve their heritage. They are actively trying to re-create Pulap and Pulapese culture in a migrant community on Moen, and they use their salary and influence to acquire reputations for generosity, the traditional route to prestige. They consciously promote patterns of behavior they believe reflect traditional values, behavior such as wearing loincloths and lavalavas, using respectful language and behavior toward senior siblings, preparing local foods and distributing them among all Pulapese on Moen, and collecting funds from all the employed workers to purchase food for the community. These reflect sharing, respect for kin, and concern for the group instead of the self.

The leader of the migrant community, the first from Pulap to obtain a college education, represents an intriguing blend of the modern and traditional. The man's elite and well-paying position is due in large part to his education. Yet he also comes from the chiefly clan, which gives him a measure of chiefly influence. He contributes the bulk of the support to the migrant community, carrying out responsibilities to care for fellow islanders. Those with an education have access to resources unavailable to others, but they have a responsibility to use their money and influence for the benefit of kin. For someone of the chiefly clan, this responsibility extends to the entire island community, not just a single kin group. The migrant community leader, for example, has helped purchase land on Moen for cultivating local foods to ease dependence on imported foods. Although this emphasis on traditional values and behavior helps Pulapese adjust to life on Moen and levels out inequalities among them, it has little effect on the larger problem of growing stratification within Chuuk and increasing dependence on a cash economy and outside assistance.

Thus, in many ways the school has disrupted Pulap's way of life and has encouraged migration from the island. Many Pulapese now strive for a college education abroad, and many live today in Chuuk Lagoon, some with jobs, some merely with hopes for one. Yet they live together in a small community in which they attempt to re-create the social and cultural setting of Pulap, with a cultural identity based on traditionalism. Their emphasis on sharing, cooperation, respect toward senior siblings, and humility all symbolize to them retention of traditional customs and values that others in Chuuk have presumably lost, at least in the eyes of Pulapese. The elementary school is, in effect, encouraging the island's young people to abandon their way of life in favor of new opportunities for wealth, prestige, and power while also encouraging maintenance of a set of traditional values.

NOTES

1. The name of the state recently changed from Truk to the indigenous term Chuuk, pronounced RUUK in the Pulap dialect. In historical discussions, however, I continue to use the labels Truk Intermediate and Truk High School, when those were the names for the schools.

2. A few Pulapese have attended other schools, including Catholic elementary and secondary schools on Moen, but most attend Pulap Elementary School, Weipat Junior High

School, and then Chuuk High School. Furthermore, since this article was written, a new junior high school has been established on the nearby atoll of Puluwat to serve students from the Western Islands.

3. Adult literacy programs also started in each district by 1966 (Smith 1968:75).

4. Elementary school teachers on contracts with the Department of Interior arrived in the 1960s, and in 1967 a number of Peace Corps Volunteers began teaching in elementary schools.

5. In 1965, a Protestant interdistrict high school opened on Moen, and the Ponape Agriculture and Trade School (PATS) opened on Ponape.

6. Previously only a few girls, chosen by an American Jesuit, had left the island for school. They attended a private Catholic elementary school on Moen for a few years during the 1950s. Each then returned home.

7. 1 arrived on Pulap in January 1980 and was able to observe activities at the school during that spring semester. Most mornings I spent several hours observing (as unobtrusively as possible) and taking notes on what I saw happening. I also spent time interviewing the teachers, but I was not a teacher myself. My research in general focused on the impact of education on cultural identity and interisland ties. I had previously been a teacher at the junior high school while in the Peace Corps, and I later spent several months observing and interviewing teachers at the high school.

8. Although the teacher aides are paid through Title I funds and assist only with math and reading courses, in the eyes of the students, staff, and community, they are in essentially the same category as the other teachers.

REFERENCES

Caughey, John Lyon. 1977. *Faanakkar: Cultural Values in a Micronesian Society*. University of Pennsylvania Publications in Anthropology, 2. Philadelphia: University of Pennsylvania.

Gale, Roger W. 1979. *The Americanization of Micronesia: A Study of the Consolidation of U.S. Rule in the Pacific*. Washington, D.C.: University Press of America.

Gladwin, Thomas, and Seymour B. Sarason. 1953. *Truk: Man in Paradise*. Viking Fund Publications in Anthropology, 20. New York: Wenner-Gren Foundation for Anthropological Research.

Goodenough, Ward H. 1951. *Property, Kin, and Community on Truk*. Yale University Publications in Anthropology, 46. New Haven, Conn.: Yale University Press.

Hezel, Francis X. 1978. The Education Explosion in Truk. *Micronesian Reporter* 26(4):24–33.

———. 1982. *Reflections on Micronesia*. Working Paper Series, Pacific Islands Studies. Honolulu, Hawai'i: Center for Asian and Pacific Studies in collaboration with the Social Science Research Institute, University of Hawai'i at Mānoa.

———. n.d. *In the Aftermath of the Education Explosion*. Unpublished MS.

Kiste, Robert. 1985. Overview of U.S. Policy. In *History of the U.S. Trust Territory of the Pacific Islands*. Working Paper Series, Pacific Islands Studies Program. K. Knudsen, ed. Pp. 1–13. Honolulu: Center for Asian and Pacific Studies, University of Hawai'i at Mānoa.

Lutz, Catherine. 1985. Ethnopsychology Compared to What? Explaining Behavior and Consciousness Among the Ifaluk. In *Person, Self, and Experience: Exploring Pacific*

Ethnopsychologies. Geoffrey M. White and John Kirkpatrick, eds. Pp. 35–79. Berkeley: University of California Press.

Nagao, Clarence M., and Masao Nakayama. 1969. A Study of School-Community Relations in Truk. In *The Truk Report*. Stephen Boggs, ed. Honolulu: University of Hawai'i Press.

Nevin, David. 1977. *The American Touch in Micronesia*. New York: Norton.

Pearse, Richard, and Keith A. Bezanson. 1970. *Education and Modernization in Micronesia: A Case Study in Development and Development Planning*. Stanford, Calif.: Stanford International Development Education Center, School of Education, Stanford University.

Singleton, John. 1974. Education, Planning and Political Development in Micronesia. In *Political Development in Micronesia*. Daniel T. Hughes and Sherwood G. Lingenfelter, eds. Pp. 72–92. Columbus: Ohio State University Press.

Smith, Donald F. 1968. *Education of the Micronesian with Emphasis on the Historical Development*. Ed.D. dissertation, American University, Washington, D.C.

Swartz, Marc J. 1965. Personality and Structure: Political Acquiescence in Truk. In *Induced Political Change in the Pacific: A Symposium*. Roland W. Force, ed. Pp. 17–39. Honolulu, Hawai'i: Bishop Museum Press.

Tolerton, Burt, and Jerome Rauch. 1949. *Social Organization, Land Tenure and Subsistence Economy of Lukunor, Nomoi Islands*. CIMA Report, 26. Washington, D.C.: Pacific Science Board.

12

The Cultural Transformation of Western Education in Sierra Leone

Caroline Bledsoe

INTRODUCTION

The most revealing moments in fieldwork often come from the least expected sources. Such an event occurred half-way through my fieldwork in Sierra Leone. I was analysing a transcript of a recent speech delivered in Mende to parents and teachers at a rural primary school by the regional Inspector of Schools for the government schools during his up-country trip. The inspector, an extremely well educated man whom I expected to present a thoroughly 'modern' view of education, asserted that the key to a child's success through modern education was ancestral blessings. He elaborated:

> If a child has blessing, he can go through whatever learning he has to go through. Whatever request he has will be granted, whatever occupation or learning; that will make him prosper and be honourable in the future. Now, in Sierra Leone, some people are educated, but they lack blessing. Some people are degree holders in engineering or have teaching certificates but they don't have the type of work that is equivalent to their education or training. And they don't have pay that is commensurate with their training. . . . If a child is educated but doesn't have blessing, he won't do anything to progress himself. He will be a problem to himself and to his family. He cannot arrange anything for himself or for the community or the nation. Blessing is the major support or lever that will lift someone to better himself.

By casting his argument in these terms the inspector offers us a fascinating glimpse into how his audience, and likely he himself, were viewing Western education. I began to realise that my own cultural notions of schooling had blinded me to broader views. Needless to say, this text spawned a whole new direction for my project on children, education, and fostering. Close attention to this and other texts

137

through extensive exegesis with a range of people, from illiterate rural elders to highly educated students and teachers, confirmed that local people appear to have interpreted and moulded education very differently from how early colonial and mission officials must have intended.

This study asks how rural Sierra Leoneans, the targets of some of the earliest educational experiments in West Africa, have used their own cultural framework to reinterpret the meaning of the new schools and learning philosophies that the colonial government and missionaries imposed on them. Using insight gained from the local perspective, the study focuses not only on *what* is taught but *how* it is taught.

I show that the Mende have situated formal education within local authority structures of obligation and mystical agency. They maintain that, since valued knowledge is a key economic and political commodity, teachers, as its proprietors or 'owners', can demand for imparting it compensation from those who benefit from it: a model of education manifested most strikingly in the so-called secret societies for which the region is famous. As with more 'traditional' knowledge the chief cultural idiom by which children acquire 'civilised' knowledge in school, and thus advance in the modern world, is through 'buying [learning] blessings' from those who teach them. By addressing ideologies of knowledge, power, and secrecy, the article seeks a sharper understanding of contemporary cultural views of education in the postcolonial era: views that often differ markedly from Western perceptions of schools and pedagogical relationships.

By emphasising the impact of local modes of thinking (especially notions of secrecy) on a Western institution, this study seeks to shed new interpretive light on the evolution of education in a country—indeed, among the very ethnic group— that comprised a keystone of nineteenth century British educational experiments in Africa. Before we turn to these questions, however, we need to ask why it is necessary to place Western education under a cultural microscope.

WESTERN EDUCATION AS A CULTURAL PHENOMENON

The Privileged Analytic Status of Western Education

One of the most common assumptions among anthropologists of previous eras was that Western innovations would inevitably supplant indigenous ways. Such assumptions lay behind Boas's and Mead's urgent efforts to galvanise anthropologists to describe traditional cultures before they became irrevocably acculturated beneath the crushing tide of modernisation. We have clearly moved beyond this, attempting to incorporate dynamism into the heart of our models of society and recognising that local societies rarely accept alien technology or domination wholesale (Scott, 1985). Instead, they seek to resist or transform undesired innovations. Recent social theory has turned from static views of culture toward theories of action or 'praxis' that ask how people continually manipulate cultural categories.

Works in this vein 'see people not simply as passive reactors to and enactors of some "system", but as active agents and subjects in their own history' (Ortner, 1984: 143).

Innovative studies of African societies are finding that strands of change have their own internal dynamics, and that local societies creatively set their own agendas for change (see Ajayi, 1969; Peel, 1983). By what processes do these societies absorb, modify, and reorder external elements? For Herskovits (1948) the answer was reinterpretation: new meanings could be read into a form that originated elsewhere. By contrast, Drewal (1989) focuses on the notion of improvisation. She argues that, far from remaining rigidly 'traditional', Yoruba ritual specialists in Nigeria constantly improvise new themes and practices:

> in a highly competitive society of operationally strong individuals, everybody is engaged in the same exercise to alter their current conditions, seizing opportunities, jockeying for position, extending their power and influence, 'playing' situations to turn them to their own advantage, in short 'making things happen'. As the oft seen adage painted on trucks and lorries in Nigeria asserts, 'NO CONDITION IS PERMANENT' [p. xxi]

As this quotation suggests, such processes, whether labelled reintepretation or improvisation, entail rhetorical struggles at multiple levels of the social spectrum for control over the meaning and interpretation of new elements. Rather than asking the usual questions about Western education, such as how it can be more effectively spread or what harm it causes, the present study treats Western education like any new source of knowledge as a component of a theory of agency (e.g., Giddens, 1976): as a potential *resource* that people may use to achieve contextually specific goals. Given insights that Mende lend to the issue, I treat as problematic not the restriction of valued knowledge but claims that it is imparted freely. This helps explain why actors have not only reinterpreted or improvised new educational forms, but used them as tools for their own ends such as succession to chieftaincy and claims to economic resources.

In delving into Sierra Leonean history to examine the relationship of power and agency to knowledge, I attempt to avoid two common fallacies of colonial studies: that (1) education and all its alleged cognitive benefits were adopted wholesale by a non-reactive population, and that (2) educational policies can be analysed simply as oppressive instruments of indirect rule (cf. Abernethy, 1969; Yates, 1982), the governance srategy that characterised British colonial policy. Contemporary studies of responses to colonial policies call for a sense of reciprocal cultural dynamics: how do local societies attempt to reshape the intentions and forms of an imposed institution?

Despite these commendable goals, perceiving the cultural assumptions underlying Western schooling and its role in African children's lives is surprisingly difficult for those of us who grew up in it. Indeed, interpretive efforts stimulated by Geertz (1983), Dolgin *et al.* (1977), and Turner (1967) have been applied largely to contexts that Clifford and Marcus (1986) would call the exotic 'other', brushing aside phenomena from Western culture as unworthy of the analytical cultural eye. As a result, Western scholarship readily detects exotica in rituals or artefacts of foreign origin, yet it can be oblivious to remarkable transformations of meaning that Western practices undergo when transplanted to new contexts.

Education is a quintessential case in point. Modern formal education—perhaps because it deals explicitly with inculcating the young with knowledge, the most fundamental element of human culture—is presumed to sweep aside prior forms of culture and replace them with alien ones. This replacement process is considered doubly effective because a child is seen as a *tabula rasa*, a blank slate upon which new societal scripts can be written. Children who are carefully taught the 'proper' knowledge are then assumed to carry out its dicta because they have no alternative knowledge to contradict or dilute the knowledge with which they have been programmed. Yet such truisms take for granted assumptions they should most explain. In the context described here, 'civilised' knowledge is treated less as a self-contained bundle of facts than as one of many sources of symbolic capital.

This article presents some preliminary research aimed at eroding the privileged status of Western schooling as a reified cultural category, whose consequences, if planted on virgin intellectual soil, follow unproblematically from its content. To overcome the problem of the insider's cultural blinkers it examines the cultural transformation of schooling in a society that appears most to challenge Western education's philosophical assumptions. Whereas it is never possible to attain a completely neutral cultural perspective, disengaging Western education from its Euro-American context and placing it under an entirely different cultural lens offers an unusual vantage point from which to examine afresh Western assumptions about socialisation.

Power and Inequality in Access to Knowledge

Inequality in access to knowledge has been a major issue in the sociology of education. Durkheim's (1961) functionalism treated educational institutions as basic to 'organic' social solidarity, which rested on compliance without force. Education created a moral order of free individualism: a prerequisite for a smooth transition to a complex modern state characterised by 'organic solidarity'. There remained, of course, the awkward problem of unequal access to education and its impact on people's life chances. Intellectual descendants of Durkheim such as Parsons (1964) tried to salvage the functionalist optimism by stressing that differential access to education served societal needs for specialisation. However, scholars influenced by the 'conflict' perspectives of Weber and Marx argued that elites exploit education and knowledge, exacerbating inequality rather than mitigating it (e.g., Willis, 1977; Ogbu, 1981). To Bourdieu and Passeron (1977) the issue became one of 'cultural capital', while Gramsci (1971) focused on 'hegemony'.

While symbolic interactionists and phenomenologists such as Berger and Luckman, Schutz, Garfinkel, and Cicourel expanded the issue of education to include the strategic management of knowledge in general, European scholars linked issues of language and discourse with Marxian concerns with power and class conflict. For Foucault (1972) in fact, power rests on the transmission—or obstruction—of knowledge through language.

Within the Mende cultural repertoire, knowledge and secrecy are key idioms wherein actors attempt to exploit the potentiality of alternative secret meanings (Murphy, 1990) and to construe some bodies of knowledge as more important than others. As Simmel pointed out, moreover, knowledge itself is of less value than the political fact of controlling access to it. He stressed the potential for hiding or intentionally distorting information: 'The sociological significance of the secret is external, namely, the relationship between the one who has the secret and another who does not' (1950:345). Similarly, Mende secrecy tenets are refreshingly straightforward in viewing knowledge with a candidness Simmel would have applauded: as a potential commodity to be imparted for gain. When cast in this framework, issues of education and classroom curricula become secondary to larger questions of power: power that determines access to allegedly valued knowledge.

Sierra Leone thus provides an exemplary case for examining the confluence of Western and West African theories of knowledge transmission and power. The next section presents a historical sketch of the advent of formal education into Sierra Leone. It makes no claim to document events exhaustively. Instead, it turns a cultural eye to history, stressing British cultural assumptions about what should be taught and how it should be taught. It then contrasts these assumptions with some contemporary Mende interpretations of education stemming from local perceptions of power and knowledge that emerged from my own research.

FORMAL EDUCATION IN EARLY SIERRA LEONE

Sierra Leone drew special attention from early British educational efforts in West Africa. It has been called 'The Athens of West Africa', because high-quality formal schooling was established there quite early, relative to the rest of the region—the first college in West Africa, Fourah Bay, opened in Freetown in 1827. Why did the British place such strong emphasis on education in West Africa? Obviously there were many agendas. The well known ones of economic exploitation and political subjugation should not be minimised. For some of the early founders, however, efforts to establish education stemmed from altruistic motives. During the eighteenth century, Enlightenment philosophies sparked popular movements in Europe centred on belief in the rationality and humanitarianism of man. Education was seen as the key to enlightenment. An educated populace could take more assertive steps toward improving its social and economic problems, a need most relevant to the poor masses who suffered appalling conditions as England began to industrialise.

Reacting to the horrors of slavery, Granville Sharp laid out a plan in 1786 for helping the black poor in England by creating a blueprint for a perfect society in West Africa, in which no one's labour could be forcibly coerced. Inspired by his utopian treatise *A Short Sketch of Temporary Regulations (until Better shall be Proposed) for the intended Settlement on the Grain Coast of Africa near Sierra Leone*, an initial group of black settlers seeking to establish such a society—together with a few whites seeking primarily their fortunes—set sail in 1787 for Sierra Leone.

In his treatise Sharp had argued that 'natural man could be civilised through reason alone' (quoted in Peterson, 1969: 21), rather than through force or slavery. Sierra Leone was thus viewed as a potential utopian frontier of the mind and the soul: a new beginning, in which humanity could rectify its past sins. The principal cornerstone for this utopian experiment was education; accordingly, the first formal schooling for settler children began quickly, dating from about 1792. Schooling specifically targeted for the indigenous population was much longer in coming because, despite the ideals that had inspired the settlement, the settlers and indigenes were often at loggerheads (see Mason, 1959, for a general discussion).

The Content of 'Civilised' Knowledge

If we step back to gain more cultural distance, two critical questions emerge about education in the early colony. The first concerns the content of the knowledge imparted. What, exactly, were schools supposed to teach, and what value was placed on this knowledge?

'Civilised' knowledge comprised the core lessons taught in schools. Government trade schools for boys focused on practical skills like agriculture and crafts, whereas elite schools sought to create African versions of English public schools: cultured ladies and gentlemen. Girls focused on handwork and homemaking while boys studied European history, literature, science, and the arts. Mission schools, on the other hand, emphasised moral and spiritual values, and they used education and literacy less as an end in themselves than as a means of religious conversion. Considerable emphasis was placed on teaching literacy so that people in the remotest areas could learn the Gospel when no missionaries were at hand. As Sumner (1963: 13) points out:

> Books may supply, in a measure, the place of missionaries, and, where nothing more is practicable, may often answer the grand purpose, and thus spare the expenses of equipments, the fatigue of long journeys, the perils of an inhospitable country, the hardships of a precarious subsistence and the risk of an unhealthy climate.

Obviously, the two general aims of colonial authorities and missionaries—gentrification and conversion, respectively—were intertwined. Missionaries insisted that students embrace the lessons imparted in school as a sign of religious and cultural conversion. And government schools viewed Christianity as basic to a civilised society. In both cases, however, children were urged to cultivate a civilised image and to renounce 'heathen' practices of polygamy and worshipping false gods.

The Value Placed on Knowledge

We have considerable evidence that educators and administrators saw the content of knowledge itself as central to shaping children as future citizens. This was manifested particularly in colonial efforts to preserve the purity of 'civilised' knowledge. Two examples will illustrate this.

Liberated Africans

After the demise of legal slave trading, Freetown became the receiving point for shiploads of recaptured slaves from ships seized after embarkation from other African ports. Incorporating and rehabilitating hundreds of liberated Africans each year into a small, insecure colony was no easy matter. Most severe were the problems of the wretchedly hungry and sick children set down from the slaving ships, often without parents or relatives. At first they were apprenticed for care to settlers who had preceded them. Yet although many settlers welcomed cheap domestic labour, few tried to improve the children's lives, and the apprenticeship system rapidly degenerated to *de facto* slavery (Sumner, 1963: 21). Recognising these problems, the London-based Church Missionary Society (the CMS), founded in 1799, joined with the government to create separate villages for liberated people, where children could be trained in trades, farming and, for the most promising, teaching or mission work.

Despite the monumental problems these parentless children presented, missionaries and government officials viewed one aspect of their condition as a bonus for the flagging utopian vision of the country's founders: the children could be separated more easily than others from the influence of 'uncivilised' elders. Pagan beliefs would be easier to hide from them, while formal education could present civilised knowledge and morals as unchallengeable truth. Sumner (1963: 25) summarises the views of the Rev. Edward Bickersteth, the assistant secretary of the CMS, as follows:

> Where the adult mind has been debased by peculiar habits, it is necessary to pay attention to the education of children. The advantage in this is that in maintaining the children they are separated from the vicious customs and practices of their parents and countrymen. Teaching softens the manners of the pupils and helps them to adopt foreign customs; this prepares the way for missionary work . . . once the children are with their parents again, they follow the same manners and customs as though they had not been to school.

Indeed, what most appealed to Governor Charles MacCarthy, whose term began in 1816, was the very fact which previous governors had found daunting: lopped off from their kin, these children's loyalties could be moulded and they could be organised into orderly Christian communities, 'each grouped round its church tower, instructed and cared for by benevolent European guidance' (Fyfe, 1962: 128). In these children, the vision of the frontier of the mind and the soul could perhaps be salvaged, as Walker and Seeley (1847: 9) later remarked. 'Church and State went hand in hand in every practical effort to convert a wilderness into a garden . . .' These children thus represented a serendipitous opportunity to rekindle the flames of the great social experiment. Removed from their native environments and families, they most closely represented an ideal *tabula rasa* state: blank slates upon which a fresh cultural order could be inscribed. A. B. C. Sibthorpe (1970: 38–9), himself probably a liberated African, recorded with approval that:

> all the children, those excepted who lived with their parents, were placed under the entire control and care of the missionaries and teachers, from the time of their being landed, and were thus preserved from the contaminating example of their heathen countrymen, while opportunity was afforded the missionaries of ascertaining the disposition of the children, and of making early impression on their youthful minds.

Mission Children

The belief that the purity of 'civilised' knowledge had to be preserved helps to explain why colonial administrators and missionaries devoted special energies to liberated children whom they regarded as the emptiest of vessels for planting the seeds of civilisation. Such belief also helps to explain the strategies of missions in the hinterland after coastal schools had gained a firmer footing. The proximity of Mende speakers to the coast and their distance from Islamic influences to the north made them logical targets of educational and missionising efforts. As they had earlier, authorities focused their civilising efforts on children, attempting to divert children's loyalties away from the old guard and its pagan ways (for the Catholic case see Gittens, 1977: 413). Physically removing children and placing them in boarding schools on mission grounds became a key strategy for missionaries trying to solve not only the problem of geographical access to schools but also that of contaminating influences from elders. As these new cohorts matured, missionaries believed, the old guard and its heathen ideas could quietly die out.

Whether the targets of education were liberated children or indigenous children who could be drawn into boarding schools, they represented the colonial notion of a frontier of the mind and soul upon which to erect the new society. Those children who could ingest 'civilised' knowledge in its purest form, uncontaminated by heathen influences, would most likely pass it on intact to subsequent generations. Hence promoters of schooling in early Sierra Leone placed considerable emphasis on the content of the knowledge taught, assuming that knowledge could affect behaviour by virtue of the logic and persuasiveness of its content alone, regardless of the social context into which it was placed. Knowledge was thus treated as 'an autonomous variable whose effects on society and cognition can be discerned from its intrinsic character', as Street (forthcoming) similarly describes literacy.

The Process of Imparting Knowledge

Having looked at *which* knowledge was to be imparted in colonial education, we now ask *how* it was supposed to be taught. For present purposes, I refer not to pedagogical techniques but to obligations that the process of education may have created between students and those who taught or supported them. Descriptions of the ideal relationships between students and teachers in early Sierra Leone are difficult to find, but may be inferred from indirect evidence.

Although teachers were expected to impart knowledge liberally to whoever sought it in order to improve humanity, their main reward from teaching, aside from a modest salary, appeared to be moral fulfilment. Teachers in government schools seemed to expect little or no recompense from the students. For them, altruism—an unselfish interest in the future welfare of the children—was a strong ideological component. For missionaries, also, altruism figured strongly. However, fulfilment of religious duties and the hope of martyrdom provided equally strong motives. Recent literature on missionaries reflects abundant evidence that many missionaries saw themselves as fulfilling divine will, regardless of personal cost. A missionary who met an untimely death or suffered the wrenching loss of a loved one could take comfort that these tests of devotion might lead to martyrdom (see, for example, Gittens 1977, on Catholics in Sierra Leone, and Beidelman, 1982, on CMS missionaries in Tanzania).

In any event, because a teacher was seen as carrying out a duty toward God or Britain, the benefits that he could expect from students themselves drew little attention. This fact, coupled with that of knowledge as intrinsically important, made the teacher a mere conduit for knowledge: an instrument of greater Godly or colonial designs. To be sure, teachers were expected to behave as good Christians and humanitarians, so that the lessons that students drew from all their educational experiences were consistent. But, as long as teachers imparted knowledge accurately, it could stand on its own in the minds and souls of students, wholly independent of relations between students and teachers. (These assumptions about knowledge and teaching, of course, are not restricted to a quaint historical epoch in colonial Sierra Leone. Contemporary Euro-Americans hold as well that 'civilised' knowledge, having intrinsic value independent of social relations, can elevate humanity and bring about technological and social development. Because of its value for humanity, knowledge should be imparted liberally by teachers who receive, in return, moral satisfaction for imbuing the younger generation with valued knowledge.)

MENDE VIEWS OF SOCIAL RECOMPENSE AND CHILD 'DEVELOPMENT'

Local Responses to Education

In one sense, efforts to bring formal education to the new colony were extraordinarily successful. As education became 'a mark of achievement and a sign of being "civilised"' (Fyle, 1981: 74) parents who could afford the cost eagerly began to enrol their children in school. But the train of historical events also revealed deep flaws in European conceptions of knowledge. First, the knowledge learned in school did not necessarily produce the expected behaviour by virtue of the logic and per-suasiveness of its content alone. Children presumed to be even the emptiest of cultural vessels quickly realised that an education gave them the authority to com-mand the labour of others. Recognising that schooling produced acute social and economic disparities, they responded in ways that differed dramatically from ideals they learned in school and church. Although they were taught, for example, that forced labour was evil, they realised that literacy and education offered a chance of freeedom from hard labour and a privileged position from which to turn around and command the labour of uneducated new arrivals. Sumner (1963: 6) vividly describes newcomers' response to education:

> Whenever there was work to be done, the lightest burdens fell to the lot of Africans who could read and write, and the more menial labour had to be done by the illiter-ate Africans. . . . Newcomers into the settlement were put to work in the public ser-vices, under the supervision of their literate companions. Seeing what hardship these conditions entailed, the illiterate Africans in the settlement were prompted to apply themselves to get 'educated' as soon as possible.

In the pragmatic political and economic reality in which children found them-selves, 'civilised' knowledge taught in schools became less a self-contained pack-age with content that stood apart from the social world than an idiom for gaining status. This view of knowledge as a social as well as a cultural phenomenon is re-flected also in the Mende belief that *how* one learns knowledge is as important as the content of the knowledge itself. To explain this, I turn to my own interviews and text analyses conducted in Sierra Leone. I focus on secondary school students and their relationships with teachers.

Social Obligation and the Learning Process

Scholars of rural West Africa have long noted that elders seeking to solidify con-trol over youth try to place tight controls on information they construe as valu-able, and protect it through rituals and powerful associations based on secrecy. In areas where the Poro and Sande societies initiate almost all boys and girls, respec-tively, into their membership, secret society elders gain power through claims to dangerous and powerful knowledge inaccessible to non-initiates and low-ranking members (for, example, d'Azevedo, 1962; Meillassoux, 1964; Terray, 1969; Bellman, 1975; MacCormack, 1979; Jedrej, 1980; Murphy, 1980; Bledsoe, 1984). One of the most important lessons children learn is 'You don't talk it' (for Liberia see Bellman, 1984; for Nigeria see Callaway, 1964: 63, and Fafunwa, 1974: 26–27). Yet *how* chil-dren learn knowledge is as important as *what* they learn. Because valued knowledge is considered a commodity, it is 'owned', and its proprietors demand recompense for imparting it (see also Bledsoe and Robey, 1986). It is here that we must take up the role of teachers.

The necessity to work for and compensate teachers comprises the backbone of a fundamental cultural theory of child development, aptly summarised in the Sierra Leonean maxim 'No success without struggle'. This maxim implies that, in order to 'develop' (as the notion of social and economic advancement is translated into English), children cannot simply *learn* knowledge through intensive study: they must *earn* it (if necessary, through tolerating hunger, beatings, and sickness) from those who legitimately possess it, through proper channels of social recompense. Adults paint this maxim on houses, taxis, and buses throughout the country, and use it to exhort children to persist in their training despite difficulties (Bledsoe, 1990a; see Ogundijo, 1970: 11–24, for Nigerian parallels, and LeVine and LeVine, 1981, for general socialisation practices in Africa).

By contrast with the Euro-American view that successful people can control their own income because they achieved their success independently, the Mende argue that even the hardest-working individuals who seek to 'develop' need help from highly placed agents in the political structure or in the mystical authority structure. They view the fact that an individual may have graduated from secondary school and secured an urban job with regular monthly wages as proof less of his own industry than of support from investors: whether patrons, kin, ancestors, or spirits. Successful children, therefore, are not free to enjoy unencumbered the rewards of their success; rather, they should bring benefits to their investors, rewarding them in proportion to the amount that the investor contributed to their eventual success. A shrewd investment in a promising student, therefore, may be repaid many times.

The chief cultural idiom by which children are said to 'earn' knowledge is through 'buying [or "earning"] blessings' from those who support them or teach them. Obviously, blessings are not exclusive to the Mende. They figure prominently in Western texts such as the Bible. Yet although most descriptions of African cosmology associate blessings with images of a more traditional era, local people hold that ancestors and blessings determine an individual's success in exploiting even contemporary urban opportunities—a belief strongly reflected in the speech by the Inspector of Schools quoted at the beginning. Ancestors and the blessings they confer are said to 'pave the way' for their living individuals to God. The content of many blessings states this explicitly: 'God help you to develop,' 'God let your old age be well provided for,' 'God let your children survive,' 'God let your riches continue,' 'God make all your ventures be fruitful,' 'God let you triumph over all your enemies,' 'God let your work progress,' and so on.

For both Muslim and Christian Mende, elders bless younger kin, parents bless children, uncles bless nephews, masters bless apprentices, teachers bless students, etc., ritually calling for their ancestors to ask God (Ngewo), the ultimate source of blessings, to ensure the good fortune and success of the subordinates who have served them well or of people who have done good deeds on their behalf. Blessing someone acknowledges that the person has fulfilled a debt or obligation. Actually receiving God's blessing, however, is no easy matter. Because God does not want to

face a barrage of individual supplicants of unproven merit, he requires requests to
come through the proper authority channels. Standing between God and a living
supplicant, therefore, is a long, hierarchical chain of mediating ancestors—living
as well as dead—through whom God confers blessings on families and the young.

While children can earn knowledge by showing respect to authority figures,
whether they can put his knowledge to use requires blessings from God. God is said
to insist that, before their new knowledge and skills can bear fruit, children must
display gratitude to their benefactors through labour, remittances, and unquestioning
loyalty. Only after benefactors have testified to the children's worthiness will God
finally bless them, thus rendering efficacious the knowledge they have learned and
allowing them to advance. The blessings that young people earn from benefactors
at each career step will produce further 'development'. A successful person who
shares generously will find yet more potential benefactors eager to contribute to his
development. Blessings produce development, which produces yet more blessings,
in a spiral of interrelated mystical and economic success.

A child is surrounded by discourse about blessings from infancy. At the naming
ceremony a few days after birth, in which the family socially incorporates its new
member, a ritual specialist offers sacrifices, asking God and the ancestors to bless
the child and to allow him to grow up to benefit the family as a whole. Later, when
a successful child comes to visit, family elders cluster round, claiming credit for his
development, construing his successes as less the outcome of his effort than of theirs.
A secondary school student elucidated:

> An old man may call a student aside and say, 'My son, you are young and you can move
> about, whereas I cannot walk anymore as you can.' This means that the student is
> greatly in his debt, because he has grown old and immobile in struggling for the stu-
> dent. 'I am not strong now to do hard work. May my blessing be on you; may you suc-
> ceed in your O-levels.'

Through their actions, then, elders claim to have earned the ancestral approval
that induced God to target the family for development. By earning blessings from
their forebears, *they* were the ones who worked and made sacrifices to send him to
school. *Their* merit led to his high test scores and to his successful job application.
Because of *their* sacrifices, *their* blessings are needed for his continued development.

All this means that the content of knowledge cannot itself bring the rewards of
education, because knowledge does not stand apart from social relations as a detached cultural package. Since blessings legitimate rights to certain domains of
knowledge, *how* children learn—that is, through earning blessings—is as important
as what they actually learn. Children who did not earn knowledge through blessings may find their knowledge a liability rather than an asset. Those who display a
precocious fund of knowledge are either ignored or regarded with acute suspicion.
Indeed, a child from a humble rural home who performs brilliantly in exams and
receives scholarships to overseas universities without benefit of his elders' blessings

is viewed less with admiration than with fear. Such extraordinary success might have been achieved through a pact with a powerful spirit that will eventually demand recompense in the form of human life. Desperate to avoid paying the price personally, the individual may sacrifice friends or family members.

The obverse of a blessing is a curse, translated locally as a 'swear'. Like blessings, curses represent crucial symbolic capital as mystical sanctions in Mende social authority structure. Curses, however, represent extreme steps for grave provocation. If children circumvent proper channels of acquiring knowledge, or fail to reward their benefactors, those benefactors may curse them. Learning that they are unworthy, God will render ineffective or even dangerous the knowledge they have learned. Nor will their ancestors risk credibility with God by lobbying for their further development. Ancestors may even curse the child who has usurped the family's resources, and turn fresh energies instead toward children more likely to help the family develop. 'Ungrateful' children will thus come to nothing despite their fancy degrees; benefactors' curses will topple their career and their fancy degrees will come to nothing. They may lose their jobs, become sick, or even die.

LOCAL CULTURAL VIEWS OF FORMAL EDUCATION

Teachers as Proprietors of 'Civilised' Knowledge

As this discussion suggests, the belief that only the legitimate proprietors of knowledge have the right to dispense it is not restricted to secret societies; this belief imbues all aspects of life, including perceptions of 'modern' formal education and its accoutrements: school buildings, teachers, students, text-books, exams, and promotional procedures. Although rural people may politely agree with the Western view that 'civilised' knowledge should be imparted freely, they regard schools as gateways through which a few privileged children pass, to gain control over powerful knowledge—in this case, knowledge of the outside cosmopolitan world and its mysterious technologies and lucrative opportunities. Because teachers are the most important points in the system for dispensing this knowledge, relationships between students and teachers have quite different expectations from what the Euro-American model would suggest.

Individuals who manage to graduate from school and get jobs as teachers are fortunate in one sense, because they have jobs with prestigious monthly cash incomes. However, Sierra Leonean teachers, like everyone else, suffer from growing inflation and economic recession. They are paid dismally low salaries, and many experience agonising delays in receiving their salary cheques. These delays are often exacerbated by principals and administrators, themselves feeling the economic pinch, who use the main means at their disposal—witholding cheques and jobs—to gain compensation. Nor can teachers easily find alternative sources of income through legal channels. In Sierra Leone the Kingsley-Davis laws, written during the colonial era, proclaim that teachers should not be engaged in any other kind of work such as large-scale trading or farming.

To survive, as well as to show gratitude to their own former benefactors, teachers must evade these laws, growing crops, trading, and so on. They also use their proprietorship over 'civilised' knowledge to make ends meet. Hence, by contrast to the Western ideal, which assumes that teachers facilitate learning and freely dispense knowledge, rural teachers become knowledge brokers for valued knowledge of the cosmopolitan world (see also Murphy, 1981: 679, on Liberia). They write the most glowing letters of recommendation for scholarships for the most submissive students rather than the best scholars, a phenomenon by no means restricted to Sierra Leone. To loyal students they dispense information on how to survive in the modern system: how to dress for interviews, make contact with powerful bureaucrats, and fill in confusing application forms. And some male teachers use their leverage to demand sexual favours from older female students. (See Bledsoe, 1990b: 301–2; for Ghana see Bleek, 1976: 53–5.)

Teachers also find ways to supplement their income and labour needs by using leverage over students—especially their ability to confer grades and promotions. Some sell advance copies of exam papers to anxious students or ask them to work on their farm and in their household. Unless compensated, teachers may fail to grade exams or threaten to grade harshly, as the following incident suggests.

During my fourteen-month stay in rural Sierra Leone I became skilled at recognising signs that the end of a school term was at hand. I lived, with my husband and son, in a house in front of a compound we shared with a husband-and-wife couple who taught at the local secondary school. When exams were imminent, students unfamiliar with the compound would knock on our door, often at night, asking for the Howards and bringing with them sacks of meat and garden produce and piles of firewood. Trying to hide our amusement, we directed them to the back of the compound. One day, watching a large pile of firewood being amassed by several teenage boys, I gathered my courage and walked out to ask the woman what was going on. Displaying fine control of the art of ambiguity, she acknowledged immediately that these were her students whose gifts were meant to persuade her to raise their scores. But she denied that the firewood would affect her grading. Instead, she confided, she had told these particular boys they had done poorly in the exam, even though they had not—then hinted that they might bring firewood for 'extra credit'. Defending her action, she drew attention to the growing economic hardship in the country and to the couple's hardship as strangers in an area with no rights to local farmland: 'We are just strangers here. There would be nobody to provide things for us during the Christmas vacation. We have no coffee, no cocoa plantations; so who will look after us?'

Although such demands on students have no legal basis in the national system of education, it would be a mistake to label them as outright 'extortion'. Instead, teachers use 'traditional' idioms to explain and legitimate their demand. They infer that they are the legitimate proprietors of 'civilised' knowledge because they themselves were clearly successful in obtaining employment and thus must have 'earned' their 'civilised' knowledge properly, through blessings, from their own teachers. (This explains why written materials such as books are regarded ambivalently. While they contain valued 'civilised' knowledge, those who read them have not necessarily earned the right to the knowledge they contain.)

Second, teachers claim that, just as they themselves 'earned' their knowledge properly, students should 'earn' their knowledge from their teachers if they hope to progress. Upon receiving testimonies of worthiness from the teachers who have imparted valued knowledge to a child, his ancestors, in turn, appeal to God to help their descendent achieve his goals. Only then will God render efficacious the 'civilised' knowledge he has learned. A secondary school boy's statement reflects this:

> if you help the teachers with their work, and are generally respectful to them, they will bless you, just as trade and Arabic masters do. They will say, 'Since this student is assisting me, O God, help him in whatever he is doing, his work, and especially in his O-levels.'. . . . Students in fact say that if you are not blessed by your teachers, you will not do well in your O-levels or get a job thereafter. This is why many students, in fact, do not get jobs. And sometimes, in fact, when a student has been abusing [insulting] his teacher, the teacher will swear [curse] him, usually in his mind but publicly if the student has abused him publicly. He will say, 'Well, you will get your reward from what you have done.' Or 'What you have done, if it was good, God will give you a good reward'. [These statements, the student stressed, are indirect curses, Since the behaviour was *not* good, God will punish the student.]

This process by which teachers bless students bears striking parallels to what we would call the 'traditional' pattern of elders blessing youths. However, it is not a mechanical carry-over of archaic cultural traditions; instead, it represents teachers' pragmatic use of important cultural idioms to legitimate their demands.

Students' Responses to Teachers' Demands

Although I have emphasised the weighty supernatural sanctions that underlie Mende notions of success, it is equally important to point out that blessings and other ritual tactics rarely work to elders' satisfaction. Adults inevitably complain about children's 'ingratitude', while children attempt to undermine the claimed necessity to earn blessings or the power of curses. This means that European assumptions that ingesting the content of knowledge was the central goal of education were flawed not only because they overlooked the importance of the process of learning. They also failed to recognise that knowledge alone does not mechanically determine behaviour. Rather, reality is socially negotiated. To see why this is so, we need to look more closely at students' responses to teachers' demands for recompense—responses ranging from outright rebellion to tricks of logic. Not surprisingly, some of the most complicated debates occur within struggles between teachers and students to define the meaning of teaching and how—or even whether—'civilised' knowledge should be paid for.

Students, of course, face a handicap in that the political weight of a school usually supports the teachers. Those who are openly hostile to or insult their teachers run the risk of receiving poor grades or of being expelled. But teachers must be careful as well. Unlike their students, many teachers come from outside the community or belong to local families of non-elite status. And many students who have reached the secondary level are launched firmly on 'civilised' career tracks, giving them greater access to powerful patrons and politicians in the wider world. Hence tactics on both sides are couched in cautious ambiguity that allows either party to deny, if neccesary, the implications of their statement.

Students must consider carefully the kind of response they will make to teachers' demands. Those fearing to challenge a teacher may capitulate and meet the demands, though they can let their anger become known indirectly by grumbling, 'We did not come here to work for teachers. We came here to learn.' Others who comply may voice scepticism about teachers' claims to political or ritual authority. In the incident described above that involved our compound, when the secondary school teacher tried to insinuate that the boys had done poorly in their exams, she revealed that the boys had asked for proof that they had done badly by asking to see the graded exams. When she refused, one boy had declared it was a trick. However, all capitulated in the end, perhaps realising they had little recourse and that an outright fight was not worth the risk.

Another way in which students deal with teachers' demands is to evade them by transferring to another school. Technically, a 'transfer certificate', necessary for registering at a new school, is available to any student in good academic standing who wishes to leave. Yet a recalcitrant student who tries to escape debts and enmities with local teachers may find his transfer certificate withheld. Moreover, like the Inspector of Schools quoted at the beginning, teachers may insinuate that transferring may do a difficult student little good because they will not bless him. A young man explained why many students reject this option: 'If you have been misbehaving at one school, you can always go somewhere else. But you are leaving your blessing behind. You are pursuing education, but leaving blessing behind.'

Yet the most interesting debates occur when students mount outright challenges to teachers' abilities to bless or curse them. Everyone involved agrees that teachers should impart knowledge, and that the recipients should compensate them for the knowledge learned. But when teachers are salaried by the government and students pay school fees, there is greater ambiguity. Knowledge is being paid for both by students and by the government on behalf of them. Therefore what debt, if any, remains, and who should pay whom? To what extent are teachers justified in making further demands on students? Mende theories of knowledge and recompense for it leave ample room for ambiguity—an ambiguity that both parties can try to manipulate.

Students argue that they have already paid their school fees to learn and, moreover, that teachers have already been compensated for imparting their knowledge because they receive a salary from the government. Hence, students allege, they are not indebted to their teachers and have no need of their blessings. As long as they have blessings from their families or care takers, to whom they actually *are* indebted, they can succeed very well without teachers' blessings. Even curses from a teacher, they argue, will be ineffective because students are not indebted to the teacher. (Note, however, that such responses do not challenge the premise that blessings from teachers are necessary to future success. They simply dispute the need for blessings in this instance.)

Teachers, of course, have their own counters to such arguments: for example, 'We were working for our teachers when we were in school, so you should help us too.' More importantly, they argue, their pitifully small salaries are incommensurate with the value of the knowledge they are imparting. A student elucidated how a teacher may express his dissatisfaction with his imbalance by cursing an 'ungrateful' student indirectly:

> If the money you have paid me is equal to the knowledge I have given you, then God will reward you in that way. If, however, the money you have paid is not equal to the knowledge I have given you, then you will be rewarded in a bad way.

Students do indeed worry about these sanctions, as a teenager admitted: 'Students often say that the reason they did badly in their O-levels or can't find a job is because teachers have not blessed them or because a teacher swore them.'

Besides implying that students are still obligated to their mentors, teachers play on the 'traditional' notion that a child owes his benefactor not what was given originally but an amount proportionate to the eventual successes attained. Explained a student, the teacher will say, 'I will not profit from [your future earnings]: just your people. So you should help me now.'

Old Idioms and New Roles

Although it is clear that teachers try to exploit their claims to legitimately 'own' 'civilised' knowledge, the final student response to teacher demands described here is not resistance but assimilation. If we make a simple cohort observation, we suddenly realise that many students themselves become teachers. At this point a striking transformation occurs. The same individuals who previously argued that teachers have no power to bless or curse students now maintain that they do, in order to make demands of their own students. Both sides, therefore, are fluent practitioners of, and deft logicians in, both 'modern' and 'traditional' discourse. It is the situation in which individuals find themselves, as well as changes in their life or career status, that determines which kind of discourse will be employed.

More surprising is the realisation that educational level seems to be inversely related to the degree of modernity individuals represent. While students advocate the 'modern' view that knowledge should be imparted freely or with minimal compensation because of government support to teachers, those same students who become highly educated teachers—administrators like the Inspector of Schools—use the 'traditional' idiom of knowledge ownership and the need for students to 'earn' blessings to reimburse teacher for the knowledge they learn.

CONCLUSIONS

The distinctions between what we might call the intellectualist view of knowledge as a self-contained set of facts versus the socially embedded nature of knowledge recalls a famous typology. Weber (1970: 296–9) argued that, with the rise of the modern state, 'traditional' personal authority gave way to 'rational-legal' authority, based on logically structured, impersonal bureaucratic rules. Applied to Sierra Leone, this typology would suggest that modern formal education, because of the sheer persuasive force of its 'rationality'—the veracity of the knowledge it imparts—would have swept aside 'irrational' socially embedded knowledge.

The evidence presented here, however, shows that what Westerners might call 'rational' education does not automatically supplant other ways of thinking. Indeed, the 'crushing tide of acculturation' theory of education fails to cope with both the dynamics of knowledge management and the fact that the social context of knowledge is as important in many cultural settings as its content. Although indigenous education, including that found in secret societies, has changed, local people have established new voices even when institutions of such apparently sweeping scope and power as formal education were imposed on them. (Gittens's insightful 1977 study concludes similarly that, despite enormous inputs of labour, money, and religious fervour, Catholic missionaries probably changed the Mende less than the Mende changed them.)

These findings suggest that inverting the usual academic procedures by using African views of knowledge can yield insightful perspectives on Western customs and beliefs. Since Mende political culture does not begin from the same lofty, even quixotic, ideals of freely disseminating knowledge, recognising these pragmatic attitudes about the benefits of hiding valued knowledge has presented a significant opportunity to pry beneath the Western ideological surface, to ask how individuals in all societies erect power bases atop edifices of alleged knowledge. That few Westerners draw such explicit conclusions about the potential uses of knowledge is a tendency that the Mende regard as curiously naive.

ACKNOWLEDGMENTS

This article is a revised version of a paper presented at the conference on La Jeunesse en Afrique: encadrement et rôle de la société à l'époque contemporaine (XIXe et XXe siècles) at the University of Paris in 1990. I am grateful to the organisers of the conference for permission to publish here. In addition I should like to thank, for their help during the fieldwork or the analysis, C. Magbaily Fyle, Murray Last,

Robert Launay, and William Murphy. Finally, I am grateful to the National Science Foundation, the Population Council, the Rockefeller Foundation, the Population Studies Center at the University of Pennsylvania, and the Department of Anthropology in Northwestern University for generous institutional support of the project.

REFERENCES

Abernethy, D. B. 1969. *The Political Dilemma of Popular Education*. Stanford, Cal.: Stanford University Press.

Ajayi, J. F. A. 1969. 'Colonialism: an episode in African history', in L. H. Gann and P. Duignan (eds.), *Colonialism in Africa*, Cambridge: Cambridge University Press.

Althusser, Louis. 1971. 'Ideology and ideological state apparatuses (notes towards an investigation)', in *Lenin and Philosophy, and other Essays*, pp. 127–86. New York: Monthly Review.

Bailey, F. G. 1983. *The Tactical Uses of Passion*. Ithaca N.Y.: Cornell University Press.

Beidelman, T. O. 1982. *Colonial Evangelism: a socio-historical study of an East African mission at the grass roots*. Bloomington: Indiana University Press.

Bellman, B. L. 1975. *Village of Curers and Assassins: on the production of Fala Kpelle cosmological categories*. The Hague: Mouton.

———. 1984. *The Language of Secrecy: symbols and metaphors in Poro ritual*. New Brunswick, N.J.: Rutgers University Press.

Bledsoe, Caroline H. 1984. 'The political use of Sande ideology and symbolism', *American Ethnologist* 11 (13), 455–72.

———. 1990a. '"No success without struggle": social mobility and hardship for Sierra Leone children', *Man* (n.s.) 25, 70–88.

———. 1990b. 'Schoolgirls and school fees among the Mende of Sierra Leone', in Peggy Sanday and Ruth Goodenough (eds.), *Beyond the Second Sex*, pp. 283–309. Philadelphia: University of Pennsylvania Press.

Bledsoe, Caroline H., and Robey, Kenneth M. 1986. 'Arabic literacy and secrecy among the Mende of Sierra Leone', *Man* (n. s.) 21, 202– 26.

Bleek, Wolf. 1976. 'Sexual Relationships and Birthcontrol in Ghana: a case study of a rural town', Ph.D. dissertation, University of Amsterdam.

Bourdieu, Pierre, and Passeron, J. 1977. *Reproduction*. Beverly Hills, Cal.: Sage Publications.

Callaway, Archibald. 1964. 'Nigeria's indigenous education: the apprenticeship system', *Odu: University of Ife Journal of African Studies* 1 (1), 62–9.

Clark, T. J. 1984. *The Painting of Modern Life*. New York: Knopf.

Clifford, James, and Marcus, George (eds.). 1986. *Writing Culture: the poetics and politics of ethnography*. Berkeley, Cal.: University of California Press.

Cole, Michael, and Griffin, Peg. 1986. A sociohistorical approach to remediation', in Suzanne de Castell, *et al*. (eds.), *Literacy, Society, and Schooling: a reader*, pp. 110–31. Cambridge: Cambridge University Press.

Collier, Jane F. 1988. *Marriage and Inequality in Classless Societies*. Stanford, Cal.: Stanford University Press.

Davies, C. B. 1974. *A Bibliography of Education in Sierra Leone*. Occasional Paper 4, Sierra Leone: Njala University College Library.

d'Azevedo, Warren L. 1962. 'Some historical problems in the delineation of a Central West Atlantic region', *New York Academy of Science* 96(2), 512–38.

Dolgin, J., Kemnitzer, D., and Schneider, D. (eds.). 1977. *Symbolic Anthropology. a reader in the study of symbols and meanings*. New York: Columbia University Press.

Drewal, Margaret T. 1989. 'Performers, Play, and Agency: Yoruba ritual process', Ph.D. dissertation, New York University Press.

Durkheim, Emile. 1961. *Moral Education: a study in the theory and application of the sociology of education*. New York: Free Press. (First published in 1925.)

Fafunwa, A. Babs. 1974. *History of Education in Nigeria*. London: Allen & Unwin.

Foucault, Michel. 1972. 'The formation of enunciated modalities', in *The Archaeology of Knowledge and the Discourse on Language*, trans. A. M. Sheridan, pp. 50–5. New York: Pantheon.

Fyfe, Christopher. 1962. *A History of Sierra Leone*. London: Oxford University Press.

Fyle, C. Magbaily. 1981. The History of Sierra Leone: a concise introduction. London: Evans.

Geertz, Clifford. 1983. *Local Knowledge*. New York: Basic Books.

Giddens, Anthony. 1976. *Central Problems in Social Theory*. London: Macmillan.

Gittens, Anthony. 1977. 'Mende and Missionary: belief, perception and enterprise in Sierra Leone'. Ph.D. dissertation, University of Edinburgh.

Goffman, Erving. 1959. *The Presentation of Self in Everyday Life*. Garden City N.Y.: Doubleday.

Goody, Jack. 1968. 'Restricted literacy in northern Ghana', in J. Goody (ed.), *Literacy in Traditional Societies*. Cambridge: Cambridge University Press.

Graff, Harvey J. 1986. 'The legacies of literacy: continuities and contradictions in Western society and culture', in Suzanne de Castell (ed.), *Literacy, Society, and Schooling: a reader*, pp. 61–86. Cambridge: Cambridge University Press.

Gramsci, Antonio. 1971. *Selection from the Prison Notebooks*. London: Lawrence & Wishart.

Herskovits, Melville J. 1948. *Man and his Works*. New York: Knopf.

Hobsbawm, Eric, and Ranger, Terence (eds.). 1983. *The Invention of Tradition*. Cambridge: Cambridge University Press.

Jedrej, M. C. 1980. 'Structural aspects of a West African secret society,' *Ethnologische Zeitschrift* 1, pp. 133–142.

LeVine, S. and LeVine, R. 1981. 'Child abuse and neglect in sub-Saharan Africa', in J. E. Korbin (ed.), *Child Abuse and Neglect: cross-cultural perspectives*, pp. 35–55. Berkeley, Cal.: University of California Press.

MacCormack, C. P. 1979. 'Sande: the public face of a secret society', in Benetta Jules-Rosette (ed.), *New Religions of Africa*. Norwood, N.J.: Ablex.

Mason, R. J. 1959. *British Education in Africa*. London: Oxford University Press.

Meillassoux, C. 1964. *Anthropologie économique des Gouro de Côte d'Ivoire*. Paris: Mouton.

Murphy, William P. 1980. 'Secret knowledge as property and power: elders versus youth', *Africa* 50 (2), 193–207.

———. 1981. 'The rhetorical management of dangerous knowledge as property and power in Kpelle brokerage', *American Ethnologist* 8, pp. 667–85.

———. 1990. 'Creating the appearance of consensus in Mende political discourse', *American Anthropologist* 92 (1), 24–41.

Ogbu, John. 1981. 'School ethnography: a multilevel approach', *Anthropology and Education Quarterly* 12 (1), 3–29.

Ogundijo, M. I. 1970. 'Indigenous Education in Ejigbo District of Oshun Division in the Pre-colonial Days and the Coming of the Missionaries.' B.A. dissertation, Faculty of Education, University of Life.

Ortner, Sherry B. 1984. 'Theory in anthropology since the sixties.' *Comparative Studies in Society and History* 26, pp. 126–66.

Parsons, Talcott. 1964. 'The school class as a social system: some of its functions in American society.' In T. Parsons (ed.), *Social Structure and Personality*. pp. 129–54. New York: Free Press.

Peel, J. D. Y. 1983. *Ijeshas and Nigerians*. Cambridge: Cambridge University Press.

Peshkin, Alan. 1972. *Kanuri Schoolchildren: education and social mobilization in Nigeria*. New York: Holt, Rinehart & Winston.

Peterson, J. 1969. *Province of Freedom: a history of Sierra Leone: 1787–1870*. London: Faber.

Schneider, David M. 1968. *American Kinship: a cultural account*. Englewood Cliffs, N.J.: Prentice-Hall.

Scott, James C. 1985. *Weapons of the Weak: everyday forms of peasant resistance*. New Haven, Conn.: Yale University Press.

Sibthorpe, A. B. C. 1970. *The History of Sierra Leone*. London: Frank Cass. (First published: 1868).

Simmel, Georg. 1950. *The Sociology of Georg Simmel*, trans. Kurt H. Wolff. Glencoe: Free Press. (First published 1906.)

Street, Brian. 1984. *Literacy in Theory and Practice*. Cambridge: Cambridge University Press.

———. (Forthcoming). 'Introduction', in B. Street (ed.), *Discourse, Context and Ideology: essays in literacy and anthropology*. Cambridge: Cambridge University Press.

Sumner, D. L. 1963. *Education in Sierra Leone*. Freetown: Government of Sierra Leone.

Terray, E. 1969. *Le Marxisme devant les sociétés 'primitives'*. Paris: Maspéro.

Turner, Victor. 1967. *The Forest of Symbols*. Ithaca, N.Y.: Cornell University Press.

Vansina, Jan. 1973. *The Tio Kingdom of the Middle Congo, 1880–1892*. London: Oxford University Press.

———. 1985. *Oral Tradition: a study in historical methodology*, second edition. Chicago: Aldine.

Walker, Rev. Samuel Abraham, and Seeley, A. M. 1847. *The Church of England Mission in Sierra Leone*. London: Burnside & Seeley.

Weber, Max. 1970. 'The sociology of charismatic authority', in H. H. Gerth and C. Wright Mills (trans.), *From Max Weber: essays in sociology*, pp. 245–52. New York: Oxford University Press. (First published 1910).

Willis, Paul E. 1977. *Learning to Labour: how working class kids get working class jobs*. Westmead: Saxon House.

Yates, Barbara A. 1982. 'Colonialism, education, and work: sex differentiation in colonial Zaire', in E. Bay (ed.), *Women and Work in Africa*, pp.127–52. Boulder, Colo.: Westview.

Section III

School Practice and Community Life
Cultural Congruence, Conflict, and Discontinuity

School Practice and Community Life: Cultural Congruence, Conflict, and Discontinuity

Michèle Foster

INTRODUCTION

As Bradley A. U. Levinson notes in the introduction, schools are a pervasive institution around the world. In every kind of society, some groups of students seem to do well in the institutions called schools, while others do not. What are the reasons that so many students from ethnic minority groups or working-class backgrounds fail in school while most others succeed? What are some of the different explanations that scholars have offered to explain this situation? Finally, what are some of the solutions that have been proposed to address this problem? In this introductory essay, I provide a historical sketch of some of the ideas and debates that have shaped the field of inquiry often referred to as cultural congruence, conflict, and discontinuity. This field of inquiry considers the relationship between schools and the communities in which students receive their primary socialization. Research in this field analyzes the cultural values, practices, and ways of speaking and relating that students learn at home and bring with them to school. Often this research contrasts community practices with those of schools to unearth whether and how community practices are recognized and accommodated, or devalued and discredited. Although I include references for several books and journal articles beyond those that comprise this section, and deliberately include texts that represent diverse perspectives, my discussion is not meant to be comprehensive, but rather reflects my view of the field. A references and reading section that includes studies across national boundaries can be found at the end of the introduction.

HISTORICAL BACKGROUND

Studies of cultural congruence, conflict, and discontinuity developed largely in response to the writing and research of psychologists who had since the 1960s advanced the idea that particular groups of ethnic minority pupils failed in school because they were culturally deprived, deficient, or disadvantaged. These psychologists grounded their research in the culture of poverty hypothesis and came to be known as cultural deficit theorists (Valencia 1997). This hypothesis maintained that some groups remain persistently poor because of cultural pathologies, deficiencies, and defects that are transmitted from parents to children, and that children are culturally deprived because their parents, families, and communities do not provide them with the kind of experience typical of those found in the families and communities of white middle-class children. One of the earliest works to denounce this hypothesis was the book *The Culture of Poverty: A Critique* (1971), edited by Eleanor Burke Leacock, an anthropologist. Many other critiques, studies, and analyses soon followed. Language, particularly how people use it in different contexts like schools to accomplish particular culture-specific goals, was a focus of much of this research. Two reasons for the focus on language were because the cultural deficit theorists had focused on language and also because language was (and still is) a ubiquitous feature of classrooms.

One of the most influential studies in this area was undertaken by William Labov, whose seminal sociolinguistic study, *Language in the Inner City* (1972), demonstrated that African American English (also called Black English and Ebonics) was a rule-governed, complete, and systematic language variety. Concurrently, John Gumperz and Dell Hymes were developing the theoretical framework for ethnography of communication, a field of study that examines the nature and function of communicative behavior in the context of culture. Grounded in the view of culture promoted by Clifford Geertz, this research focused on how language is used in particular contexts to construct and interpret meaning and identities, and to sustain relationships. Hymes challenged Noam Chomsky's "scientific" study of language—analysis of language units, sounds, morphemes, and the rules by which these units are organized to produce speech—that had dominated the field of linguistics. An anthropologist, Hymes argued that it was impossible to understand language without reference to its cultural underpinnings and, moreover, that parsing only the linguistic features without also investigating the ways that different groups of people use language in their everyday life was insufficient. He thus reconnected linguistics to the field of anthropology through linguistic anthropology, one of the four fields of anthropology.

MICROETHNOGRAPHIC STUDIES

Shirley Brice Heath's article "What No Bedtime Story Means: Narrative Skills at Home and School," is a classic example of an ethnography of communication study.

She examines in detail how children are socialized *through* language as well as *to* language, and then shows how such language socialization can result in miscommunication between children and their teachers who come from different cultural and class backgrounds. In particular, she illustrates how along with learning how to talk, preschoolers in two different working-class communities learn different ways of using language—conceptions of a "good story," asking questions, and ways of interacting with texts—through interactions with their caregivers. Contrasting these community ways of using language with those used by the mainstream and valued in school, Heath subsequently explores how community literacy practices may become obstacles to students' mastery of schooled literacy practices and attendant school achievement. Other studies within this microethnographic tradition include articles in several edited volumes (Cazden, John, and Hymes 1972; Gilmore and Glatthorn 1982; Schieffelin and Ochs 1986), and articles, chapters, and books by Sarah Michaels (1981), Karen Watson-Gegeo (1992), Susan Philips (1983), Frederick Erickson and Jeffrey Schultz (1982), and Hugh Mehan (1982). Concerned with documenting moment to moment, face-to-face interactions between and among individuals, and analyzing materials gathered on video and audio tapes, microethnographic studies have been conducted in classrooms, families, and other community settings.

Research within this tradition has made us mindful of the culturally specific nature of interactions within particular settings such as churches, courtrooms, and classrooms. It has also illustrated how cultural and linguistic differences can both produce and exacerbate conflict between teachers and pupils and lead to unfavorable schooling outcomes.[1]

MUTILEVEL ETHNOGRAPHIES

Because they concentrate on verbal and nonverbal communication, studies within this tradition are typically microethnographic, that is, they focus on face-to-face interactions at the expense of macrosocial processes. Studies that take macrolevel processes and mechanisms into account represent another paradigm of research in this field. Although there are differences among them, the articles by John U. Ogbu ("Understanding Cultural Diversity and Learning"), Carlos Vélez-Ibáñez and James B. Greenberg ("Formation and Transformation of Funds of Knowledge among U.S.–Mexican Households"), and Deborah Reed-Danahay ("Habitus and Cultural Identity: Home/School Relationships in Rural France") that appear in this volume are examples of research that has widened its lens to include some of the historical, political, and economic forces that both shape and give rise to particular cultural practices.

For example, Velez-Ibáñez and Greenberg's article links the macrosocial—historical, political, and economic circumstances—to the development of particular cultural systems within Mexican American border communities. The article also illustrates how these cultural systems—or "funds of knowledge"—comprise part of a social network in which children acquire their cultural identity and personality.

The ecological research of Ogbu is perhaps the most comprehensive and illustrative of this tradition. He contends that differential achievement among ethnic minority groups cannot be fully explained by discontinuities between students' cultural and linguistic socialization and the cultural backgrounds of the dominant groups comprising schools. He distinguishes between two kinds of students and theorizes that these different groups possess different cultural characteristics and frames of reference. Immigrant students, whom Ogbu calls "voluntary minorities," possess primary cultural characteristics—developed in their native lands. In contrast, involuntary or castelike minorities possess secondary cultural characteristics that developed in response to their subordination. He argues that the problem of underachievement does not result from differences per se, but rather from students' interpretation of these differences either as cultural borders to be crossed or cultural boundaries to be maintained. Voluntary minorities are more likely to consider the differences as cultural borders to be crossed and therefore will be more academically successful than involuntary minorities, who are more inclined to regard such differences as boundaries to be maintained. Other research within this tradition includes Margaret Gibson's (1988) on Sikh immigrants, and Signithia Fordham's (1988; Fordham and Ogbu 1986) on African American students.

Because it attempts to link microethnographic research with structural forces, Ogbu's research is often considered more comprehensive than studies of face-to-face interaction. Still, his research grows out of the theoretical orientations of structural functionalism, which means that it stresses unified, synchronous, and coherent accounts of cultures. Critical theorists have chided research on cultural discontinuity for paying insufficient attention to the power relations that are part of cultural action. Some groups, critical theorists contend, have more power than others and this enables more powerful groups to impose their meanings on subordinate groups, meanings that always serve dominant interests and are oppressive to subordinate groups. Dominant groups not only create structures that serve to oppress subordinate groups, but they also create meanings that normalize these structures. Subordinate groups, however, continually resist these structures and regimes of domination and truth. And while this resistance contains the possibility of propelling change, it can also unwittingly serve to reinforce the status quo. Researchers working within the critical theory tradition believe that the task of the scholar is not merely to collect the insiders' perspectives without exposing the power relations that often remain hidden from view. Some examples of studies grounded in the critical theory paradigm include Paul Willis (1977), Michelle Fine (1991), and Jay MacLeod (1987).

Reed-Danahay's article addresses several of these points. Taking into account both structure and agency, her research illustrates how even as the French school attempts to impose the state values of individualism and competition by enforcing behavioral and linguistic codes, the students covertly resist this domination. Not only does their resistance enable students to distance themselves from the values of the school and middle-class, urban, French culture, it also serves to maintain their connections with their regional and local cultures.

CONTRIBUTIONS TO CLASSROOM PRACTICE

Most of the studies in this area have concentrated primarily on documenting and explaining cultural discontinuity and cultural conflict. A smaller set of studies has documented and analyzed instances of culturally compatible interactions between teachers and their students (Foster 1995, 1987; Lipka 1991; Erickson and Mohatt 1992; Au 1980; Piestrup 1973). Researchers have spent less attention trying to apply these findings to classrooms. Regardless of whether they emerge from micro- or macroparadigms, however, where suggestions for instructional applications have been made, they have been remarkably similar. Cooperative learning and using the cultural and linguistic practices of the home, including funds of knowledge, as a bridge to school practices are some of the recommendations that researchers have suggested (González, Moll, and Amanti 1995; Lee 1993; Tharp and Gallimore 1989). For many years Ogbu held off making recommendations, but here has offered several suggestions bifurcated for voluntary and involuntary group students.

CONCLUSION

While studies of cultural congruence, conflict, and discontinuity have contributed much to our understanding of school inequality, they have sometimes inadvertently and unwittingly reinforced the notion of culture as sets of traits and static behaviors applicable to all members of a particular ethnic group, with little attention to the other identities, such as class, gender, and region, that produce variations within particular ethnic groups. One of the significant differences between the early studies of discontinuity and conflict in the United Kingdom and the United States is that until recently studies in the former have tended to examine class conflicts at secondary schools where these conflicts have been more salient (Woods 1990). Meanwhile, studies in the United States have tended to examine cultural conflicts at the primary and elementary schools where these conflicts are more prevalent (Cazden 1986). Now, however, studies of racial conflict in the United Kingdom have become more abundant, especially in light of postcolonial immigration (Gillborn 1990). Nonetheless, because the anthropological tradition within the United Kingdom has tended toward the social, rather than the cultural as it has in the United States, the sociolinguistic tradition has been stronger in the United States.

By no means do the readings in this section represent the totality of this field. Those readers finding that the articles pique their interest and wishing to read more broadly can consult the works listed in the references and readings section.

NOTE

1. Ethnography of communication and sociolinguistic studies have expanded such that they are now used to examine literacy events (events that involve the use of written language) and literacy practices (the culturally shared ways of people interacting with and interpreting written materials). One result of these inquiries is that reading and writing have come to be understood as more than a set of decontextualized cognitive skills. Rather, they are social practices that vary both across and within cultures, are shaped by the cultures that give rise to them, and shape individuals' ways of participating in literacy events, making some ways seem more normal than others. Some of this research has also raised questions about why some literacy practices are privileged over others.

Jonathan Boyarin's (1993) book, especially the article in it by Sarris (1993), is one example of this research. Using events from the Kashaya Pomo Reservation, Sarris's article contemplates the common practice of including "culturally relevant" materials into classrooms in order to motivate and raise the academic achievement of ethnic minority students. When the teacher presents the students with a "culturally relevant" story, they react with antagonism. This article contains a caveat for educators: since all students including those from ethnic minority backgrounds have multiple identities, teachers should not expect them to respond to culturally relevant materials in predictable, identical, or fixed ways. Rather, teachers should not only expect but also be open to the multiple ways in which students bring their identities to bear on their interactions with texts. Other examples of this research can be found in edited volumes such as those by Brian Street (1993), David Barton and Roz Ivanic (1991), and Beverly Moss (1994), and an article by Adrian Bennett and Michele Sola (1985).

REFERENCES AND READINGS

Au, Kathryn. 1980. Participation Structures in a Reading Lesson with Hawaiian Children: Analysis of a Culturally Appropriate Instructional Event. *Anthropology and Education Quarterly* 11 (2): 91–115.

Barton, David, and Roz Ivanic. 1991. *Writing in the Community.* Newbury Park, Calif.: Sage.

Bennett, Adrian, and Michele Sola. 1985. The Struggle for Voice: Narrative, Literacy, and Consciousness in an East Harlem School. *Journal of Education* 167 (1): 88–110.

Boyarin, Jonathan, ed. 1993. *The Ethnography of Reading.* Berkeley: University of California Press.

Cazden, Courtney. 1986. Classroom Discourse. In *Handbook of Research on Teaching.* 3rd ed. Edited by M. Wittrock. New York: Macmillan.

Cazden, Courtney, Vera John, and Dell Hymes, eds. 1972. *Functions of Language in the Classroom.* New York: Teachers College Press.

Erickson, Frederick, and Gerald Mohatt. 1992. Participant Structures in Two Communities. In *Doing the Ethnography of Schooling,* edited by G. D. Spindler. New York: Holt, Rinehart and Winston.

Erickson, Frederick, and Jeffrey Schultz. 1982. *The Counselor as Gatekeeper: Social Interaction in Interviews.* New York: Academic.

Fine, Michelle. 1991. *Framing Dropouts: Notes on the Politics of an Urban High School.* Albany: SUNY Press.

Fordham, Signithia. 1988. Racelessness as a Factor in Black Students' School Success: Pragmatic Strategy or Pyrrhic Victory. *Harvard Educational Review* 58 (1): 54–84.

Fordham, Signithia, and John Ogbu. 1986. Black Students' School Success: Coping with the "Burden of 'Acting White'." *Urban Review* 18 (3): 176–206.

Foster, Michele. 1987. "It's Cookin' Now": A Performance Analysis of the Speech Events of a Black Teacher in an Urban Community College. *Language in Society* 18 (1): 1–29.

———. 1995. Talking that Talk: The Language of Control, Curriculum, and Critique. *Linguistics and Education* 7:129–150.

Gibson, Margaret. 1988. *Accommodation without Assimilation: Sikh Immigrants in an American High School*. Ithaca, N.Y.: Cornell University Press.

Gillborn, David. 1990. *Race, Ethnicity, and Education*. London: Unwin and Hyman.

Gilmore, Perry, and Alan Glatthorn, eds. 1982. *Children in and out of School*. Washington, D.C.: Center for Applied Linguistics.

González, Norma, Luís Moll, and Cathy Amanti. 1995. Funds of Knowledge for Teaching in Latino Households. *Urban Education* 29 (4): 443–470.

Gumperz, John J., and Dell Hymes, eds. 1964. The Ethnography of Communication. *American Anthropologist* 66:6 (part 2): 1–86 (special publication).

———, eds. 1972. *Directions in Sociolinguistics: The Ethnography of Communication*. New York: Holt, Rinehart and Winston.

Hymes, Dell. 1974. *Foundations of Sociolinguistics: The Ethnography of Communication*. Philadelphia: University of Pennsylvania Press.

Labov, William. 1972. *Language in the Inner City*. Philadelphia: University of Pennsylvania Press.

Leacock, Eleanor Burke, ed. 1971. *The Culture of Poverty: A Critique*. New York: Simon and Schuster.

Lee, Carol. 1993. *Signifying as a Scaffold for Literary Interpretation: The Pedagogical Implications of an African American Discourse Genre*. Urbana, Ill.: National Council of Teachers of English.

Lipka, Jerry. 1991. Toward a Culturally Based Pedagogy: A Case Study of One Yup'ik Eskimo Teacher. *Anthropology of Education Quarterly* 22 (3): 203–223.

MacLeod, Jay. 1987. *Ain't No Makin' It: Aspirations and Attainment in a Low-income Neighborhood*. Boulder, Colo.: Westview.

Mehan, Hugh. 1982. The Structure of Classroom Events and Their Consequences for Student Performance. In *Children in and out of School*, edited by P. Gilmore and A. Glatthorn. Washington, D.C.: Center for Applied Linguistics.

Michaels, Sarah. 1981. "Sharing Time": Children's Narrative Styles and Differential Access to Literacy. *Language in Society* 10 (3): 423–442.

Moss, Beverly. 1994. *Literacy across Communities*. Cresskill, N.J.: Hampton Press.

Ogbu, John. 1981. School Ethnography: A Multilevel Approach. *Anthropology and Education Quarterly* 12 (1): 3–29.

Philips, Susan. 1983. *Invisible Culture: Communication in Classroom and Community on the Warm Springs Indian Reservation*. New York: Longman.

Piestrup, Ann McCormick. 1973. *Black Dialect Interference and Accommodation of Reading Instruction in the First Grade*. Monograph No. 4. Berkeley: University of California Language Behavior Research Lab.

Reed-Danahay, Deborah. 1987. Farm Children at School: Educational Strategies in Rural France. *Anthropology Quarterly* (April): 83–89.

Sarris, Greg. 1993. Keeping Slug Woman Alive: The Challenge of Reading in a Reservation Classroom. In *The Ethnography of Reading*, edited by J. Boyarin. Berkeley: University of California Press.

Schieffelin, Bambi, and Elinor Ochs. 1986. *Language Socialization across Cultures*. Cambridge: Cambridge University Press.

Street, Brian, ed. 1993. *Cross-cultural Approaches to Literacy*. Cambridge: Cambridge University Press.

Tharp, Roland, and Ronald Gallimore. 1989. *Rousing Minds to Life: Teaching, Learning, and Schooling in Social Context*. Cambridge: Cambridge University Press.

Valencia, Richard, ed. 1997. *The Evolution of Deficit Thinking*. London: Falmer.

Watson-Gegeo, Karen. 1992. Thick Explanations in the Ethnographic Study of Child Socialization: A Longitudinal Study of the Problem of Schooling for Kwara'ae (Solomon Islands) Children. *New Directions for Child Development* 58:51–66.

Willis, Paul. 1977. *Learning to Labour: How Working-class Kids Get Working Class Jobs*. Aldershot, U.K.: Gower.

Woods, Peter. 1990. *The Happiest Days? How Pupils Cope with School*. London: Falmer.

13

What No Bedtime Story Means: Narrative Skills at Home and School

Shirley Brice Heath

In the preface to *S/Z*, Roland Barthes' work on ways in which readers read, Richard Howard writes: "We require an education in literature . . . in order to discover that *what we have assumed*—with the complicity of our teachers—*was nature is in fact culture, that what was given is no more than a way of taking*," (emphasis not in the original; Howard 1974:ix).[1] This statement reminds us that the *culture* children learn as they grow up is, in fact, "ways of taking" meaning from the environment around them. The means of making sense from books and relating their contents to knowledge about the real world is but one "way of taking" that is often interpreted as "natural" rather than learned. The quote also reminds us that teachers (and researchers alike) have not recognized that ways of taking from books are as much a part of learned behavior as are ways of eating, sitting, playing games, and building houses.

As school-oriented parents and their children interact in the pre-school years, adults give their children, through modeling and specific instruction, ways of taking from books which seem natural in school and in numerous institutional settings such as banks, post offices, businesses, or government offices. These *mainstream* ways exist in societies around the world that rely on formal educational systems to prepare children for participation in settings involving literacy. In some communities these ways of schools and institutions are very similar to the ways learned at home; in other communities the ways of school are merely an overlay on the home-taught ways and may be in conflict with them.[2]

Just how does what is frequently termed "the literate tradition" envelop the child in knowledge about interrelationships between oral and written language, between knowing something and knowing ways of labelling and displaying it? We have even less information about the variety of ways children from *non-mainstream* homes learn about reading, writing, and using oral language to display knowledge in their preschool environment. The general view has been that whatever it is that mainstream school-oriented homes have, these other homes do not have it; thus these children are not from the literate tradition and are not likely to succeed in school.

A key concept for the empirical study of ways of taking meaning from written sources across communities is that of _literacy events:_ occasions in which written language is integral to the nature of participants' interactions and their interpretive processes and strategies. Familiar literacy events for mainstream preschoolers are bedtime stories, reading cereal boxes, stop signs, and television ads, and interpreting instructions for commercial games and toys. In such literacy events, participants follow socially established rules for verbalizing what they know from and about the written material. Each community has rules for socially interacting and sharing knowledge in literacy events.

This chapter briefly summarizes the ways of taking from printed stories families teach their preschoolers in a cluster of mainstream school-oriented neighborhoods of a city in the Southeastern region of the United States. We then describe two quite different ways of taking used in the homes of two English-speaking communities in the same region that do not follow the school-expected patterns of bookreading and reinforcement of these patterns in oral storytelling. Two assumptions underlie this chapter: (1) Each community's ways of taking from the printed word and using this knowledge are interdependent with the ways children learn to talk in their social interactions with caregivers. (2) There is little or no validity to the time-honored dichotomy of "the literate tradition" and "the oral tradition." This chapter suggests a frame of reference for both the community patterns and the paths of development children in different communities follow in their literacy orientations.

MAINSTREAM SCHOOL-ORIENTED BOOKREADING

Children growing up in mainstream communities are expected to develop habits and values which attest to their membership in a "literate society." Children learn certain customs, beliefs, and skills in early enculturation experiences with written materials: the bedtime story is a major literacy event which helps set patterns of behavior that recur repeatedly through the life of mainstream children and adults.

In both popular and scholarly literature, the "bedtime story" is widely accepted as a given—a natural way for parents to interact with their child at bedtime. In a series of "reading cycles," mother and child alternate turns in a dialogue: the mother directs the child's attention to the book and/or asks what-questions and/or labels items on the page. In a "scaffolding" dialogue (cf. Cazden 1979), the mother points and asks "What is x?" and the child vocalizes and/or gives a nonverbal signal of attention. The mother then provides verbal feedback and a label. Before the age of two, the child is socialized into the "initiation-reply-evaluation sequences" repeatedly described as the central structural feature of classroom lessons (e.g., Sinclair and Coulthard 1975; Griffin and Humphrey 1978; Mehan 1979). Teachers ask their students questions which have answers prespecified in the mind of the teacher. Students respond, and teachers provide feedback, usually in the form of an evaluation. Training in ways of responding to this pattern begins very early in the labelling activities of mainstream parents and children.

Maintown Ways

This patterning of "incipient literacy" (Scollon and Scollon 1979) is similar in many ways to that of the families of fifteen primary-level school teachers in Maintown, a cluster of middle-class neighborhoods in a city of the Piedmont Carolinas. These families (all of whom identify themselves as "typical," "middle-class," or "mainstream") had preschool children, and the mother in each family was either teaching in local public schools at the time of the study (early 1970s), or had taught in the academic year preceding participation in the study. Through a research dyad approach, using teacher-mothers as researchers with the ethnographer, the teacher-mothers audio-recorded their children's interactions in their primary network—mothers, fathers, grandparents, maids, siblings, and frequent visitors to the home. Children were expected to learn the following rules in literacy events in these nuclear households:

1. As early as six months of age, children *give attention to books and information derived from books.* Their rooms contain bookcases and are decorated with murals, bedspreads, mobiles, and stuffed animals which represent characters found in books. Even when these characters have their origin in television programs, adults also provide books which either repeat or extend the characters' activities on television.
2. Children, from the age of six months, *acknowledge questions about books.* Adults expand nonverbal responses and vocalizations from infants into fully formed grammatical sentences. When children begin to verbalize about the contents of books, adults extend their questions from simple requests for labels (What's that? Who's that?) to ask about the attributes of these items (What does the doggie say? What color is the ball?).
3. From the time they start to talk, children *respond to conversational allusions to the content of books; they act as question-answerers who have a knowledge of books.* For example, a fuzzy black dog on the street is likened by an adult to Blackie in a child's book: "Look, there's a Blackie. Do you think he's looking for a boy?" Adults strive to maintain with children a running commentary on any event or object which can be book-related, thus modelling for them the extension of familiar items and events from books to new situational contexts.
4. Beyond two years of age, children *use their knowledge of what books do to legitimate their departures from "truth."* Adults encourage and reward "book talk,"

even when it is not directly relevant to an ongoing conversation. Children are allowed to suspend reality, to tell stories which are not true, to ascribe fiction-like features to everyday objects.

5. Preschool children *accept book and book-related activities as entertainment*. When preschoolers are "captive audiences" (e.g., waiting in a doctor's office, putting a toy together, or preparing for bed), adults reach for books. If there are no books present, they talk about other objects as though they were pictures in books. For example, adults point to items, and ask children to name, describe, and compare them to familiar objects in their environment. Adults often ask children to state their likes or dislikes, their view of events, and so forth, at the end of the captive audience period. These affective questions often take place while the next activity is already underway (e.g., moving toward the doctor's office, putting the new toy away, or being tucked into bed), and adults do not insist on answers.

6. Preschoolers *announce their own factual and fictive narratives* unless they are given in response to direct adult elicitation. Adults judge as most acceptable those narratives which open by orienting the listener to setting and main character. Narratives which are fictional are usually marked by formulaic openings, a particular prosody, or the borrowing of episodes in story books.

7. When children are about three years old, adults discourage the highly interactive participative role in bookreading children have hitherto played and children *listen and wait as an audience*. No longer does either adult or child repeatedly break into the story with questions and comments. Instead, children must listen, store what they hear, and on cue from the adult, answer a question. Thus, children begin to formulate "practice" questions as they wait for the break and the expected formulaic-type questions from the adult. It is at this stage that children often choose to "read" to adults rather than to be read to.

A pervasive pattern of all these features is the authority which books and book-related activities have in the lives of both the preschoolers and members of their primary network. Adults jump at openings their children give them for pursuing talk about books and reading.

The Mainstream Pattern

A close look at the way bedtime story routines in Maintown taught children how to take meaning from books raises a heavy sense of the familiar in all of us who have acquired mainstream habits and values. Throughout a lifetime, any school-successful individual moves through the same processes described above thousands of times. Reading for comprehension involves an internal replaying of the same types of questions adults ask children of bedtime stories. We seek *what-explanations*, asking what the topic is, establishing it as predictable and recognizing it in new situational contexts by classifying and categorizing it in our minds with other phenomena. The what-explanation is replayed in learning to pick out topic sentences, write outlines, and answer standardized tests which ask for the correct titles to stories, and so on. In learning to read in school, children move through a sequence of skills designed to teach what-explanations. There is a tight linear order of instruction which recapitulates the bedtime story pattern of breaking down the story into small bits of information and teaching children to handle sets of related skills in isolated sequential hierarchies.

In each individual reading episode in the primary years of schooling, children must move through what-explanations before they can provide *reason-explanations* or *affective commentaries*. Questions about why a particular event occurred or why a specific action was right or wrong come at the end of primary-level reading lessons, just as they come at the end of bedtime stories. Throughout the primary grade levels, what-explanations predominate, reason-explanations come with increasing frequency in the upper grades, and affective comments most often come in the extra-credit portions of the reading workbooks or at the end of the list of suggested activities in text books across grade levels This sequence characterizes the total school career. Thus, reliable and successful participation in the ways of taking from books that teachers view as natural must, in the usual school way of doing things, precede other ways of taking from books.

These various ways of taking are sometime referred to as "cognitive styles" or "learning styles." It is generally accepted in the research literature that they are influenced by early socialization experiences and correlated with such features of the society in which the child is reared as social organization, reliance on authority, male-female roles, and so on. These styles are often seen as two contrasting types, most frequently termed "field independent–field dependent"(Witkin et al. 1966) or "analytic-relational" (Kagan, Sigel, and Moss 1963; Cohen 1968, 1969, 1971). The analytic field-independent style is generally presented as that which correlates positively with high achievement and general academic and social success in school. Several studies discuss ways in which this style is played out in school—in preferred ways of responding to pictures and written text and selecting from among a choice of answers to test items.

Much of the literature on learning styles suggests a preference for one or the other is learned in the social group in which the child is reared and in connection with other ways of behaving found in that culture. But how is a child socialized into an analytic/field-independent style? What kinds of interactions does he enter into with his parents and the stimuli of his environment which contribute to the development of such a style of learning? How do these interactions mold selective attention practices such as "sensitivity to parts of objects," "awareness of obscure, abstract, nonobvious features," and identification of "abstractions based on the features of items" (Cohen 1969: 844–45)?

Close analyses of how mainstream school-oriented children come to learn to take from books at home suggest that such children learn not only how to take meaning from books, but also how to talk about it. In doing the latter, they repeatedly practice routines which parallel those of classroom interaction. By the time they enter school, they have had continuous experience as information-givers; they have learned how to perform in those interactions which surround literate sources throughout school. They have had years of practice in interaction situations that are the heart of reading—both learning to read and reading to learn in school. They have developed habits of performing which enable them to run through the hierarchy of preferred knowledge about a literate source and the appropriate sequence of skills to be displayed in showing knowledge of a subject. They have developed ways of decontextualizing and surrounding with explanatory prose the knowledge gained from selective attention to objects.

They have learned to listen, waiting for the appropriate cue which signals it is their turn to show off this knowledge. They have learned the rules for getting certain services from parents (or teachers) in the reading interaction (Merritt 1979). In nursery school, they continue to practice these interaction patterns in a group rather than in a dyadic situation. There they learn additional signals and behaviors necessary for getting a turn in a group, and responding to a central reader and to a set of centrally defined reading tasks. In short, most of their waking hours during the preschool years have enculturated them into: (1) all those habits associated with what-explanations, (2) selective attention to items of the written text, *and* (3) appropriate interactional styles for orally displaying all the know-how of their literate orientation to the environment. This learning has been finely tuned and its habits are highly interdependent. Patterns of behaviors learned in one setting or at one stage reappear again and again as these children learn to use oral and written language in literacy events and to bring their knowledge to bear in school-acceptable ways.

ALTERNATIVE PATTERNS OF LITERACY EVENTS

Are there ways of behaving which achieve other social and cognitive aims in other sociocultural groups?

The data below are summarized from an ethnography of two communities—Roadville and Trackton— located only a few miles from Maintown's neighborhoods in the Piedmont Carolinas. Roadville is a white working-class community of families steeped for four generations in the life of the textile mill. Trackton is a working-class black community whose older generations have been brought up on the land, either farming their own land or working for other landowners. However, in the past decade, they have found work in the textile mills. Children of both communities are unsuccessful in school; yet both communities place a high value on success in school, believing earnestly in the personal and vocational rewards school can bring and urging their children "to get ahead" by doing well in school. Both Roadville and Trackton are literate communities in the sense that the residents of each are able to read printed and written materials in their daily lives, and on occasion they produce written messages as part of the total pattern of communication in the community. In both communities, children go to school with certain expectancies of print and, in Trackton especially, children have a keen sense that reading is something one does to learn something one needs to know (Heath 1980). Nonetheless there are radical differences between the two communities in the ways in which children and adults interact in the preschool years; each of the two communities also differs from Maintown. Roadville and Trackton view children's learning of language from two radically different perspectives: in Trackton, children "learn to talk," in Roadville, adults "teach them how to talk."

Roadville

In Roadville, babies are brought home from the hospital to rooms decorated with colorful, mechanical, musical, and literacy-based stimuli. The walls are decorated with pictures based on nursery rhymes, and from an early age, children are held and prompted to "see" the wall decorations. Adults recite nursery rhymes as they twirl the mobile made of nursery-rhyme characters. The items of the child's environment promote exploration of colors, shapes, and textures: a stuffed ball with sections of fabrics of different colors and textures is in the crib; stuffed animals vary in texture, size, and shape. Neighbors, friends from church, and relatives come to visit and talk to the baby, and about him to those who will listen. The baby is fictionalized in the talk to him: "But this baby wants to go to sleep, doesn't he? Yes, see those little eyes gettin' heavy." As the child grows older, adults pounce on word-like sounds and turn them into "words," repeating the "words," and expanding them into well-formed sentences. Before they can talk, children are introduced to visitors and prompted to provide all the expected politeness formulas, such as "Bye-bye," "Thank you," and so forth. As soon as they can talk, children are reminded about these formulas, and book or television characters known to be "polite" are involved as reinforcement.

In each Roadville home, preschoolers first have cloth books, featuring a single object on each page. They later acquire books which provide sounds, smells, and different textures or opportunities for practicing small motor skills (closing zippers, buttoning buttons, etc.). A typical collection for a two-year-old consisted of a dozen or so books—eight featured either the alphabet or numbers, others were books of nursery rhymes, simplified Bible stories, or "real-life" stories about boys and girls (usually taking care of their pets or exploring a particular feature of their environment). Books based on Sesame Street characters were favorite gifts for three- and four-year-olds.

Reading and reading-related activities occur most frequently before naps or at bedtime in the evening. Occasionally an adult or older child will read to a fussy child while the mother prepares dinner or changes a bed. On weekends, fathers sometimes read with their children for brief periods of time, but they generally prefer to play games or play with the children's toys in their interactions. The following episode illustrates the language and social interactional aspects of these bedtime events; the episode takes place between Wendy (2;3 at the time of this episode) and Aunt Sue who is putting her to bed.

[Aunt Sue (AS) picks up book, while Wendy (W) crawls about the floor, ostensibly looking for something]

W: uh uh

AS: Wendy, we're gonna read, uh, read this story, come on, hop up here on this bed.

[Wendy climbs up on the bed, sits on top of the pillow, and picks up her teddy bear]

[Aunt Sue opens book, points to puppy]

AS: Do you remember what this book is about? See the puppy? What does the puppy do?

[Wendy plays with the bear, glancing occasionally at pages of the book, as Aunt Sue turns. Wendy seems to be waiting for something in the book]

AS: See the puppy?

[Aunt Sue points to the puppy in the book and looks at Wendy to see if she is watching]

W: uh huh, yea, yes ma'am

AS: Puppy sees the ant, he's a li'l

[Wendy drops the bear and turns to book.]

fellow. Can you see that ant? Puppy has a little ball.

W: ant bite puppy

[Wendy points to ant, pushing hard on the book]

AS: No, the ant won't bite the puppy, the [turns page] puppy wants to play with the ant, see?

[Wendy tries to turn the page back; AS won't let her, and Wendy starts to squirm and fuss]

AS: Look here, here's someone else, the puppy

[Wendy climbs down off the bed and gets another book]

W: read this one

AS: Okay, you get back up here now. [Wendy gets back on bed]

AS: This book is your ABC book. See the A, look, here, on your spread, there's an A. You find the A. [The second book is a cloth book, old and tattered, and long a favorite of Wendy's. It features an apple on the cover, and its front page has an ABC block and ball. Through the book, there is a single item on each page, with a large representation of the first letter of the word commonly used to name the item. As AS turns the page, Wendy begins to crawl about on her quilt, which shows ABC blocks interspersed with balls and apples. Wendy points to each of the A's on the blanket and begins talking to herself. AS reads the book, looks up, and sees Wendy pointing to the A's in her quilt.]

AS: That's an A, can you find the A on your blanket?

W: there it is, this one, there's the hole too. [pokes her finger through a place where the threads have broken in the quilting]

AS: [AS points to ball in book] Stop that, find the ball, see, here's another ball.

This episode characterizes the early orientation of Roadville children to the written word. Bookreading time focuses on letters of the alphabet, numbers, names of basic items pictured in books, and simplified retellings of stories in the words of the adult. If the content or story plot seems too complicated for the child, the adult tells the story in short, simple sentences, frequently laced with requests that the child give what-explanations.

Wendy's favorite books are those with which she can participate: that is, those to which she can answer, provide labels, point to items, give animal sounds, and "read" the material back to anyone who will listen to her. She memorizes the passages and often knows when to turn the pages to show that she is "reading." She holds the book in her lap, starts at the beginning, and often reads the title, "Puppy."

As Wendy grows older, she wants to "talk" during the long stories, Bible stories, and carry out the participation she so enjoyed with the alphabet books. However, by the time she reaches three and a half, Wendy is restrained from such wide ranging participation. When she interrupts, she is told:

> Wendy, stop that, you be quiet whcn someone is reading to you. You listen; now sit still and be quiet.

In Roadville's literacy events, the rules for cooperative discourse around print are repeatedly practiced, coached, and rewarded in the preschool years. Adults in Roadville believe that instilling in children the proper use of words and understanding of the meaning of the written word are important for both their educational and religious success. Adults repeat aspects of the learning of literacy events they have known as children. In the words of one Roadville parent: "It was then that I began to learn . . . when my daddy kept insisting I *read* it, *say* it right. It was then that I *did* right, in his view."

The path of development for such performance can be described in three overlapping stages. In the first, children are introduced to discrete bits and pieces of books—separate items, letters of the alphabet, shapes, colors, and commonly represented items in books for children (apple, baby, ball, etc.). The latter are usually decontextualized, not pictured in their ordinary contexts, and they are represented in two-dimensional flat line drawings. During this stage, children must participate as predictable information-givers and respond to questions that ask for specific and discrete bits of information about the written matter. In these literacy events, specific features of the two-dimensional items in books which are different from their "real" counterparts are not pointed out. A ball in a book is flat; a duck in a book is yellow and fluffy; trucks, cars, dogs, and trees talk in books. No mention is made of the fact that such features do not fit these objects in reality. Children are not encouraged to move their understanding of books into other situational contexts or to apply it in their general knowledge of the world about them.

In the second stage, adults demand an acceptance of the power of print to entertain, inform, and instruct. When Wendy could no longer participate by contributing her knowledge at any point in the literacy event, she learned to recognize bookreading as a performance. The adult exhibited the book to Wendy: she was to be entertained, to learn from the information conveyed in the material, and to remember the book's content for the sequential followup questioning, as opposed to ongoing cooperative participatory questions.

In the third stage, Wendy was introduced to preschool workbooks which provided story information and was asked questions or provided exercises and games based on the content of the stories or pictures. Follow-the-number coloring books and preschool "push-out and paste" workbooks on shapes, colors, and letters of the alphabet reinforced repeatedly that the written word could be taken apart into small pieces and one item linked to another by following rules. She had practice in the linear, sequential nature of books: begin at the beginning, stay in the lines for coloring, draw straight lines to link one item to another, write your answers on lines, keep your letters straight, match the cutout letter to diagrams of letter shapes.

The differences between Roadville and Maintown are substantial. Roadville adults do not extend either the content or the habits of literacy events beyond bookreading. They do not, upon seeing an item or event in the real world, remind children of a similar event in a book and launch a running commentary on similarities and differences. When a game is played or a chore done, adults do not use literate sources. Adults do not talk about the steps and procedures of *how* to do things; if a father wants his preschooler to learn to hold a miniature bat or throw a ball, he says "Do it this way." He does not break up "this way" into such steps as "Put your fingers around here," "Keep your thumb in this position," "Never hold it above this line." Over and over again, adults do a task and children observe and try it, being reinforced only by commands such as "Do it like this," "Watch that thumb."

Adults at tasks do not provide a running verbal commentary on what they are doing. They do not draw the attention of the child to specific features of the sequences of skills or the attributes of items. They do not ask questions of the child, except questions which are directive or scolding in nature ("Did you bring the ball?" "Didn't you hear what I said?"). Children do not ask questions of the type "But I don't understand. What is that?"

Both boys and girls during their preschool years are included in many adult activities, ranging from going to church to fishing and camping. They spend a lot of time observing and asking for turns to try specific tasks, such as putting a worm on the hook or cutting cookies. Talk about the task does not segment its skills and identify them, nor does it link the particular task or item at hand to other tasks. Reason-explanations such as "If you twist the cutter, the cookies will be rough on the edge," are rarely given, or asked for.

Neither Roadville adults nor children shift the context of items in their talk. They do not tell stories which fictionalize themselves or familiar events. In Roadville, a story must be invited or announced by someone other than the storyteller, and only certain community members are designated good storytellers. It is a true story, an actual event which occurred to either the storyteller or to someone else present.

The sources of stories are personal experience. They are tales of transgressions which make the point of reiterating the expected norms of behavior of man, woman, fisherman, worker, and Christian. They are true to the facts of the event.

Roadville parents provide their children with books; they read to them and ask questions about the books' contents. They choose books which emphasize nursery rhymes, alphabet learning, animals, and simplified Bible stories, and they require their children to repeat from these books and to answer formulaic questions about their contents. They use proverbs and summary statements to remind their children of stories and to call on them for simple comparisons of the stories' contents to their own situations. Roadville parents coach children in their telling of a story, forcing them to tell about an incident as it has been pre-composed or pre-scripted in the head of the adult. Thus, in Roadville, children come to know a story as either an accounting from a book, or a factual account of a real event in which some type of marked behavior occurred and there is a lesson to be learned. Any fictionalized account of a real event is viewed as a *lie*; reality is better than fiction. Thus children cannot decontextualize their knowledge or fictionalize events known to them and shift them about into other frames.

When these children go to school they perform well in the initial stages of each of the three early grades. They often know portions of the alphabet, some colors and numbers, can recognize their names, and tell someone their address and their parents' names. They will sit still and listen to a story, and they know how to answer questions asking for what-explanations. They do well in reading workbook exercises which ask for identification of specific portions of words, items from the story, or the linking of two items, letters, or parts of words on the same page. When the teacher reaches the end of story-reading or the reading circle and asks questions such as "What did you like about the story?" relatively few Roadville children answer. If asked questions such as "What would you have done if you had been Billy [a story's main character]?" Roadville children most frequently say "I don't know" or shrug their shoulders.

Near the end of each year, and increasingly as they move through the early primary grades, Roadville children can handle successfully the initial stages of lessons. But when they move ahead to extra-credit items or to activities considered more advanced and requiring more independence, they are stumped. They turn frequently to teachers asking "Do you want me to do this? What do I do here?" If asked to write a creative story or tell it into a tape recorder, they retell stories from books; they do not create their own. They rarely provide emotional or personal commentary on their accounting of real events or book stories. They are rarely able to take knowledge learned in one context and shift it to another; they do not compare two items or events and point out similarities and differences. Thus their initial successes in reading, being good students, following orders, and adhering to school norms of participating in lessons begin to fall away rapidly about the time they enter the fourth grade. As the importance and frequency of questions and reading habits

with which they are familiar decline in the higher grades, they have no way of keeping up or of seeking help in learning what it is they do not even know they don't
know.

Trackton

Babies in Trackton come home from the hospital to an environment which is
almost entirely human. Infants are held during their waking hours, occasionally
while they sleep, and they usually sleep in the bed with parents until they are about
two years of age. They are held, their faces fondled, their cheeks pinched, and they
eat and sleep in the midst of human talk and noise from the television, stereo, and
radio. Encapsuled in an almost totally human world, they are in the midst of constant human communication, verbal and nonverbal. They literally feel the body
signals of shifts in emotion of those who hold them almost continuously; they are
talked about and kept in the midst of talk about topics that range over any subject. As children make cooing or babbling sounds, adults refer to this as "noise,"
and no attempt is made to interpret these sounds as words or communicative attempts on the part of the baby.

When a child can crawl and move about on his own, he plays with the household objects deemed safe for him—pot lids, spoons, plastic food containers. Only
at Christmastime are there special toys for very young children; these are usually
trucks, balls, doll babies, or plastic cars, but rarely blocks, puzzles, or books. They
never request nor do they receive manipulative toys. such as puzzles, blocks, take-
apart toys or literacy-based items, such as books or letter games.

Adults read newspapers, mail, calendars, circulars (political and civic-events related), school materials sent home to parents, brochures advertising new cars, television sets, or other products, and the Bible and other church-related materials.
There are no reading materials especially for children (with the exception of
children's Sunday School materials), and adults do not sit and read to children.
Since children are usually left to sleep whenever and wherever they fall asleep, there
is no bedtime or naptime as such. At night. they are put to bed when adults go to
bed or whenever the person holding them gets tired. Thus, going to bed is not
framed in any special routine. Sometimes in a play activity during the day, an older
sibling will read to a younger child, but the latter soon loses interest and squirms
away to play. Older children often try to "play school" with younger children, reading to them from books and trying to ask questions about what they have read.
Adults look on these efforts with amusement and do not try to convince the small
child to sit still and listen.

Signs from very young children of attention to the nonverbal behaviors of others are rewarded by extra fondling, laughter, and cuddling from adults. For example,
when an infant shows signs of recognizing a family member's voice on the phone
by bouncing up and down in the arms of the adult who is talking on the phone,

adults comment on this to others present and kiss and nudge the child. Yet when children utter sounds or combinations of sounds which could be interpreted as words, adults pay no attention. Often by the time they are twelve months old, children approximate words or phrases of adults' speech; adults respond by laughing or giving special attention to the child and crediting him with "sounding like" the person being imitated. When children learn to walk and imitate the walk of members of the community, they are rewarded by comments on their activities: "He walks just like Toby when he's tuckered out."

Children between the ages of twelve and twenty-four months often imitate the tune or "general Gestalt" (Peters 1977) of complete utterances they hear around them. They pick up and repeat chunks (usually the ends) of phrasal and clausal utterances of speakers around them. They seem to remember fragments of speech and repeat these without active production. In this first stage of language learning, the repetition stage, they imitate the intonation contours and general shaping of the utterances they repeat. Lem 1;2 in the following example illustrates this pattern.

> *Mother:* [talking to neighbor on porch while Lem plays with a truck on the porch nearby] But they won't call back, won't happen=
> *Lem:* =call back
> *Neighbor:* Sam's going over there Saturday, he'll pick up a form =
> *Lem:* =pick up on, pick up on [Lem here appears to have heard *form* as *on*]

The adults pay no attention to Lem's "talk," and their talk, in fact, often overlaps his repetitions.

In the second stage, repetition with variation, Trackton children manipulate pieces of conversation they pick up. They incorporate chunks of language from others into their own ongoing dialogue, applying productive rules, inserting new nouns and verbs for those used in the adults' chunks. They also play with rhyming patterns and varying intonation contours.

> *Mother:* She went to the doctor again.
> *Lem (2;2):* [in a sing-song fashion] went to de doctor, doctor, tractor, dis my tractor, doctor on a tractor, went to de doctor.

Lem creates a monologue, incorporating the conversation about him into his own talk as he plays. Adults pay no attention to his chatter unless it gets so noisy as to interfere with their talk.

In the third stage, participation, children begin to enter the ongoing conversations about them. They do so by attracting the adult's attention with a tug on the arm or pant leg, and they help make themselves understood by providing nonverbal reinforcements to help recreate a scene they want the listener to remember. For example, if adults are talking, and a child interrupts with seemingly unintelligible utterances, the child will make gestures, extra sounds, or act out some outstanding features of the scene he is trying to get the adult to remember. Children try to create a context, a scene, for the understanding of their utterance.

This third stage illustrates a pattern in the children's response to their environment and their ways of letting others know their knowledge of the environment. Once they are in the third stage, their communicative efforts are accepted by community members, and adults respond directly to the child, instead of talking to others about the child's activities as they have done in the past. Children continue to practice for conversational participation by playing, when alone, both parts of dialogues, imitating gestures as well as intonation patterns of adults. By 2;6 all children in the community can imitate the walk and talk of others in the community, or frequent visitors such as the man who comes around to read the gas meters. They can feign anger, sadness, fussing, remorse, silliness, or any of a wide range of expressive behaviors. They often use the same chunks of language for varying effects, depending on nonverbal support to give the language different meanings or cast it in a different key (Hymes 1974). Girls between three and four years of age take part in extraordinarily complex stepping and clapping patterns and simple repetitions of hand clap games played by older girls. From the time they are old enough to stand alone, they are encouraged in their participation by siblings and older children in the community. These games require anticipation and recognition of cues for upcoming behaviors, and the young girls learn to watch for these cues and to come in with the appropriate words and movements at the right time.

Preschool children are not asked for what-explanations of their environment. Instead, they are asked a preponderance of analogical questions which call for nonspecific comparisons of one item, event, or person with another: "What's that like?" Other types of questions ask for specific information known to the child but not the adults: "Where'd you get that from?" "What do you want?" "How come you did that?" (Heath 1982). Adults explain their use of these types of questions by expressing their sense of children: they are "comers," coming into their learning by experiencing what knowing about things means. As one parent of a two-year-old boy put it: "Ain't no use me tellin' 'im: learn this, learn that, what's this, what's that? He just gotta learn, gotta know; he see one thing one place one time, he know how it go, see sump'n like it again, maybe it be the same, maybe it won't." Parents do not believe they have a tutoring role in their child's learning; they provide the experiences on which the child draws and reward signs of their successfully coming to know.

Trackton children's early stories illustrate how they respond to adult views of them as "comers." The children learn to tell stories by drawing heavily on their abilities to render a context, to set a stage, and to call on the audience's power to join in the imaginative creation of story. Between the ages of two and four years, the children, in a monologue-like fashion, tell stories about things in their lives, events they see and hear, and situations in which they have been involved. They produce these spontaneously during play with other children or in the presence of adults. Sometimes they make an effort to attract the attention of listeners before they begin the story, but often they do not.

Preschool storytellers have several ways of inviting audience evaluation and interest. They may themselves express an emotional response to the story's actions; they may have another character or narrator in the story do so often using alliterative language play; or they may detail actions and results through direct discourse or sound effects and gestures. All these methods of calling attention to the story and its telling distinguish the speech event as a story, an occasion for audience and storyteller to interact pleasantly, and not simply to hear an ordinary recounting of events or actions.

Trackton children must be aggressive in inserting their stories into an ongoing stream of discourse. Storytelling is highly competitive. Everyone in a conversation may want to tell a story, so only the most aggressive wins out. The content ranges widely, and there is "truth" only in the universals of human experience. Fact is often hard to find, though it is usually the seed of the story. Trackton stories often have no point—no obvious beginning or ending; they go on as long as the audience enjoys and tolerates the storyteller's entertainment.

Trackton adults do not separate out the elements of the environment around their children to tune their attentions selectively. They do not simplify their language, focus on single-word utterances by young children, label items or features of objects in either books or the environment at large. Instead, children are continuously contextualized, presented with almost continuous communication. From this ongoing, multiple-channeled stream of stimuli, they must themselves select, practice, and determine rules of production and structuring. For language, they do so by first repeating, catching chunks of sounds, intonation contours, and practicing these without specific reinforcement or evaluation. But practice material and models are continuously available. Next the children seem to begin to sort out the productive rules for speech and practice what they hear about them with variation. Finally, they work their way into conversations, hooking their meanings for listeners into a familiar context by recreating scenes through gestures, special sound effects, etc. These characteristics continue in their story-poems and their participation in jump-rope rhymes. Because adults do not select out, name, and describe features of the environment for the young, children must perceive situations, determine how units of the situations are related to each other, recognize these relations in other situations, and reason through what it will take to show their correlation of one situation with another. The children can answer questions such as "What's that like?" ["It's like Doug's car"] but they can rarely name the specific feature or features which make two items or events alike. For example, in the case of saying a car seen on the street is "like Doug's car," a child may be basing the analogy on the fact that this car has a flat tire and Doug's also had one last week. But the child does not name (and is not asked to name) what is alike between the two cars.

They fictionalize their "true stories," but they do so by asking the audience to identify with the story through making parallels from their own experiences. When adults read, they often do so in a group. One person, reading aloud, for example, from a brochure on a new car decodes the text, displays illustrations and photographs, and listeners relate the text's meaning to their experiences asking questions and expressing opinions. Finally, the group as a whole synthesizes the written text and the negotiated oral discourse to construct a meaning for the brochure (Heath forthcoming a).

When Trackton children go to school, they face unfamiliar types of questions which ask for what-explanations. They are asked as individuals to identify items by name, and to label features such as shape, color, size, number. The stimuli to which they are to give these responses are two-dimensional flat representations which are often highly stylized and bear little resemblance to the "real" items. Trackton children generally score in the lowest percentile range on the Metropolitan Reading Readiness tests. They do not sit at their desks and complete reading workbook pages; neither do they tolerate questions about reading materials which are structured along the usual lesson format. Their contributions are in the form of "I had a duck at my house one time." "Why'd he do that?" or they imitate the sound effects teachers may produce in stories they read to the children. By the end of the first three primary grades, their general language arts scores have been consistently low, except for those few who have begun to adapt to and adopt some of the behaviors they have had to learn in school. But the majority not only fail to learn the content of lessons, they also do not adopt the social interactional rules for school literacy events. Print in isolation bears little authority in their world. The kinds of questions asked of reading books are unfamiliar. The children's abilities to metaphorically link two events or situations and to recreate scenes are not tapped in the school; in fact, *these abilities often cause difficulties*, because they enable children to see parallels teachers did not intend, and indeed, may not recognize until the children point them out (Heath 1978).

By the end of the lessons or by the time in their total school career when reason-explanations and affective statements call for the creative comparison of two or more situations, it is too late for many Trackton children. They seem not to know how to take meaning from reading; they do not observe the rules of linearity in writing, and their expression of themselves on paper is very limited. Orally taped stories are often much better, but these rarely count as much as written compositions. Thus, Trackton children continue to collect very low or failing grades, and many decide by the end of the sixth grade to stop trying and turn their attention to the heavy peer socialization which usually begins in these years.

FROM COMMUNITY TO CLASSROOM

Learning how to take meaning from writing before one learns to read involves repeated practice in using and learning from language through appropriate participation in literacy events such as exhibitor/questioner and spectator/respondent dyads (Scollon and Scollon 1979) or group negotiation of the meaning of a written text.

Children have to learn to select, hold, and retrieve content from books and other written or printed texts in accordance with their community's rules or "ways of taking," and the children's learning follows community paths of language socialization. In each society, certain kinds of childhood participation in literacy events may precede others, as the developmental sequence builds toward the whole complex of home and community behaviors characteristic of the society. The ways of taking employed in the school may in turn build directly on the preschool development, may require substantial adaptation on the part of the children, or may even run directly counter to aspects of the community's pattern.

At Home

In *Maintown* homes, the construction of knowledge in the earliest preschool years depends in large part on labelling procedures and what-explanations. This pattern of linking old and new knowledge is reinforced in narrative tales which fictionalize the teller's events or recapitulate a story from a book. Thus for these children the bedtime story is simply an early link in a long chain of interrelated patterns of taking meaning from the environment. In particular, children learn that written language may represent not only descriptions of real events, but decontextualized logical propositions, and the occurrence of this kind of information in print or in writing legitimates a response in which one brings to the interpretation of written text selected knowledge from the real world. Moreover, readers must recognize how certain types of questions assert the priority of meanings in the written word over reality. The "real" comes into play only after prescribed decontextualized meanings; affective responses and reason-explanations follow conventional presuppositions which stand behind what-explanations.

Roadville also provides labels, features, and what-explanations, and prescribes listening and performing behaviors for preschoolers. However, Roadville adults do not carry on or sustain in continually overlapping and interdependent fashion the linking of ways of taking meaning from books to ways of relating that knowledge to other aspects of the environment. They do not encourage decontextualization; in fact, they proscribe it in their own stories about themselves and their requirements of stories from children. They do not themselves make analytic statements or assert universal truths, except those related to their religious faith. They lace their stories with synthetic (nonanalytic) statements which express, describe, and synthesize actual real-life materials. Things do not have to follow logically so long as they fit the past experience of individuals in the community. Thus children learn to look for a specific moral in stories and to expect that story to fit their facts of reality explicitly. When they themselves recount an event, they do the same, constructing the story of a real event according to coaching by adults who want to construct the story as they saw it.

Trackton is like neither Maintown nor Roadville. There are no bedtime stories; in fact, there are few occasions for reading to or with children specifically. Instead, during the time these activities would take place in Maintown and Roadville homes, Trackton children are enveloped in different kinds of social interactions. They are held, fed, talked about, and rewarded for nonverbal, and later verbal, renderings of events they witness. Trackton adults value and respond favorably when children show they have come to know how to use language to show correspondence in function, style, configuration, and positioning between two different things or situations. Analogical questions are asked of Trackton children, although the implicit questions of structure and function these embody are never made explicit. Children do not have labels or names of attributes of items and events pointed out for them, and they are asked for reason-explanations not what-explanations. Individuals express their personal responses and recreate corresponding situations with often only a minimal adherence to the germ of truth of a story. Children come to recognize similarities of patterning, though they do not name lines, points, or items which are similar between two items or situations. They are familiar with group literacy events in which several community members orally negotiate the meaning of a written text.

At School

In the early reading stages, and in later requirements for reading to learn at more advanced stages, children from the three communities respond differently, because they have learned different methods and degrees of taking from books. Knowing more about how these alternatives are learned at early ages in different sociocultural conditions can help the school to provide opportunities for *all* students to avail themselves of these alternatives early in their school careers. For example, mainstream children can benefit from early exposure to Trackton's creative, highly analogical styles of telling stories and giving explanations, and they can add the Roadville true story with strict chronicity and explicit moral to their repertoire of narrative types.

In conclusion, if we want to understand the place of literacy in human societies and ways children acquire the literacy orientations of their communities, we must recognize two postulates of literacy and language development.

1. Strict dichotomization between oral and literate traditions is a construct of researchers, not an accurate portrayal of reality across cultures.
2. A unilinear model of development in the acquisition of language structures and uses cannot adequately account for culturally diverse ways of acquiring knowledge or developing cognitive styles.

Roadville and Trackton tell us that the mainstream type of literacy orientation is not the only type even among Western societies. They also tell us that the mainstream ways of acquiring communicative competence do not offer a universally applicable model of development. They offer proof of Hymes' assertion a decade ago that "it is impossible to generalize validly about 'oral' vs. 'literate' cultures as uniform types" (Hymes 1973: 54).

"We need, in short, a great deal of ethnography" (Hymes 1973: 57) to provide descriptions of the ways different social groups "take" knowledge from the environment. For written sources, these ways of taking may be analyzed in terms of *types of literacy events*, such as group negotiation of meaning from written texts, individual "looking things up" in reference books, writing family records in Bibles, and the dozens of other types of occasions when books or other written materials are integral to interpretation in an interaction. These must in turn be analyzed in terms of the specific *features of literacy events*, such as labelling, what-explanations, affective comments, reason-explanations, and many other possibilities. Literacy events must also be interpreted in relation to the *larger sociocultural patterns* which they may exemplify or reflect. For example, ethnography must describe literacy events in their sociocultural contexts, so we may come to understand how such patterns as time and space usage, caregiving roles, and age and sex segregation are interdependent with the types and features of literacy events a community develops. It is only on the basis of such thoroughgoing ethnography that further progress is possible toward understanding cross-cultural patterns of oral and written language uses and paths of development of communicative competence.

NOTES

One of a series of invited papers commemorating a decade of *Language in Society*.

1. First presented at the Terman Conference on Teaching at Stanford University, 1980, this paper has benefitted from cooperation with M. Cochran-Smith of the University of Pennsylvania. She shares an appreciation of the relevance of Roland Barthes' work for studies of the socialization of young children into literacy; her research (1981) on the story-reading practices of a mainstream school-oriented nursery school provides a much needed detailed account of early school orientation to literacy.

2. Terms such as *mainstream* or *middle-class* cultures or social groups are frequently used in both popular and scholarly writings without careful definition. Moreover, numerous studies of behavioral phenomena (for example, mother-child interactions in language learning) either do not specify that the subjects being described are drawn from mainstream groups or do not recognize the importance of this limitation. As a result, findings from this group are often regarded as universal. For a discussion of this problem, see Chanan and Gilchrist 1974, Payne and Bennett 1977. In general, the literature characterizes this group as school-oriented, aspiring toward upward mobility through formal institutions, and providing enculturation which positively values routines of promptness, linearity (in habits ranging from furniture arrangement to entrance into a movie theatre), and evaluative and judgmental responses to behaviors which deviate from their norms.

In the United States, mainstream families tend to locate in neighborhoods and suburbs around cities. Their social interactions center not in their immediate neighborhoods, but around voluntary associations across the city. Thus a cluster of mainstream families (and not a community—which usually implies a specific geographic territory as the locus of a majority of social interactions) is the unit of comparison used here with the Trackton and Roadville communities.

REFERENCES

Basso, K. (1974). The ethnography of writing. In R. Bauman & J. Sherzer (eds.), *Explorations in the ethnography of speaking*. Cambridge University Press.

Cazden, C. B. (1979). Peekaboo as an instructional model: Discourse development at home and at school. *Papers and Reports in Child Language Development* 17: 1–29.

Chanan, G., & Gilchrist, L. (1974). *What school is for*. New York: Praeger.

Childs, C. P., & Greenfield, P. M. (1980). Informal modes of learning and teaching. In N. Warren (ed.), *Advances in cross-cultural psychology*, vol. 2. London: Academic Press.

Cochran-Smith, M. (1981). The making of a reader. Ph.D. dissertation. University of Pennsylvania.

Cohen, R. (1968). The relation between socio-conceptual styles and orientation to school requirements. *Sociology of Education* 41: 201–20.

——. (1969). Conceptual styles, culture conflict, and nonverbal tests of intelligence. *American Anthropologist* 71 (5): 828–56.

——. (1971). The influence of conceptual rule-sets on measures of learning ability. In C. L. Brace, G. Gamble, & J. Bond (eds.), *Race and intelligence*. (Anthropological Studies, No. 8, American Anthropological Association), 41–57.

Glaser, R. (1979). Trends and research questions in psychological research on learning and schooling. *Educational Researcher* 8 (10): 6–13.

Goody, E. (1979). Towards a theory of questions. In E. N. Goody (ed.), *Questions and politeness: Strategies in social interaction*. Cambridge University Press.

Griffin, P., & Humphrey, F. (1978). Task and talk. In *The study of children's functional language and education in the early years*. Final report to the Carnegie Corporation of New York. Arlington, Va.: Center for Applied Linguistics.

Heath, S. (1978). *Teacher talk: Language in the classroom*. (Language in Education 9.) Arlington, Va.: Center for Applied Linguistics.

——. (1980). The functions and uses of literacy. *Journal of Communication* 30 (1): 123–33.

——. (1982). Questioning at home and at school: A comparative study. In G. Spindler (ed.), *Doing ethnography: Educational anthropology in action*. New York: Holt, Rinehart & Winston.

——. (forthcoming a). Protean shapes: Ever-shifting oral and literate traditions. To appear in D. Tannen (ed.), *Spoken and written language: Exploring orality and literacy*. Norwood, N.J.: Ablex.

——. (forthcoming b). *Ways with words: Ethnography of communication in communities and classrooms*.

Howard, R. (1974). A note on S/Z. In R. Barthes, *Introduction to S/Z*. Trans. Richard Miller. New York: Hill and Wang.

Hymes, D. H. (1973). On the origins and foundations of inequality among speakers. In E. Haugen & M. Bloomfield (eds.), *Language as a human problem*. New York: W. W. Norton & Co.

————. (1974). Models of the interaction of language and social life. In J. J. Gumperz & D. Hymes (eds.), *Directions in sociolinguistics*. New York: Holt, Rinehart and Winston.

Kagan, J., Sigel, I., & Moss, H. (1963). Psychological significance of styles of conceptualization. In J. Wright & J. Kagan (eds.), *Basic cognitive processes in children*. Monographs of the society for research in child development 28 (2): 73–112.

Mehan, H. (1979). *Learning lessons*. Cambridge, Mass.: Harvard University Press.

Merritt, M. (1979). Service-like events during individual work time and their contribution to the nature of the rules for communication. NIE Report EP 78-0436.

Ninio, A., & Bruner, J. (1978). The achievement and antecedents of labelling. *Journal of Child Language* 5: 1–15.

Payne, C., & Bennett, C. (1977). "Middle class aura" in public schools. *The Teacher Educator* 13 (1): 16–26.

Peters, A. (1977). Language learning strategies. *Language* 53: 560–73.

Scollon, R., & Scollon, S. (1979). The literate two-year old: The fictionalization of self. *Working Papers in Sociolinguistics*. Austin, TX: Southwest Regional Laboratory.

Sinclair, J. M., & Coulthard, R. M. (1975). *Toward an analysis of discourse*. New York: Oxford University Press.

Sutton-Smith, B. (1981). *The folkstories of children*. Philadelphia: University of Pennsylvania Press.

Umiker-Sebeok, J. D. (1979). Preschool children's intraconversational narratives. *Journal of Child Language* 6 (1): 91–110.

Witkin, H., Faterson, F., Goodenough, R., & Birnbaum, J. (1966). Cognitive patterning in mildly retarded boys. *Child Development* 37 (2): 301–16.

14

Understanding Cultural Diversity and Learning

John U. Ogbu

Cultural diversity has become a household phrase in education, especially minority education. I suspect, however, that there is some misunderstanding about what it means and its relevance to minority education. As an anthropologist, I am sensitive to the use of the phrase *cultural diversity*; as a student of minority education, I am concerned about its application or misapplication with respect to the school adjustment and performance of minority children.

The problem is not merely one of cultural and language differences, although these differences are important. What is even more significant, but thus far unrecognized, is the nature of the relationship between minority cultures/languages and the culture and language of the dominant White Americans and the public schools they control. The relationship between the minority cultures/languages and the mainstream culture and language is different for different minorities. And it is this difference in the relationship that is problematic in the ability of the minorities to cross cultural and language boundaries and that calls for understanding in order to enhance the success of intervention and other efforts. What is the nature of this intercultural relationship and what are its implications for minority education?

CULTURAL DIVERSITY AND DIFFERENTIAL SCHOOL SUCCESS

Societal and School Influences on Minority Education

The school learning and performance of minority children are influenced by complex social, economic, historical, and cultural factors. Therefore, before describing the cultural forces, I want to make it categorically clear that I am focusing on only one group of forces. I have described elsewhere other forces at work, namely,

190

how American society at large, the local communities, and the schools all contribute to minority problems in school learning and performance. Societal contributions include denying the minorities equal access to good education through societal and community educational policies and practices and denying them adequate and/or equal rewards with Whites for their educational accomplishments through a job ceiling and other mechanisms. Schools contribute to the educational problems through subtle and not so subtle policies and practices. The latter include tracking, "biased" testing and curriculum, and misclassification (see Ogbu, 1974, 1977, 1978, 1991). Here we are focusing on cultural forces, specifically, on the relationship between minority cultures and mainstream culture and the implications of that relationship for minority schooling.

Differential Influence of Cultural Forces

There is evidence from comparative research suggesting that differences in school learning and performance among minorities are not due merely to cultural and language differences. Some minority groups do well in school even though they do not share the language and cultural backgrounds of the dominant group that are reflected in the curriculum, instructional style, and other practices of the schools. Such minorities may initially experience problems due to the cultural and language difference, but the problems do not persist.

The reason some minorities do well in school is not necessarily because their cultures are similar to the mainstream culture. For example, Gibson (1988) reports that in Valleyside, California, the Punjabis do well even though judged by mainstream culture they would be regarded as being academically at risk.

One cultural feature, namely, differential interpretation of eye contacts by White teachers and minority-group members, has been offered as an explanation for the learning difficulties among Puerto Rican children in New York (Byers & Byers, 1972) but has not had similar adverse effects on the Punjabis. Other examples of differential academic influence of minority cultural differences have been found in studies of minority education in Stockton (Ogbu, 1974), Watsonville (Matute-Bianchi, 1986), and San Francisco (Suárez-Orozco, 1987).

Studies outside the United States have also found that minority children do not fail in school because of mere cultural/language differences or succeed in school because they share the culture and language of the dominant group. In Britain, students of East Asian origins, for whom the British language and culture are different, do considerably better in school than West Indian students, who have much longer been privy to the British language and culture (Ogbu, 1978). In Japan (DeVos & Lee, 1981) and New Zealand (Penfold, conversation with author, 1981), minority groups—even if they have similar cultures and languages but different histories— differ in school learning and academic success.

There are cases where a minority group does better in school when it is away from its country of origin, residing in a host society where its language and culture differ greatly from the language and culture of the dominant group. Take the case of the Japanese Buraku outcaste. In Japan itself, Buraku students continue to do poorly in school when compared with the dominant Ippan students (Hirasawa, 1989; Shimahara, 1991). But the Buraku immigrants in the United States are doing just as well as the Ippan immigrants (DeVos, 1973; Ito, 1967). The Koreans in Japan are another example. In Japan, where they went originally as colonial forced labor, they do very poorly in school. But in Hawaii and the continental United States, Korean students do as well as other Asians; yet Korean culture is more similar to Japanese culture than to American mainstream culture (DeVos, 1984; DeVos & Lee, 1981; Lee, 1991; Rohlen, 1981). The Koreans' case is further instructive because of their differential school success as a minority group in the United States, Japan, and China (see Kristoff, 1992, for Koreans in China). Korean peasants relocated to these three countries about the same time as emigrants, except the group that went to Japan. The Koreans are academically successful in China and Hawaii, but not in Japan. West Indians are a similar example. They are academically successful in the continental United States and in the U.S. Virgin Islands, where they regard themselves as "immigrants" (Fordham, 1984; Gibson, 1991); less successful in Canada, where they regard themselves as members of "the Commonwealth" (Solomon, 1992); and least successful in Britain, which they regard as their "motherland" (Ogbu, 1978).

As these studies suggest, mere cultural and language differences cannot account for the relative school failure of some minorities and the school success of others. Minority status involves complex realities that affect the relationship between the culture and language of the minority and those of the dominant groups and thereby influence the school adjustment and learning of the minority.

TYPES OF MINORITY STATUS: A PREREQUISITE FOR UNDERSTANDING CULTURAL DIVERSITY AND LEARNING

To understand what it is about minority groups, their cultures and languages that makes crossing cultural boundaries and school learning difficult for some but not for others, we must recognize that there are different types of minority groups or minority status. Our comparative study has led us to classify minority groups into (a) autonomous, (b) immigrant or voluntary, and (c) castelike or involuntary minorities.

1. Autonomous minorities are people who are minorities primarily in a numerical sense. American examples are Jews, Mormons, and the Amish. There are no non-White autonomous minorities in the United States, so we will not discuss this type further (see Ogbu, 1978).

2. Immigrant or voluntary minorities are people who have moved more or less voluntarily to the United States—or any other society—because they desire more economic well-being, better overall opportunities, and/or greater political freedom. Their expectations continue to influence the way they perceive and respond to events, including schooling, in the host society. Voluntary minorities usually experience initial problems in school due to cultural and language differences as well as lack of understanding of how the education system works. But they do not experience lingering, disproportionate school failure. The Chinese and Punjabi Indians are representative U.S. examples. Refugees are not voluntary minorities; they are not a part of this classification or the subject of this paper (see Ogbu, 1990, for a full discussion of the distinction).

3. Castelike or involuntary minorities are people who were originally brought into the United States or any other society against their will. For example, through slavery, conquest, colonization, or forced labor. Thereafter, these minorities were often relegated to menial positions and denied true assimilation into the mainstream society. American Indians, Black Americans, early Mexican-Americans in the Southwest, and native Hawaiians are U.S. examples. Puerto Ricans may qualify for membership in this category if they consider themselves "a colonized people." The Burakumin and Koreans in Japan and the Maoris in New Zealand are examples outside the United States. It is involuntary minorities that usually experience greater and more persistent difficulties with school learning.

MINORITY STATUS, CULTURE, AND IDENTITY

The different types of minorities are characterized by different types of cultural differences as well as social or collective identities. Voluntary minorities are characterized by primary cultural differences and involuntary minorities by secondary cultural differences.

Primary cultural differences are differences that existed before two groups came in contact, such as before immigrant minorities came to the United States. For example, Punjabi Indians in Valleyside, California, spoke Punjabi; practiced the Sikh, Hindu, or Muslim religion; had arranged marriages, and wore turbans, if they were male, before they came to the United States. In Valleyside they continue these beliefs and practices to some extent (Gibson, 1988). The Punjabis also brought with them their distinctive way of raising childing, including teaching children how to make decisions and how to manage money.

We gain a better understanding of primary cultural differences when we examine non-Western children who attend Western-type schools in their own countries. The Kpelle of Liberia are a good example. John Gay and Michael Cole (1967) found that the arithmetic concepts in Kpelle culture were similar in some respects to those used in the American-type school but differed in other ways. The Kpelle had few geometrical concepts, and although they measured time, volume, and money, their culture lacked measurements of weight, area, speed, and temperature. These differences in mathematical concepts and use existed *before* the Kpelle were introduced to Western-type schools.

Secondary cultural differences are differences that arose after two populations came into contact or after members of a given population began to participate in an institution controlled by members of another population, such as the schools controlled by the dominant group. Thus, secondary cultural differences develop as a response to a contact situation, especially one involving the domination of one group by another.

At the beginning of the culture contact the two groups are characterized by primary cultural differences; later, the minorities develop secondary cultural differences to cope with their subordination. The secondary culture develops in several ways: from a reinterpretation of previous primary cultural differences or through the emergence of new types of cultural norms and behaviors.

Several features of secondary cultural differences are worth noting for their effects on schooling. First, it is the differences in style rather than in content that involuntary minorities emphasize: cognitive style (Ramirez & Castenada, 1974; Shade, 1982), communication style (Gumperz, 1981; Kochman, 1982; Philips, 1972, 1983), interaction style (Erickson & Mohatt, 1982), and learning style (Au, 1981; Boykin, 1980; Philips, 1976).

Another feature is cultural inversion. Cultural inversion is the tendency for involuntary minorities to regard certain forms of behavior, events, symbols, and meanings as inappropriate for them because these are characteristic of White Americans. At the same time the minorities value other forms of behavior, events, symbols and meanings, often the opposite, as more appropriate for themselves. Thus, what is appropriate or even legitimate behavior for in-group members may be defined in opposition to White out-group members' practices and preferences.

Cultural inversion may take several forms. It may be in-group meanings of words and statements (Bontemps, July 1969, conversation with author), different notions and use of time (Weis, 1985), different emphasis on dialects and communication style (Baugh, 1984; Holt, 1972; Luster, 1992), or an outright rejection of White American preferences or what Whites consider appropriate behavior in a given setting (Fordham & Ogbu, 1986; Petroni, 1970). Cultural inversion, along with other oppositional elements, results in the co-existence of two opposing cultural frames of reference or ideals orienting behavior, from the perspectives of involuntary minorities.

Involuntary minorities sometimes use cultural inversion to repudiate negative White stereotypes or derogatory images. Sometimes they use it as a strategy to manipulate Whites, to get even with Whites, or, as Holt (1972) puts it for Black Americans, "to turn the table against whites."

Secondary cultural differences seem to be associated with ambivalent or oppositional social or collective identities vis-a-vis the White American social identity.

Voluntary minorities seem to bring to the United States a sense of who they are from their homeland and seem to retain this different but non-oppositional social identity at least during the first generation. Involuntary minorities, in contrast, develop a new sense of social or collective identity that is in opposition to the social identity of the dominant group after they have become subordinated. They do so in response to their treatment by White Americans in economic, political, social, psychological, cultural, and language domains. Whites' treatment included deliberate exclusion from true assimilation or the reverse, namely, forced superficial assimilation (Castile & Kushner, 1981; DeVos, 1967, 1984; Spicer, 1966, 1971). Involuntary minorities, such as Black Americans, developed oppositional identity because for many generations they realized and believed that the White treatment was both collective and enduring. They were (and still are) not treated like White Americans regardless of their individual differences in ability, training, education, place of origin or residence, economic status, or physical appearance. They could not (and still cannot) easily escape from their birth-ascribed membership in a subordinate and disparaged group by "passing" for White or by returning to a "homeland" (Green, 1981). Native Americans and native Hawaiians have no other "homeland" to return to. In the past some Black Americans sought an escape by returning to Africa (Hall, 1978) and, more recently, by converting to the Muslim religion (Essien-Udom, 1964).

CULTURAL DIFFERENCES, IDENTITY, AND SCHOOL LEARNING

I have identified different types of cultural differences characteristic of the voluntary and involuntary minorities and have described the relationship between these cultural differences and mainstream (White) American culture. I turn now to the way the relationship between the minority cultures and mainstream culture affects minority schooling.

The primary cultural differences of voluntary minorities and the secondary cultural differences of involuntary minorities affect minority school learning differently. My comparative research suggests that involuntary minorities experience more difficulties in school learning and performance partly because of the relationship between their cultures and the mainstream culture. As I have come to understand it, they have greater difficulty with school learning and performance partly because they have greater difficulty crossing cultural/language boundaries in school than voluntary minorities with primary cultural differences.

Primary Cultural Differences and Schooling

What kinds of school problems are associated with primary cultural differences and why do the bearers of these differences overcome these problems and learn more or less successfully? Why do voluntary minorities successfully cross cultural boundaries?

In school, primary cultural differences may initially cause problems in interpersonal and intergroup relations as well as difficulties in academic work for several reasons. One is that children from different cultural backgrounds may begin school with different cultural assumptions about the world and human relations. Another is that the minorities may come to school lacking certain concepts necessary to learn math and science, for instance, because their own cultures do not have or use such concepts. Still another problem is that the children may be non-English-speaking. Finally, there may be differences in teaching and learning styles.

However, the relationship between the primary cultural differences and White American mainstream culture helps voluntary minority children to eventually overcome the initial problems, adjust socially, and learn and perform academically more or less successfully. First, the cultural differences existed before the minorities came to the United States or entered the public schools; the differences did not arise to maintain boundaries between them and White Americans. They are different from, but not necessarily oppositional to, equivalent features in mainstream culture in the schools.

Furthermore, because primary cultural differences did not develop in opposition or to protect their collective identity and sense of security and self-worth, voluntary minorities do not perceive learning the attitudes and behaviors required for school success as threatening their own culture, language, and identities. Instead, they interpret such learning (e.g., English) instrumentally and as additive, as adding to what they already have (their own language), for use in the appropriate context (Chung, 1992). They also believe that the learning will help them succeed in school and later in the labor market. Voluntary minorities, therefore, tend to adopt the strategy of "accommodation without assimilation" (Gibson, 1988) or "alternation strategy" (Ogbu, 1987). That is, while they may not give up their own cultural beliefs and practices, voluntary minorities are willing, and may even strive, to play the classroom game by the rules and try to overcome all kinds of schooling difficulties because they believe so strongly that there will be a payoff later (Gibson, 1987). With this kind of attitude, they are able to cross cultural boundaries and do relatively well in school.

Still another factor in favor of voluntary minorities is that they interpret the cultural and language differences they encounter as barriers to be overcome in order for them to achieve their long-range goals of obtaining good school credentials for future employment. They did not come to the United States expecting the schools to teach them in their own culture and language, although they are grateful if the schools do. Usually, they go to the school expecting and willing to learn the culture and language of the schools, and they also expect at least some initial difficulty in doing so.

Finally, primary cultural differences and the problems they cause are often specific enough to be identified through careful ethnographic research This specificity and identifiability facilitate developing educational policies, programs, and practices to eliminate their negative impact.

Secondary Cultural Differences and Schooling

Many of the "cultural problems" caused by secondary cultural differences are on the surface similar to those caused by primary cultural differences: conflicts in interpersonal/intergroup relations due to cultural misunderstandings, conceptual problems due to absence of certain concepts in the ethnic-group cultures, lack of fluency in standard English, and conflicts in teaching and learning style.

However, the underlying factor that distinguishes these problems from those of primary cultural differences is the style, not the content. Sociolinguists stress differences in communication style; cognitive researchers emphasize cognitive styles, styles of thought, or a mismatch between teacher and minority students in cognitive maps; interactionists and transactionists locate the problem in differences in interactional style. Researchers working among native Hawaiians traced their reading problems to differences in learning style.

What needs to be stressed is that secondary cultural differences do not merely cause initial problems in the social adjustment and academic performance of involuntary minorities but the problems appear to be extensive and persistent. One reason for this is that these minorities find it harder to cross cultural and language boundaries.

This difficulty occurs because of the nature of the relationship between the minority culture and the dominant White American culture. The cultural differences arose initially to serve boundary-maintaining and coping functions under subordination. As boundary-maintaining mechanisms, they do not necessarily disappear or change when involuntary minorities and Whites are brought together, as in desegregated schools. Secondary cultural differences evolved as coping mechanisms under "oppressive conditions," and the minorities have no strong incentives to give up these differences as long as they believe that they are still oppressed; some of the cultural differences have taken on a life of their own, and the minorities are not necessarily aware of their boundary-maintaining functions or oppositional quality.

Involuntary minorities interpret the cultural and language differences as markers of their collective identity to be maintained, not as barriers to be overcome. This results partly from coexistence of opposing cultural frames of reference discussed earlier. There is, again, no incentive to learn or behave in a manner considered consciously and unconsciously as inappropriate for the minorities.

Among involuntary minorities, school learning tends to be equated with the learning of the culture and language of White Americans, that is, the learning of the cultural and language frames of reference of their "enemy" or "oppressors." Consider the current argument by some that school curriculum and textbooks are reflective of White culture. (Note that for their part, White Americans also define minority school learning in terms of learning White culture and language as reflected in the school curriculum and practices.) Thus, involuntary minorities may consciously or unconsciously interpret school learning as a displacement process detrimental to their social identity, sense of security, and self-worth. They fear that by learning the White cultural frame of reference, they will cease to act like minorities and lose their identity as minorities and their sense of community and self-worth. Furthermore, reality has demonstrated that those who successfully learn to act White or who succeed in school are not fully accepted by the Whites; nor do such people receive rewards or opportunity for advancement equal to those open to Whites with similar education.

The important point here is that unlike voluntary minorities, involuntary minorities do not seem to be able or willing to separate attitudes and behaviors that result in academic success from those that may result in linear acculturation or replacement of their cultural identity with White American cultural identity.

There are social pressures discouraging involuntary minority students from adopting the standard attitudes and behavior practices that enhance school learning because such attitudes and behaviors are considered "White." In the case of Black students, for example, the social pressures against "acting White" include accusations of Uncle Tomism or disloyalty to the Black cause and to the Black community, fear of losing one's friends and one's sense of community (Fordham & Ogbu, 1986; Luster, 1992; Ogbu, 1974; Petroni, 1970).

The same phenomenon has been described for American Indian students—the tendency to "resist" adopting and following school rules of behavior and standard practices (Dumont, 1972; Kramer, 1991; Philips, 1972, 1983). According to some studies, Indian students enter the classroom with a cultural convention that dictates that they should not adopt the expected classroom rules of behavior and standard practices. A good illustration is Philips's study of Indian children in Warm Springs Reservation in Oregon referred to earlier. She found that the Indian students and their White teachers in an elementary school held different views about how students should interact with teachers and among themselves; they also held different views about how students should participate in classroom activities. Although the teachers' views apparently prevailed, the teachers were not particularly effective in classroom management and in getting the children to learn and perform.

There are also psychological pressures against "acting White" that are just as effective in discouraging involuntary minority students from striving for academic success. An involuntary minority individual who desires to do well in school may also define the behavior enhancing school success or the success itself as "acting White." Thinking that attitudes and behaviors associated with academic success and the success itself may result in loss of peer affiliation and support and at the same time uncertain of White acceptance and support if he or she succeeds in learning to act White, a student may feel a personal conflict. Put differently, an involuntary minority student desiring and striving to do well in school is faced with the conflict between loyalty to the minority peer group, which provides a sense of community and security, and the desire to behave in ways that may improve school performance but that the peer group defines as "White."

The dilemma of involuntary minority students, then, is that they may have to choose between "acting White" (i.e., adopting "appropriate" attitudes and behaviors or school rules and standard practices that enhance academic success but that are perceived and interpreted by the minorities as typical of White Americans and therefore negatively sanctioned by them) and "acting Black," "acting Indian," "acting Chicano," and so on (i.e., adopting attitudes and behaviors that the minority students consider appropriate for their group but that are not necessarily conducive to school success).

We noted earlier that researchers among involuntary minorities repeatedly emphasize conflicts and discontinuities in teaching and learning due to differences in style, rather than content. Stylistic differences are more diffuse and less specific than the content differences of primary cultural differences. The differences in manifest contents are not the overriding problem, because they also exist within the primary cultural differences of voluntary minorities. Rather, the differences that are more problematic among involuntary minorities are differences in style and are oppositional in relation to White or mainstream culture. Moreover, it is more difficult for interventionists and teachers without special training to detect the problems and help the students.

Involuntary minorities lack some instrumental factors that motivate voluntary minorities to cross cultural boundaries. The latter try to overcome cultural, language, and other barriers because they strongly believe that there will be a material payoff later. Involuntary minorities—who did not choose to come to the United States motivated by hope of economic success or political freedom—believe less strongly. Furthermore, they lack the positive dual frame of reference of the immigrants who compare their progress in the United States with that of their peers "back home." Involuntary minorities compare their progress—if at all—with that of White Americans, and they usually conclude that they are worse off than they should be and blame Whites, the schools, and other societal institutions controlled by Whites. Thus, these minorities do not have as strong incentives merely to play the classroom game by the rules (Gibson, 1988).

THE INDIVIDUAL IN COLLECTIVE ADAPTATION

We have described what appears to be the dominant pattern for each type of minority. But when we enter a minority community, whether of voluntary or involuntary minorities, we usually find some students who are doing well in school and other students who are not. We also find that the members of each community know that some strategies enhance school success and other strategies do not. We may even learn about the kinds of individuals and subgroups who use the different strategies. However, the strategies of a voluntary minority community are not necessarily the same as those of the involuntary minorities (Ogbu, 1989).

Among the voluntary minorities there appears to be a collective orientation toward making good grades in school and there also appear to be social pressures, including peer pressures, that encourage making good grades. In addition, community gossips promote striving for school success. Partly to avoid ridicule (which may extend to one's family), criticism, and isolation, voluntary minority youths tend to utilize those strategies that enhance their chances to succeed in school. The community also appears to use both tangible and symbolic means to encourage school striving. While successful members of the group may live outside the ethnic neighborhood, they tend to maintain social membership there and participate in activities in which they mix informally with the residents. They thus provide concrete evidence to the youth both that they can succeed through education and that they can be bona fide members of the community in spite of their success. Finally, voluntary minority students are eager to utilize information and resources available in school.

For involuntary minorities the situation is somewhat different. Although making good grades is strongly verbalized by students, parents, and the community as a desirable goal, there is less community and family pressure to achieve it. For example, there rarely is any stigma attached to being a poor student, and there are no community gossips criticizing a poor student or his or her family. As for peer groups, their collective orientation is probably against academic striving. Therefore, peer pressures discourage making good grades. Students who adopt attitudes and behaviors enhancing school success or who make good grades may be subjected to negative peer pressures, including criticism and isolation.

Under this circumstance, involuntary minority youths who want to succeed academically often consciously choose from a variety of secondary strategies to shield them from the peer pressures and other detracting forces of the community. The secondary strategies are over and above the conventional strategy of adopting proper academic attitudes, hard work, and perseverance. These strategies provide the context in which the student can practice the conventional strategy.

WHAT CAN BE DONE

Prerequisites

Recognize that there are different kinds of cultural/language differences and that the different types arise for different reasons or circumstances.

Recognize that there are different types of minority groups and that the minority types are associated with the different types of cultural/language differences.

Recognize that all minority children face problems of social adjustment and academic performance in school because of cultural/language differences. However, while problems faced by bearers of primary cultural differences are superficially similar to those of bearers of secondary cultural differences, they are fundamentally different. The reason lies in the difference in the relationship between the two types of cultural differences and White American mainstream culture.

Helping Children with Primary Cultural/Language Differences

Most problems caused by primary cultural differences are due to differences in cultural content and practice. One solution is for teachers and interventionists to learn about the students' cultural backgrounds and use this knowledge to organize their classrooms and programs, to help students learn what they teach, to help students get along with one another, to communicate with parents, and the like. Teachers and interventionists can learn about the students' cultures through (a) observation of children's behavior in the classroom and on playgrounds, (b) asking children questions about their cultural practices and preferences, (c) talking with parents about their cultural practices and preferences, (d) doing research on various ethnic groups with children in school, and (e) studying published works on children's ethnic groups.

Some problems caused by primary cultural differences can also be solved through well-designed and implemented multicultural education. Such multicultural education must be based on actual knowledge of the cultures and languages of the children's ethnic groups, how they differ from mainstream culture and language, and the kinds of problems they generate.

Helping Children with Secondary Cultural/Language Differences

First, teachers and interventionists must recognize that involuntary minority children come to school with cultural and language frames of reference that are not only different from but probably oppositional to those of the mainstream and school. Second, teachers and interventionists should study the histories and cultural adaptations of involuntary minorities in order to understand the bases and nature of the groups' cultural and language frames of reference as well as the children's sense of social identity. This knowledge will help them understand why these factors affect the process of minority schooling, particularly their school orientations and behaviors.

Third, special counseling and related programs should be used (a) to help involuntary minority students learn to separate attitudes and behaviors enhancing school success from those that lead to linear acculturation or "acting White" and (b) to help the students to avoid interpreting the former as a threat to their social identity and sense of security.

Fourth, programs are needed to increase students' adoption of the strategy of "accommodation without assimilation," "alternation model," or "playing the classroom game." The essence of this strategy is that students should recognize and accept the fact that they can participate in two cultural or language frames of reference for different purposes without losing their own cultural and language identity

or undermining their loyalty to the minority community. They should learn to practice "when in Rome, do as the Romans do," without becoming Romans.

We have found from ethnographic studies (Ogbu & Hickerson, 1980) that
whereas voluntary minority students try to learn to act according to school norms
and expectations, involuntary minority students do not necessarily do so. Instead,
they emphasize learning how to manipulate "the system," how to deal with or respond to White people and schools controlled by White people or their minority
representatives. This problem should be addressed. A related approach that can be
built into multicultural education programs is teaching the students their own responsibility for their academic performance and school adjustment.

Finally, society can help reorient minority youths toward more academic striving for school credentials for future employment by (a) creating more jobs in general, (b) eliminating the job ceiling against minorities, and (c) providing better
employment opportunities for minorities.

The Role of the Involuntary Minority Community

The involuntary minority community can and should play an important part in
changing the situation for three reasons. First, some of the needed changes can be
most effectively brought about through community effort. Second, minority children do not succeed or fail only because of what schools do or do not do, but also
because of what the community does. Third, our comparative research suggests that
the social structure and relationship within the minority communities could be a
significant influence on students' educational orientations and behaviors.

At this point in my research I suggest four ways in which the involuntary minority community can encourage academic striving and success among its children.
One is to teach the children to separate attitudes and behaviors that lead to academic success from attitudes and behaviors that lead to a loss of ethnic identity and
culture or language. This can be achieved partly by successful members of the group
retaining their social membership in the community and not dissociating themselves
from the neighborhood, labeling the less successful invidiously as "underclass," and
so on. Second, the involuntary minority community should provide the children
with concrete evidence that its members appreciate and value academic success as
much as they appreciate and value achievements in sports, athletics, and entertainment.

Third, the involuntary minority community must teach the children to recognize and accept the responsibility for their school adjustment and academic performance. One difference between voluntary and involuntary minorities is that the
former place a good deal of responsibility on the children for their school behavior
and academic performance (Gibson, 1988).

Finally, the involuntary minority middle class needs to reevaluate and change
its role vis-a-vis the community. We have discovered in our comparative research

two contrasting models of middle class relationship with minority community which we suspect have differential effects on minority school success. The first model is, apparently, characteristic of voluntary minorities. Here successful, educated, and professional individuals, such as business people, doctors, engineers, lawyers, social workers, and university professors, appear to retain their social membership in the community, although they generally reside outside predominantly minority neighborhoods. Such people regard their accomplishments as a positive contribution to their community, a community, not just individual, achievement. The community, in turn, interprets their accomplishments in a similar manner. The successful members participate in community events where they interact with the youth and less successful adults informally and outside their official roles as representatives of the welfare, police, school district, or White-controlled companies. In this community, the middle class provides concrete evidence to young people that school success pays *and* that school success and economic and professional success in the wider society are compatible with collective identity and bona fide membership in the minority community.

In contrast, involuntary minorities seem to have a model that probably does not have much positive influence on schooling. Members of involuntary minorities seem to view professional success as "a ticket" to leave their community both physically and socially, to get away from those who have not "made it." People seek education and professional success, as it were, in order to leave their minority community. White Americans and their media reinforce this by praising those who have made their way out of the ghetto, barrio, or reservation. The middle-class minorities do not generally interpret their achievements as an indication that "their community is making it"; neither does the community interpret their achievements as an evidence of the "development" or "progress" of its members. The middle class may later return to or visit the community with "programs," or as "advocates" for those left behind or as representatives of White institutions. They rarely participate in community events where they interact outside these roles with the youth and the less successful community members. Thus, the involuntary minority middle class does not provide adequate concrete evidence to the youth and the less successful that school success leads to social and economic success in later adult life. The involuntary minority middle class must rethink its role vis-a-vis the minority youth. What is needed is for the middle class to go beyond programs, advocacy, and institutional representation to reaffiliate with the community socially.

NOTE

An earlier version of this article was presented as an invited address to Division D, AERA, Annual Meeting, Chicago, March 1991. This article was revised June 1992.

REFERENCES

Au, K. H. (1981). Participant structure in a reading lesson with Hawaiian children: Analysis of a culturally appropriate instructional event. *Anthropology and Education Quarterly*, 10(2), 91–115.

Baugh, J. (1984). *Black street speech: Its history, structure, and survival*. Austin, TX: University of Texas Press.

Bennett, W. J. (1984). To *reclaim a legacy: A report on the humanities in higher education*. Washington, DC: National Endowment for the Humanities.

Boykin, A. W. (1980, November). *Reading achievement and the sociocultural frame of reference of Afro American children*. Paper presented at NIE Roundtable Discussion on Issues in Urban Reading. Washington, DC: The National Institute of Education.

Bullock, H. A. (1970). *A history of Negro education in the South from 1619 to the present*. New York: Praeger.

Byers, P., & Byers, H. (1972). Non-verbal communication and the education of children. In C. B. Cazden, D. Hymes, & V. John (Eds.), *Functions of language in the classroom*. New York: Teachers College Press.

Castile, G. P., & Kushner, G. (Eds.). (1981). *Persistent peoples: Cultural enclaves in perspective*. Tucson, AZ: University of Arizona Press.

Chung, J. P-L. (1992). The *out-of-class language and social experience of a clique of Chinese immigrant students: An ethnography of a process of social identity formation*. Unpublished Doctoral Dissertation, State University of New York at Buffalo.

DeVos, G. A. (1967). Essential elements of caste: Psychological determinants in structural theory. In G. A. DeVos & H. Wagatsuma (Eds.), *Japan's invisible race: Caste in culture and personality* (pp. 332–384). Berkeley, CA: University of California Press.

DeVos, G. A. (1973). Japan's outcastes: The problem of the Burakumin. In B. Whitaker (Ed.), *The fourth world: Victims of group oppression* (pp. 307–327). New York: Schocken.

DeVos, G. A. (1984, April). *Ethnic persistence and role degradation: An illustration from Japan*. Paper presented at the American-Soviet Symposium on Contemporary Ethnic Processes in the USA and the USSR. New Orleans, LA.

DeVos, G. A., & Lee, C. (1981). *Koreans in Japan*. Berkeley, CA: University of California Press.

Dumont, R. V., Jr. (1972). Learning English and how to be silent: Studies in Sioux and Cherokee classrooms. In C. B. Cazden, D. Hymes, & V. John (Eds.), *Functions of language in the classroom*. New York: Teachers College Press.

Erickson, F., & Mohatt, G. (1982). Cultural organization of participant structure in two classrooms of Indian students. In G. D. Spindler (Ed.), *Doing the ethnography of schooling: Educational anthropology in action* (pp. 132–175) New York: Holt.

Essien-Udom, E. U. (1964). *Black nationalism: A search for identity in America*. New York: Dell.

Fordham, S. (1984, November). *Ethnography in a Black high school: Learning not to be a native*. Paper presented at the 83rd Annual Meeting of the American Anthropological Association, Denver.

Fordham, S., & Ogbu, J. U. (1986). Black students' school success: Coping with the "burden of 'acting white.'" *The Urban Review*, 18(3), 176–206.

Gay, J., & Cole, M. (1967). *The new mathematics and an old culture: A study of learning among the Kpelle of Liberia*. New York: Holt.

Gibson, M. A. (1987). Playing by the Rules. In G. D. Spindler (Ed.), *Education and cultural process* (2nd ed., pp. 274–281). Prospect Heights, IL: Waveland Press.

Gibson, M. A. (1988). *Accommodation without assimilation: Sikh immigrants in an American high school*. Ithaca, NH: Cornell University Press.

Gibson, M. A. (1991). Ethnicity, gender and social class: The social adaptation patterns of West Indian youths. In M. A. Gibson & J. U. Ogbu (Eds.), *Minority status and schooling: A comparative study of immigrants and involuntary minorities* (pp. 169–203). New York: Garland.

Gibson, M. A., & Ogbu, J. U. (Eds.). (1991). *Minority status and schooling: A Comparative study of immigrants and involuntary minorities*. New York: Garland.

Green, V. (1981). Blacks in the United States: The creation of an enduring people? In G. P. Castile & G. Kushner (Eds.), *Persistent peoples: Cultural enclaves in perspective* (pp. 69–77). Tucson, AZ: University of Arizona Press.

Gumperz, J. J. (1981). Conversational inference and classroom learning. In J. Green & C. Wallat (Eds.), *Ethnographic approaches to face-to-face interaction* (pp. 3–23). Norwood, NJ: Ablex.

Hall, R. A. (1978). *Black separatism in the United States*. Hanover, NH: The New England University Press.

Hirasawa, Y. (1989). *A policy study of the evolution of Dowa education in Japan*. Unpublished Doctoral Dissertation, Harvard University.

Holt, G. S. (1972). "Inversion" in Black communication. In T. Kochman (Ed.), *Rappin' and stylin' out: Communication in urban Black America* (pp. 152–159). Chicago: University of Illinois Press.

Ito, H. (1967). Japan's outcastes in the United States. In G. A. DeVos & H. Wagatasuma (Eds.), *Japan's invisible race: Caste in culture and personality* (pp. 200–221). Berkeley, CA: University of California Press.

Kochman, T. (1982). *Black and White styles in conflict*. Chicago: University of Chicago Press.

Kramer, B. J. (1991). Education and American Indians: The experience of the Ute Indian tribe. In M. A. Gibson & J. U. Ogbu (Eds.), *Minority status and schooling: A comparative study of immigrants and involuntary minorities* (pp. 287–307). New York: Garland.

Kristoff, N. D. (1992, February 7). In China, the Koreans shine ("It's Our Custom"). *New York Times*, p. A7.

Lee, Y. (1991). *Koreans in Japan and United States*. In M. A. Gibson & J. U. Ogbu (Eds.), *Minority status and schooling: A comparative study of immigrants and involuntary minorities* (pp. 131–167). New York: Garland.

Luster, L. (1992). *Schooling, survival, and struggle: Black women and the GED*. Unpublished Doctoral Dissertation, Stanford University.

Matute-Bianchi, M. E. (1986). Ethnic identities and patterns of school success and failure among Mexican-descent and Japanese-American students in a California high school: An ethnographic analysis. *American Journal of Education*, 95(1), 233–255.

Ogbu, J. U. (1974). *The next generation: An ethnography of education in an urban neighborhood*. New York: Academic Press.

Ogbu, J. U. (1977). Racial stratification and education: The case of Stockton, California. *ICRD Bulletin*, 12(3), 1–26.

Ogbu, J. U. (1978). *Minority education and caste: The American system in cross-cultural perspective*. New York: Academic Press.

Ogbu, J. U. (1987). Variability in minority school performance: A problem in search of an explanation. *Anthropology and Education Quarterly*, 18(4), 312–334.

Ogbu, J. U. (1988). Diversity and equity in public education: Community forces and minority school adjustment and performance. In R. Haskins and D. Macrae (Eds.), *Policies for America's public schools: Teachers, equity, and indicators* (pp. 127–170). Norwood, NJ: Ablex.

Ogbu, J. U. (1989). The individual in collective adaptation: A framework for focusing on academic underperformance and dropping out among involuntary minorities. In L. Weis, E. Farrar, & H. G. Petrie (Eds.), *Dropouts from schools: Issues, dilemmas and solutions* (pp. 181–204). Buffalo, NY: State University of New York Press.

Ogbu, J. U. (1990). Minority status and literacy in comparative perspective. *Daedalus.* 119(2), 141–168.

Ogbu, J. U. (1991). Low school performance as an adaptation: The case of Blacks in Stockton, California. In M. A. Gibson & J. U. Ogbu (Eds.), *Minority status and schooling: A comparative study of immigrants and involuntary minorities* (pp. 249–285). New York: Garland.

Ogbu, J. U., & Hickerson, R. (1980). *Survival strategies and role models in the ghetto.* University of California-Berkeley, Department of Anthropology, Special Project.

Ogbu, J. U., & Matute-Bianchi, M. E. (1986). Understanding sociocultural factors in education: Knowledge, identity, and adjustment in schooling. In California State Department of Education, Bilingual Education Office, *Beyond language: Social and cultural factors in schooling language minority students* (pp. 73–142). Sacramento, CA: California State University-Los Angeles, Evaluation, Dissemination and Assessment Center.

Petroni, F. A. (1970). Uncle Toms: White stereotypes in the Black movement. *Human Organization, 29,* 260–266.

Philips, S. U. (1972). Participant structure and communicative competence: Warm Springs children in community and classroom. In C. B. Cazden, D. Hymes, & V. John (Eds.), *Functions of language in the classroom.* New York: Teachers College Press.

Philips, S. U. (1976). Commentary: Access to power and maintenance of ethnic identity as goals of multi-cultural education. *Anthropology and Education Quarterly, 7*(4), 30–32.

Philips, S. U. (1983). *The invisible culture: Communication in classroom and community on the Warm Springs Indian Reservation.* New York: Longman.

Ramírez, M., & Castañeda, A. (1974). *Cultural democracy, bicognitive development and education.* New York: Academic Press.

Rohlen, T. (1981). Education: Policies and prospects. In C. Lee & G. A. DeVos (Eds.), *Koreans in Japan: Ethnic conflicts and accommodation* (pp. 182–222). Berkeley, CA: University of California Press.

Shade, B. J. (1982). *Afro-American patterns of cognition.* Unpublished manuscript, Wisconsin Center for Educational Research, Madison, WI.

Shimahara, N. K. (1991). Social mobility and education: Buraku in Japan. In M. A. Gibson & J. U. Ogbu (Eds.), *Minority status and schooling: A comparative study of immigrants and involuntary minorities* (pp. 249–285). New York: Garland.

Sleeter, C. E., & Grant, C. A. (1987). An analysis of multicultural education in the United States. *Harvard Educational Review, 57*(4), 421–444.

Solomon, R. P. (1992). *The creation of separation: Black culture and struggle in an American high school.* Albany, NY: State University of New York Press.

Spicer, E. H. (1966). The process of cultural enslavement in Middle America. *36th Congress International de Americanistas, Seville, 3,* 267–279.

Spicer, E. H. (1971). Persistent cultural systems: A comparative study of identity systems that can adapt to contrasting environments. *Science, 174,* 795–800.

Suárez-Orozco, M. M. (1987). Becoming somebody: Central American immigrants in U. S. inner-city schools. *Anthropology & Education Quarterly, 18*(4), 287–299.

Weis, L. (1985). *Between Two Worlds.* New York: Routledge and Kegan, Paul.

15

Formation and Transformation of Funds of Knowledge among U.S.-Mexican Households

Carlos G. Vélez-Ibáñez and James B. Greenberg

INTRODUCTION

Our purpose in this work is to provide a broad anthropological context for possible educational reforms of the public schools that serve U.S.-Mexican[1] populations in the southwestern United States. Our position is that public schools often ignore the strategic and cultural resources, which we have termed *funds of knowledge*, that households contain. We argue that these funds not only provide the basis for understanding the cultural systems from which U.S.-Mexican children emerge, but that they also are important and useful assets in the classroom. Many assumptions about these cultural systems informing policy and practice in public schools are not supported by the actual nature of these populations, since, as Greenberg has said, "the difficulty in educating our children begins in the separation in industrial societies of the work place from the home" (1990:317). This separation makes an understanding of the cultural system necessary to build constructive relationships between teachers, students, and parents, relationships which are needed to improve the educational quality and equity in schools that serve U.S.-Mexican populations.

We argue that grasping the social relationships in which children are ensconced and the broad features of learning generated in the home are key if we are to understand the construction of cultural identity and the emergence of cultural personality among U.S.-Mexican children. We will explain why educational structures and practices often militate against such cultural identity and why we should consider alternative policies. By examining the historical processes by which U.S.-Mexican cultural identity has been constructed, we hope to provide a critical perspective on the deficiency model or a minority model of instruction used for culturally different students.[2]

As case material will show, each generation struggled against different historical forces, yet their defenses, for the most part, were invariant—human creativity coupled with an enormous ability to mobilize and expand social relations. The case study illustrates the effect of struggles on households and their ability to maintain their security and support the emergence of personal and cultural identity.

HISTORICAL DIMENSIONS OF FUNDS OF KNOWLEDGE FOR U.S. MEXICANS

The key to understanding the forces that shape U.S. Mexicans lies in the historical struggle of their households over control of their labor and resources, and for economic security. We shall argue that the economic and political transformations that accompanied the rise of capitalism in the southwestern United States have profoundly shaped such households. We also will argue that, since the late-19th century, the combination of the historical forces of industrialization and their accompanying immigration policies has contributed binationally to the rise of U.S.-Mexican ethnicity. As well, these forces have led both to the formation of binational families and to the distribution of Mexican households in residential clusters. These forces have also led to repeated transformations of the cultural and behavioral practices, or funds of knowledge (Vélez-Ibáñez 1987, 1988a, 1989, 1992b; Vélez-Ibáñez and Greenberg 1990), that form the core of regional U.S.-Mexican cultural identity.

The best way to explain what we mean by funds of knowledge is to relate them to Wolf's (1966) discussion of household economy. Wolf distinguishes several funds that households must juggle: caloric funds, funds of rent, replacement funds, ceremonial funds, social funds. Entailed in these are wider sets of activities requiring specific strategic bodies of essential information that households need to maintain their well-being. If we define such funds as those bodies of knowledge of strategic importance to households, then we may ask such pertinent questions as: How were such assemblages historically formed? How variable are they? How are they transformed as they move from one context to another? How are they learned and transmitted? How are they socially distributed?

SETTING

Since the late-19th century there has been a continual struggle for control of U.S.-Mexican households in the border region. Large-scale and industrially organized technologies (Vélez-Ibáñez 1992a) have been drawn to the 2,000-mile-long political border and have created a region that includes 52 million persons in the ten border states,[3] half of whom live within a 400-mile-wide belt dissected by the border (Martinez 1988). Since 1950 the population of the six Mexican border states has increased threefold, while the population of the four U.S. states has increased from 20 million to 42 million since 1980. Such growth stems from uncontrolled industrialization on both sides of the border, created by a series of symbiotic economic and technological relations in manufacturing, processing, industrial agriculture, labor markets, and twin plants development (Diez-Canedo 1981; Fernández-Kelly 1987; García y Griego 1983; Gonzalez-Archegia 1987; Martínez 1983; Porras n.d.; Tiano 1985). Such relations in the borderlands continue to shape the formation of Mexican households as well as their cultural and social responses.

United States border policy exacerbates such structural conditions and influences how Mexican households on both sides cope with changing economic and political fortunes. Whether yesterday's Mexican national becomes today's U.S. citizen is very much dependent upon the region's economic health. Even ethnicity among U.S. Mexicans in the Southwest, and its attending political implications (Vélez-Ibáñez 1992a), is of very recent origin and largely a product of post-Depression border policies.

DYNAMIC OF FUNDS: HISTORICAL FORMATION

The historical conditions that produced the dynamic qualities of the border region have their roots in the incessant introduction of large-scale technological and capital-intensive investments (Vélez-Ibáñez 1992). Such development created binational labor markets that proletarianized rural populations and pushed persons back and forth across the border. As new technologies and productive activities, such as mining, construction, railroads, and industrial forms of agriculture, were introduced into the borderland arena, populations responded in kind. For most of the 19th century and the early 20th century, labor markets were open to both U.S.- and Mexican-born workers.

Before 1929, the north and south movement of persons between border communities was relatively uninterrupted. *Cross-border families*, with portions of large extended kin networks residing on both sides, were common (Alvarez 1987; Heyman n.d.). It still is not uncommon for parents who reside in a Mexican borderland town or city to send children to elementary and secondary schools in the United States. Such cross-border kinship systems, as Heyman points out, were really "a series of bilaterally related households and networks scattered between similar types of neighborhoods on both sides of the border" (n.d.:7).

Yet, after 1929, the massive repatriation and deportation policies and practices of the 1930s began to interfere with the formation and maintenance of the cross-border families. As Heyman points out, the new legal context of visa regulation that was put into effect during the heyday of the repatriation period "caused the differentiation of documented and undocumented entrants, and divided Mexican from Mexican American kin in a manner not seen in the period before 1929" (n.d.:1).

After 1929, legal citizenship rather than culture became the hallmark of ethnic identity. For many Mexicans born in the United States, immigration restrictions on Mexican kin created a they-us differentiation that interrupted the easy flow of kin between extended cross-border familial networks. As American schools under the guise of "Americanization" programs relegated the Spanish language to a secondary position and denigrated its use, self-denial processes set in. This experience led some U.S. Mexicans to change their names, anglicize their surnames, and internalize self-hatred and self-deprecation (Rodríguez 1982).

Differentiation has been repeatedly accentuated by systematic processes of deportation, repatriation, and voluntary departure, such as "Operation Wetback in 1954,"[4] or the recent immigration sweep, "Operation Jobs," in 1982. The intent of the Immigration Reform and Control Act (IRCA) passed in 1986 was to stem undocumented immigration. IRCA, however, has had no striking impact on the labor sectors of which Mexican undocumented workers are a part (Chávez 1988; Chávez et al. 1992; Cornelius 1988). What it has done is to legalize Mexican migrants, guarantee their permanent settlement, and increase the flow of individual workers and families back and forth to the United States with newly acquired legality (Cornelius 1988:4).

The more profound consequence of IRCA is that it has created further division between eligible and noneligible Mexicans. Even within the same extended family, the legalization of one family member sharply contrasts with the illegality of others. Because reform bills such as IRCA are usually followed by immigration sweeps, each roundup further emphasizes the "foreignness" of the population in Mexico, and further differentiates them from U.S. Mexicans.[5] Such demographic and political splitting between Mexican-born and U.S.-born Mexicans establishes the cultural basis for the creation of an ethnic U.S. Mexican, and the denial of cultural continuity between these populations.

CROSS-BORDER RELATIONS

Yet, despite the political and cultural divisions that have arisen, cross-border families and *clustered households*[6] continue to balance the effect of the disruption of identity and self-reference. As a result, Mexican households typically are nested within extensive kinship networks that actively engage them in the lives of relatives on both sides of the border. Because many Mexicans work in highly unstable labor markets, in their struggle to make a living they are not only forced to crisscross national boundaries, but they must also depend on one another to gain access to resources found on each side.

As Mexican families have crisscrossed the border in response to the intermittent booms and busts in the border economy, they have produced an associated phenomenon, one we term generational *hop-scotching* (Vélez-Ibáñez 1992a). In such families, one or more members of a given household are born in Mexico, and others are born in the United States. As well, one generation may be born in the United States, a second in Mexico, and a third in the United States. Although such hop-scotching has both negative and positive consequences for members of a given household, the phenomenon provides a legal advantage in gaining access to personal or institutional resources on either side of the U.S.-Mexico border.

FORMATION PROCESSES

The dynamic processes of the border economy directly impact the way local populations respond to the loss of control over the means of production. One manifestation of this loss is an increasing separation between the functions of knowledge in the workplace and the home. We may better understand the impact of this separation by examining their previous integration. For example, most Mexican families in the Southwest either have ancestors who were farmers and ranchers or were engaged in commercial or craft and manufacturing activities in a rural setting, or they have relatives who are engaged in these activities now.

Historically, these households not only produced or bartered for much of what they consumed, but their members also had to master an impressive range of knowledge and skills. To cope and adapt to changing circumstances and contexts, household members had to be generalists and possess a wide range of complex knowledge. In the countryside, many segments of the population understood the characteristics of local ecosystems—soils, plants, pets, hydrology, and weather (Sheridan 1988). Given the frailty and complexity of arid land environments, water management, flood control, and climate variations were important parts of the knowledge base for survival. As cattle producers, animal husbandry, range management, and veterinary medicine were topics that were part of the "natural systems" of household information. The maintenance of equipment made knowledge of blacksmithing and mechanics essential. As well, to avoid reliance on specialists, some knowledge and skills in construction and repair were mandatory (i.e., bodies of knowledge about building plans, masonry, carpentry, and electrical wiring, and also formulas for mixing cement, mortar, and adobe). Where there was a lack of physicians or where medical costs were prohibitive, rural and folk medical knowledge of remedies, medicinal herbs, and first aid procedures were often extensive. In time of economic and labor crises, such skills become crucial in adjusting income and searching for work. For instance, after the "Great Arizona Mine Strike" of 1983, many striking U.S.-Mexican miners still skilled in ranching became cowboys to make ends meet (O'Leary, interview with author 1991).

Taken together, these largely rural skills, experience, technical knowledge of habitat and survival, make up the adaptive strategies that we have called funds of knowledge for much of the Arizona-Sonora Mexican population.

THE IMPACT OF CAPITALIST DISLOCATIONS AND
TECHNOLOGICAL CHANGES ON ADAPTATIONS OF HOUSEHOLDS

As households became dependent on wages, the locus of work activities moved away from the home, and the funds of knowledge required of workers became increasingly specialized. Moreover, funds of knowledge that households needed for their survival and reproduction were increasingly found not within them, but distributed in their social networks or located in a variety of formal institutions to which they had to turn to solve their everyday problems. Such institutions included government offices, labor unions, and, of course, schools.

CLASS CHANGES

One paradox of funds of knowledge in urban contexts is that, although they help households, depending on their content and breadth, to be independent of the marketplace, individuals gain funds through work and through participation in labor markets. Yet, even as such funds help households obtain a degree of independence of the marketplace, there are major obstacles to their permanency or transmission from one generation to another. Succeeding generations often do not gain a complete and functional understanding of the funds that their ancestors had unless they remain within the same class segment or are able to transliterate such knowledge into a new, rewarding labor arena. Urban residents, nevertheless, often attempt symbolically to retain such funds by constructing equivalent conditions and contexts for their maintenance and transmission. Such attempts take the form of economic and ideological investments in small ranching and farming projects, which are often not profitable, but which aim to recapitulate early childhood experience. Because wages in highly segmented labor markets are low and unstable, working-class households have had to jump from one sector of the labor market to another, holding several jobs and pooling their wages to make ends meet. However, because the independence is problematic, the broad funds of knowledge alone, which they have acquired in this process, cannot guarantee their well-being or survival. Thus, the ability of households to cope in rough economic seas rests equally on the exchange relationships among them.

Depending on kin or friends also is fraught with problems. Besides the uncertainty experienced in the search for work, the frailty of having to depend on others for assistance with child care, household maintenance, and transportation leads people to make very determined efforts to enter primary labor markets. Such formal-sector jobs are prized not just because they pay better, but because they provide formal benefits that help underwrite the households' reproduction and lessen their dependence on others. This quest for stability is of single importance for U.S.-Mexican households. If they cannot find employment within primary labor markets, then they are willing to make extreme investments in education in the hope that their children will gain such an entrée. The irony is that educational institutions also serve as important mechanisms of denial for access to such labor markets.

SOCIAL DISTRIBUTION OF FUNDS OF KNOWLEDGE

Significantly, nevertheless, funds of knowledge do become part of the implicit operational and cultural system of daily life. Friends and kin often provide a safety net and substantial aid in time of crisis. Such exchanges occur in such a routine and constant fashion that people are hardly aware of them. These exchanges take a variety of forms: labor services; access to information or resources (including help in finding jobs or housing or dealing with government agencies or other institutions); and various forms of material assistance besides money, such as putting up visitors.

Small favors are a constant feature of exchange relations. However, because they are reciprocal, they balance out in the long term and are less important economically than is the exchange of information and special funds of knowledge. Indeed, help in finding jobs, housing, and better deals on goods and services, and in dealings with institutions and government agencies, is of far greater significance to survival than are the material types of aid that these households usually provide one another.

Because households depend on their social networks to cope with the borderland's complex political and changing economic environment, they are willing to invest considerable energy and resources in maintaining good relations with their members. One way they do this is through family rituals: birthdays, baptisms, confirmations, "coming out" rituals (*quinceaneras*), wedding showers, weddings, Christmas dinners, outings, and visitations. Not only do these events bring members of one's network together ritually to reaffirm their solidarity, but staging them also often requires members to cooperate by investing their labor or pooling their resources. Moreover, such rituals broadcast an important set of signals both about the sponsor's economic well-being and about the state of social relations with other members—through both lavishness and attendance.

As well, the willingness to help stage family rituals is a measure of who one can count upon for other things. These rituals form a calendrical cycle where Christmas, New Year's, and Easter are major rituals in which almost everyone participates. Life-cycle rituals, such as baptisms, confirmations, quinceaneras, weddings, and funerals, mark a secondary level of minor rituals that fit between the major rituals. Interspersed throughout these are myriad other, yet smaller, celebrations, such as birthdays, anniversaries, house warmings, and ritualized visitations. This entire calendrical cycle is carefully monitored by the households involved and gives meaning to the social relations articulated through such events. Great effort, resources, and energies go into not only organizing such events, but also evaluating their social success.

Such formal rituals are but one mechanism through which social networks are maintained. Household visits, which are as important, are themselves informal rituals. Like their more formal counterparts, the frequency of visiting and the treatment that the visitor receives are important signals about the state of social relations. This frequent contact helps both to maintain social ties and to provide a context for the exchange of information through which funds of knowledge constantly are renewed and updated.

The Emergence of the Mexican Child in Social Density

There is one other dynamic aspect that should be considered. The probability that the funds of knowledge that such clusters contain will be transmitted to the following generation rests not only on an appropriate economic and social context for their application, but also on the early expectations for learning that children gain in such contexts. Our evidence suggests that these clusters provide U.S.-Mexican children with a social platform in which they internalize these "thick" social relations and learn to have analogously "thick" social expectations.

However, because most studies of early childhood socialization have been attitudinal and not observational, the empirical record of process for Mexican children is scant. A recent study by Vélez (1983) of mother-infant interaction, however, provides some insights into the possible genesis of Mexican expectations and potentialities. Her work provides the probable link between early childhood experience and the formation of these expectations in clustered household settings, and establishes the theoretical basis for understanding the phenomenon.

The original postulate in the work asserted that there would be significant variations in the mothering styles of Mexican-American mothers and those of Anglo mothers that could be attributed to cultural expectations, and that such expectations included the probability that Mexican mothers provide more proximal stimulation to infants, are more responsive to their infants' signals, and express such differences about infant rearing in their beliefs and values (Vélez 1983:11).

In her findings, there was little difference in the frequency or quality of the actual interaction between mothers and infants. Of greater significance for the emergence of the Mexican infant's social personality was the social context of interactions, and the role that others played in the infant's early social experience (1983:80). Vélez found that, although she introduced a variety of social and economic controls to match her sample, the Mexican mothers' social density was much greater, contact with infant and mother by other relatives was significantly more frequent, and greater stimulation of the infant by others was also statistically significant. The Mexican infant had a social context packed with tactile and sound stimulation. The child was surrounded by a variety of relatives, and at the behavioral level, was seldom really alone. This last finding also was supported by the observation that, although Mexican children had their own rooms available, 92% of the Mexican children slept in their parents' room, whereas 80% of the Anglo children slept in their own rooms.

Although this was a working-class sample, we have the impression from our present study that the same phenomenon extends to middle-class Mexican-American households. It would appear that the early "thick" social context that surrounds Mexican children leads to the emergence of social expectations that are different from those of non-Mexican populations that do not have equivalent social characteristics. Such differences, we suggest, may include the internalization of many other significant object relations with more persons, an expectation of more relations with the same persons, and expectations of being attentive to, and investing emotionally in, a variety of relations. Such psychodynamic and psychosocial processes entailed in cultural expectations of *confianza* (mutual trust)[7] are the cradle from whence anticipations for exchange relations emerge. Such early experiences give cultural expectation for exchange its substance, expectations that are reinforced by ritual and other forms of exchange throughout the life cycle.

Such "thick contexts" are the social platforms in which the funds of knowledge of the cluster of households are transmitted. So, by examining how such knowledge is transmitted, we gain some insight into the cultural conflicts that may arise when Mexican children confront educational models of the dominant society that seek to reshape Mexican children culturally and socially according to its values.

FUND TRANSMISSION AND THE BASIS FOR CULTURAL CONFLICT

Further analysis of how information is transmitted to children in U.S.-Mexican households suggests that such knowledge is passed on through culturally constituted methods, that these methods have emotive implications for the self-esteem of children, and that they are possible sources of cultural conflict in the schools.

Because Mexican children are ensconced within "thick" multiple relations, they visit and become familiar with other households, households that contain other funds of knowledge and with whom they carry on a variety of social relationships. Such clustered households provide the opportunity for children to become exposed to an array of different versions of such funds. However, what is important is that the children not only are exposed to multiple domains in which funds of knowledge are used, but that they are afforded also the opportunity to experiment with them in each domain. Our studies (Vélez-Ibáñez and Greenberg 1984; Moll et al. 1988) show that the transmission process is largely an experimental one. Although adults may manifest specific portions of a fund, the organization of learning is in the hands of the children themselves. Children are expected to ask questions during the performance of household tasks. Thus, the question-answer process is directed by the child rather than by the adult. Once children receive an answer, they may emulate adults by creating play situations for practicing the learned behavior.

Another important aspect in the transmission of funds of knowledge is the wide latitude allowed for error and the encouragement that children are given to experiment further. For instance, a child's observing and "assisting" an adult repair an automobile leads to attempts by the child to experiment on other mechanical devices, as well as on "junk" engines that may be available. The usual adult direction is to "finish it yourself and try your best, no matter how long it takes." Even when the child is stuck at one point, the adult usually does not volunteer either the question or the answer. Such sequences teach children to persevere, to experiment, to manipulate, and to delay gratification.

Because there are multiple occasions for experimentation, there are also multiple opportunities to fail and to overcome that failure in different domains. Because there are a variety of contexts in which children may observe and learn to do tasks adequately, children have more than one domain in which they may be successful. A major characteristic of the transmission of funds of knowledge is that multiple household domains provide children with a zone of comfort that is familiar yet experimental, where error is not dealt with punitively and where self-esteem is not endangered. Because such transmission occurs in multiple domains, children usually can find nonstressful domains or neutral zones of comfort, where little criticism is expressed and where they will not be faulted. When an adult is impatient and judgmental, children often go to other adults in other domains who are more patient. Children thus learn very early to use a comparative approach to evaluate adults, avoiding discouraging or punitive persons because there are others available who are not so.

Because the feedback process is in the hands of the child, such zones of comfort also allow self-evaluation and self-judgment. The only exceptions are when children would be in danger or cannot physically do the tasks. Similarly, if their errors would prove costly, then children are not encouraged to experiment. Nonetheless, the outstanding characteristic of such experimentation is that children eventually develop enough familiarity with various domains to predict and manipulate them. Children learn quickly that there are constraints, but these are so obviously in their favor that such an understanding becomes the underlying basis for zones of comfort. In economic terms, such zones of comfort, and the relationships that support their expression, become the basis of confianza and place children within the appropriate cultural frame for adulthood.

The use of traditional pedagogical approaches to learning in public schools threatens the cultural frame of such zones of comfort. Our observations show that when little girls "play school" they emulate teacher-originated and -directed sequences. The children taking the role of teacher allow for markedly little active student-controlled interaction, and imitate as well the expectations of rote or uncreative responses to instruction (Tapia 1989). In addition, the school model of instruction is emphasized by parents during homework periods, with strong punitive measures either threatened or carried out if tasks are not completed. This use of the schooling model created one of the few sources of adult-child conflict in the households we observed. Such basic cultural conflict becomes further exacerbated when understood within a larger cultural framework of human emergence. For the U.S.-Mexican adult, who has emerged within both culturally constituted zones of comfort and formal educational settings, self-doubt, negation, and cultural resistance will emerge together.

CONCLUSIONS

The funds of knowledge that Mexican populations have historically acquired in the U.S.-Mexico borderland reflect the ongoing character of the organization of production and its technological basis. Consequently, the agrarian pursuits that the population followed in the rural countryside included a broad range of skills that also could be marketed in urban and industrial settings. Yet, their very success in adapting to the unstable labor markets contained the seeds of cultural demise. In moving from the countryside to the city, the social and cultural context in which their identities were forged was fundamentally altered, and the transmission of funds of knowledge, in some instances, was lost.

Yet, social exchange between households, clusters of households, and kinship networks not only continues to provide individuals access to historic funds of knowledge, but also provides them the cultural matrix for incorporating new understandings and relationships in a "Mexican" way. These funds and their functions in social relationships, thus, will continue to be characteristically "shaped" by the Mexican experience of structural changes in the economic and political environment. Case studies of Mexican families highlight differences in degrees of patriotism and religiosity. Yet, in spite of these differences, the basis of social density and the multiplicity of relations, regardless of rural-urban dimensions, occupation, or language preference, remain at the core of the way households have unfolded within the life cycle. Identity formation and emergence as Mexicans in the United States thus arises from the matrix of social relations in the clusters of households, and not from "cultural" iota as such. Such identity becomes implicitly "cultural," in that, as other works (Vélez-Ibáñez 1988) have shown, these matrices become the social platforms from whence children emerge.

POLICY IMPLICATIONS

There are several policy implications that flow from an understanding of the full range of household strategies and their probable outcomes as mentioned in this study.

Educational Policy Reform

The implications of our finding for educational policy reform seem clear. What is needed is a critical reexamination of the cultural basis of evaluation and assessment of U.S.-Mexican children, a close analysis of the cultural basis of instruction and pedagogy, and field testing of the nature of the social relations between U.S.-Mexican children, their parents, and the educational institutions that serve them.

Concerning evaluation and assessment, we should pay some attention to more dynamic forms of assessment that seek to measure children's learning potential. The process would use mediated learning practices within the assessment context, with the assessor actively participating in the teaching of skills to the examinee. Such an approach is based on the modification of the examinee, not on stable, easily measurable characteristics. Using this approach, Feurestein (1979) shows significant gains for educable mentally retarded students through instruction based on learning potential.

Second, the very basis of instruction should be reexamined. In contrast with the traditional, highly individualized competitive instruction systems, "cooperative learning systems" might be more appropriate for children for whom such social interaction is both a highly developed skill and an expectation. Such systems are based on the idea that students accomplish their academic tasks in heterogeneous groups, where, although the tasks are usually assigned by the teacher, each student's effort contributes to the total group effort. Cooperative learning may be an important innovation in relation to education and culture for three reasons. First, it may be more compatible with the cultural norms and values of U.S.-Mexican children, and it seems highly compatible with their learning experiences. Second, it may contribute to their interethnic relations in the classroom. Third, and most important, such approaches lead to much higher academic gains for minority students (Kagan 1986).

Next, both the social basis of instruction between children and teachers and the social basis of relations between teacher and parents must be carefully considered. If, as we have pointed out, the expectations of children and parents in relations with others are based on social density, then the school-based model of instruction is in direct contradiction and opposition to these expectations. If anything, the school-based model of instruction is organized around single-stranded teacher-to-student interaction, in which parental involvement is restricted to occasional contact or is defined within highly formalized contexts such as parent-teacher organizations. There is little in the triad of children, teacher, and parents that cross-cuts either generational, class, educational, ethnic, or status differences except the single strand of informational and assessment authority directed by the teacher.

Last, the implications for teacher training and the elimination of institutionalized "literacy fracturing" seem paramount. We should pay greater attention to providing teachers with opportunities to learn how to incorporate the funds of knowledge from their student's households into learning modules that approximate the total reality of the population. As well, literacy instruction must maximize its use of the available literacy and skills within the home as a means to tap the vast funds of knowledge that parents have, but are seldom given the opportunity to share and express.

NOTES

1. We use the term Mexican to describe both those born in Mexico and those of Mexican parentage born in the United States. Although Chicano or Mexican American also are used for those born in the United States of Mexican heritage, Mexican is the generally preferred term used by the U.S.-born population. While there is an extended discussion that links the rise of ethnic consciousness to the collapse of rural and commercial control by Mexicans in the United States in the 1880s (see Camarillo 1979; Griswold de Castillo 1984) and their encapsulation in urban ghettos, our position is that this leaves out the importance of cross-border relations both due to the constant re-introduction of kin and culture from Mexico and due to the obvious retention of the Spanish language over time. Mexican households continue to define themselves as Mexicans culturally and, more important, socially (see Garcia 1982:295–314; Vélez-Ibáñez 1983).

2. The deficiency model of minority groups, either directly or indirectly, underlies most instructional strategies concerning culturally different populations. For example, Spanish-speaking "minority" students placed in so-called ability groups are exposed to learning based on the assumption that they are not "ready" for comprehension and must be treated to an array of decoding exercises in which text-bound skills are underscored and a generally reductionist, "tiny-bite" approach to skills acquisition is emphasized. Despite the fact that many Spanish-speaking students have great comprehensive abilities in Spanish, the deficiency model excludes already-developed comprehension as a strength and substitutes a learning model that is non-contextual, piecemeal, and hierarchical.

3. The ten states that make up the U.S.-Mexican border region are, on the Mexican side, Baja California Norte, Baja California Sur, Sonora, Chihuahua, Nuevo Leon, and Tamaulipas; and on the U.S. side, California, Arizona, New Mexico, and Texas.

4. "Operation Wetback" was an INS-sponsored program of expulsion of undocumented Mexican labor during fiscal year 1954 and allegedly resulted in the departure of 1,300,000 "illegals," according to INS authorities. See U.S. Department of Justice (1954:31).

5. The cultural implication for some U.S. Mexicans is to differentiate themselves as "American Mexicans" from the *mojados* (wetbacks). Analogous processes become set in motion for Mexicans in Mexico with differentiations made between themselves as real Mexicanos and the despised *pochos* from the United States.

6. One important type of variant further removed from the border in this regard is that familial "clustering" of households, or extension of families beyond the nucleated household, increases rather than lessens with each succeeding generation. We have termed these *cross-border clustered households* because 77.1% of our sample have relatives in Mexico, and of the total sample, a significant proportion (61%) organize their extended kin relations in the United States in a clustered household arrangement of dense bilateral kin and maintain kin ties with their Mexican relatives. Recent studies (Keefe 1979:360; Keefe et al. 1978, 1979; Griswold del Castillo 1984:129-132) have shown that, despite class, Mexican extended families in the United States become more extensive and stronger with generational advancement, acculturation, and socioeconomic mobility. These findings as well are supported by findings in a national study that has found that the clustered residential households we will be describing for Tucson, Arizona, were more common among U.S.-born Mexicans than they were among Mexican immigrants or Anglos (see Vélez-Ibáñez 1992).

7. *Confianza* is a cultural construct indicating the willingness to engage in generalized reciprocity. For a full discussion, see Vélez-Ibáñez and Greenberg (1984:10–16).

REFERENCES

Alvarez, Robert. 1987. *Familia: Migration and Adaptation in Baja and Alta, California.* Berkeley: University of California Press.

Camarillo, Albert. 1979. *Chicanos in a Changing Society: From Mexican Pueblos to American Barrios in Santa Barbara and Southern California, 1848–1930.* Cambridge, Mass.: Harvard University Press.

Chávez, Leo R. 1988. Settlers and Sojourners: The Case of Mexicans in the United States. *Human Organization* 47(2):95–108.

Chávez, Leo R., Esteban T. Flores, and Marta López-Garza. 1992. Here Today, Gone Tomorrow? Undocumented Settlers and Immigration Reform. *Human Organization* (in press).

Cook-Gumperz, John, and J. J. Gumperz. 1992. From Oral to Written Culture: The Transition to Literacy. In *Variation in Writing.* M. F. Whitehead, ed. Hillsdale, N.J.: Lawrence Erlbaum.

Cornelius, Wayne A. 1988. *The Role of Mexican Labor in the North American Economy of the 1990s.* Paper prepared for the Fourth Annual Emerging Issues Program for State Legislative Leaders: "The North American Economy in the 1990s." University of California, San Diego.

Diéz-Canedo, Jesus. 1981. *Undocumented Migration to the United States: A New Perspective.* Dolores E. Mills, trans. Albuquerque: Center for Latin American Studies, University of New Mexico.

Fernández-Kelly, Patricia. 1987. Technology and Employment along the U.S. Mexican Border. In *The United States and Mexico: Face to Face with New Technology.* Cathryn L. Thorup, ed. Pp. 149–166. New Brunswick, N.J.: Transaction Books.

Feurestein, Reuven. 1979. *The Dynamic Assessment of Retarded Performers: The Learning Potential Assessment Device, Theory, Instruments, and Techniques.* Baltimore, Md.: University Park Press.

García, John A. 1982. Ethnicity and Chicanos: Measurement of Ethnic Identification, Identity, and Consciousness. *Hispanic Journal of Behavioral Sciences* 43(4):295–314.

García y Griego, Manuel. 1983. *Mexico and the United States: Migration, History, and the Idea of Sovereignty.* El Paso: Center for Interamerican and Border Studies, University of Texas.

González-Archegia, Bernardo. 1987. *California-Mexico Linkages.* Paper presented at the First Annual California-Mexico Business Conference, Los Angeles.

Greenberg, James B. 1990. Funds of Knowledge: Historical Constitution, Social Distribution, and Transmission. In *Restructuring to Promote Learning in America's Schools: Selected Readings.* Vol. II. William T. Pink, Donna S. Ogle, and Beau F. Jones, eds. Pp. 317–326. Elmhurst, Ill.: North Central Regional Educational Laboratory.

Griswold del Castillo, Richard. 1984. *La Familia: Chicano Families in the Urban Southwest, 1848 to the Present.* Notre Dame, Ind.: University of Notre Dame.

Heyman, Josiah. n.d. The Power of the United States Border Over Mexican Lives: The Case of Cross-Bordership. In *The U.S.-Mexico Border in Anthropological Context.* C. Vélez-Ibáñez, J. Greenberg, and R. Trotter, eds. (in press).

Kagan, Susan. 1986. Cooperative Learning and Socio-Cultural Factors in Schooling. In *Young Language: Social and Cultural Factors in Schooling Language Minority Students.* S. Kagan, ed. Pp. 36–47. Los Angeles: California State University.

Keefe, Susan E. 1979. Urbanization, Acculturation, and Extended Family Ties: Mexican Americans in Cities. *American Ethnologist* 6(2):349–365.

Keefe, Susan E., Amado Padilla, and Manuel L. Carlos. 1978. *Emotional Support Systems in Two Cultures: A Comparison of Mexican Americans and Anglos Americans*, Occasional Paper No. 7, Los Angeles: Spanish Speaking Mental Health Research Center, UCLA.

———. 1979. The Mexican American Extended Family as an Emotional Support System. *Human Organization* 38(2):144–152.

Martínez, Oscar. 1983. *The Foreign Orientation of the Mexican Border Economy. Border Perspectives, 2*. El Paso: Center for Interamerican and Border Studies, University of Texas.

———. 1988. *Troublesome Border*. Tucson: University of Arizona Press.

Moll, Luís C., Carlos G.Vélez-Ibáñez, and James B. Greenberg. 1988. *Community Knowledge and Classroom Practice: Combining Resources for Literacy Instruction*. Unpublished MS, Innovative Approaches Research Project Grant, Development Associates.

Porras, A. Salas. n.d. *Crisis, Maquiladoras y Estructura Sociopolitica en Chihuahua, Sonora y Baja California*. Unpublished MS.

Rodríguez, Richard. 1982. *Hunger of Memory. The Education of Richard Rodriguez: An Autobiography*. New York: D. R. Godine.

Sheridan, Thomas E. 1988. *Where the Dove Calls: The Political Ecology of a Peasant Community in Northwestern Mexico*. Tucson: University of Arizona Press.

Tapia, Javier. 1989. *The Recreation of School at Home Through Play*. Unpublished MS, Bureau of Applied Research.

Tiano, Susan B. 1985. *Export Processing, Women's Work, and the Employment Problem in Developing Countries: The Case of the Maquiladora Program in Northern Mexico, 22*. El Paso: Center for Interamerican and Border Studies, University of Texas.

U.S. Department of Justice. 1954. *Annual Report of the Immigration and Naturalization Service*. Washington, D.C.: U.S. Department of Justice.

Vélez, Maria T. 1983. *The Social Context of Mothering: A Comparison of Mexican American and Anglo Mother Infant Interaction Patterns*. Ph.D. dissertation, Wright Institute of Psychology.

Vélez-Ibáñez , Carlos G. 1983. *Bonds of Mutual Trust: The Cultural Systems of Rotating Credit Associations among Urban Mexicans and Chicanos*. New Brunswick, N.J.: Rutgers University Press.

———. 1987. Mecanismos de intercambio incorporados entre los mexicanos en la zona fronteriza de Estados Unidos. In *Memoria XII, Simposio de Historia y Antropologia de Sonora*. O. Martinez et al., eds. Pp. 413–482. Hermosillo, Sonora: Universidad de Sonora.

———. 1988a. *Forms and Functions among Mexicans in the Southwest: Implications for Classroom Use*. Paper presented at the Invited Session, Forms and Functions of Funds of Knowledge within Mexican Households in the Southwest, American Anthropological Association Annual Meeting, Phoenix.

———. 1988b. Networks of Exchange Among Mexicans in the U.S. and Mexico: Local Level Mediating Responses to National and International Transformation. *Urban Anthropology and Studies of Cultural Systems and World Economic Development* 17(1):27–51.

———. 1989. *Transmission and Patterning of Funds of Knowledge: Shaping and Emergence of Confianza in U.S. Mexican Children*. Paper presented at Society for Applied Anthropology, Annual Meeting, Santa Fe.

———. 1992a. Plural Strategies of Survival and Cultural Formation in U.S. Mexican Households in a Region of Dynamic Transformation: The U.S.- Mexico Borderlands. *In Diagnosing America*. Shep Foreman, ed. (in press).

———. 1992b. Problem Solving and Collaboration: A Model for Applied Anthropology from the Field. In *Discovering Anthropology*. Daniel R. Gross, ed. Pp. 402–403. Mountain View, Calif.: Mayfield Publishing.

Vélez-Ibáñez, Carlos G., and James B. Greenberg. 1984. *Multidimensional Functions of Non-Market Forms of Exchange among Mexicans/Chicanos in Tucson, Arizona*. Unpublished MS, National Science Foundation.

———. 1990. *Formation and Transformation of Funds of Knowledge Among U.S. Mexican Households in the Context of the Borderlands*. Paper presented at the American Anthropological Association Annual Meeting, Washington, D C.

Wolf, Eric R. 1966. *Peasants*. Englewood Cliffs, N.J.: Prentice Hall.

16

Habitus and Cultural Identity: Home/School Relationships in Rural France

Deborah Reed-Danahay

Discontinuity between the culture of the school and the culture of the home, particularly at the level of the elementary school, is an important theme in education. The theory of "habitus" as developed by Pierre Bourdieu, with its related concepts of cultural capital and symbolic violence,[1] helps us to understand some of the structural forces shaping educational outcomes that are rooted in class-based discontinuities between home and school. Ethnographic studies by Shirley Brice Heath (1983), Annette Lareau (1989), and Régine Sirota (1988) provide further evidence of the ways in which home/school differences in modes of communication, knowledge and uses of literacy, and cultural values can place some children at a disadvantage. These studies have, however, given less attention to the active role of peers in shaping responses to schooling than to the attitudes of parents and teachers.[2] In this chapter, I adopt a "child-centered" analysis that examines the ways in which children negotiate between the values of the school and the values of their parents. I argue that educational outcomes for children in the rural French *commune* of Lavialle cannot be sufficiently understood with a theory of habitus alone. From the fall of 1980 to the end of 1981, I lived in Lavialle and conducted an ethnographic and historical study of this community, its families, and its school. I have since returned for visits to follow up on this research, most recently in the summers of 1996 and 1998. My research in Lavialle suggests that home/school discontinuity can be reinforced by families as well as by schools. Moreover, it is the children at school who must cope with the conflicting demands of each setting. This approach is informed by a situational approach to cultural identity, which views it as shifting and multiple.

My main focus here is on the importance of peer groups and of local cultural values on the educational strategies of children and their families in Lavialle, which I have also explored in much detail elsewhere (cf. Reed-Danahay 1996). The children in this community do not, as a rule, excel in school. Few acquire a university-level education, and most enter farming or work in trades. In order to understand the link between the educational strategies of families and children in Lavialle and the poor school performance of Lavialle children, it is necessary to rethink the school versus home dichotomy. It cannot be argued that Lavialle's children do not continue on to higher education or succeed in school simply because there is discontinuity between the home environment and the school environment. This discontinuity must be the object of study and not taken for granted. We must examine, for instance, why teachers continue to criticize parents as indifferent to schooling (see also Reed-Danahay and Anderson-Levitt 1991), and why parents continue to criticize teachers as being indifferent to their children.

France is an interesting and instructive place to examine these issues, because it has had a long and highly centralized primary education system that reinforced "distance" between home and school in several ways. First, educational policies and curriculum in France are formed at national or regional levels, with no room for the input of local families. Second, teachers are hired by educational authorities at regional administrative levels, so that local people have no say over the hiring of teachers. And third, what goes on in the classroom is not officially open to discussion with parents in most French schools. Formal channels exist at national levels for some parent advocacy groups to influence policy, but at the level of the local elementary school, official parental input is quite limited. This system is highly stratified, as well as centralized, and has been subject to repeated criticisms for its rigid hierarchy.[3]

The French system of education, which had built a primary school in every French commune by the beginning of the twentieth century, must be viewed within the context of the social, economic, and cultural conditions in which these schools operated. Linguistic and cultural diversity has long been characteristic of rural France, and France retained a significant rural population much longer into the twentieth century than did other industrial nations, such as England or the United States. Each commune (the smallest administrative unit) in France was required to maintain a public primary school beginning in the 1880s. These schools spread the French language and French national identity at the same time that they taught basic literacy skills. Men and women who have attended French village schools frequently mention the abrupt discontinuity between home and school that they experienced. For children who had learned regional languages and dialects at home, schooling often meant their first exposure to the French language and to the culture of literacy in general. This is expressed by Breton writer Pierre-Jakèz Hélias, who describes his introduction to schooling in the beginning of the twentieth century: "The first day of school was, of course, approached with apprehension. We would have barely crossed the threshold and there we were, in another world" (1978, 143). Hélias, who eventually became a university professor at a time when very few rural children even completed primary school, is ambivalent about becoming educated, however, and writes of the costs of estrangement from social origins that this entails (see Reed-Danahay 1997a).

For a long time, French education operated on a two-tiered system, one geared toward high school and university, the other geared toward the completion of schooling at the primary level. This system persisted well into the middle of the twentieth century. In order to enter high school, a child had to attend a school that provided a class oriented toward secondary education and had to pass an exam, the Certificat d'Etudes Primaires (CEP). During the early part of the twentieth century, most farm children in France failed to pass or even take this exam, in large part because there were not many rural schools offering this type of instruction or encouraging children to take it. Even now, the educational levels of rural children are much lower than those of middle-class urban or suburban children. A recent survey (Estrade 1995) shows that a father's profession is closely correlated with a child's attainment of a high school diploma or its equivalent (in France, the *Bac* or *Baccalaureat*). Only 28 percent of adults aged twenty-eight to thirty-nine whose fathers are farmers have this diploma. In contrast, 72 percent of the adult children of men who work in upper-level management (*les cadres*) have reached this level of credentialing.

HABITUS AND CULTURAL IDENTITY

Pierre Bourdieu and his colleagues (Bourdieu and Passeron 1964, 1977; Sirota 1988) have argued that home/school discontinuity in the French educational system perpetuates social inequality because it favors middle-class students and their families. Middle-class homes have more in common with the school environment than those of children from other social classes. Members of the working classes in France fail to succeed in school, Bourdieu argues, because they lack the types of social knowledge and symbolic capital valued by the schools, which operate as "credentialing" mechanisms to officially validate the social power of those who already have power. Those who fail to succeed in school mainly do so by opting out of the system, rather than being forced to leave. Because of their "misrecognition" (Bourdieu's term) of the objective structures of power and symbolic violence encountered at school, children from minority and lower-class families internalize their failures and "choose" to enter low-level careers—thereby contributing to social and cultural reproduction. It is the habitus that shapes one's orientations toward the future, and this is formed in the milieu of the family. Those with a more middle-class habitus are more likely to succeed in schooling because their class habitus most closely resembles that of the teachers and school. In this line of reasoning, Lavialle's children do not succeed in school because they have acquired a habitus that does not equip them for school success.

For Bourdieu, habitus is defined as a system of predispositions to action and belief acquired through what he calls "inculcation" in the family. External "conditions of existence" (which include class position), mediated by the family, determine the structures of the habitus "which in turn become the basis of perception and appreciation of all subsequent experience" (Bourdieu and Passeron 1977, 78). Social

systems and social actors are closely linked in this theory. Bourdieu has more recently written that "the legitimization of the social order . . . results from the fact
that agents apply to the objective structures of the social world structures of perception and appreciation that have emerged from these objective structures and tend
therefore to see the world as self-evident" (1990, 135). Bourdieu argues that the
educational strategies of families from different social strata, determined by their
variously inculcated habituses, play a major role in educational outcomes. All strategies, according to his theory, are primarily aimed at processes of social and cultural reproduction. Bourdieu writes that strategies are used by families "to produce
and reproduce themselves, that is, to create and perpetuate their unit, and thus their
existence as groups, which is almost always, and in all societies, the condition of
the perpetuation of their position in the social space" (1990, 74).

Bourdieu's theory of habitus has made significant contributions to a structural
analysis of social hierarchy, and points toward the direction of understanding social practice, but it does not sufficiently capture the dynamic nature of "everyday"
behavior by social actors. The concept of habitus implies that each person has one
socially acquired habitus. There is no room in this theory for an understanding of
the educational strategies of children, and of the ways in which they straddle the
demands of their families and those of the school. The notion of inculcated
predispositons to behavior does not easily explain the complexities of situational
identity or of multiple cultural and social identities acquired by an individual over
time, or the active role that children can play in their own socialization. Children
and their parents cannot, however, be viewed as having just one cultural identity.
One type of identity may be appropriate for children at school, while another might
be appropriate at home.

Growing up in class-stratified and multiethnic societies is, in part, a process of
learning to manipulate one's "selfhood" in various settings (Giddens 1991; Cohen
1994). John Ogbu (1982) has usefully addressed issues of minority/dominant class
education by clarifying the role that cultural discontinuities between home and
school play in school outcomes. He suggests that members of minority groups may
adopt a stance of opposition to dominant culture, and writes that

> subordinate group members . . . may . . . create certain cultural and linguistic features
> that differentiate them from their superiors in order to maintain their identity and sense
> of security or out of dislike for their superiors. . . . They know a good deal about the
> culture of the dominant group but do not necessarily practice it, because their con-
> vention dictates that they should not act like members of the dominant group. (300)

Ogbu suggests that members of subordinate groups are "bicultural" because of their
knowledge of dominant culture. Such a concept of one person being able to manipulate different social identities depending upon the situation avoids dichotomies
like school culture versus home culture.

What Ogbu describes is very similar to the case in Lavialle. Most inhabitants of
Lavialle do not want to practice the culture of the middle classes. Lavialle's school

is a site for the negotiation of social and cultural identity, and for the construction of relationships between family, community, and state. It is around these processes that relations of power and resistance are shaped in Lavialle. The school and home environments of Lavialle's children have coexisted for a very long time. Childhood is in large part defined during the late twentieth century as the time when one is in school, with adulthood being partly defined by the completion of formal education. There continues to be a wide gap in Lavialle between the ways of the school (values and modes of communication and material culture) and the ways of the home, despite, however, years of mutual contact. Part of this is due to the refusal of inhabitants in Lavialle to adopt the middle-class modes of communication and values promoted by the teachers.

LAVIALLE: PLACE AND IDENTITY

Lavialle is a dairy farming community in the Auvergne region of south central France. It is a composed of seventeen small hamlets or villages that are spread out over an area of several miles, and its population is approximately 370. While there are residents who are not farmers, and who work in either artisanal occupations or for small firms in the area, almost all of Lavialle's residents are native to the local region and connected through kin ties to farm families. The center of Lavialle, from the nearest urban area, is about a three-quarters-of-an-hour drive by car along a two-lane highway that cuts through the township, and is a place of fields, trees, houses, and barns. Due to the winding roads within Lavialle, it might take up to twenty minutes to drive from one end of the township to the other. The houses and barns are clustered into the villages, and a series of fields separate each village.

Social identity in Lavialle is connected primarily to family and kinship ties, with occupational, spatial, residential, gender, and political divisions being secondary to kinship. Identity for the people who live in Lavialle and consider themselves to be "natives" (and this characterizes the vast majority of the population) is formed in relationship to various levels—that of the family (household as well as kindred), that of the village where one lives, that of the township, that of the local region (where most social life occurs), and that of the wider region of Auvergne. Beyond that, there is French identity. People in Lavialle most often refer to their village as the place where they live, rather than to Lavialle as a larger unit, except for those who live in the main village, also called "Lavialle." In order to understand home/school relationships, these multiple levels of identity must be taken into consideration, as must the multiple sites for the formation of identity. School is just one of these sites. It occupies many hours during a child's life, but is only one among many settings for social learning, which include households, Catholic religious instruction (catechism lessons), mass media, and peer groups.

Lavialle's school was built in the late 1880s, and is located in the central village. For several decades, there were three public schools in Lavialle. There were also various religious schools (Catholic) that some children attended in nearby towns.

My historical research has shown that these different schools, located in different parts of the township of Lavialle, had different constellations of home/school relationships. With population decline in Lavialle, especially following World War II, two of the schools closed in the 1960s, leaving only the main primary school in the central village open. When I first studied this school, the teachers lived in an apartment on the top floor, which they shared with the mayor's office, the communal archives, and the school's kitchen. This arrangement reinforced the role of the school building as a symbol for the identity of the *commune* as a political unit, and as a secular counterpoint to the Catholic Church as symbol of the *commune* as a religious unit.

Despite its small size, Lavialle has persisted as a vital social and economic system up until the present. The population has aged, but there are a significant number of young families. The school had about thirty students when I first studied it in 1980–81, and today in the late 1990s, even though total population of the *commune* has decreased by about fifty. This is an indication of the relative stability of the active adult population, as well as of the birthrate. Those children who attended Lavialle's primary school during my first fieldwork there in the early 1980s have now entered adulthood. Several of these former pupils are married and have children of their own. Children from that cohort have remained interested in farming, and in each case where a farm family needed an heir, this has been ensured. There are, therefore, several young farm households, and farms that might have been predicted two decades ago to die out are still managing to persist.

SCHOOLING IN LAVIALLE

The educational levels of children in Lavialle, particularly that of boys, is much lower than the national average. Few adults there have attended college, or even completed a high school education (*lycée*). Those with diplomas most often have technical degrees. The children who do attend college tend to leave and enter professional careers in urban areas. In order to understand how the educational strategies of Lavialle children and their parents are linked to life trajectories for these children, it is necessary to rethink some common assumptions about the nature of school versus home relationships. Often, school and home are assumed to be at odds with each other, with the values of school conflicting with those at home. We often lose sight of the fact that schools and contemporary families have developed in relationship (and in reaction) to one another. If we take a child-centered approach to this relationship, rather than one based on the perspectives of adults, this becomes clearer. Children spend time at home and at school, and they must balance the demands of parents and teachers.

Children in Lavialle must adjust to new rules, meanings, behavioral codes, and symbols of authority and power when they enter school. At home, they learn to be members of families. At school, they learn how to be both French and Laviallois—and begin to form a view of themselves in relation to people outside the local region. Schooling has existed in Lavialle for over a century, and although most people in Lavialle do not wholly identify with the values of the school, it would be misleading to see home and school in purely antithetical terms. They are best seen in relation to each other.

The teachers whom I have observed and interviewed in Lavialle reinforce the chasm between urban middle-class life and rural life in Lavialle. Through subtle and not so subtle ways, they criticize Lavialle families and their mode of life. At the same time, however, the families and children of Lavialle have adopted modes of resisting these messages. The pupils in Lavialle's primary school undermine the "symbolic violence" (Bourdieu and Passeron 1977) of the school through active strategies of peer group solidarity and passive strategies of resistance to teachers. For all children in Lavialle, going to school has to do with growing up, and it is, in many ways, a part of local culture. Most of the pupils in Lavialle's school have parents and grandparents who attended the same classrooms in the same building when they were children, which instills an important sense of continuity. Schooling is an expected part of everyone's life, and an institution through which all members of the community have passed.

There are three main "sites" of learning in the school: the classroom, the school lunchroom, and the playground (see Reed-Danahay 1996). Each of these settings has a particular constellation of home and school relationship. The children, therefore, receive a variety of sometimes-conflicting messages at school. In the classroom, the emphasis is on the intentional teaching of various literacy skills and moral values. In the lunchroom, the emphasis is on middle-class codes of etiquette, historically based bourgeois family forms, and self-control. On the playground, the emphasis is on the division between work and play, peer interaction, and the culture of childhood in Lavialle. As the children move throughout the space and time of the school day, they negotiate their identities with each other and with the teachers in these different contexts. Here, I will only discuss these issues as they are played out in the classroom setting.

CLASSROOM STRATEGIES

Let me turn to some illustrative examples of student behavior at Lavialle's elementary school as I first observed it in the 1980–81 and 1981–82 school years. In the classroom, the teacher tried to foster values of individualism and competition among the students, but the children resisted this through covert forms of cooperative behavior. Such behaviors reflected family- and peer-based forms of socialization. Group behavior was closely monitored by the teacher, in an attempt to reinforce his authority. For example, after the class had taken a *dictée* from the teacher (dictation for grammar and handwriting practice), the teacher would later harshly judge and criticize each child for his or her faults in front of the entire class. The teacher made use of the techniques of ridicule and embarrassment with the hopes of sham-ing the students to do better. Such a technique relies upon a notion of competi-tion and values of individualism. From the perspectives of both children and their parents, who harshly criticized such methods, this was not a highly valued form of behavior. Lavialle parents do not use methods of ridicule to discipline their chil-dren.[4] They are especially lax in their discipline of young children.

Similar methods of teaching by use of public ridicule were used by the teacher during a math lesson that I have described in detail elsewhere (Reed-Danahay 1987 and 1996). In a typical situation, the students worked on math problems in unison as the teacher gave each assignment. They were to work out their problems on a slate at the same time, and then show their answers in unison when the teacher shouted a prompt. Those who got wrong answers were subject to critical comments in an attempt to shame them in front of their peers. This competitive atmosphere of the French classroom, which has also been described in French fiction and mem-oir, was resisted by the students in Lavialle.

I have observed both in my earlier fieldwork and in more recent visits that par-ents in Lavialle frequently criticize teachers in the presence of their children, and set up a "we-they" dichotomy between the families and the teachers. The children construct a similar boundary between home and school. They accomplish this not through outright resistance, but through passive forms of resistance. Children be-haved in an overtly passive manner while actively pursuing social ties and aid from peers. The children did not openly resist schoolwork; rather, they tried to provide proper answers in class, and did their homework. In many ways, however, they did no more than the minimum that was expected of them by their teachers. The chil-dren also behaved as a group, through cooperative behaviors that undermined the teachers' authority and influence. For example, pupils often helped each other with problems if the teacher had to leave the room for a few minutes. Older pupils guided younger ones. Whenever possible, children made sure that their work conformed to that of their peers—straining their necks to see what the others were doing. Rarely did a child go to the teacher for help; most often it was to another child that one would turn. This is understandable, since a child was in danger of being mocked by the teacher if he or she did not follow instructions carefully. From the child's perspective, the safest route was to rely on peers. Through this, the teacher's emphasis on the individual learner competing with her or her peers for achieve-ment was constantly undermined. A strategy of encouraging children to come and work with him on an individual basis would have enabled the teacher to establish better individual rapport with children and to encourage the better students. But this did not occur.

Two of the children's speech behaviors in class illustrate their passive resistance to the teacher. First, the children commonly used the third-person pronoun (on or one) to refer to themselves, rather than the first person singular (je or I). The teacher often tried to correct them in this usage, with such questions as "Why do you say *on?* Was it not you alone who did this? Come now, say 'je.' " This use of a more passive voice is common among inhabitants of Lavialle, who use the *on* form to connote both I and we. This speech form allows for vagueness of meaning, and emphasizes a group rather than the individual. In the classroom, it subverts the emphasis on individual learning and achievement at the same time that it connects the child/speaker to a social group. Other cultural values support the use of *on* in Lavialle. First, those who are pretentious and who put on airs are criticized in Lavialle, where the value of being *simple* (modest and down-to-earth) is high. To use the first-person pronoun accents the individual and his or her achievements, something to be discouraged. Second, people in Lavialle are also secretive and discreet in giving out information about each other—a consequence of living in a face-to-face society where privacy is at a premium. Using the more vague form of speech *on* also fits in with this value. Although *on* appears to be a passive form of speech in comparison with *je*, if viewed within the wider context of Lavialle social life, it can be seen as part of an active, defensive strategy aimed at guarding local culture from outside intrusions. With their use of the form *on* in class, the children were using a local speech form associated with "home" culture in the context of school. Their continued use of this form despite the teacher's protests shows their desire to conform to their parents' speech behaviors rather than to those of their teacher.

Children also had a habit of whispering in the classroom, especially during formal instruction in math and French lessons. They spoke very softly to the teacher, seeming to adopt a posture of timidity and respect. This was not encouraged by the teacher, however, who often demanded that children speak up more loudly. When I asked the teacher about this, he told me that he had observed the new children who entered the school taking their cue from their older peers. He was frustrated at not being able to change this pattern, despite repeated reprimands. Whispering behavior was, thus, learned from peers, and younger children adopted the habit after observing the older students. Although this behavior appears, at first glance, to reflect timidity and does show that children were somewhat fearful of the teacher, it had the effect of strengthening group ties among the children (all whispering) versus the teacher. Again, this undermined the teacher's attempts to encourage individual children to outshine their peers. Whispering in class and the use of the *on* as a personal pronoun are both cultural practices pointing toward group, rather than individual identity.

PEER RELATIONS AND CULTURAL IDENTITY

These classroom strategies adopted by the children reflect two important factors in home/school relationships in Lavialle: the peer group and the cultural value of social manipulation associated with the verb *se debrouiller* (meaning variously to "make out" or to "make do").[5] Boys and girls of the same age make the transitions between home and school together; they also provide each other with a bridge between the two realms. Parents are not present at school, and teachers are not present at home. But other children are present in both places. It is the peer group that provides the continuity between the seeming discontinuity of the home and school. Strong peer group solidarity is encouraged by Lavialle families, but discouraged by the teachers. This solidarity persists into adulthood and plays a significant role alongside the family in the social and cultural reproduction of Lavialle social life. It is clearly demonstrated through the behaviors of the children at school, who reinforce this strong peer solidarity among themselves. It is also reinforced through other local cultural practices in Lavialle outside of schooling. Older children and adolescents in Lavialle—*les jeunes*—are encouraged by families to socialize together as a group. Strong peer friendships are formed during this time. Successive cohorts of eighteen year olds organize a community festival, which is accompanied by ritual activities accenting the group's transition to young adulthood (Reed-Danahay 1997b). Agemates (known as *les classards*) continue to have strong bonds well into adulthood, expressed ritually through regular meals that they organize together in local restaurants.

The concept of *se debrouiller*, while not specifically dealing with identity per se, captures the fluid nature of social life in Lavialle and expresses strategies of resistance to forms of power and social control. This French term is used by the inhabitants of Lavialle to express various means of coping, making do, and outwitting obstacles. It is central to an understanding of strategies of resistance and accommodation in Lavialle, and implies both "making do" and "making out." When children are helping each other behind the backs of the teachers in Lavialle's primary school, they are practicing *debrouillardise*, which is a culturally acceptable way of "making do" or coping with the teachers. The person who is good at this practice is highly valued among the Laviallois, and believed to be successful. *Se debrouiller* is a form of what James C. Scott (1985) labels "everyday forms of resistance" and also of what Michel de Certeau (1988) calls "tactics." The value of "making do," which can imply both simply coping with adversity or more actively outwitting it, involves an active strategy of behavior that helps one adapt to new circumstances.

PROFILE: LUC

Twenty-year-old Luc Bissot is now completing his training in agriculture. He didn't do well in school, something attributed by his mother both to bad teachers and to his own lack of motivation. She considers him smart, but says that he just isn't motivated to do things he has no interest in. He is, however, interested in agriculture. When I visited his family at their farm in Lavialle during the summer of 1998, Luc was busily taking care of his animals and other activities, while the rest of us were at the table enjoying a Sunday dinner. His father runs the dairy farm, but Luc has his own animals that he raises for slaughter, he also cures ham, and has beehives, and is able to sell his products for some income. It is becoming obvious that Luc will want to assume the family farm when his father retires in about fifteen years.

The Bissot family is prosperous, and politically important in Lavialle. Luc's father, Marc Bissot, is a dairy farmer in his late forties who sits on the town council, as did his father. Marie Bissot, Luc's mother, is from a dairy farming family in a nearby village, also in the *commune* of Lavialle and is active at church. Luc is the eldest of two children. For the time being, as his father did before him, he will work along with his father, and manage his own small activities on the side. When Luc was a toddler, Marc drove a truck for a local dairy, and picked up milk from the local farms. When his own father retired, Marc began to devote full-time attention to the farm, even though his father continued to assist him in his retirement.

Considered a "youth" in Lavialle (a loose category that includes both older adolescents and young adults), Luc has a group of friends in the local region (who are still unmarried like him) with whom he socializes on the weekends. When asked, his parents will say that they want Luc to be free to choose his own career. They are, in fact, not receptive to my own musings to them about socialization strategies that encourage children to stay in farming. They are, however, glad that Luc has chosen agriculture. Given the socialization strategies of his family and of Lavialle in general, and the economic strength of his family's farm in particular, it is not surprising that he made this "choice."

One could explain this in terms of habitus. Bourdieu (1972) has examined the marriage strategies of French farmers, in which the "right" mate is generally chosen in a seemingly effortless way, in terms of habitus. He has also, as I referred to previously, used habitus as an explanation for the discontinuity between home and school that results in low educational levels for farm children. According to this theory, Luc acquired a habitus in his milieu that predisposed him to want a farming career and put him at a disadvantage vis-à-vis schooling because his class habitus was not the one valued by the school. It is, as Bourdieu would put, a choice that wasn't a choice. But I think this is too simplistic. To get from birth to the stage he is in now, Luc was exposed to many settings for social learning—school, his peer group, television, and music, in addition to his family. He has not blindly followed in his father's footsteps due to an internalized predisposition. Both his father and grandfather are well-read and astute observers of the world. It is necessary to recognize that Luc has been a social actor in his own right in this process. In an era of continuing decline in farming occupations in France and the rest of the Western world, the fact that Luc wants to be a farmer is as much due to his family's educational strategies and to the strength of peer group solidarity in Lavialle (both of which encourage attachment to place) as it is due to an educational system that is stratified and class-based and that has excluded him. Luc is not simply reproducing his family and their farm; he is actively involved in a process of cultural production, and adapted to new social conditions that are not exactly those his father faced at his age almost three decades ago. Distance between the culture of Luc's home and the culture of the school in Lavialle are as much a product of the active strategies of his family and of Luc himself to keep some distance from the values of the school as they are a product of the centralized and class-based nature of French schooling.

CONCLUSION

The dairy farming community of Lavialle has persisted as a vital agricultural community with strong family ties and peer ties in large part due to educational and socialization strategies that encourage children to identify with the local region and with local social life. This conclusion is based on observations in a variety of settings in Lavialle—including classrooms, households, and community organizations. The persistence of these families, which is a form of social and cultural reproduction, is based on active strategies used by parents and children in Lavialle to selectively resist certain forms of social control connected to state power and the school. It is also, however, based on an adaptive strategy of coexistence with national institutions and state power. Families in Lavialle do not reject schooling outright, rather, they attempt to shape it to their own perceived needs.

Cultural identity within nation-states can be multiple and shifting. The residents of Lavialle practice a form of "cultural diglossia" in which they participate both in a local, regional culture and in a national French culture. School and home, therefore, constitute different sites for social interaction that are best viewed not in total opposition to each other, but rather as places that have developed in response to each other. In my research in Lavialle, I have been interested not only in the socialization strategies of parents and teachers, but in the ways that children have coped with these sometimes-conflicting messages. Children, like adults, are social actors who must make sense of their environment and adapt to it. From the perspective of children, in Lavialle and elsewhere, growing up means learning to adjust to the conflicting demands of the family and of the school—and learning to cope with the contradictions that this implies. Luc, the young man profiled at the end of this chapter, is a product of peer socialization, family socialization, and socialization by teachers at school. That he will follow in his father and mother's footsteps and become a farmer is as much a product of his own ability to *se debrouiller* (to "make out" and "make do"), as it is a product of "inculcated predispositions" or habitus.

NOTES

1. It would not be possible to reference all writings by Bourdieu on these concepts, because they are so central to his work. I refer the reader, in particular, to Bourdieu and Passeron (1977); Bourdieu (1990); and Bourdieu (1977).

2. Willis (1981) was one of the first to draw attention to the role of peers ("the lads") in forms of cultural resistance and cultural (re)production. There have been several studies since then that examine the active role of adolescents—for example, see the recent edited collection by Amit-Talai and Wulff (1995). At the level of elementary schooling, however, there is less work on the role children themselves play in home/school relationships.

3. There are several historical overviews of French education that address these issues

in more depth than I can accomplish here: Prost (1968); and Furet and Ozouf (1982). See also the historical chapters in Reed-Danahay (1996). Recent work in the history of French education challenges previous approaches that stressed the monolithic nature of an educational system insensitive to local populations. See, for instance, Chanet (1996) and Grew and Harrigan (1991).

4. Wylie (1975) also describes methods of using ridicule and shame in the classrooms of Peyrane. He reports, however, that parents mostly shared the same values and attitudes toward education as did the teachers. The reasons for the differences between Peyrane and Lavialle are most likely due to the regional differences between the two settings and to the greater role that agriculture plays in Lavialle social life. I also suspect that Wylie's own role as teacher in Peyrane may have discouraged parents from expressing their criticisms of teachers to him.

5. I have discussed this concept and its relationship to theories of resistance at some length in Reed-Danahay (1993) and also in Reed-Danahay (1996).

REFERENCES

Amit-Talai, Vered, and Helena Wulff, eds. 1995. *Youth Cultures: A Cross-cultural Perspective*. London and New York: Routledge.

Bourdieu, Pierre. 1972. Les stratégies matrimoniales dans le système de reproduction. *Annales: Economies, Societés, Civilisations* 4–5:1105–1125.

———. 1977. *Outline of a Theory of Practice*, translated by Richard Nice. Cambridge: Cambridge University Press.

———. 1990. *In other Words*, translated by Matthew Adamson. Stanford, Calif.: Stanford University Press.

Bourdieu, Pierre, and Jean-Claude Passeron. 1964. *Les Héritiers, les étudiants et la culture*. Paris: Editions de Minuit.

———. 1977 [1972]. *Reproduction in Education, Society and Culture*. Trans. Richard Nice. London: Sage.

Certeau, Michel de. 1988. *The Practice of Everyday Life*, translated by S. Randall. Berkeley: University of California Press.

Chanet, J-F. 1996. *L'Ecole républicaine et les petites patries*. Paris: Aubier.

Cohen, Anthony P. 1994. *Self-consciousness: An Alternative Anthropology of Identity*. London: Routledge.

Estrade, Marc-Antoine. 1995. *Les inegalités devant l'école: influence du milieu social et familiale*. INSEE Premiere, no. 400. Paris: Institute National de la Statistique et des Etudes Economiques.

Furet, François, and Jacques Ozouf. 1982. *Reading and Writing: Literacy from Calvin to Jules Ferry*. Cambridge: Cambridge University Press; Paris: Editions de la Maison des Sciences de l'Homme.

Giddens, Anthony. 1991. *Modernity and Self-identity: Self and Society in the Late Modern Age*. Stanford, Calif.: Stanford University Press.

Grew, Raymond, and Patrick Harrigan. 1991. *School, State and Society: The Growth of Elementary Schooling in 19th Century France—A Qualitative Analysis*. Ann Arbor: University of Michigan Press.

Heath, Shirley Brice. 1983. *Ways with Words: Language, Life and Work in Communities and Classrooms.* Cambridge: Cambridge University Press.

Hélias, Pierre-Jakèz. 1978 [1975]. *The Horse of Pride: Life in a Breton Village,* translated by June Guicharnaud. New Haven, Conn., and London: Yale University Press.

Lareau, Annette. 1989. *Home Advantage: Social Class and Parental Intervention in Elementary Education.* New York: Falmer.

Ogbu, John. 1982. Cultural Discontinuities and Schooling. *Anthropology and Education Quarterly* 13 (4): 290–307.

Prost, Antoine. 1968. *Histoire de l'enseignement en France, 1800–1967.* Paris: Librairie Armond Colin.

Reed-Danahay, Deborah. 1987. Farm Children at School: Educational Strategies in Rural France. *Anthropological Quarterly* 60 (2): 83–89.

———. 1993. Talking about Resistance: Ethnography and Theory in Rural France. *Anthropological Quarterly* 66 (4): 221–229.

———. 1996. *Education and Identity in Rural France: The Politics of Schooling.* Cambridge: Cambridge University Press.

———. 1997a. Leaving Home: Schooling Stories and the Ethnography of Autoethnography in Rural France. In *Auto/Ethnography: Rewriting the Self and the Social,* edited by Deborah Reed-Danahay. Oxford and New York: Berg.

———. 1997b. Persistence et adaptation d'un rite de passage: La Fête Communale et les "conscrits" dans une commune du Puy-de-Dôme. *Revue d'Auvergne* 539 (2): 130–136.

Reed-Danahay, Deborah, and Kathryn M. Anderson-Levitt. 1991. Backward Countryside, Troubled City: Teachers' Images of Families in Rural and Urban France. *American Ethnologist* 18 (3): 546–564.

Scott, James C. 1985. *Weapons of the Weak: Everyday Forms of Peasant Resistance.* New Haven, Conn.: Yale University Press.

Sirota, Régine. 1988. *L'Ecole primaire au quotidien.* Paris: Presses Universitaires de France.

Willis, Paul. 1981. Reprint. *Learning to Labor: How Working Class Kids Get Working Class Jobs.* New York: Columbia University Press.

Wylie, Laurence. 1975. Reprint. *Village in the Vaucluse.* 3rd ed. Cambridge, Mass.: Harvard University Press, 1957.

Section IV

Cultural Production and Reproduction in Contemporary Schools

Cultural Production and Reproduction in Contemporary Schools

Kathryn M. Borman, Amy E. Fox, and Bradley A. U. Levinson

The articles included in this section include a wide range of topical areas and theoretical frameworks. A common set of organizing ideas links the articles that, taken together, cover the life course of school-aged children and young adults engaged in formal schooling arrangements. Three important concepts related to schooling in a capitalist society constitute overlapping themes. These themes are: (1) persistent and inherent inequities in the educational delivery system, resulting in equally persistent gaps in academic achievement between groups of students; (2) inadequacies of current pedagogical and administrative practices; and (3) the continuing importance of race, ethnicity, gender, and socioeconomic status (SES) in structuring students' life experiences and opportunities.

These conceptions of school and society have their roots in the earliest sociological literature, particularly analyses by Karl Marx, Max Weber, and Emile Durkheim. For Marx and his coauthor Friedrich Engels (1978), the rise of the bourgeoisie in the nineteenth century signaled the "rapid improvement of all instruments of production" (477), and this required the refinement of skills for workers who fueled the process of production with their labor. Although their analyses did not interrogate the institution of schooling per se, Marx and Engels examined how the growing division of labor, the bourgeoisie's concern for control of the means of production, and the exploitation of labor in the name of economic progress, all served to justify a system that ensured the economic and social advancement of the few on the backs of the many. Thus, inequities along class lines with respect to access to skills and knowledge is a Marxian concern, and such inequities continue to be played out in schools through grouping and tracking practices that result in differential skill acquisition.

In contrast to Marx, Durkheim's preoccupation with the relationship between the individual and society led him to emphasize the importance of institutions such

239

as education and religion in binding individuals to the social fabric (see Bradley A. U. Levinson, section I). This binding would decrease the likelihood of *anomie* (drift and confusion in values) and a potential disassociation of the individual from the common good. The "cooperation of particular wills" was so important to Durkheim as a mechanism to increase social solidarity that he was reluctant throughout his work to suggest a liberatory role for education. Instead, he saw the moral life of the child as inextricably bound to early socialization in the family, church, and school.

Weber's concern with status issues, as these are tied to social class, prompted him to recognize, value, and expand upon Marx's contributions to intellectual thought (Roth and Wittich 1978). Weber didn't think that inequalities were determined solely by a person's relationship to the means of production (Marx). He defined social class more broadly in terms of status, occupation, and lifestyle. By elaborating how tastes, habits, and preferences are largely linked to the individual's position in the social hierarchy, Weber opened the door to examining the school's role in validating certain kinds of status and style over others. He is an important precursor to the current postmodern focus on habitus (Bourdieu 1977), cultural capital, and other aspects of the individual's relationship to the social order.

By the early 1960s, scholars from the sociological tradition began to analyze the reproductive function of schooling (Karabel and Halsey 1977). The goal was to identify the ways schools served to reproduce basic features of the social order. From a so-called functionalist perspective, like that offered by Durkheim, social reproduction was an important and valuable process. The reproduction of the social structure, and the cultural values supporting this structure, were seen as a requirement of coherent social systems, good and necessary for generational continuity. (You can see a parallel here with earlier anthropological work stressing the "conservative" dimension of education and the relatively smooth transmission of knowledge for the preservation of society—see section I.) Yet from a so-called conflict perspective, such as that offered by Marx and Weber, social reproduction ensures the dominance of certain groups over others. The process of social reproduction maintains an exploitative and oppressive social structure characterized by fundamental inequalities in resources and life opportunities. From the conflict perspective, the reproduction cycle ought to be broken to encourage the liberation of dominated groups and the creation of a more equitable society.

Until the 1970s, educational scholars of either sort tended to view reproduction as a process that was more or less "automatically" accomplished by the whole social system. Functionalist sociologists saw social reproduction as built in to the nature of society, and for the good, whereas conflict sociologists saw social reproduction as a negative but perhaps inevitable feature of modern capitalism. Among the latter, the American economists Samuel Bowles and Herbert Gintis (1976) wrote about the injustices of *Schooling in Capitalist America* (cf. Baudelot and Establet 1975), and the French Marxist thinker Louis Althusser (1971) characterized schools as the primary "ideological state apparatus" under capitalism. In this vision, there wasn't much that could be done about changing the social order through changing schools; reproductive schooling could only be challenged through a total transformation of the capitalist system. Pierre Bourdieu and Jean-Claude Passeron (1977), also writing about modern capitalist France, emphasized the cultural dimension of reproduction. Not only did schools reproduce the social class system, they also reproduced the cultural values and styles associated with dominant and subordinate social classes.

Yet even as this body of work was beginning to exercise considerable influence among scholars, there was growing unease about how schools were portrayed in such functionalist terms. The picture was too deterministic, the school too much an instrument of powerful political and economic interests (Liston 1988). Teachers and textbook writers appeared as guileless agents of the state, or handmaidens of the ruling class. Students appeared as passive dummies, marching off to their respective fates. Critical ethnographic research in schools sought largely to correct this imbalance (Anderson 1989; Mehan 1992). Paul Willis's (1981) striking study of working-class students at a British comprehensive high school is often cited as a watershed moment in this ethnographic wave, but in reality the 1970s and 1980s saw a flurry of nearly concurrent activity (Anyon 1981; Apple and Weis 1983; Everhart 1983; Rosenbaum 1976). Willis's primary achievement was to show how the working-class lads produced their own culture valuing labor and tough masculinity. They ended up being "reproduced" socially (i.e., they stayed in the working class), but this happened through their active intervention in school and the production of cultural meanings, not through a passive acceptance of their working-class fate. In these studies, both teachers and students demonstrated great agency, the ability to intervene creatively in their circumstances and even "resist" the dominant script. Yet there was still an exclusive emphasis on social class. Feminists and critical race theorists also broadened the question of reproduction to include structures of gender and racial inequality, focusing ethnographic research on the agency of women and racial minorities (Holland and Eisenhart 1990; Lesko 1988; Valli 1986; McRobbie 1992; Gillborn 1990; see also Signithia Fordham, section V).

Meanwhile, educational theorists reflected on the findings of this ethnographic research and developed a more nuanced picture of how power operated within schools to shape particular student outcomes (Apple 1982; Giroux 1983; Morrow and Torres 1995; Shapiro 1990). They attempted to understand the range and modalities of human agency in schools without losing sight of the structures and circumstances conditioning that agency. Increasingly, ethnographers enriched theory by exploring the process of *cultural production* as the making of meanings by reflexive social actors in specific and diverse contexts of structured power. Theorists now agreed that social and cultural reproduction, if and where it occurred, could not be foreordained; it had to pass through the dynamics of cultural production, the consequential making of meanings.[1]

Within the last decade, social theory has expanded even more to take into account divergent voices whose perspectives consciously set about dismantling white male privilege to instead honor diversities of experience (Agger 1998; Andersen and Collins 1992). The most important of these theorists is arguably Patricia Hill Collins, whose *Black Feminist Thought* (1990) revolutionized social theory by calling into question a number of important concepts, including social action, community, and male-female relations. She argues that society is characterized by multiple sites of domination and resistance, noting that in addition to

> being structured along axes such as race, gender, and social class, the matrix of domination is structured on several levels. People experience and resist oppression on three levels: the level of personal biography, the group or community level of the cultural context created by race, class and gender, and the systemic level of social institutions. Black feminist thought emphasizes all three levels as sites of domination and as potential sites of resistance. (1990, 223)

Collins's analysis allows us to envision individuals as actively creating and resisting social structure and cultural forms in diverse racial and ethnic communities.

The authors of the selections included in this section, like the social theorists we have reviewed here, explore inequalities in education and society and demonstrate how an active engagement in teaching and learning is centrally important if children and young adults are to participate meaningfully in school.

Donna Eder's article, "Ability Grouping as a Self-fulfilling Prophecy: A Microanalysis of Teacher-student Interaction," examines the influence of learning environments on student achievement. She demonstrates the inadequacies of pedagogical practices that sort and separate students according to ability level. Eder draws from her in-depth research in a first-grade classroom to investigate the effects of learning contexts on different ability groups and their performance on tests. By combining interviews, observations, and videotaped interactions of different reading ability groups, Eder captures the dynamics operating in these groups and focuses on within- and among-group variation. She utilizes a sociolinguistic approach to analyze and explore both teacher-student interactions within the classroom and behavioral differences across varying ability groups. Eder's detailed analysis of videotaped interactions allows her to investigate the verbal and nonverbal cues as they unfold within the context of these differing ability groups.

She contends that by separating children into ability groups, teachers provide a disservice to students and risk creating ineffective learning environments. Her analysis suggests that those students placed into lower-level ability groups struggle with lower attention spans and are more likely to engage in inattentive behavior than those in accelerated groups. Students in lower-ability groups tend to require more direct teacher management and experience a greater number of disruptions in turn taking, thus compounding inattentive behavior. The author argues that children in lower-ability groups are often placed in learning contexts that impede the learning process. This article has important implications for sorting and tracking students. The author challenges schools to reconceptualize the organization of classrooms so students are not classified and "sorted" according to ability.

In the article "Beneath the Skin and between the Ears: A Case Study in the Politics of Representation," Hugh Mehan examines the process of creating student identities by focusing on the case of the construction of learning disabled (LD) students. Mehan and his colleagues conducted research in a school district in southern California from 1978 to 1979. The researchers employed multiple methods, including observations, interviews, review of documents (e.g., student records), and videotaping. Mehan utilizes a linguistic perspective to examine how student identities are constructed, focusing on the institutional processes and practices involved in classifying LD students. The political aspect of representing others is evident through an examination of the terms and the process used to label students.

Mehan's analysis incorporates two interrelated levels that provide a context for understanding the politics and power involved in the classification of students into regular or special education tracks. The first layer examines the historical, social, and political context for the development of terms related to special education, disability, and mental retardation. The second level investigates the practical use of such terms. Students defined as LD are placed into special classes for part of their day and in "normal" classrooms for the remainder of the day. In order to determine the final assessment and placement of a student, schools hold meetings with various stakeholders to discuss the individual; those attending such meetings include parents, teachers, the psychologist, and other school personnel. The dialogue about the student being evaluated incorporates various perspectives and different discourses. Mehan examines such dialogue, paying particular attention to the *ways* in which students are represented and *how* certain types of discourse are considered dominant. For example, in reviewing the case of one student, the psychologist provides a technical, uninterrupted report laden with numbers and jargon. In contrast, the parent and teacher describe the student in an informal manner, utilizing anecdotal information to provide a profile of the student. Such informal presentations are interrupted and questioned, but the psychologist is not. We thus see how, during the process of classifying students, children become objects of the institutionalized system and translated into a kind of objective text.

Both Mehan and Eder utilize a linguistic analysis to criticize the process of sorting and labeling students. Although each researcher focuses on a different population of students, they underscore the importance of investigating school practices that encourage the separation of students into groupings. Such groupings have long-term implications for students, since labels according to perceived ability influence the types and levels of courses students can subsequently take.

Dorothy Holland and Margaret Eisenhart explore gender inequalities in institutions of higher education in their article "Moments of Discontent: University Women and the Gender Status Quo." Through their interviews with black and white women at two universities in the South, Holland and Eisenhart explore aspects of the women's lives that are problematic with respect to their future plans and current experiences. Women interviewed during the course of the project were concerned about two dimensions of their lives: (1) not being taken seriously academically, and (2) romantic relationships. Some complained that their professors refused to take them seriously as students. Most, however, discussed the paramount importance of peer relationships, especially romantic relationships, and pointed to their critical salience in the women's self-definition and experiences at the university. Attractiveness emerges as a particularly important element related to social prestige, and therefore necessary in developing and maintaining romantic relationships. According to the women interviewed, people find romantic partners based on their relative attractiveness.

Interestingly, unlike the findings for other types of inequality, such as class and ethnicity, the women do not blame institutional structures for gender inequality, but rather seek in themselves or in their relationships with others the "causes" for their lack of academic recognition and achievement. Although some women complain about their treatment, few resist or challenge the status quo, in part because there does not appear to be a clear system of domination to confront. Despite historical patterns of gender discrimination, and ongoing reports of a chilly academic climate for women, these university students are not critical of patriarchy or the system.

R. W. Connell and his coauthors examine the intersection of class and gender in educational settings in their article "Class and Gender Dynamics in a Ruling-class School." In order to conduct research on the effects of class on education, the authors study both working-class and ruling-class schools in Australia for comparative purposes. The authors posit that educational systems embody class stratification systems and in turn reproduce these relations.

Income, occupational status, and education define "ruling class." Within ruling-class schools, education encompasses preparation in three areas: (1) moral order, (2) academic performance, and (3) well-rounded education. The social organization of schools and school structure are shaped by market forces and therefore reflect the capitalist interest in individual achievement, as well as competition and conflict over scarce resources—in this case, high grades. According to the researchers, parents play an active role in ruling-class schools through the demands they place on administrators and teachers, as well as their social relations and networks in the community. This finding from Connell and his coauthors' early research has been documented repeatedly in subsequent studies in a wide range of settings. For example, through her case studies of working and middle-class schools in California and Philadelphia, Annette Lareau (1989) demonstrates that upper-middle-class parents, especially those whose children are not doing well in school, attempt to take an aggressive role in their children's schooling. They neither depend on the school for authorization nor automatically defer to teachers' professional expertise. As a result, these parents both closely supervise and frequently intervene in their children's schooling.

By contrast, working-class parents, lacking the skills and confidence to assist their children in school, rarely challenge the authority of the school, and thus infrequently confront their children's teachers or school principals. Ironically, working-class parents are often more respectful of teachers' "professionalism" and authority than are upper-middle-class parents. The findings of Lareau and others that have carried out similar studies are particularly important in highlighting the influence on children's school achievement of family-based cultural capital, including resources such as a well-developed academic vocabulary and a circle of well-schooled family friends and relatives.

Taken together, the readings in this section provide the reader with a good sense of how inequalities are created and/or reinforced in schools. If we can understand how processes of cultural production in schools lead to unfortunate social and cultural reproduction, then we can design strategies for achieving greater justice through schools.

NOTE

1. Two articles originally to be published in this book illustrate the point well: William Corsaro's (1993) work challenges notions of socialization that envision children as passive recipients of information transmitted by adults. He argues that children actively engage in the production and reproduction of culture through their interactions with adults and peers. Direct observations coupled with analyses of videotapes reveal that children create their own peer culture by utilizing elements of adult culture and in turn reproducing adult culture. To illustrate his perspective, Corsaro draws upon videotapes of two different groups of children (one with white, economically privileged children, and the other with black, low-income children) as they informally take on dramatic role-play situations in school. Themes that emerge from the children's informal play center on family life and occupational demands. Conversations and interactions reflect the children's own lived experiences, thus demonstrating the interplay between their play with peers, their understanding of the adult world, and their integration of these in their peer relations. The contrasting cases illustrate how the children interpret, react to, and "reproduce" power inequalities in existing structures.

In his article, "Student Culture and the Contradictions of Equality at a Mexican Secondary School" (1998), Bradley Levinson compares "official" school structures and policies with student subjectivity. Levinson draws from his ethnographic study of a Mexican secondary school, *Escuela Secundaria Federal* (ESF), to examine the interplay between school structures that promote equality and solidarity and student viewpoints on these ideals. Levinson utilizes the concept of agency to investigate students' participation in school and argues that they actively participate in the formation of school culture through their responses to the official school structures. Cultural production theory frames the analysis, interpretation, and understanding of strategies employed by students within the context of ESF.

The secondary school where Levinson conducted his ethnographic research is comprised of a heterogeneous student population with a diverse range of class, gender, and ethnic backgrounds. Despite the social differences among students at this school, subcultures do not develop; rather there is a sense of equality and solidarity among students. Levinson explores how the school builds solidarity and creates a connection among the students despite their social differences. School administrators and teachers established the *grupo escolar*, a cohort of students who are placed into groups and remain together for their three years of schooling. These groups consist of a heterogeneous selection of students in terms of academic ability, social class, ethnicity, and gender. The author argues that the school culture embodies the national discourse about developing cohesion among citizens in building a national identity. Education, therefore, is linked to the formation of a united national persona as teachers and administrators emphasize that students are working for the good of Mexico. ESF utilizes the *grupo escolar* as a strategy to reinforce the official ideology of the school and reiterates a commitment to equality by requiring school uniforms to erase social class differences. Although students embrace the concepts of equality and solidarity, they do not focus on the nation as a whole. Rather, they appropriate such concepts to organize their own strategies and social relationships in the school. Levinson's article contributes to our understanding of the interplay between school structures and student cultures.

REFERENCES AND READINGS

Agger, Ben. 1998. *Critical Social Theories: An Introduction*. Boulder, Colo.: Westview.

Althusser, Louis. 1971. Ideology and Ideological State Apparatuses. In *Lenin and Philosophy and other Essays*. New York: Monthly Review Press.

Anderson, Gary. 1989. Critical Ethnography in Education: Origins, Current Status, and New Directions. *Review of Educational Research* 59:249–270.

Andersen, Margaret L., and Patricia Hill Collins. 1992. *Race, Class, and Gender: An Anthology*. Belmont, Calif.: Wadsworth.

Anyon, Jean. 1981. Social Class and School Knowledge. *Curriculum Inquiry* 11 (1): 3–42.

Apple, Michael, ed. 1982. *Cultural and Economic Reproduction in American Education: Essays in Class, Ideology, and the State*. Boston: Routledge and Kegan Paul.

Apple, Michael W., and Lois Weis, eds. 1983. *Ideology and Practice in Schooling*. Philadelphia: Temple University Press.

Baudelot, Christian, and Roger Establet. 1975. *La escuela capitalista*. Madrid: Siglo Veintiuno Editores.

Bourdieu, Pierre. 1977. *Outline for a Theory of Practice*. Cambridge: Cambridge University Press.

Bourdieu, Pierre, and Jean-Claude Passeron. 1977. *Reproduction: In Education, Society, Culture*. Beverly Hills, Calif.: Sage.

Bowles, Samuel, and Herbert Gintis. 1976. *Schooling in Capitalist America*. New York: Basic.

Cobb, P. 1994. Constructivism in Mathematics and Science Education. *Educational Researcher* 23 (7): 4.

Collins, Patricia Hill. 1990. *Black Feminist Thought*. Boston: Unwin-Hyman.

Corsaro, William. 1993. Interpretive Reproduction in Children's Role-play. *Childhood* 1:64–74.

Driver, R., H. Asoko, J. Leach, E. Mortimer, and P. Scott. 1994. Constructing Scientific Knowledge in the Classroom. *Educational Researcher* 23 (7): 5–12.

Durkheim, Emile. 1965. *The Elementary Forms of the Religious Life*. New York: The Free Press.

Everhart, Robert. 1983. *Reading, Writing, and Resistance: Adolescence and Labor in a Junior High School*. London: Routledge and Kegan Paul.

Gillborn, Paul. 1990. *Race, Ethnicity, and Education*. London: Unwin-Hyman.

Giroux, Henry. 1983. *Theory and Resistance in Education: A Pedagogy for the Opposition*. Massachusetts: Bergin and Garvey.

Holland, Dorothy, and Margaret Eisenhart. 1990. *Educated in Romance: Women, Achievement, and College Culture*. Chicago: University of Chicago Press.

Karabel, Jerome, and A. H. Halsey. 1977. *Power and Ideology in Education*. Oxford: Oxford University Press.

Lareau, Annette. 1989. *Home Advantage: Social Class and Parental Intervention in Elementary Education*. London: Falmer.

Lesko, Nancy. 1988. *Symbolizing Society: Stories, Rites, and Structure in a Catholic High School*. New York: Falmer.

Levinson, Bradley A. 1998. Student Culture and the Contradictions of Equality at a Mexican Secondary School. *Anthropology and Education Quarterly* 29 (3): 1–30.

Liston, Daniel. 1988. *Capitalist Schools: Explanation and Ethics in Radical Studies in Schooling*. London: Routledge and Kegan Paul.

Marx, Karl, and Friedrich Engels. 1978. Manifesto of the Communist Party. In *The Marx-Engels Reader*. 2d ed. Edited by R. C. Tucker. New York: Norton.

McRobbie, Angela. 1992. *Feminism and Youth Culture*. London: Unwin-Hyman.

Mehan, Hugh. 1992. Understanding Inequality in Schools: The Contribution of Interpretive Studies. *Sociology of Education* 65 (1): 1–20.

Morrow, Raymond Allen, and Carlos Alberto Torres. 1995. *Social Theory and Education: A Critique of Theories of Social and Cultural Reproduction*. Albany: SUNY Press.

Rosenbaum, James. 1976. *Making Inequality*. New York: Wiley.

Roth, G., and C. Wittich, eds. 1978. *Economy and Society, Vol. II. The Writings of Max Weber*. Berkeley: University of California Press.

Shapiro, Svi. 1990. *Between Capitalism and Democracy*. New York: Bergin and Garvey.

Valli, Linda. 1986. *Becoming Clerical Workers*. London: Routledge and Kegan Paul.

Willis, Paul. 1981. *Learning to Labor: How Working Class Kids Get Working Class Jobs*. New York: Columbia University Press.

17

Ability Grouping as a Self-fulfilling Prophecy: A Microanalysis of Teacher-Student Interaction

Donna Eder

INTRODUCTION

The extent to which students' academic achievements are influenced by the environment in which learning occurs is an important issue for the sociology of education. Much of the research in this area has focused exclusively on across-school comparisons of social contexts and has been the subject of considerable methodological and theoretical debate (Sewell and Armer, 1966; Hauser, 1971; Jencks, Smith, Acland, Bane, Cohen, Gintis, Heyns, and Michelson, 1972; Hauser, Sewell, and Alwin, 1976). One outcome of this debate is an increased understanding of the importance of examining differential environments *within* schools as well as the practice by which students are allocated to tracks or ability groups and thus to different learning environments (Richer, 1975; Kerckhoff, 1976; Rosenbaum, 1976; Alexander and McDill, 1976).

At the high school level, assignment to tracks would result in exposure to differential social contexts within schools. Alexander and McDill (1976) found that students in college tracks had more high status friends, more high ability friends, and more friends who planned to go to college and that this, in turn, had an influence on their own aspirations to attend college. In a later study which controlled for peer relations in ninth grade, tracking continued to influence twelfth-grade friendships but to a lesser degree (Alexander, Cook and McDill, 1978). However, the impact of tracking on ninth-grade friendships is not considered, although Rosenbaum's (1976) study suggests that initial exposure to tracking may have the most dramatic effect on peer relations.

So far research on within-school contexts has been restricted mainly to high school tracks, even though as Alwin and Otto (1977) point out, context effects are likely to be greater for younger children. Also, the practice of assigning students to ability-based instructional groups within classrooms is almost as common at the elementary level as tracking is at the high school level. Use of ability grouping for reading instruction is especially common, occurring in between 74 to 80 percent of all classrooms (Austin and Morrison, 1963; Wilson and Schmits, 1978). This practice is extremely important in that it determines which other students will be present when students are actually being instructed. While previous studies have looked mainly at student characteristics when examining differences in social contexts, this study will focus on the ways in which these characteristics differentially affect the nature of teacher-student interaction during group lessons.

A closer examination of ability grouping is important since research on the effects of grouping indicates that it may have different effects on students of different ability levels. Studies of both across-classroom grouping and within-classroom grouping have found a significant effect of group assignment on ability and/or achievement, controlling for initial ability (Douglas, 1964; Rosenbaum, 1976; Alexander and McDill, 1976; Weinstein, 1976). While comparisons of schools which used across-classroom grouping with those which did not have found no or little difference in average achievement, most have found greater variance in achievement in schools with ability-grouped classrooms (Daniels, 1961; Borg, 1966; Baker Lunn, 1970). In other words, bright students performed better in ability-grouped schools than in other schools while slower students performed worse in ability-grouped schools than in schools without ability grouping. Also, in a study comparing adolescent achievement in twelve countries Pidgeon (1970) found the most variance in achievement among British students at a time when British schools were the most rigidly streamed. Thus, while bright students may benefit from ability-grouped instruction, it appears that slower students do not. Since ability grouping is aimed at improving instruction at all levels, it is important to examine why grouping has a differential effect at different levels.

One explanation for this differential effect is variation in teachers' behaviors across group levels (Rist, 1970; McDermott, 1976). Furthermore, McDermott's work suggests that this variation may be directly related to differences in students' behavior across groups. In a study of ability-based reading groups, he found that the teacher called on each student to read in the high group whereas the students in the low group were required to "bid" for reading turns by raising their hands. While the first procedure was less time consuming, it could not be used in the low group without embarrassing those students who were unable to read. Further observational studies are needed to determine other ways in which differences in student characteristics across ability groups affect interaction during lessons.

The purpose of this paper is to examine the nature and extent of differences in the learning contexts of ability-based reading groups in a first-grade classroom. First, the importance of perceived ability and maturity levels for assignment decisions will be discussed. Then, the nature of teacher-student interaction will be examined as well as differences in interaction patterns across group levels. Finally, group differences in actual and perceived reading achievement will be analyzed. It will be argued that it is differences in learning contexts which makes ability grouping a self-fulfilling prophecy.

AN IN-DEPTH STUDY OF ABILITY GROUPING

The design for this study involved observation in a first-grade classroom for an entire academic year. A first-grade classroom was selected because students' initial school experiences are likely to be especially influential and first-grade represents most students' first experience with ability grouping for formalized instruction. The study involved an entire year period so that any changes in either the students' or teacher's behavior over the year could be identified. Observation was begun with the teacher's previous class so that she would be used to my presence before studying this classroom intensively. The target classroom was observed an average of three days per week for an entire school year. Observational periods were usually three hours long and included all days of the week and both morning and afternoon sessions. Brief notes were made in the classroom, while more complete notes were recorded after the observational period. Because observation was started prior to the study and occurred on a frequent basis, it is unlikely that my presence substantially affected the interactions observed, especially given the routine nature of many of the interactions.

Initial observations indicated the relative importance of reading instruction. For example, one to two hours a day were typically spent in formal reading instruction compared to five to ten minutes in formal math instruction. Since all reading instruction occurred in ability-based groups, later observations focused more on reading lessons.

Group lessons were video-taped on eight days during the year, four days in the fall and four in the spring. Taping was done on different days of the week at approximately two-week intervals in order to obtain data that would be representative of each time period. A comparison of video-taped data with field notes from days in which video-taping did not occur indicated that the video-taped data were typical of interaction in this classroom.

During the first stage of analysis four video-taped lessons, one from each of the four reading groups, were viewed repeatedly to determine differences in the behavior of the teacher and students across groups as well as their impact on group interaction. A sociolinguistic approach will be used to analyze these data. While this approach is useful for examining the nature of teacher-student interaction as well as differences across group levels, it does not demonstrate the degree to which these patterns are representative of interaction in this classroom. This necessitated a second stage of analysis in which relevant behaviors were coded on all 32 video-taped lessons to determine their relative frequency across group levels. (This stage will be discussed in detail later in the chapter.)

Ability Group Assignments

Two weeks before school began the teacher met with the students' kindergarten teachers. During these discussions the kindergarten teachers indicated how they thought each child would do in reading, *i.e.*, whether they could start above grade level, at grade level, or below grade level. Based on these discussions and her own observation of the students, the teacher assigned the students to four relatively equal-size groups during the first week of school.[1] Although the four groups could be placed on a continuum from high to low, the two high groups began reading in the same level book and the two low groups began reading in the same level book. Altogether, 13 students were in high groups (eight males and five females) and ten students were in low groups (five males and five females). Students in both high and low groups were primarily from middle-class backgrounds.

Interviews with the kindergarten teachers who had made the recommendations indicated that these recommendations were based on perceptions of students' maturity as well as their ability. Although the teachers differed to some degree regarding which factors most influenced the level at which a child could begin reading, maturity, as indicated by a child's ability to pay attention, was clearly an important factor for some of the teachers. In fact, one teacher considered it to be the most important factor: "I think attention span is extremely important and good listening skills are extremely important and those are the two most important—more important than knowing the names of the letters." Other studies have found that maturity as well as ability factors were influential in determining a child's reading aptitude and/or group assignment (Leiter, 1974; Austin and Morrison, 1963). It appears that many teachers view group instruction as being a social as well as an academic event, requiring both social and academic skills.

Differences in Inattentive Behavior and Management across Ability Groups

According to Goffman (1963), many encounters involve a shared focus of attention as well as requirements for attending to this central or main involvement. During reading group lessons, the lesson itself is the main involvement to which students are required to attend. While this requirement exists for all group levels, lower groups are likely to have more inattentive behavior due in part to the fact that students who are perceived to be immature and inattentive are often assigned to lower groups.

The inattentive behavior of these students, however, is likely to generate further inattentiveness. To begin with, students often imitate each other's behavior. Also, the more inattentive behavior in a group, the greater the likelihood that other members will either be directly involved in such behavior themselves or simply become more interested in watching it rather than following along in their books, further contributing to a greater degree of inattentiveness in low ability groups.

Attentiveness is also likely to be affected by the ability level of other group members. If a student has little or no difficulty reading, other members are less likely to become bored or inattentive. However, if a student is having a lot of difficulty reading, it is harder for others to follow the story line and maintain interest in the material, resulting in less attentive behavior on their part. Also, the longer it takes for a student to read, the more others will tend to stop paying attention because they see no opportunity for their direct participation in the near future.

When someone becomes inattentive during an interaction, one or more participants are generally responsible for regaining that person's attention. In the case of classroom interaction, the main responsibility of maintaining the attention of others lies with the teacher. However, as Goffman (1967) has noted, managing the attention of others is itself a form of inattention in that it, too, is a departure from the central focus of the interaction. Thus, in order to regain the attention of students, the teacher must also become temporarily distracted. Because of the higher rate of inattention in lower groups, more teacher management is also likely to occur.

Management acts may contribute, in turn, to further student inattention. For one thing, students are likely to attend to the behavior being managed rather than to the ongoing lesson. Also, if management occurs frequently, the interruptions are likely to weaken the overall quality of the lesson by making it less coherent and thus more difficult to follow as well as to understand resulting in increased inattention.[2]

Reading Turn Disruption

One way in which teachers may attempt to minimize distracting effects of management acts is to perform them simultaneously with academic acts. For example, teachers frequently ask questions of inattentive students in order to regain their attention as well as obtain academic information. If several students have become inattentive, teachers may open the floor to general participation by addressing all students with questions such as "Who knows the next word?" However, when this practice occurs during students' reading turns, it may interfere with their reading performance as in the following example:[3]

> [Cynthia is the current reader, while Robin and Jennifer are other group members. Robin is folding her book-marker and looking away from her book.]
> *Cynthia:* run
> *Teacher:* run . . . That's right. You can run . . . [Becky turns around to look at something in the classroom.] Who knows that little word, a-n-d? [Points to Becky's book.]
> *Jennifer:* and
> *Teacher:* and Robin, get your marker under the right row of words. [Points to Robin's book, then to Cynthia's.] You can run and . . .

Another way in which teachers may attempt to minimize the distracting effect of management is to use non-verbal management while asking academic questions as in the next example from Jeff's reading turn.

[Gary and Ted are playing with their book-markers. Sara is looking around.]
Teacher: Here we go. Li . . . [Points to Gary's book then to Jeff s book.] What kind of dogs?
Jeff: Little
Teacher: little . . .
Jeff: dogs
[Gary and Ted continue to play with markers.]
Teacher: [Points to Jeff's book.] What are they doing? Now let's look at the s-word. [Points to Gary's book.] Little dogs s-s-s . . .
Group: sit
Teacher: sit. All right.

Throughout this reading turn the teacher attempts to regain Gary's attention by pointing to his book, at the same time providing the reader with clues. While, in this example, the teacher does not explicitly invite other members to participate, her non-verbal orientations away from the reader while managing may have been interpreted by students as an invitation for general participation.

In general, whenever the teacher was oriented away from the reader while asking a question or providing a clue, other students were more likely to provide the correct word (Eder, forthcoming). Thus, while performing management and academic activities may minimize the distracting effect of management, it also tends to disrupt students' reading turns by limiting their opportunities to successfully complete turns on their own. Since management is expected to occur more frequently in lower groups, there is also likely to be more reading turn disruption in those groups.

In both of the above cases reading turn disruption was due to the teacher's direct or inadvertent invitation for participation by others. Students may also read during another's turn without an invitation from the teacher. When this occurred, students were often reprimanded by the teacher as in the following example:

Rob: Rides
Teacher: Rides
Rob: the bus
Paula: . . . bus
Teacher: Let him do it.
Rob: to the [pause]
Brien: park
Rob: park
Brien: park
Teacher: Let's just let Rob do it.

However, not all reading turn violations were reprimanded as shown in the next example from the medium low group:

Peter: the . . . dogs . . .
Teacher: The dogs l-l-l-like . . . The dogs like . . . to . . . run [To Group] What kind of dogs are these?

Group: Little
Teacher: Little
Group: dogs
Teacher: Dale, are you watching? Little dogs . . .
Peter: can
Teacher: can . . . run . . .
Group: and
Teacher: and
Group: jump

While Paula and Brien are reminded that it is Rob's turn to read in the first example from a reading turn in the high group, the interaction shown in the second
example from the medium low group provides a marked contrast. Although group
members read out of turn several times, not once are they reminded that it is Peter's
turn to read.

There are a number of reasons why reading turn violations may be reprimanded
less often in lower groups than in higher groups. For one thing, reading turn violations are an indication of attention, showing that the other members have been
following along. Thus a teacher may be more hesitant to reprimand such violations
in lower groups where attention is more problematic. Also, teachers are sometimes
more concerned with completing a turn than with who completes it, knowing that
if turns become too long there is a danger of losing all attention (Mehan, 1979).
This is more likely to be such a concern in lower groups where students are expected
both to have more difficulty reading and to be more inattentive. However, if turn
violations are reprimanded less often in lower groups, they are more likely to continue to occur and thus further limit a student's opportunity to complete successfully his (her) reading turn.

The greater frequency of turn disruptions and violations in lower groups is likely
to affect both the actual and perceived achievement of students. Since one way
students learn to read is by figuring out difficult words on their own, reading turn
disruptions and violations would interfere with this important learning experience.
Furthermore, if other group members read during students' turns, it may appear that
they are having more difficulty reading than if they had the opportunity to read
without interference from other members.

In summary, learning contexts of lower ability groups are likely to differ from
learning contexts of higher ability groups in several crucial ways. First, lower ability groups are likely to have more inattention than higher ability groups due both
to assignment on the basis of perceived maturity and the influence of other group
members. Secondly, lower ability groups should have more management activities
than higher ability groups because of the greater amount of inattention in lower
groups. Since management activities are sometimes combined with academic activities which often result in the disruption of students' reading turns, lower ability groups are also expected to have more reading turn disruptions than higher ability
groups. At the same time, reading turn violations are expected to be reprimanded

less often in lower ability groups than in higher groups, contributing to a higher rate of reading turn violations in lower groups. The greater degree of inattention, management and reading turn disruptions and violations are all likely to contribute to lower levels of reading achievement in students assigned to low ability groups.

DISCUSSION

The results of this study indicate that learning contexts varied dramatically across ability groups. While students in low groups were instructed in an environment characterized by disruption from the teacher as well as from other members, high group members were instructed in a much less disruptive environment. In other words, those students who were likely to have more difficulty learning were inadvertently assigned to groups whose social contexts were much less conducive to learning.

A comparison of reading achievement across ability groups indicated that high group members performed better on reading tests and were assessed as being better readers by the teacher. While these analyses do not indicate the extent to which differences in learning contexts accounted for differences in achievement, it is likely that they did contribute to this difference, especially since none of the students knew how to read prior to beginning first grade.

Most of the previous research on the self-fulfilling prophecy in education has focused on only a few of the possible mechanisms by which initial perceptions become self-fulfilling prophecies (Wilkins, 1976). For example, Rosenthal and Jacobson's (1968) classic study suggested that a change in teachers' expectations was sufficient to alter student performance. Considerable research has been devoted to identifying the linkages between teacher expectation and student performance, with an emphasis on teacher attention and evaluation. However, this line of research has produced mixed results. While some teachers have been found to give more attention and praise to brighter students (Rist, 1970; Brophy and Good, 1970; Rubovits and Maehr, 1971), other teachers were found to give more attention and praise to slower students[4] (Weinstein, 1976).

Labeling theory has suggested another mechanism by which self-fulfilling prophecies might operate. In the educational arena, it is expected that students who are assigned to lower groups will come to view themselves as less able and will perform in accordance with those self-conceptions. However, again the research on the effects of ability grouping on students' self-concepts has led to mixed results, in part because group differences may be more or less visible to students (see Goldberg, Passow, and Justman, 1966, for a review of this literature). Recent evidence indicates that many students may be unaware of their ability group assignment or curriculum track placement (Eder, 1979b; Rosenbaum, 1980).

Because students are exposed to different learning contexts when they are assigned to ability groups, their behavior is likely to be differentially influenced in line with their group assignments. The crucial mechanism in this process is differences in teacher-student interaction, where differences in teacher behavior are viewed as resulting mainly from differences in students' behavior.

Further support for the idea that ability group assignment is a self-fulfilling prophecy comes from studies which have examined the rate of mobility across groups. Although the flexibility of ability groups has been emphasized in theory, little movement across groups has been found either during the academic year or between years (Groff, 1962; Hawkins, 1966; Mackler, 1969; Rist, 1970). If students tend to remain in the groups to which they are assigned initially, it is important that these assignments be accurate. However, since most students are assigned to ability groups within the first few weeks of first grade, it is highly unlikely that accurate assessments of student aptitudes have been made.

The lack of accurate measures of academic aptitude in early grades is particularly important since it increases the likelihood of ethnic and class bias in ability group assignment. Rist (1970) found that family background was strongly related to initial ability group assignment. Since there is little mobility across groups, it is not surprising that an independent effect of family background on ability group assignment has been found through elementary and high school (Baker Lunn, 1970; Alexander and McDill, 1976; Hauser et al., 1976; and Rosenbaum, 1976).

In general, the results of this study indicate that the common practice of ability grouping should be questioned. While homogeneous grouping has long been considered more efficient in terms of the teacher's time and the use of instructional resources, the results of this study clearly indicate that homogeneous grouping compounds initial learning problems by placing those children who have learning problems in the same groups. One alternative would be to use some form of heterogeneous grouping. This might make learning somewhat more difficult for brighter children, but would benefit slower students by reducing the amount of inattention, management, and turn disruptions during their reading lessons. Another alternative would be more reliance on one-to-one instruction. Although this might seem more time consuming; it may prove in the long term to be a more efficient means of instruction, particularly for slower students. Either of these alternatives would be superior to the current practice of ability grouping which is least advantageous for the very students who are most in need of a positive learning environment.

The results of this study also indicate that interaction with others is amazingly complex; that we are often engaged in a variety of activities during a single interaction. For example, the teacher simultaneously instructed students, managed their inattentive behavior, and allocated speaking turns. Because other activities were performed simultaneously with academic activities, students' academic turns were affected in unintended ways. Since other types of interaction are likely to be equally complex, much of our impact on others is likely to be unintentional. Only through detailed examinations of interactions can these unintended effects be identified.

In summary, the social context of learning in low ability groups was found to be dramatically different from that in high ability groups. Although the study is limited to a single classroom, similar results are likely to be found in other elementary classrooms, since students are typically grouped on the basis of ability and maturity levels. More importantly, this study demonstrates the importance of examining the processes by which schools affect students, rather than focusing solely on the extent of school effects. Hopefully, it will encourage more research which directly examines the processes by which the internal organization of schools affects students and will generate interest in research which attempts to link social process with social structure in other areas.

NOTES

1. The teacher did not have any other information about the students such as reading readiness or intelligence test scores.

2. Group size is also likely to affect the degree of inattentiveness. However, ability groups generally tend to be relatively equal in size due to time and size constraints (Eder, 1979a).

3. Related non-verbal behaviors are shown in square brackets.

4. The teacher in this classroom gave more praise to students in lower groups than to high group members (Eder, 1979b).

REFERENCES

Alexander, K., M. Cook, and E. McDill. 1978. "Curriculum tracking and educational stratification: Some further evidence." *American Sociological Review* 43:47–68.

Alexander, K. L., and E. L. McDill. 1976. "Selection and allocation within schools: Some causes and consequences of curriculum placement." *American Sociological Review* 41:969–80.

Alwin, D. F., and L. B. Otto. 1977. "High school context effects on aspirations." *Sociology of Education* 50:259–73.

Austin, M., and C. Morrison. 1963. *The First R: The Harvard Report on Reading in Elementary School*. New York: MacMillan.

Baker Lunn, J. D. 1970. *Streaming in the Public School*. London: National Foundation for Educational Research in England and Wales.

Borg, W. R. 1966. *Ability Grouping in the Public Schools*. Madison, WI: Dembar Education Research Services.

Brophy, J., and T. Good. 1970. "Teachers' communication of differential expectations for children's classroom performance: Some behavioral data." *Journal of Educational Psychology* 61:365–74.

Daniels, J. G. 1961. "The effect of streaming in the primary school." *British Journal of Educational Psychology* 31:67–78.

Douglas, J. 1964. *The Home and the School*. London: MacGibben and Kee.

Eder, D. 1979a. *Stratification Within the Classroom: The Formation and Maintenance of Ability Groups*. Unpublished Ph.D. dissertation. University of Wisconsin, Madison, Wisconsin.

———. 1979b. "Ability grouping and students' self-esteem." Presented at the American Sociological Association Convention, Boston.

———. Forthcoming. "The impact of management and turn-allocation activities on student performance." *Discourse Processes*.

Goffman, Erving. 1963. *Behavior in Public Places*. New York: The Free Press.

———. 1967. *Interaction Ritual*. New York: Doubleday.

Goldberg, M., A. H. Passow and J. Justman. 1966. *The Effects of Ability Grouping*. New York: Teachers College Press.

Groff, P. J. 1962. "A survey of basic reading group practices." *Reading Teacher* 15:232–35.

Hauser, R. M. 1971. *Socioeconomic Background and Educational Performance*. Rose Monograph Series. Washington, DC: American Sociological Association.

Hauser, R. M., W. H. Sewell and D. F. Alwin. 1976. "High school effects on achievement." Pp. 309–41 in W. H. Sewell, R. M. Hauser and D. L. Featherman (eds.), *Schooling and Achievement in American Society*. New York: Academic Press.

Hawkins, M. L. 1966. "Mobility of students in reading groups." *Reading Teacher* 20:136–40.

Jencks, C., M. Smith, H. Acland, M. Bane, D. Cohen, H. Gintis, B. Heyns and S. Michelson. 1972. *Inequality: A Reassessment of the Effect of Family and Schooling in America*. New York: Basic Books.

Kerckhoff, A. C. 1976. "The status attainment process: Socialization or allocation?" *Social Forces* 55:368–81.

Leiter, K. 1974. "Ad hocing in the schools." In A. V. Cicourel (ed.)., *Language Use and School Performance*. New York: Academic Press.

McDermott, R. P. 1976. *Kids Make Sense*. Unpublished Ph.D. dissertation. Stanford University, Stanford, California.

Mackler, B. 1969. "Grouping in the ghetto." *Education and Urban Society* 2:80–96.

Mehan, H. 1979. *Learning Lessons*. Boston: Harvard University Press.

Pidgeon, D. 1970. *Expectation and Pupil Performance*. Slough, Great Britain: N F & R.

Richer, S. 1975. "School effects: The case for grounded theory." *Sociology of Education* 48:383–99.

Rist, R. 1970. "Student social class and teacher expectations: The self-fulfilling prophecy in ghetto education." *Harvard Educational Review* 40:411–51.

Rosenbaum, J. E. 1976. *Making Inequality: The Hidden Curriculum of High School Tracking*. New York: Wiley.

———. 1980. "Track misperceptions and frustrated college plans: An analysis of the effects of tracks and track perceptions in the national longitudinal survey." *Sociology of Education* 53:74–87.

Rosenthal, R., and J. Jacobson. 1968. *Pygmalion in the Classroom*. New York: Holt, Rinehart, and Winston.

Rubovits, P., and M. Maehr. 1971. "Pygmalion analyzed: Toward an explanation of the Rosenthal-Jacobson findings." *Journal of Personality and Social Psychology* 19:197–203.

Sewell, W. H., and J. M. Armer. 1966. "Neighborhood context and college plans." *American Sociological Review* 31:159–68.

Weinstein, R. 1976. "Reading group membership in first grade: Teacher behavior and pupil experience over time." *Journal of Educational Psychology* 68:103–16.

Wilkins, W. 1976. "The concept of a self-fulfilling prophecy." *Sociology of Education* 49: 175–83.

Wilson, B., and D. Schmits. 1978. "What's new in ability grouping?" *Phi Delta Kappan* 59: 535–36.

18

Beneath the Skin and between the Ears: A Case Study in the Politics of Representation

Hugh Mehan

CONSTRUCTING SOCIAL FACTS: CLARITY FROM AMBIGUITY

Events in the world are ambiguous. We struggle to understand these events, to imbue them with meaning. The choice of a particular way of representing events gives them a particular meaning. There is often a competition over the correct, appropriate, or preferred way of representing objects, events, or people. In fact, although there are many possible modes of representing the world and communicating them to people, the course of history can be envisioned as successive attempts to impose one mode of representation upon another.

Proponents of various positions in conflicts waged in and through discourse attempt to capture or dominate modes of representation. They do so in a variety of ways, including inviting or persuading others to join their side, or silencing opponents by attacking their positions. If successful, a hierarchy is formed, in which one mode of representing the world (its objects, events, people, etc.) gains primacy over others, transforming modes of representation from an array on a horizontal plane to a ranking on a vertical plane. This competition over the meaning of ambiguous events, people, and objects in the world has been called the "politics of representation" (Holquist, 1983; Shapiro, 1987; Mehan & Wills, 1988; Mehan, 1989).

For example, there are many ways in which nonresident laborers can be represented: "guest workers," "potential citizens," "illegal aliens," "undocumented workers." Each formulation or way of representing this group of people does not simply reflect its characteristics. Each mode of representation defines the person making the representation and constitutes the group of people, and does so in a different way. To be a GUEST worker is to be an invited person, someone who is welcome and in a positive relationship to the employer; to be a guest WORKER is to be someone who is contributing to the economy, productively, by laboring. The for-

259

mulation: POTENTIAL CITIZEN invokes similar positive connotations. It does so within the realm of citizenship and politics, however, rather than in the realm of market economics, as the guest worker formulation does. The "potential citizen" is not yet a complete citizen, but is on the path of full participation in the society. The ILLEGAL ALIEN designation invokes many opposite ways of thinking. "Illegal" is simple and clear: a person outside of society, an idea reinforced by the "alien" designation—foreign, repulsive, threatening. Finally, representing this group as UNDOCUMENTED WORKERS implies a person or persons who contribute economically, but do so in an extralegal capacity.

So, too, a recent "surrogate mother case" illustrates that a new-born baby is subject to multiple and competing interpretations. The case turned on the issue of whether the baby's mother had the right to retain her after she had agreed to give her over to the (artificially inseminating) father. Those who favored her right to do so resisted the use of the "surrogate mother" term in favor of the "natural mother" designation. They drew the analogy between the surrogate mother case and disputes over adoption or custody after divorce. This language portrays custody as an issue involving interpersonal relationships and commitments involving parents and children. Those who favored the (artificially inseminating) father's claim to the child (and therefore opposed the "surrogate" mother) invoked language associated with contracts and legally binding arguments. This mode of representation led one commentator to say "it made the Baby M case bear an uncanny resemblance to 'the all sales final style of the used car lot'" (Pollitt, 1987, p. 682).

A similar competition over the meaning of a group is played out in schools every day when educators try to decide whether a certain child is "normal" or "deviant," belongs in a "regular educational program" or in a "special education program." Deciding whether students are "normal" or "special" is a practical project that occurs routinely in U.S. schools. Although this activity is as old as schools themselves, in response to recently enacted state and federal legislation this classification and sorting activity has become more formalized. There are now procedures mandated by law, especially PL 94-142, "The Education for All Handicapped Students Act," concerning the referral of students to special education. This law, established to provide an equitable education to handicapped youngsters in the least restrictive environment possible, imposes time limits for the assessment of students and specifies the participants involved in decision making. For example, final placement decisions are to be made by a committee composed of the student's teacher, a school psychologist, a representative from the district office, the child's parents, and, in some cases, a medical official.

In general, I am interested in how the clarity of social facts such as "intelligence," "deviance," "health," or "illness" are produced from the ambiguity of everyday life. In the work described in this chapter, I concentrate on a particular instantiation of that general interest—the production of student identities. In short, I am asking: How are student identities produced? How does a student become a "special education" or a "regular education" student?

This line of questioning places my investigation in the "social constructionist" tradition of research, which is concerned with the ways in which the stable and enduring features of our everyday world are assembled through historical processes and in concrete social settings. The constructivist is interested in how the stable features of social institutions such as schooling (e.g., Mehan, Hertweck, & Meihls, 1986; McDermott et al., 1978; Erickson & Shultz, 1982), science (e.g., Latour & Woolgar, 1986; Knorr-Cetina, 1981), medicine (e.g., Cicourel, 1981; Fisher & Todd, 1983; West, 1984), politics (e.g., Nathanson, 1984; Mehan & Wills, 1988), and the family (e.g., Laing, 1967; Pollner & McDonald-Wikler, 1985; Gordon, 1988) are both generated in and revealed by the language of the institution's participants.

In this line of work, people's everyday practices are examined for the way in which they exhibit, indeed, generate, the social structures of the relevant domain. The notion of structures is meant in a Durkheimian sense, that is, they are "external to and constraining upon" the immediate social situation (Durkheim, 1895/1950). In addition, they are not subject to change as an act of will or volition by individuals (Garfinkel & Sacks, 1970). Furthermore, the structures must be more than an analytic device of the researcher. Inferences about social structure are permissible only when the workings of the structure can be located in people's interaction.

A SOCIAL FACT OF THE SCHOOL SYSTEM: HANDICAPPED STUDENTS

In order to understand the process by which students are considered for placement in one of a number of special education programs or are retained in regular classrooms, we (Mehan, et al., 1986) followed the progress of students' cases through the special education referral process mandated by federal law (PL 94-142). During the 1978–1979 school year in which my colleagues and I observed this sorting and classification process in a midsize school district in southern California, 141 students out of a total school population of 2,700 students were referred for "special education"; 53 of these cases were considered by the committee with responsibility for final placement decisions. Most (38) of the students considered by the "eligibility and placement" (E&P) committees were placed into the "learning disabilities" (LD) program (a "pullout" education program in which students spend a part of their school day in their regular classroom and the other part of the day in a special classroom), and 7 were placed in the "educationally handicapped" (EH) program (a program in which students spend all of their school day in a special classroom). Notably, no students were placed in special programs outside the district and only one student considered by the committee was retained in his regular classroom.

These figures, which represent the aggregate number of students placed into educational programs, would conventionally be accepted as an example of a "social fact." Furthermore, each number represents a point in a student's educational career, that is, his or her identity as a "special education" or a "regular education" student. Hence, we have two senses of social structure here: one represented as aggregate data, the other represented as social identities.

Given this statistical distribution, I am asking: What practices produce this array, these careers, these identities? In answering this question, I propose to show that these "social facts" of the school system are constructed in the practical work of educators in their person-to-person and person-to-text interaction. In the analysis that follows, I explore a way of showing how the routine practices of educators as they carry out their daily work construct a "handicapped" student by tracing one student's case through the special education referral process. The major steps in this process are "referral," "educational testing," and "placement decision."

In order to uncover the discursive and organizational arrangements that create descriptions of students as handicapped, my colleagues and I employed an interconnected set of research methods. In addition to observing in classrooms, teachers' lounges, testing rooms, and committee meetings, we interviewed educators and parents, reviewed students' records, and videotaped events that were crucial in the construction of students' identities. Students' records provided such baseline data as the age, sex, and grade of students, the official reason for referral, the name of the person making the referral, the date of referral, psychological assessment information, and final disposition of cases. Information available from school records was checked against information that became available to us through observation, videotaping, informal discussions, and more formal interviews with educators in the district.

Observations in classrooms and analysis of lessons videotaped there gave us insight into the reasons teachers referred students and the relationship between teachers' accounts of student behavior and students' classroom behavior. Videotape of educational testing sessions and Eligibility and Placement Committee meetings served as the behavioral record we examined for the educators' sorting and classifying practices. It also served as a multipurpose document for interviews with participants in these key events in the referral process.

CONSTRUCTING AN LD STUDENT: THE CASE OF SHANE

We discovered, upon the analysis of the materials gathered by these diverse research techniques, that the student classification process in the Coast District had a number of components. The schools' work of sorting students most frequently started in the classroom, continued through psychological assessment, and culminated in evaluation by the E&P Committee. Thus, as Collins (1981) suggested, a "social structure"—the aggregate number of students in various educational programs or their identity as "special" or "regular" students—was generated in a sequence of organizationally predictable interactional events (classroom, testing session, meetings).

An important feature of this process is the transformation of discourse into texts. Discourse from one setting in the sequence of events in the referral process becomes the text used for discussion in the next session. So, for example, after a teacher and students interact in the classroom (discourse), the teacher fills out a form (text). That text is introduced into the discourse of the School Appraisal Team (SAT) meeting. From the discourse of the participants in that meeting, another piece of text is generated, this time a "summary of recommendation," which instructs the school psychologist to begin educational testing. The administration of the educational test transpires as face-to-face interaction between tester and student. Based on that discourse, the tester writes a report. That text is sent to the placement committee, where it becomes part of the file, which, representing the child, becomes the basis of the final placement decision. Such texts, generated from a particular event in the sequential process (e.g., a testing encounter), become the basis of the interaction in the next step in the sequence (e.g., a placement committee meeting). These texts become divorced from the social interaction that created them as they move through the system, institutionally isolated from the interactional practices that generated them in the preceding events.

Step 1: Calling for Help

The process by which a child becomes "educationally handicapped" usually begins in the classroom when, for whatever reasons, a teacher refers a child by completing a referral form. Completing the form and making the referral do not automatically make the child LD or educationally handicapped; but unless that bureaucratic step is taken, the child cannot be eligible to achieve that status. On October 10, approximately 1 month after the start of school, the fourth-grade teacher at the Desert Vista School referred "Shane" for possible placement in special education for his "low academic performance" and his "difficulty in applying himself to his daily class work."[1]

In order to gain more insight into the teachers' reasons for referring students than was available on official referral forms, we videotaped classroom lessons and viewed them with the teachers. Following guidelines concerning these "viewing sessions" that have proved productive in the past (e.g., Cicourel et al., 1974; Erickson & Shultz, 1982), teachers were asked to "stop the tape any time they found anything interesting happening." While watching a videotape of a math lesson in which Shane and others were participating, the teacher stopped the tape just after Shane said "no way" while assembling a pattern with geometric shapes called tangrams:

130 *Teacher:* Yeah, he, he starts out like that on a lot of things. It's like, I can't do it. He's just glancing at it. . . . He's very apprehensive about approaching anything. But once he gets into it, and finishes something he's just so pleased with himself. And I'll say, hey I thought you said "No way." "Well?"

Later in the interview, the teacher stopped the tape again and commented:

406 *Teacher:* I mentioned before, yeah, that whenever he's given some new task to do it's always like, too hard, no way I can do it, until we, oh, come on, you just get into it and try it. When he finishes, I mean its like fantastic, you know that he did it.[2]

These comments reinforced the teacher's representation of the child as one who has trouble applying himself to his school work. It is interesting to note, however, that all the other students in the lesson expressed similar consternation with the difficulty of the task. Nevertheless, the teacher did not treat the comments by the other students as instances of the concern over work difficulty; she did, however, treat the comments by Shane as exemplifying this reason for referring him. This gap between referral reason and students' behavior was a general pattern in our study (Mehan et al., 1986, pp. 69–97), which implicates the problematic nature of the behavioral record beneath special education referrals and the important role that teachers' expectations and conceptions play in forming judgments about students' behavior.

Step 2: Refining the Definition

The referral was forwarded to the next step in the referral system, the School Appraisal Team, a committee composed of educators at the Desert Vista School. At its first meeting in October, the school psychologist was instructed to assess Shane. For a variety of practical reasons that plague bureaucratic processes such as this referral system, including a large backlog of cases, difficulty in obtaining parental permission, and necessary records from another school district, the recommended assessment did not take place until December and January—2 months after the original referral.

The school psychologist administered a battery of tests to Shane on December 6, including an informal assessment called the "Three Wishes," the Goodenough Draw A Man Test, and portions of the Wechsler Intelligence Scale For Children— Revised (WISC-R). The SAT met again on January 4. After hearing the results of the first round of assessment, the committee recommended that the psychologist complete testing. In response to that instruction, the school psychologist completed the WISC-R and administered the California Assessment Test (CAT) and the Bender Gestalt. On February 2, the committee heard the psychologist's report of testing. The psychologist reported that Shane had a verbal IQ of 115. He was reading at a fourth-grade level. His arithmetic and spelling tested at 3.0 and 3.5, which "put him below grade level." His test age on the Bender Gestalt was 7.0–7.5, while his actual age (at the time) was 9.0, which put him "considerably below his age level." Based on this assessment, the SAT recommended that Shane be considered by the "Eligibility and Placement" (E&P) Committee for possible placement into a program for the learning disabled.[3]

We see illustrated here the process by which general calls for help from a class-room teacher become refined and specified in official language. The teacher had said Shane "has difficulty in applying himself to classwork." That vague observa-tion is now transformed into a technical assessment: Shane's academic skill is ex-pressed in numerical terms (IQ of 115, test age of 7.5). He is compared with a nor-mative standard: He is "behind grade level." No longer is he a child "who needs help"; now he is a candidate "learning disabled child."

This refining is fundamental to the way in which the diagnostic process creates handicapped students and handicapped students' careers. Students' identities are sharpened as they move from regular education classrooms to testing rooms and finally to meeting rooms.

Step 3: Resolving Competing Representations of the Student

When the E&P Committee met on February 16 to discuss Shane's case, the fol-lowing dialogue took place:

92 *Psychologist:* does the uh, committee agree that the, uh learning disability place-ment is one that might benefit him?
93 *Principal:* I think we agree.
94 *Psychologist:* We're not considering then a special day class at all for him?
95 *Special Education Teacher:* I wouldn't at this point//
96 *Many:* = No.

The committee decided to place Shane into an LD group, a pullout educational program in which students spend a part of the school day in the regular classroom and the other part of the day in a special program. The "special day class" indexed by the psychologist (line 94) is the EH program in which students spend the en-tire school day in a special classroom.

When we observed these E&P meetings, we were struck by a prominent feature of the interaction. Although committee members came to meetings with a variety of opinions about the appropriate placement of students, by meeting's end one view of the children, that one recommended by the district, prevailed. Furthermore, this agreement was reached without debate or disagreement. For example, before the E&P meeting reviewed in this chapter, the classroom teacher, reflecting on the changes in the student she referred in October, was no longer convinced that Shane needed special education. The mother, worried about the stigmatizing effect of even a mild placement such as an LD group, did not want any special education for her child. Although definite and vocal before the meeting, they were silent during the meeting. In trying to understand how committee members (including parents) lost their voices while routinely coming to agreement with the school's recommenda-tion, we turned our attention to the discourse of the placement committee meet-ings prior to the "decision to place" students occurred (see transcript lines 92–96).

During the course of the meeting, four reports were made to the committee, one by the school psychologist, one by the child's teacher, one by the school nurse, and one by the child's mother. These reports varied along three dimensions: (1) the manner in which they presented information, (2) the manner in which they grounded their assertions, and (3) the manner in which they represented the child. By arraying the reports along these dimensions, I found three "languages" being spoken in the meeting: a psychological language, a sociological language, and a historical language. Competing versions of the child are presented in these "languages" or idioms, but only one, the version of the child presented in the psychological language, prevails.

Mode of Presentation

The information that the committee obtained from the classroom teacher and the mother appeared in a different form than the information made available by the school psychologist. The information that the psychologist had about the student was presented to the committee in a single uninterrupted report whereas information was elicited from both the classroom teacher and the mother. Here is the psychologist's opening statement to the committee:

> 1 *Psychologist:* Um. What we're going to do is, I'm going to have a brief, an overview of the testing because the rest of, of the, the committee has not, uh, has not an, uh, been aware of that yet. And uh, then each of us will share whatever, whatever we feel we need to share.
> 2 *Principal:* Right.
> 3 *Psychologist:* And then we will make a decision on what we feel is a good, oh (3) placement (2) for an, Shane.

The school psychologist then provided the committee members with the information she had about the student:

> 3 *Psychologist:* Shane is ah nine years old, and he's in fourth grade. Uh, he, uh, was referred because of low academic performance and he has difficulty applying himself to his daily class work. Um, Shane attended the Montessori School in kindergarten and first grade, and then he entered Carlsberg-bad in, um, September of 1976 and, uh, entered our district in, uh, '78. He seems to have very good peer relationships but, uh, the teachers, uh, continually say that he has difficulty with handwriting. 'kay. He enjoys music and sports. I gave him a complete battery and, urn, I found that, uh, he had a verbal IQ of 115, performance of 111, and a full scale of 115, so he's a bright child. Uh, he had very high scores in, uh, information which is his long-term memory. Ah, vocabulary, was, ah, also, ah, considerably over average, good detail awareness and his, um, picture arrangement scores, he had a seventeen which is very high//
> 4 *Special Education Teacher:*   = Mmmm//
> 5 *Psychologist:* = very superior rating, so he, his visual sequencing seems to be good and also he has a good grasp of anticipation and awareness of social situations. Urn, he (5)

(she is scanning her notes) scored in reading at 4.1, spelling 3.5, and arithmetic 3.0, which gave him a standard score of 100 in, uh, reading, 95 in spelling, and 90 in arithmetic. When compared with his [overall] score, it does put him somewhat ah below his, you know, his capabilities. I gave him the Bender Gestalt (clears throat) and he had six errors. And his test age was 7.0 to 7.5 and his actual age is nine, so it, uh, he was considerably beneath his, uh, his uh, age level. (2) His, I gave him the, uh VADS and his, um (5 or 6) (looking through notes) both the oral-aural and the visual-written modes of communication were high but the visual oral and the oral written are low, so he, uh, cannot switch channels. His expressive vocabulary was in the superior range (6). Uh, visual perception falls above age level, so he's fine in that area (6). And fine motor skills appear to be slightly lower than, uh, average (voice trails off slightly), I saw them. (3) He read words very quickly when he was doing the academics but I didn't see any reversals in his written work. Uh, I gave him several projective tests and, um, the things that I picked up there is that, um he [does] possibly have some fears and anxieties, uh, (5). So I had felt ah, that perhaps he might, uh, uh, benefit, um, (3) from special help. He also was tested, um, in 1976 and at that time he was given the WISC-R and his IQ was slightly lower, full scale of a 93 (3 or 4). His, um, summary of that evaluation, uh, was, uh, he was given the ITPA and he had high auditory reception, auditory association, auditory memory. (2) So his auditory skills are good. (3) He was given another psychol- psychological evaluation in 1977. He was given the Leiter and he had an IQ of 96 (6). And, um (3 or 4) they concluded that he had a poor mediate recall (2) but they felt that was due to an emotional overlay and they felt that some emotional conflicts were, uh, interfering with his ability to concentrate.

At the end of this presentation, the psychologist asked the student's teacher to provide information:

5 *Psychologist*: Kate, would you like to share with u:s?
6 *Classroom Teacher*: What, the problems I see ( ) Um. . .
7 *Psychologist*: Yes.
8 *Classroom Teacher*: Um. Probably basically the fine motor types of things are difficult for him. He's got a very creative mi:ind and expresses himself well ( ) orally and verbally and he's pretty alert to what's going on. (2) Maybe a little bit [too] much, watching EVERYthing that's (hh) going (hh) on, and finds it hard to stick to one task. And [mostly] I've been noticing that it's just his writing and things that he has a, a block with. And he can rea:ad and comprehend some things when I talk to him, [but] doing independent type work is hard for him.
9 *Principal*: mhmmm, putting it down on paper . . .
10 *Classroom Teacher*: Yeah::, and sticking to a task//
11 *Principal*:   = mmhmmm//
12 *Classroom Teacher*:   = and getting
it done, without being distracted by (hehhehheh)
13 *Special Education Teacher*: How does he relate with what the other kids do?
14 *Classroom Teacher*: Uh, very well. He's got a lot of frie:ends, and, uh, especially, even out on the playground he's, um (3), wants to get in on the games, get on things and is well accepted. So:o, I don't see too many problems there.

In this sequence, we have the classroom teacher beginning to present some of the conditions under which Shane has trouble (8), being interrupted by the principal (9), then the special education teacher took the floor (13). From that point on, the special education teacher asked the classroom teacher a series of questions about Shane's peer relations, reading level, and performance in spelling and math.

After the school psychologist asked how Shane handled failure, the questioning shifted to the mother, who was asked about her son's fine motor control at home:

46 *Special Education Teacher:* How do you find him at [home] in terms of using his fingers and fine motor kinds of things? Does he do//
47 *Mother:*   = He will, as a
small child, he didn't at all. He was never interested in it, he wasn't interested in sitting in my lap and having a book read to him, any things like that//
48 *Special Education Teacher:* = mhmmm//
49 *Mother:*   = which I think is part of it you
know. His, his older brother was just the opposite, and learned to write real early. [Now] Shane, at night, lots of times he comes home and he'll write or draw. He's really doing a lot//
50 *Special Education Teacher:* ( )
51 *Mother:*   = he sits down and is writing love notes to
his girl friend (hehheh). He went in our bedroom last night and turned on the TV and got out some colored pencils and started writing. So he, really likes to, and of course he brings it all in to us to see//
52 *Special Education Teacher:* =mhmmm//
53 *Mother:*   = and comment on, so I think, you
know, he's not [NEGAtive] about//
54 *Special Education Teacher:*   = no//
55 *Mother:*   = that any more//
56 *Special Education Teacher:*   =uh huh
57 *Mother:* He was before, but I think his attitude's changed a lot.

These transcript excerpts show that the information that the psychologist had about the student was presented to the committee in a single, uninterrupted report, while the mother's and classroom teacher's information was elicited by other members of the committee. The school psychologist's presentation of the case to the committee was augmented by officially sanctioned props, including the case file itself (a bulky manila folder on display in front of the psychologist), test results, carefully prepared notes. When she spoke, she read from notes. By contrast, neither the mother nor the teacher had such props. They spoke from memory, not from notes.

Grounds of Assertions

The members of the committee supported their claims about the child in different ways. The psychologist provided a summary of the results of a given test or subtest in a standard format. She named the subtest, reported the student's score, and gave her interpretations of the results. For example:

I gave him a complete battery, and I found that, uh, he had a verbal IQ of 115, performance of 111, and a full scale of 115, so he's a bright child.

He had very high scores in, uh, information, which is his long-term memory.

His, um, picture arrangement scores, he had a seventeen, which is very high, very superior rating.

While the psychologist reported information about the student gained from the use of quasi-scientific tools, the classroom teacher and mother based their reports on firsthand observations. For example, the teacher provided general statements, "he's got a very creative mind and expresses himself well" (8), as well as some more specific assertions: "he can read and comprehend some things when I talk to him, but doing independent type work is hard for him" (8). While the psychologist's observations were confined to a relatively short period of time (hours of testing) and a circumscribed setting, the classroom teacher's and mother's observations were based on a longer period of time and a less circumscribed spatial and social arrangement. For the teacher, this period was a school year and the space was the classroom, while the mother's observations concerned the child's actions in a wide variety of situations spanning a lifetime.

Thus, information gathered by systematic, albeit indirect, observations (i.e., that from specialized tests) *was presented to* the committee, whereas information gathered by direct, albeit unguided or unstructured, observation (which included information about classroom experiences and home life) *was elicited from* participants. Furthermore, the mode in which information was presented to the committee varied according to the status and official expertise of the participants in the meeting. The most highly technical information (that from tests) was made available by the most highly trained and highest-ranking people in attendance at the meeting, whereas the personal observations were made available by the participants with the least technical expertise and lowest ranking. Speakers of officially higher rank and who spoke with their authority grounded in technical expertise presented their information, whereas speakers of lower rank, who spoke with authority based on firsthand observations, had information elicited from them.

Mode of Representation

Shane's mother, his teacher, the school psychologist, and the school nurse discussed the student and his academic performance differently. The student was characterized by the psychologist as having "troubles" and "problems." This mode of representation is constituted by her syntax and her vocabulary: "he has difficulty applying himself to his daily work" (3), "he cannot switch channels" (5), "he has some fears and anxieties" (5). The verbs "have" and "is" make the "troubles" and "problems" Shane's; they are beneath his skin, between his ears. The classroom teacher characterized the problem in a similar way: "the fine motor types of things are difficult for him" (8), "doing independent type work is hard for him" (8).

While the student's problem is the focus of attention for the entire committee, the mother and teacher discussed the student in a different language than did the psychologist and the nurse. Notable in this regard are comments about the student's motivation: "he enjoys math" (28), "he enjoys handwriting and wants to learn it" (30), "he seems to enjoy handwriting and wants to learn it" (30), "he really tries at it hard and seems to wanna learn it better" (34). She also introduced a number of contingencies that influenced the student's performance. First, his performance varies as a function of preparation: "If he studies his spelling and concentrates on it he can do pretty well" (22). Second, his performance varies according to the kinds of materials and tasks: "It's hard for him to copy down [math] problems . . . if he's given a sheet where he can fill in answers and work them out he does much better" (28); he does better on group tasks, "but doing independent type work is hard for him" (8). If the tasks at hand are a means to some other end desired by the student, then his performance improves: "if there's something else he wants to do and knows he needs to do and knows he needs to get through that before he can get on to something else, he'll work a little more diligently at it" (45).

The mother's language contrasts even more sharply with the psychologist's than does the teacher's. The mother spoke about changes through time, continually contrasting her son as he was at an earlier age with how he is now. In each of these contrasts, she emphasized improvements and changes for the better. Although she seems to acknowledge the official committee position about Shane's problem, she provided an alternative explanation about the source of the problem. For her, the locus of difficulty was not within him ("it's not physical," "it's not functional"), but it was to be found in his past experience and the situations he had been in.

In short, the teacher, like the psychologist, characterized the issue before the committee as "Shane's problem." The teacher's characterization, unlike the psychologist's, however, had a contingent quality. She spoke sociologically, providing contextual information of a locally situated sort. The mother's language, by contrast, has a historical dimension; she spoke in terms that implied changes through time.

STRATIFYING LANGUAGES OF REPRESENTATION

Committee members often came to E&P meetings with differing views of the student's case and attitudes about the student's placement. During this meeting, the various members of this committee perceived Shane differently. The psychologist located the child's problem beneath his skin and between his ears, whereas the classroom teacher saw the student's problem varying from one classroom situation to another, and the mother saw the child's problem changing through time. That is, the teacher and the mother provided accounts about the student's performance in languages that were different than the psychologist's version of the student's academic difficulties.

This discussion, if left here, would be at best an interesting example of perspectival differences in representation that occur in face-to-face interaction. That is, psychologists, teachers, and parents have different languages for talking about children because of their different experiences and backgrounds. Although the perspectival dimension of representation is certainly an important aspect of the social construction of this child's identity, closing the discussion at this point would leave out a crucial ingredient: These modes of representation are not equal. By meeting's end, one mode of representation, that voiced in a psychological language, prevailed. The psychological representation of the student supplanted both the sociological and historical representations of the student.

So, the question that must be asked is: How did the psychologist control the discourse, dominating the other voices in the conversation? Or, asking this question in another way: How does this mode of representation achieve its privileged status?

In order to determine how the stratification of these modes of representation is accomplished discursively, it is instructive to look at the manner in which the committee treated the descriptions of the child offered by the committee members. The reports by the psychologist and the nurse were accepted without question or challenge, while those of the mother and the teacher were interrupted continuously by questions. This differential treatment is at first surprising, especially in light of the differences in the manifest content of the three descriptions. The psychologist's description is replete with technical terms ("VADS," "Bender," "detail awareness," "ITPA," "WISC-R") and numerical scales ("IQ of 96," "full scale of 93," "test age was 7.0 to 7.5"), while both the mother and the teacher describe the student in lay terms ("he has a creative mind," "doing independent work is hard for him," "he wasn't interested in sitting in my lap and having a book read to him").

Thus, the speaker who includes technical terms in her language *is not asked* to clarify terms, whereas the speakers of a vernacular *are asked* to clarify their terms. No one in the meeting asked the psychologist for more details or further information. In fact, the mother only requested clarification once during the course of the entire meeting and that was just as the formal business was being concluded. Her question was about "PE":

422 *Special Education Teacher:* check over ((( ))) (5–6) I don't think I addressed PE
423 *Psychologist:* I don't think we uh, [oh], ok, we do not need that, okay, he does not need physical edu//
424 *Mother:* = (I want to ask something about that while
you mentioned PE. You mean physical education)
425 *???:* mmhmmm
426 *Mother:* Does the school have a soccer program or is that just totally separate from um, you know, part of the boys' club o::r//
427 *Principal:* = Right. It's a parent organized, um,
association//
428 *Mother:* = Is there something (one?) at the school that would have information on it if it comes up in the season, because Shane really has expressed an interest in that

Here we see the mother ask her only question in the session, about a nontechnical topic, at the end of the meeting, after the placement decision had been reached.

The differences in the way in which the three reports were treated, especially the requests for clarification of technical terms during the committee meeting, help us understand why the psychologist's representation was accorded privileged status by the committee. The psychologist's report gains its authority by the very nature of its construction. The psychologist's language obtains its privileged status *because* it is ambiguous, because it is full of technical terms, *because* it is difficult to understand. The parents and the other committee members do not challenge the ambiguity of the psychologist's report because the grounds to do so are removed by the manner in which the psychologist presents information, grounds assertions, and represents the child in discourse.

Meaning is said to be negotiated in everyday discourse. Speakers and hearers are both responsible for the construction of understanding. According to observers from a wide variety of perspectives, a first maxim of conversation is that speakers intend to make sense and be understood (Merleau-Ponty, 1964; Sacks, Schegloff, & Jefferson, 1974; Grice, 1975; Searle, 1969; Gumperz, 1982). Hearers contribute to meaning in discourse by making inferences from the conversational string of utterances. They display their understanding actively through "back channel work" (Duncan, 1972), which includes eye contact, head nods, and vocalics such as uh huhs and lexical items like "I see," or "I understand." When the hearer does not understand, "a request for clarification" is in order. The manifest purpose of such requests is to obtain more information. The request for clarification is generated by hearers when they do not think that the speaker is speaking clearly.

The grounds for this kind of negotiation of meaning are removed from the committee by the way in which language is used by the psychologist. When the psychologist speaks, it is from an institutionally designated position of authority. Furthermore, the psychologist's representation of the child is based on her professional expertise. The privileged status of the psychologist's expertise, in turn, is displayed in the technical language of her report.

There is a certain mystique in the use of technical vocabulary, as evidenced by the high status that the specialized language of doctors, lawyers, and scientists is given in our society (West, 1984; Philips, 1977; Shuy & Larkin, 1978; Latour & Woolgar, 1986; Wertsch, 1986; Cohn, 1987). The use of technical language indicates a superior status and a special knowledge based on long training and specialized qualifications.

A certain amount of this mystique is evident in the psychologist's language and is apparent in the committee's treatment of it. When technical language is used and embedded in the institutional trappings of the formal proceedings of a meeting, the grounds for negotiating meaning are removed from under the conversation. Because the speaker and hearers do not share the conventions of a common language, hearers do not have the expertise to question, or even to interrupt the speaker. To request a clarification of the psychologist, then, is to challenge the authority of a clinically certified expert. The other members of the committee are placed in the position of assuming the psychologist is speaking knowledgeably and the hearer does not have the competence to understand.

When technical language is used, even though the possibility for active negotiation of meaning is removed, the guise of understanding remains. To be sure, the understanding is a passively achieved one, not the active one associated with everyday discourse. Instead of signaling a lack of understanding via such implicit devices as back-channel work and explicit ones like requests for clarification, the committee members (including the parents) remain silent, thereby tacitly contributing to the guise that common understanding has been achieved.

CONCLUSIONS

In addition to making some specific points about the research I have been conducting on the institutional construction of identities, I conclude by making some more general points about the constitutive model of discourse that is implied by this work and then speculating on the reason that the psychological language is so powerful in educational decision making.

The Institutional Construction of Identities

By looking at the language of groups of educators as they engage in the work of sorting students, I have tried to demonstrate the situated relevance of social structures in the practical work activities performed by people in social interaction. Educators carry out the routine work of conducting lessons, assigning students to ability groups or special programs, administering tests, and attending meetings. The notion of *work* stresses the constructive aspect of institutional practice. Educators' work is repetitive and routine. Its mundane character should not overshadow the drama of its importance, however, because steps on students' career ladders are assembled from such practice. The enactment of routine bureaucratic practices structures students' educational careers by opening or closing their access to particular educational opportunities.

Essentially, the teacher is calling for help. Her call is cast in general not specific terms. This call starts the process that constructs students' institutional identities. These often undifferentiated appeals become refined and specified in official language as they move from regular education classrooms to testing rooms and finally to meeting rooms. Through this process, the child becomes an object. The members of the committee do not have access to the teacher-student interaction; only the residue of that interaction is represented in a file, a decentered text. At the outset, the child was a participant in discourse with his teacher and his classmates. But, from that point on, the child's contribution to his own career status drops out.

The child becomes represented in text. The only way we gain access to the child is in textual representations of his interactions. Thus, the child becomes objectified as the case moves from the classroom to testing to committee meeting.

I found three languages spoken in the committee meeting, which is the last step in this identity construction process: a psychological, a sociological, and a historical language. The psychological language included absolute and categorical statements about the student's abilities. On the basis of information from systematic, albeit indirect, techniques of observation, the locus of the problem was placed within Shane. The result was a "context-free" view of the child, one who had a general disability that cuts across situations. The classroom teacher spoke in a sociological idiom; she tempered her report with contingent factors of a situational sort. According to information from unsystematic, albeit direct, observation, she said that the student's performance was influenced by his state of motivation, kinds of classroom tasks, and types of materials. The result was a "context-bound" view of the child, one who had specific problems, which appeared in certain academic situations, but who operated more than adequately in other situations. The mother's language was historical. Based on years of direct observation, she provided particulars about the biography and history of her son and noted changes and improvements across time as well as situational circumstances as the source of his difficulties.

The psychologist's recommendations were accepted without challenge or question, while the sociological and historical recommendations were routinely interrupted with requests for clarification and further information. I propose that the resolution of competing versions of the child can be understood in terms of the authority that reports gain by their manner of presentation, method of grounding truth claims, and modes of representation.

The psychological language gained its authority from the mastery and control of a technical vocabulary, grounded in a quasi-scientific idiom. Because of the fact that the psychologist's report was obscure, difficult to understand, and ambiguous, not in spite of it, the grounds for questioning or challenging were removed from the conversation. It is this technical, quasi-scientific authority that contributes to the stratification of languages of representation and thereby the construction of children's identities.

When people have competing versions of ambiguous events that transpire in the world, they often try to negotiate a commonly agreed upon definition of the situation. Often, consensus is achieved when one or another of the protagonists relinquishes his or her representation of the world as the preferred version, after having heard superior information or having been convinced of the efficacy of an argument. In the case considered here, the resolution of competing modes of representation was not negotiated. The members of the committee resolved the disjuncture among sociological, historical, and psychological versions by credentialing the psychological version as the official version of this student. Thus, an institutionally sanctioned version of experience is superimposed upon multiple and competing versions of experience.

Language as Constitutive Activity

The constructivist view of social life poses mutually constitutive relations between modes of thought, modes of discourse, and modes of action. Discourse does not passively reflect or merely describe the world. Because language is action, different uses of language constitute the world differently. Events in the world do not exist for people independently of the language people use to make sense of them. Instead, objects are defined through elaborate enactments of cultural conventions, which lead to the establishment of such well-documented "institutional facts" (Searle, 1969) as "touchdowns," "marriages," "insults," "banishments," "property rights" (D'Andrade, 1984), and, as I have proposed, "learning disabilities" and "educational handicaps." When the constitutive rules of discourse are in effect, behavior becomes action, and actions become "touchdowns," "marriages," "illness," "schizophrenia," "deviance," "intelligence," and "educational handicaps."

Modes of Representation

When discourse is viewed as activity that culturally constructs clarity out of ambiguity, then we should not be surprised to find multiple modes of representation. Marriage, schizophrenia, and learning disabilities are constructed by cultural conventions in much the same way that touchdowns are constructed by the constitutive rules of football. Just as crossing the goal line only counts as a touchdown if the appropriate players are present and it has been duly constituted by the referee, so, too, a student's behavior only counts as a learning disability if the appropriate institutional officials apply the appropriate institutional machinery (educational testing, parent conferences, placement meetings, etc.). Without the application of that institutional machinery, educational handicaps do not exist.[4]

In the case we have considered, there were many ways in which Shane could have been formulated: "normal student," "educationally handicapped student," "gifted student," "learning disabled student." Each formulation or way of representing Shane does not simply reflect or merely describe his characteristics; each mode of representation constitutes him, and does so in a different way. A "normal student" is constituted as fitting within the parameters or norms of intelligence; a "gifted student" is constituted as having exceptional talents. An "educationally handicapped" or "learning disabled" student is constituted to have an inherent disorder. Importantly, each of these formulations characterizes intelligence or talent in terms that place it inside the student. Intelligence, whether normal, exceptional, or lacking, is treated as a personal and private property of the individual. This way of characterizing people exemplifies the use of dispositional properties in the explanation of people's behavior. Each of these modes of representation naturalizes the child, thereby masking the social construction work that generated the designation in the first place.

In short, we know the world through the representations we make of it (Bakhtin, 1981). A particular way of representing events in language influences, first, the way we think about the events represented, and, second, the way we act toward the events.

The Politics of Representation

Modes of representing events vary according to the perspective from which a representation is constructed. Perspective here refers to the standpoint from which a person is participating in discourse. One dimension of perspective is the person's physical location in the here-and-now of face-to-face situations (Gurwitsch, 1966). Another is the person's location in social institutions, cultural arrangements, and sociohistorical space-time (Bakhtin, 1981).

We have found that professional educators (i.e., school psychologists), for a variety of biographical, historical, and cultural reasons, described students in dispositional terms, whereas parents and, to a lesser extent, classroom teachers formulated students in more contextual terms (Mehan et al., 1986, pp. 109-157). Although there are many possible modes of representing the world and communicating them to others constructed from particular biographical, historical, and social-cultural perspectives, the course of history can be envisioned as successive attempts to impose one mode of representation upon another. Proponents of various political positions attempt to capture or dominate modes of representation. If successful, a hierarchy is formed, in which one mode of representing the world (its objects, events, people) gains primacy over others, transforming modes of representation from an array on a horizontal plane to a ranking on a vertical plane.

It is not accidental in this "politics of representation" (Holquist, 1983; Shapiro, 1987; Mehan & Wills, 1988; Mehan, 1989) that institutionally grounded representations predominate, for example, psychiatrists' representations prevail over patients', professional educators' representations override parents' formulations. Institutional officials speak with a technical vocabulary grounded in professional expertise. Ordinary people speak in a common vernacular grounded in personal experience. More and more often in our increasingly technological society, when a voice speaking in formalized, rationalistic, and mathematical terms confronts a voice grounded in personal, commonsense, or localized particulars, the technical prevails over the vernacular.

When categorizing a student, these educators reproduced the status relations among the different discourses that exist in society. A universalizing language that is given higher status in the meeting and whose variables are read into the child, thereby decontextualizing the child, is the same language we see gaining power and authority in recent times. Thus, the concrete face-to-face encounters that generate an instance of a category are constitutive moments and reproduce the relations among categories that we see gaining ascendancy historically.

The Prevalence of the Psychological Idiom

As a closing note to this chapter, 1 would like to speculate on the reason why the psychological language is privileged over the other languages in educational decision making. The privileging of the psychological language speaks to the prevalence of the psychological idiom in our society. This psychological idiom has two important dimensions: one, a focus on the individual and, two, a base in the technological.

Since Tocqueville, observers of American society (e.g., Williams, 1960; Bellah, Madsen, Sullivan, Swidler, & Tipton, 1985) have identified individualism as a core value in American society. We see the causes of human behavior in terms of states and traits (D'Andrade, 1984). These states and traits are in the heads and between the ears of people. We say that people are successful or unsuccessful because of their personal effort and hard work—which are rabidly individualistic terms (Bellah et al., 1985).

Commentators such as Gould (1981) and Noble (1977) have identified a second politically relevant theme in American society: the increasing reliance on technical solutions to the problems facing our mass, democratic society. We turn to instruments such as the IQ test to sort students for political, educational, and medical programs. We turn to medical, legal, and scientific experts for guidance on a wide variety of problems in American society. We employ missiles, rockets, and computer-based command and control systems to ward off foreign aggressors. The inventor is a cultural hero—as embodied in the myths of Benjamin Franklin and Thomas Edison. Mastery over nature is a way to progress (Williams, 1960).

Individualism and technical knowledge constitute two of the most important dimensions of a psychological account of human behavior. Both of these dimensions are readily apparent in the discourse that dominates special education selections. Thus, there is a strong affinity between the idiom that predominates educational discourse and a dominant metaphor in American society. Both cite personal and individual characteristics as the basis of success and failure. Both rely on technical knowledge and expertise in decision making.

This power of the individualistic and technological dimensions of the psychological account of human behavior in the dominant idiom in a decision-making situation suggests there is a linkage between what happens in a mundane, everyday social situation (e.g., a meeting within a school) and an important albeit ephemeral aspect of social structure (i.e., American core values or ideology). The linkage is expressed in the psychologist's language. The psychologist is speaking with a voice that unites the concerns and activities of a particular time and place with those of the wider cultural belief system.

To do more than speculate about this linkage, of course, it is necessary to ground any such claims about the workings of ideology in discourse. The approach taken in this study (an ethnographically grounded study of the modes of representation in everyday discourse) is suggestive of a way to proceed to connect social discourse with social structure and ideology without reducing one to the other.

NOTES

1. Source: referral form in student's school record.
2. Source: interview of teacher conducted by Alma Hertweck. A number of conventions have been used in the transcripts reproduced in this chapter: ( ) = unclear talk; EVERYbody = emphasis; (hehheh) = laughter; rea:ad = stretched talk; // = overlapping utterances; (3) = pause measured in seconds.
3. Source: School Psychologist's Assessment Summary. This report was also read to the E&P Committee on February 16 (see my discussion of this report in the context of the E&P meeting).
4. See Searle (1969, pp. 34–35) for an important discussion of the "count as" relationship, i.e., how behavior becomes instances of cultural categories.

REFERENCES

Bahktin, M. M. (1981). *The dialogic imagination*. Austin: University of Texas Press.

Bellah, R. N., Madsen, R., Sullivan, W. M., Swidler, A., & Tipton, S. M. (1985). *Habits of the heart*. Berkeley: University of California Press.

Cicourel, A. V. (1981). Language and medicine. In C. A. Ferguson & S. B. Heath (Eds.), *Language in the USA* (pp. 347–367). Cambridge: Cambridge University Press.

Cicourel, A. V., Jennings, K., Jennings, S., Leiter, K., MacKay, H., Mehan, H., & Roth, D. (1974). *Language use and school performance*. New York: Academic Press.

Cohn, C. (1987). Sex and death in the rational world of defense intellectuals. *Signs, 12,* 687–718.

Collins, R. (1981). On the microfoundations of macrosociology. *American Journal of Sociology, 86,* 984–1004.

D'Andrade, R. G. (1984). Cultural meaning systems. In R. A. Shweder & R. A. LeVine (Eds.), *Culture theory: Essays on mind, self and emotion* (pp. 88–119). Cambridge: Cambridge University Press.

Duncan, S. (1972). Some signals and rules for taking speaking turns in conversation. *Journal of Personality and Social Psychology, 23,* 283–292.

Durkheim, E. (1950). *The rules of sociological method*. Glencoe, IL: Free Press. (Original work published 1895)

Erickson, F., & Shultz, J. (1982). *The counselor as gatekeeper: Social interactions in interviews*. New York: Academic Press.

Fisher, S., & Todd, A. (1983). *The social organization of doctor-patient communication*. Washington, DC: Center for Applied Linguistics.

Garfinkel, H., & Sacks, H. (1970). On formal structures of practical actions. In J. C. McKinney & E. A. Tiryakian (Eds.), *Theoretical sociology* (pp. 337–366). New York: Appleton-Century-Crofts.

Gordon, L. (1988). *Heroes of their own lives*. New York: Viking.

Gould, S. J. (1981). *The mismeasure of man*. New York: W. W. Norton.

Grice, H. P. (1975). Logic and conversation. In P. Cole & J. Morgan (Eds.), *Syntax and semantics: Vol. 3. Speech acts* (pp. 41–58). New York: Academic Press.

Gumperz, J. (1982). *Strategies of discourse*. Cambridge: Cambridge University Press.

Gurwitsch, A. (1966). *Studies in phenomenology and psychology*. Evanston, IL: Northwestern University Press.

Holquist, M. (1983). The politics of representation. *Quarterly Newsletter of the Laboratory of Comparative Human Cognition*, 5(1), 2–9.

Knorr-Cetina, K. (1981). *The manufacture of knowledge: An essay on the constructivist and contextualized nature of science*. Oxford: Pergamon Press.

Laing, R. D. (1967). *The politics of experience*. New York: Pantheon.

Latour, B., & Woolgar, S. (1986). *Laboratory life: The construction of scientific facts*. Princeton: Princeton University Press.

McDermott, R. P., Gospodinoff, K., & Aron, J. (1978). Criteria for an ethnographically adequate description of concerted activities in context. *Semiotica*, 24, 245–275.

Mehan, H. (1989). Oracular reasoning in a psychiatric setting: The resolution of conflict in language. In A. D. Grimshaw (Ed.), *Conflict talk* (pp. 160–177). Cambridge: Cambridge University Press.

Mehan, H., Hertweck, A., & Meihls, J. L. (1986). *Handicapping the handicapped: Decision making in students' careers*. Stanford, CA: Stanford University Press.

Mehan, H., & Wills, J. (1988). MEND: A nurturing voice in the nuclear arms debate. *Social Problems*, 35, 363–383.

Merleau-Ponty, M. (1964). *Signs*. Evanston, IL: Northwestern University Press.

Nathanson, C. E. (1984, August). *The social construction of the Soviet threat*. Paper presented at the meeting of the American Sociological Association, San Antonio, TX.

Noble, D. (1977). *America by design*. Oxford: Oxford University Press.

Philips, S. (1977). *The role of spatial positioning and alignment in defining interactional units: The American courtroom as a case in point*. Paper presented at the meeting of the American Anthropological Association, Houston, TX.

Pollitt, K. (1987, May 23). The strange case of Baby M. *Nation*, 667, 682–688.

Pollner, M., & McDonald-Wikler, M. (1985) The social construction of unreality: A case study of a family's attribution of competence to a severly retarded child. *Family Process*, 24, 241–254.

Sacks, H., Schegloff, E. A., & Jefferson, G. (1974). A simplest systematics for the organization of turn-taking in conversation. *Language*, 50, 696–735.

Searle, J. (1969). *Speech acts*. Cambridge: Cambridge University Press.

Shapiro, M. (1987). *The politics of representation*. Madison: University of Wisconsin Press.

Shuy, R.,& Larkin, D. L. (1978). Linguistic considerations in the simplification/clarification of insurance policy language. *Discourse Processes*, 1, 305–321.

Wertsch, J. (1986). Modes of discourse in the nuclear arms debate. *Current Research on Peace aud Violence*, 10, 102–112.

West, C. (1984). *Routine complications: Troubles in talk between doctors and patients*. Bloomington: Indiana University Press.

Williams, R. (1960). *American society*. New York: Knopf.

19

Moments of Discontent: University Women and the Gender Status Quo

Dorothy C. Holland and Margaret A. Eisenhart

In this chapter we examine university women's apprehension of and response to the gender status quo in the United States. Our larger question concerns the role of schools in the reproduction of patriarchy. Researchers and social theoreticians have made important contributions to our appreciation of the role of schools in the reproduction of class. To what extent—we ask—can these contributions also illuminate our understanding of the recreation from one generation to the next of male privilege in the United States?

Our questions about gender and schooling are inspired by the work on cultural reproduction in Britain by Willis (1981b) and McRobbie (1978), for example, and the work of anthropologists of education in the United States—especially that of John Ogbu on minority status and schooling. To a degree the findings of the two approaches have converged.

Comparing the work of Willis (1981a, 1981b) with that of Ogbu (1974, 1978, 1985), we find a convergence in methods—namely, reliance upon ethnographic techniques—and a convergence in analyses of the responses of oppressed groups—working-class males in Willis's case, ethnic and racial minorities in Ogbu's studies—to schooling. In essence, both conclude that students are likely to act in school from a collective sense of the (lack of) "opportunities" afforded to people of their group by the society. The students' discontent may lead to an oppositional stance that disrupts the social status quo, but often, for various reasons and despite its oppositional character, their response results in reproducing cultural values and patterns that contribute to the reproduction of structured inequalities and traditional class and group relationships.

In this chapter, we begin from a framework similar to the one arrived at by Ogbu and Willis. But we focus on gender—a category that neither Willis nor Ogbu has studied explicitly. We discuss the apprehension of gender-related structural barriers by women at two southern universities: Bradford,[1] a historically black school, and SU, a historically white school. We look specifically at the women's complaints about gender-related features of their lives at college and at their responses to these discontents. Our principal aim is to understand what the women in the study see as the gender-related problems in their lives. Then we turn to asking how their apprehensions affect their response to schooling and how schools figure in the re-creation of the gender status quo. Our findings suggest that the school provides an important setting for learning and enacting gender, but in distinction to the case for class and race, it is not a primary target for women's opposition.

THE STUDY

The primary data on which this chapter is based were obtained from analyses of the experiences of 23 women during their first three semesters of college. Seventeen of these—roughly half from each university—were analyzed in depth for this paper. The data were gathered in 1979–1980 as part of an ethnographic study designed to investigate the college experiences and future plans of black and white women on the two campuses. The samples included women with a range of majors, extracurricular interests, size of peer networks, and ideas about their futures; and all of the women selected had strong academic records in high school.

A three-semester period, from near the beginning of the informants' freshman year to the middle of their sophomore year, was chosen for intensive study. During the three-semester period, researchers conducted monthly observations of informants engaged in campus activities. Informants were also interviewed nine times over the course of the three semesters.

In 1983 when members of the ethnographic sample should have been graduating from college, and again in 1987, an attempt was made to recontact them and learn about their current activities and plans. Fifteen of the informants were reinterviewed.

Women's Discontents

The women at Bradford and SU did complain about the treatment they received as women. A few expressed dissatisfaction with not being taken seriously as students. But mostly, they complained about the things that happened to them in romantic relationships with men. A very few expressed discontent with the system of gender relations as they knew it.[2]

Not Being Taken Seriously

Several of the women had experiences in which they were not taken seriously as students. Della's experience is an example. One day Della went to class dressed in a skirt and blouse.

> And I sits in front . . . of the class, and my teacher says, "What's this? What's this? Della, where's she at?" And I just sat there looking at him cause he looked dumb looking around me . . . and he said, "Oh, there's Della." He looked my legs up and down, up and down, and the whole class [was] looking at him. He said, "Oh, oh, I see. I see, Della, I see. Oh, oh. . . ." I was so embarrassed; the whole class was looking at me.

Della complained about the professor's interest in her body and clothes and wondered why he had to emphasize that aspect of her in class. Della's response, as described in the longer interview, was to feel uncomfortable and embarrassed by the incident—but to refrain from acting out her opposition to the status quo.

Karla, who took a lot of courses in which she was one of only a few women, complained that at least some of her science professors failed to take their female students seriously (Holland and Eisenhart, in press [b]). Karla's response to this situation was more active than Della's, but it was still a personal one; she decided to make sure that all of her science professors knew her name and that during each class period, she asked at least one question. This way, she reasoned, the professors would not be able to ignore her like they did other female students.

Karla also complained about a former teacher (married) who wanted her to become his lover. After several attempts, Karla was able to get the man to leave her alone, but she did not stop thinking about the experience, and it made her distrustful of other male teachers' interests in her.

These examples illustrate the nature of the women's complaints about not being taken seriously as students and their responses to these situations. The cases suggest that the women do not experience *direct* barriers to school success, but they are liable to encounter assumptions that they are not serious. When older male teachers treat them as sex objects or as incompetent, they know that they are not being taken seriously as students in school.

In addition, the examples reveal who the women blamed for the situation. In Della's case, she accused the particular professor, not the school or the society, for her problem. Other women with similar complaints tended to do the same thing. Unlike the others, Karla's understanding brought the school and gender systems—specifically the link between them—into question. She seemed to realize that the practices of male authority figures in the school might not be in her best interest as a student; however, she seemed to conclude that the solution lay in her own vigilance and not in altering the school or gender systems.

As indicated previously, there are few examples in our data of complaints about not being taken seriously in school. We might interpret this to mean that schools, in general, do take their women students seriously and thus provide no target for dissatisfaction or opposition. However, our analyses here and elsewhere (Eisenhart and Holland 1983) indicate that a better explanation is that the school and its representatives were not very salient features of these women's lives. Their focus was primarily on their problems with their peers.

Why School-Related Complaints Are Not More Prevalent: The Role of Peers

It is impossible to make sense of most of the women's discontents without first understanding the student (peer) cultures at Bradford and SU. We must describe some of the relevant aspects of these cultures before turning again to the women's complaints. Although there were some differences between the student cultures on the two campuses, they were similar in that they dominated the lives of most of the women in our study, and they were organized at least in part around romantic relationships and attractiveness.

For women students, peer group activities and relationships tended to focus on male/female relationships. Popular activities involved opportunities for getting together with men or enacting romantic relationships. So, for example, being a fraternity little sister or sweetheart was considered more interesting and prestigious than being a sorority sister. Sororities were viewed positively but as a secondary source of entertainment, support, and opportunities to meet men and not primarily as an opportunity for sisterhood.

A consequence of the importance of the student culture and the culture's emphasis on male/female relationships was that other aspects of college life were relegated to secondary positions. On both campuses women's relationships with other women were peripheral to their relationships with men. Although female-female relationships were different at Bradford and SU, the outcome was the same: weak and secondary relationships among women (Holland and Eisenhart, in press [a]). The women at Bradford emphasized self-direction and self-reliance in such a way that it was difficult for them to achieve trusting relationships with women. The women at SU relied on their female friends to support them in their efforts to find and keep desirable men, but once a romantic partner was found, they tended to spend time with female friends only when their boyfriends were unavailable.

The peer-group emphasis on romantic relationships was associated with a peer-ranking system that was similar on both campuses. For women and men, *attractiveness to the opposite sex* was a very desirable quality to have, and prestige was gained by having (potential) romantic partners. The pivotal position of attractiveness was explained in what seemed to be a shared notion of intimate cross-gender relationships.

Other research at SU—summarized in Holland and Skinner (1987)—suggested that the students have a "cultural model of intimate male/female relationships" that consists of a taken-for-granted scenario of such relationships. Relationships were not dictated by the model, but understood and evaluated in light of the model. According to the model, a man and woman of roughly equivalent looks and prestige are attracted to one another. The man learns and appreciates the woman's special qualities and shows his affection by treating her well. She in turn shows her interest and affection by allowing the relationship to become more intimate.

The model portrays a prototypical relationship that is right, that needs no explanation. It gives meaning to the acts of the participants and supplies evaluations and expectations: when a man is drawn to an attractive woman, he is supposed to treat her well by appreciating her special qualities as a woman and a person, being responsive to her concerns, and giving her nice things. Bad treatment is being appraised as an object or without individual characteristics. Bad treatment from the man implies that the woman is not very attractive—relative to the man's prestige and attractiveness. Unattractive women cannot expect much good treatment. They are expected to reveal their good feelings about the man and allow the relationship to become more intimate without concomitant attention and special treatment from the man. Likewise, if the man is not considered attractive relative to the woman, then she can expect very good treatment and need not put up with a lot of demands from him.

Because men and women, according to these cultural ideas, tend to match up by attractiveness and prestige, the attractiveness of one's suitor(s) validates one's own attractiveness. The motives for pursuing romantic relationships—also specified in the peer culture—are intimacy and prestige.

Especially for women, attractiveness was the main source of prestige or "symbolic capital," to use Bourdieu's (1977) term (see Holland and Eisenhart, n.d.). Excellence in schoolwork or sports received notice, but those pursuits were regarded as personal or idiosyncratic interests; every woman, in contrast, was subjected to being ranked by attractiveness (see also Horowitz 1987).

It was in this peer-defined context that women encountered most of the gender-related problems that they considered important. Their problems concerned the treatment they received from potential romantic partners.

Primary Discontents Are with Intimate Male-Female Relationships

Most of the women at Bradford and SU were involved with men in relationships that were either newly formed or newly forming. Eleven of the seventeen women were in such relationships, and most of the complaints about intimate relationships had to do with new or developing relationships. In the earliest stages of trying to establish intimate male/female relationships, the black and white women's complaints were similar: men are not sensitive to women. As relationships developed, however, the black women at Bradford tended to react differently than the white women at SU. In the long-term well-established relationships, complaints and responses coming from the two campuses were also similar: men make decisions that women do not particularly like.

The women at both Bradford and SU complained about the potential romantic partners they were meeting on their respective campuses. One woman said:

> When I first came here during orientation . . . I met these two guys. They were going to show me around campus . . . and then one came up to me and said, "Why don't you come over to my house . . . come by yourself." He wanted to start, just to jump right into, a real serious relationship. I told him, "No"; I didn't think that would be a good idea and then he told me I was silly. . . . And, then [he] got all upset and he wouldn't talk to me the whole school term . . . just [because I said] that I won't ball with him. I guess that hurt his feelings. But, it was orientation!

Another woman said she didn't like to go out with new guys because:

> They're full of hot air . . . like to run from bedpost to bedpost . . . I know what's going on . . . I don't want any part of that.

A third talked about the earliest stage of romantic relationships as follows:

> We go out, and see the same guys, and talk, but they're not even sincere anymore . . . we know the way they are. . . . They'll come up and flirt with you all night long, and they really don't care—just as long as they're seen talking to a girl.

The women at Bradford and SU felt that many of the men they met expected too much intimacy too soon or were not very sensitive to women's personal concerns and characteristics. These men's behavior—as interpreted according to the cultural model—implied that they were using the women and/or that they thought they were more attractive than the women and so could take the women for granted.

In one case, the woman's discontent began after she joined her boyfriend at college. The two had "gone steady" since her junior year of high school, when he was a college freshman. Once at college and with the support of her dormmates, she began to experiment with her clothing styles and her makeup. Her boyfriend was not happy with these changes and told her so. One day during her freshman year, a representative of a modeling agency came to campus and picked the woman out of a crowd in the cafeteria. The agent promised her a beauty "make over" and the chance to model for a fashion magazine. Without her boyfriend's knowledge, she had her hair cut, restyled, and her makeup done by the agency's expert. She viewed this experience as fun and exciting, but when he saw her, "he just went crazy . . . he hated it . . . and he told me, if my picture came out, he'd never look at it." Instead of objecting to his right to make decisions about what she should do, she interpreted the situation to mean that she and he did not have the same tastes or enjoy the same things.

Another woman had been "going with" her boyfriend since she was a high school sophomore and he a senior. She chose her university in order to be close to him and fully intended to marry him sometime in the future. Throughout the period of the study, she looked up to him, relying on him to give her advice about her coursework and counting on him to give direction to their social life and future. For example, once when she expressed an interest in the same major he was pursuing (social science), he discouraged her, and she accepted his advice. "He told me that I just wasn't cut out for that . . . that I probably wouldn't like it at all in the long run." On another occasion, she mentioned that she would like to have more time to spend with her dormmates but that she ended up spending most of her time at her boyfriend's apartment with his friends. . . . She also displayed some uneasiness when asked to speculate about what she'd be doing in the future. She said,

> I'll probably end up getting married, like when he gets done with [graduate] school. . . . I know it sounds bad to say it, but I'd rather not think about it; I'd rather go out and . . . just go all over the place and enjoy it . . . until I'm 28 or so, and then settle down. That's what I would like to do, but I don't think he would like that too much. Sometimes he even talks about [marriage] now, and I don't want to.

The final example is also from a woman who was in a long-standing relationship that she expected would turn into marriage, although sooner than she really wanted it to.

> We are planning on getting married in at least two to two-and-a-half years . . . [but] as far as I'm concerned, I'd let marriage hang in the air. . . . It's not that marriage isn't important to me because of course someday I do want to get married so I'll have a family. He would rather get married this year. . . . But, we both decided it was just best that he complete school. . . . He gave me my limit, you know: two to two-and-a-half [years]. I asked for three to four, trying to be greedy, but he gave me my limit.

In the first case, the woman ended up concluding that the source of her discontent with her boyfriend was the "clash" of their interests. In the last two cases, the source of the discontent seemed to be a vague sense of foreboding about marriage. In all three cases, the man's position as leader was accepted; the woman responded by trying to postpone actualization of the man's decision.

These cases are important because they probably portend situations that many of the women will encounter once married. It is particularly clear in these cases that the men were disregarding or actively opposing the women's development of certain interests. In addition to the examples given above, there is evidence that women in long-term intimate relationships are ignored in more subtle ways, too. Once in an interview, one of the women talked about her opposition to the Equal Rights Amendment. Later in the study, her boyfriend told the interviewer that he was in favor of ERA. He did not appear aware that his girlfriend held a different opinion or why she might. Later during the same observation, he brought up the women's movement again. This time his girlfriend was present and heard his comments, although they were directed to the interviewer. The woman made no comment. At another time, the same woman expressed interest in working for a presidential campaign and went to two organizational meetings. According to her, when she told her boyfriend (and her family) about her activities, "everyone made fun of me," and she decided not to work for that campaign and to reconsider her presidential choice.

It seems important to note that, at least in the case of some women, these struggles with a (future) husband over who she will not be or what she will not become begin relatively early. All of the women who had steady boyfriends at the beginning of college had dated the men for at least a year and came to a college already attended by or near their older boyfriends. Of these six women, we are sure that at least three of them married their boyfriends after graduation. Thus at the time of marriage, these relationships and their implications for the women had been developing for at least five years.

At Bradford, a woman's response to bad treatment in a new or developing relationship was often to reprimand the man and hope for better treatment (if she found him attractive) or to take a man's gifts and attention but maintain her emotional distance (especially if she did not find him particularly attractive). One of the Bradford women talked about how she handled the first situation:

> I can't stand him now. . . . I hate him. I could beat him up . . . he just humiliated me so bad. . . . See . . . he was in the cafeteria, talking about me. . . . Well, he had made it all up. . . . And then, he had tried to [apologize]; . . . and I said, "Well! I've had enough. I've had it up to here. I don't want to talk to you no more." So, later he tries to call me, and so I told him, "I saw you with two different girls . . . explain that to me . . . I want some answers." But he couldn't explain. So, I said to myself, "that's a boy; no man would play those childish games."

Another Bradford woman, in talking about a friend, Earl, illustrated the second situation:

> He's all right, like, he told me that he was gonna take me somewhere tonight, and he's going to buy me what I want. . . . He give me everything I want. . . . I told him I wanted me some blue shoes, and I said I ain't been to no steak house lately, "you gonna take me?" And he say, "sure." But, he ain' t my type, you know. [When the interviewer asks the woman why she has Earl do these things for her, she responds] Don't have nobody else right now. My other honey at work. My other one, he probably [left school] already.

The most common response to these sorts of problems in intimate relationships at Bradford was to try to outmaneuver the man; that is, to manage the relationship so that one's attractiveness appeared to be greater than the man's and one could receive better treatment. Some of the women maneuvered by juggling relationships with several men at once to get the things they wanted. One had at least three relationships at once. If she wasn't treated right by one man, she would leave him for awhile and try another. These maneuvers seemed to serve a regulating function for the women (i.e., to correct an imbalance in the man's treatment of her).

Trying to outmaneuver men occurred at SU as well. The SU women were especially concerned that the men see them as attractive and so treat them well. A woman in the study at SU described by Holland and Skinner (1987) spoke of "keeping the upper hand" as a means of making sure the man treated her well. The interviewer had just asked the woman to talk more about the idea of keeping the upper hand:

> I didn't want him [a man she had just started to go out with] to think that I was really crazy about him and that he could just use me . . . he'd say something about going out and I'd say, "Well just . . . we probably will, but it's a little early right now." I'd do stuff like that, and he'd ask me . . . if I had . . . a boyfriend back home and I didn't say anything, and he says, "Well, I figured you did."

She went on to explain other ways in which she tried to give the man the impression that she had other boyfriends, including such subterfuges as sometimes leaving the dorm when she thought he was going to call.

Although SU women did sometimes respond to or try to prevent bad treatment from (potential) romantic partners by maneuvering to increase their status in the relationship, they more often took a different route. They gave up on the relationship in order to search for a more responsive man. They tended to interpret bad treatment as a function of the particular man that they were going out with and attempted to remedy the situation by looking for a guy who would be better.

Women who did not leave men who treated them badly were a topic of discussion among their friends. One woman in our study, Linda, "put up with" bad treatment during the entire duration of the study. Her boyfriend was judged by her friends to be not all that attractive relative to her, and they often told her that he was a "jerk." He was not worth all the bad treatment she was exposing herself to by continuing to go with him. They urged her to get out of the relationship.

Discontent with the Peer System of Intimate Male-Female Relationships

There were two women in the study who refused, or at least questioned, the kinds of intimate relationships emphasized by their peers. Susan resisted romantic relationships by feigning commitment to an absentee boyfriend. Several other women in our study seemed to be using the same strategy. Susan, however, was the most straightforward about the tenuous nature of her relationship to Howard, her "boyfriend." In interviews she would make statements about Howard that could have come from grade-B movies, using tones of voice that indicated she was not serious. For example, in describing her feelings about Howard's decision to attend a university two thousand miles from her university, she said:

I don t know exactly when he's going but, um, I'm sure I'll see him some time. So . . . heartbreak, sob and everything like that!

In another instance when an "older" man from a nearby city tried to persuade her to go out with him, she told the interviewer:

I don't want to go out with someone who's 30. . . . I don't want to go out with anybody but Howard. He's worth the wait.

From other things Susan said, it appeared that the motives for romance—intimacy and prestige—as culturally defined had not become sufficiently attractive to her. In fact, she explicitly objected to one of the motives. She purposefully took the researcher to her dorm to show her the way in which the girls there "showed off" their boyfriends. Susan said that she did not think boyfriends were for showing off. She objected to the part of the cultural model that related boyfriends to prestige.

Susan did not entirely give up on romantic relationships. Their attractiveness continued to pull at her throughout the course of the study and beyond. She began to try to find a boyfriend in her sophomore year and in her last followup interview was happy about a present boyfriend. When asked then how she thought she was different from how she had been in college, she replied, "I never had a boyfriend for so long before."

The experiences of Sandy, the second woman, were somewhat different from Susan's. During the early part of the study Sandy mentioned having "a crush" on the younger brother of a high school girl-friend but being unwilling to pursue the relationship for fear of offending her friend. She described a similar experience that occurred in college.

At the beginning of the study, Sandy seemed interested, along with her dormmates, in finding a male romantic partner ("You can have the blonds, I get the dark-haired . . . cute ones"). But, as alluded to above, she seemed to have trouble finding the kind of relationship she wanted with men at college. At the same time, she began to feel that she did not fit in with the student culture at SU.

In my hometown, I was pretty much respected in the community and accepted for what I am, or was, in that community. [I was] basically your nonconformist, and I dressed to suit me. But when I came down here I . . . got the impression that here I was a sloppy little girl and I didn't have any class or I didn't have any style . . . and I didn't like that.

As the study progressed, she came to develop a very special friendship with one woman.

I have a lot of good friends, but they couldn't help with the deep things. [They] are afraid to be that deep . . . and you can't have a friend that is unwilling to give some of their area just because they might get hurt. You can never reach someone that way. And so consequently I turned to Leslie and . . . Leslie and I have become very close.

Soon, Sandy's other friends became jealous of the time she and Leslie spent together, but Sandy felt that her friendship with Leslie was too precious to jeopardize. Sandy said that she wanted to spend as much time as possible with Leslie:

Our relationship is terrific . . . I just would like to spend more time . . . [so far] it's all been crammed into one semester . . . probably not gonna be another time in my life when I can just sit down and just be friends.

Sandy's relationship with Leslie is unusual in our data. It is the only example of such a special bond being formed between two women. This relationship became the major focus of Sandy's activities during the remainder of the study; she and Leslie became virtually inseparable and rarely interacted with others.

Unlike Susan, who at first rejected an aspect of the system of romantic relationships but did not turn entirely away from it, Sandy really seemed to abandon the pursuit of a romantic relationship with a man. And, in doing so, she received little encouragement. Her former female friends were jealous, and her parents complained that she was missing out on many opportunities by spending so much time in one exclusive relationship. Apparently, she and Leslie found no support group for the kind of relationship they wanted to have and simply retreated into their own private world. Before the study ended, Sandy had stopped going to class and had moved into an apartment with Leslie, who had dropped out of school and was working to support the two of them.

DISCUSSION: WHY DON'T MORE OF THE WOMEN RESIST THE SYSTEM?

Most of the women *did* have complaints about the treatment they received as women. However, if "resistance" is reserved for the acting out of discontent in oppositionary behavior, we must conclude that the women in our study exhibited very little. Certainly there was nothing on the level of or of the intensity of the oppositionary behavior exhibited by the lads of Hammertown (Willis 1981b).

Valli (1986:21–24) has provided a useful summary of several schemes for classifying stances of resistance and accommodation. Using terms from her summary scheme, the women in our study engaged in negotiation or "strategic redefinition" (Lacey 1977:73) primarily, not resistance. The women, except for Susan and Sandy, treated the system of romantic relationships and ranking by attractiveness as given. Most of their complaints had to do with romantic relationships and with their boyfriends' treatment of them in those relationships. Within the parameters of the system they attempted to better their position. They tried to convince their romantic partners that they deserved better treatment, and those in long-term relationships tried to postpone implementation of males' decisions.

Given the amount of "peer pressure" to participate in the system of romance and attractiveness it is probably amazing that any of the women opposed the system. As pointed out, most of the women were constantly immersed in peer activities that emphasized romance and attractiveness, and they had probably been immersed in groups with similar themes for many years.

Nonetheless, the question of why there was no evidence of women's resistance to the peer ranking system is worth exploring in relation to the kinds of oppositional groups that adolescents form in other situations, such as those described by Lacey (1976), Willis (1981b), and Anyon (1981). Why, in particular, did the unattractive, low-prestige women who would seem to be disadvantaged by the system not oppose and act out their opposition to the system?

First, it seems that in the present case, the peer ranking system did not provide as clear a target for opposition as existed in the other studies. It provided neither visible and external raters such as teachers, nor a standard symbol system such as grades for rating attractiveness. There was no quantified standard—perhaps because of the partial emotional basis for the ranking—and a tendency to rank according to a relative scale. Women had ideas about which men might be out of their league campuswide, but any given woman's position was relatively vague. Further, the same rankings that were applied campuswide were applied in a relative fashion within groups of friends. Thus a woman who might have been in a low group campuswide— if such ratings had been collected—was not necessarily in a low position within her group of friends. There were no absolute definitions of "jerks," "nice-looking guys," "dogs," or "babes." A man who was a "jerk" in one group would be considered a "nice-looking guy" in another group. The vagueness of the ranking system provided no target for opposition and no unequivocal bottom group as found in the schools described by Lacey and Willis.

Besides the vagueness of the ranking itself, the student system of ranking by attractiveness had ameliorative features. In the cultural system described by the model, a woman, courted by a man whose prestige and attractiveness were roughly equivalent to her own, could expect to be well treated by him. And, she could avoid bad treatment from more attractive men by avoiding them. She could be embarrassed or "put down" by approaching a man who was more attractive than she was, but once she found a man of attractiveness comparable to her own and established a relationship with him, she could expect, according to the model, good treatment.

Clearly there were disadvantages to being in the unattractive group of women, especially if one became enamored of a high-status male like a basketball player or realized that one's beaus were considered low status by everyone else. However, the peer ranking system was sufficiently vague and sufficiently ameliorative that it was difficult to grasp or to oppose.

SUMMARY AND CONCLUSIONS

In this chapter we have described two groups of women at two universities in the American South. We have explored their discontent with the treatment they received because they were women. We have also described their response to this discontent.

Given historical events such as the women's movement and the appearance of some evidence from recent studies (e.g., Connell, et al.'s 1982 study of middle school students in Australia in 1977–78), it would seem that gender attitudes, especially of middle-class, privileged young women, would be more critical of patriarchy now than in the past. In our study this change was not evident. It appears that despite the visibility of affirmative action programs and the women's movement, the conditions that promote women's acceptance of patriarchy have not been substantially altered.

For the women at Bradford and SU, the main concern was peer relations, especially romantic relationships. The women spent most of their time with age mates; were constantly exposed to peer-organized activities; learned age mates' interpretations and evaluations of all aspects of university life; had most of their close, intimate relationships with age mates on campus, and learned ways to understand and evaluate themselves from these age mates. In this peer system women were ranked by attractiveness to males. Women's relationships with other women in almost every case were subordinated to their relationships with men, although in different ways at both universities. Many student activities included getting together with men and were treated as settings for enacting romantic relationships.

It is in this peer-defined context that women encountered most of the gender-related problems that they considered important. Their problems concerned the treatment they received from (would-be) romantic partners. In beginning relationships the women's problems had to do with not receiving good treatment from the men. In established relationships, the problems—from the women's viewpoints— were that the men were trying to make decisions about the women's futures that they disliked. In both situations, the women tried to negotiate or strategically redefine the situation.

Overall, the women showed very few signs of overt resistance against the peer system of ranking by attractiveness or against the culturally defined system of intimate male/female relationships.

In Connell's criticism of Willis' study of male adolescents, McRobbie's study of females, and others' work at the Centre for Contemporary Cultural Studies, he pointed out that the premature acceptance of an overly rigid theory of social reproduction prevented them from seeing what their ethnographic studies on youth really had to offer:

> The eventual result [of their analyses] is an abstract theory of social reproduction (see Women Take Issue, and Willis 1981a), not a theory of what the field material so beautifully demonstrates, sexual power structure. [1983:225]

Presumably Connell is referring to the importance of the adolescent world as a crucial arena for the enactment of gender relations. Schwartz (1972) has also suggested that youth groups are one of the primary settings in which American children learn to enact gender roles. . . .

The school's contribution to creating a patriarchical system is not absent, but for these women at the point they were in their school careers, the university's role was not extremely salient. Perhaps more important was the fact that the intense peer-group life was made possible by the universities. The universities, as we also argued for the elementary school we studied (Eisenhart and Holland 1983), provided a benign context for the development and importance of the peer group in the lives of youth—in this case, young adults.

The college women in our study were not terribly discontent with the gender status quo as they conceived it. However, that they will remain fairly content with their lives is by no means certain. Linda, we know, married her college boyfriend (the one her friends considered a "jerk") and left him within a year. When last interviewed she was expecting to marry someone else. The strategies of looking for Mr. Right and outmaneuvering men can be continued for a long time. However, we expect that gender-related discontent will grow as more of the women encounter episodes of not being taken seriously in their work situation, and perhaps by husbands, and as they become older and less and less like the prototypical woman in American culture who is young and beautiful and, thereby, attractive (Holland and Eisenhart, in press [a]). Their future discontent and their future responses are by no means determined.

NOTES

1. All proper names used in reference to the study are pseudonyms.
2. We use "discontent" as general term to summarize the ethnographic data. We postpone the application of the analytic term "resistance" until the Discussion section because, as McRobbie suggests, not all complaints lead to great consequence: "So, to summarize, although aspects of the female role were constantly being questioned, such criticism precluded the possibility of more radical restructuring of the female role. . . ." (1978:98).

REFERENCES

Althusser, L. 1971. *Lenin and Philosophy*. London: New Left Books.
Anyon, J. 1981. Social Class and School Knowledge. *Curriculum Inquiry* 11 (1):3–42.
Bourdieu, P. 1977. *Outline of a Theory of Practice*. London: Cambridge University Press.
Bourdieu, P., and J. C. Passeron. 1977. *Reproduction in Education, Society and Culture*. London: Sage.
Bowles, S., and H. Gintis. 1976. *Schooling in Capitalist America: Educational Reform and the Contradictions of Economic Life*. London: Routledge and Kegan Paul.

Connell, R. W. 1983. *Which Way Is Up? Essays on Sex, Class and Culture*. Sydney: George Allen and Unwin.

Connell, R. W., D. J. Ashenden, S. Kessler, and G. W. Dowsett. 1982. *Making the Difference: Schools, Families and Social Division*. Sydney: George Allen and Unwin.

Eisenhart, M., and D. Holland. 1983. Learning Gender from Peers: The Role of Peer Groups in the Cultural Transmission of Gender. *Human Organization* 42(4):321–322.

Folb, E. 1980. *Runnin' Down Some Lines: The Language and Culture of Black Teenagers*. Cambridge: Harvard University Press.

Gallimore, R., J. W. Boggs, and C. Jordan. 1974. *Culture, Behavior and Education: A Study of Hawaiian-Americans*. Beverly Hills: Sage.

Gearing, F., T. Carroll, L. Richter, et al. 1979. Working Paper 6. In *Toward a Cultural Theory of Education and Schooling*. F. Gearing and L. Sangree, eds. Pp. 1–38. The Hague: Mouton.

Griffin. C. 1985. *Typical Girls? Young Women from Schools to the Job Market*. London: Routledge and Kegan Paul.

Heath, S. B. 1983. *Ways with Words: Language, Life, and Work in Communities and Classrooms*. New York: Cambridge University Press.

Holland, D., and M. Eisenhart. 1981. *Women's Peer Groups and Choice of Career*. Final Report. Washington, D.C.: National Institute of Education.

———. in press (a). On the Absence of Women's Gangs in Two Southern Universities. In *Women in the South*. Proceedings of the Southern Anthropological Society. H. Matthews, ed. Athens: University of Georgia Press.

———. in press (b). Women's Ways of Going to School: Cultural Reproduction of Women's Identities as Workers. In *Class, Race, and Gender in U.S. Education*. L. Weis, ed. Buffalo: SUNY Press.

———. n.d. *Schooling, Romance and Resistance: University Women and the Gender Status Quo*. Manuscript in preparation.

Holland, D., and D. Skinner. 1987. Prestige and Intimacy: The Cultural Model Behind America's Talk about Gender Types. In *Cultural Models in Language and Thought*. D. Holland and N. Quinn, eds. Pp. 78–111. New York: Cambridge University Press.

Horowitz, H. 1987. *Campus Life: Undergraduate Cultures from the End of the Eighteenth Century to the Present*. New York: Knopf.

Jenkins, R. 1983. *Lads, Citizens, and Ordinary Kids: Working-Class Lifestyles in Belfast*. London: Routledge and Kegan Paul.

Komarovsky, M. 1985. *Women in College*. Glencoe, Ill.: Free Press.

Lacey, C. 1976. Intragroup Competitive Pressures and the Selection of Social Strategies: Neglected Paradigms in the Study of Adolescent Socialization. In *The Anthropological Study of Education*. C. J. Calhoun and F. A. J. Ianni, eds. Pp. 189–216. The Hague: Mouton.

———. 1977. *The Socialization of Teachers*. London: Methuen.

Laing, R. D. 1967. *The Politics of Experience*. New York: Ballantine Books.

———. 1971. *Self and Others*. Harmondsworth: Penguin.

Leacock, E. 1969. *Teaching and Learning in City Schools*. New York: Basic Books.

McRobbie, A. 1978. Working Class Girls and the Culture of Femininity. In *Women Take Issue: Aspects of Women's Subordination*. Centre for Contemporary Cultural Studies, Women's Studies Group, ed. Pp. 96–108. London: Hutchinson.

———. 1980. *Settling Accounts with Subcultures: A Feminist Critique*. Screen Education 34 (Spring 1980):37–49.

Ogbu, J. 1974. *The Next Generation: An Ethnography of Education in an Urban Neighborhood.* New York: Academic Press.

———. 1978. *Minority Education and Caste: The American System in Cross-Cultural Perspective.* New York: Academic Press.

———. 1985. *Crossing Cultural Boundaries: A Perspective on Minority Education.* Paper prepared for the symposium "Race, Class, Socialization, and the Life Cycle," University of Chicago, October 1983, revised 1985.

Philips, S. 1983. *The Invisible Culture: Communication in Classroom and Community on the Warm Springs Indian Reservation.* New York: Longman.

Rist, R. 1973. *The Urban School: A Factory for Failure.* Cambridge: MIT Press.

Schwartz, G. 1972. *Youth Culture: An Anthropological Approach.* Addison-Wesley Module in Anthropology, No. 17. Reading, Mass.: Addison-Wesley Publishing.

Valli, L. 1986. *Becoming Clerical Workers.* Boston: Routledge and Kegan Paul.

Waller, W. 1937. The Rating and Dating Complex. *American Sociological Review* 2:727–734.

Willis, P. 1981a. Cultural Production Is Different from Cultural Reproduction Is Different from Social Reproduction Is Different from Reproduction. *Interchange* 12(2/3):48–67.

———. 1981b. *Learning to Labor: How Working Class Kids Get Working Class Jobs.* Morningside Edition. New York: Columbia University Press.

20

Class and Gender Dynamics in a Ruling-Class School

R. W. Connell, G. W. Dowsett, S. Kessler, and D. J. Ashenden

ON CLASS AND EDUCATION

In practical terms, class and education have never been separate. The construction of modern mass education systems in the nineteenth century coincided with the emergence of modern class structures; and those systems were class-segregated from the start. Nor was this simply a matter of private schools for the rich and state-provided elementary instruction for the workers. Many of the elite schools had been government foundations; and in most parts of the capitalist world, publicly-funded universities were set up well before a secondary system existed that could get the workers' children into them. The capitalist state, in short, was involved from the start, as *a matter of policy*, in the construction of a class-divided education system.

There was, then, no particular reason to be socially curious about class differences in education—they were implicit in the rationale of the system. It is only since the rise of notions of common schooling in the twentieth century that any questions could have much point. The debate over class effects in education is, at bottom, a sociological enquiry into a failure of educational policy—the progressives' policy of democratizing education by making provision and access more equal. For even the huge post–World War II expansion of formal education did not eliminate the old inequalities. It relocated them and added to them new forms of credentialling, exclusion, and privilege.

The sociological argument about this seems to have taken two main steps. The first step was in direct response to the postwar growth and was concerned first to document, then to explain, the persistence of class inequalities through this growth period—and finally to suggest how the inequalities could be ironed out. This set of issues, for want of a more evocative label, we may call the "inequality problematic"; the work done within it includes most of the classic investigations in the sociology of education of the 1950s and 1960s.[1]

The concept of class that underlay most of this work was the stratificationist conception current in academic sociology at the time. Classes, or better "strata", were conceived of as categories of people who had more or less of some attribute—money, prestige, authority, or what have you; surveys allowed every individual to be located at their correct address up or down any given totem-pole.[2] The idea of social *structure*, thus reduced to a set of categories, was sharply separated from any idea of social *practice* or of what people actually do once in the categories. This was measured separately on a new set of scales: IQ, academic achievement, level of completed education, etc. Correlations between "structure" scales and "performance" scales were the basic output of educational sociology governed by the inequality problematic—and still are.

This intellectual framework led naturally enough to a view of what to do about the inequalities revealed: provide *remediation* for those categories of people who turned out to have the lowest scores on the performance measures. The resulting programs (such as Educational Priority Areas in the U.K. and the Disadvantaged Schools Programme in Australia) are familiar, as is the controversy about their effects. It was in the uncertainty created by this argument that a second paradigm began to get a grip in educational sociology.

Where disillusioned liberals saw in the inequality statistics evidence that the education system was *failing*, theorists of another stamp saw it as *succeeding*—in carrying out its normal social function of reproducing capitalist class relations. Accordingly we will call this approach the "reproduction problematic." It had the advantage of drawing on a very much more sophisticated and powerful theory of class than stratificationism. A revived marxism pointed to the importance of the overall structure of class relations, stressed that class was a system of power and not just of difference, and above all, saw education in the context of a wider process of putting people in their places, reproducing the subordination of workers and bolstering the power of capital.[3]

This impulse has not yet worked itself out; the reproduction paradigm remains highly influential in radical educational circles, in Australia at least. It has solid virtues: its recognition that the state is an actor in class relations, not just a re-actor; its stress that *power* relations, not just social differences, operate through education; and its tough-minded recognition of the sheer intractability of education systems as a result.

Yet it also has serious difficulties. The structuralist theory of class from which it sprang tends, like stratificationism, to think of classes as categories which exist prior to the people who inhabit them. Structuralism tends to become determinism, people merely the puppets in a ballet of cosmic categories. And this perpetuates the split between structure (where people are) and practice (what they do). Focussing on the structures, reproduction theorists consistently find it hard to say anything very practical to teachers or students. Where the inequality problematic at least pointed to a scheme of compensatory education, the reproduction problematic leads to a profound pessimism. The main message is that whatever reformers do will have little effect, because the schools will go on reproducing class relations, in accordance with the structural demands upon them, until the bright day of revolution dawns.[4]

Where to go? We suggest (a) that there is some basis for a more adequate way of thinking about the relations between structures (such as class) and practices (such as teaching and learning) in the theory of practice emerging from the work of theorists such as Habermas (1974), Giddens (1976), and the later Sartre (1976); (b) that this ties in with the constructivist approach to class, which sees classes and class structures as constantly in process of formation—as outlined by Thompson (1968), Lefebvre (1976), and others (Connell and Irving, 1980); and (c) that these can be related to work on class and education, which escapes the problematics outlined above because the focus is on process—see Bernstein (1971) and Sennett and Cobb (1973). Whether this amounts to a shiny new third paradigm remains to be seen. But at all events that is the direction in which our research has led.

THE IMPORTANCE OF STUDYING RULING-CLASS SCHOOLS

Most of the good detailed research in the class-and-education literature has concerned itself with working-class schools or working-class kids. There are excellent reasons for this: the basic purpose of the research has been reform, and it is natural to focus on the situation of the oppressed. But it is also dangerous—so close a focus may distort. If we study only working-class schooling, how can we know what is specifically "working class" about it? One of the sound lessons of structuralism is that a class only exists in relation to another class; and it is the whole system, not one of its parts, that ultimately makes sense. And one of the simpler lessons of the history of education is that working-class schools have developed in a system that also contains elite state schools, private schools, universities, etc., and are powerfully shaped by this context.

We would argue, then, that to *understand* working-class education, we must take serious account of ruling-class education; and this is also true if our purpose is to *reform* working-class education. In the relation between the ruling class and its schools, there is a pattern that is markedly more constructive, and better adapted to the collective purposes of the class, than the usual relation between contemporary western workers and their schools (as we hope to show by a case study in this paper). This pattern can't be taken over directly; but there is certainly something to be learnt from how the ruling class does it.

Of theorists in the field, it is Bourdieu who comes closest to providing an analysis of the relation between the ruling class and its education; or at least a warrant to be interested in it. Although his discussion of actual institutions focusses on universities far more than on schools, he is clear that there is a specific and interesting relation between the character of the class and the content and authority structure of its education. We must note, however, that his conception of "class" is strictly in the structuralist framework: that he sees schooling basically as functional (or dysfunctional) to a pre-constituted class, educational institutions being given their place by the system of relations as a whole; and his basic explanation of class differences has to do with correspondences between a pre-existing class character ("habitus", in his language) and the system of evaluation current in schools and universities. Our material suggests a rather different approach, as will be seen.

THIS STUDY

For the past few years, we have been working on a study of Australian secondary students. Its basis is a sample of Year 9 and 10 (ages 14–15) pupils in Sydney and Adelaide, equally divided by sex, and equally divided between two contrasting class milieux: English-speaking working class on the one hand, professional or entrepreneurial ruling class on the other. The first group was drawn from state schools in predominantly working-class suburbs, the second from protestant private schools—being, in both cases, the schools to which most of these groups go.

In almost all cases we interviewed the student, both parents, and some of that student's classroom teachers, as well as the principals of the schools. The interviews were extended explorations of current situations and personal histories, focussing on education and work but attempting to move back from immediate details to fill in their contexts and seeking as much narrative detail as the interviewees cared to give us. All interviews (424) were handled by the authors; almost all were tape-recorded, and we have built up our analyses mainly from these tapes and their transcriptions. The fieldwork was done in 1977–78.

The rich and complex material that our interviewees gave us has, we think, some virtues for the study of the relation between class and education. It allows most obviously a direct comparison of processes in two class milieux.

Having interviews with four of the parties to the same educational transactions (the kids, the parents, the teachers, and the school administrators) allows us to cross-check and validate information (which isn't common in survey research) and even more important, to see how differently the same events register with the different participants. The life-history approach in the interviews allows us to key in to class processes, not just class positions. And the fact that the study includes both sexes in both generations, and the interviews dealt with sexuality and family relationships, gives us an opportunity to investigate the connections between class relations and gender relations—an interaction whose importance and complexity has become increasingly obvious as we have got deeper into the analysis.

There are also serious drawbacks. Work at this level of detail is extremely slow—which means small scale, problems of representativeness, and a narrow band of situations covered. (The poorest parts of the Australian working class, the very large

Southern European immigrant part of it, the mass of white-collar workers, and the lower levels of management are mostly unrepresented in our sample.) The fact that the interviews were done at one time means we have a slice through a process— we know a lot about what went before, but have as yet no follow-up. Finally, for various reasons, we are short of information about peer groups: we have a good many indications, but nothing like the wealth of information that, say, Robins and Cohen (1978) provide.

Our original intention was to build up a study with the individual student and her network of relations as the primary unit of analysis. This is the way in which we have been initially working through the material, and it is illustrated in a paper (Ashenden et al., 1980) that presents some "case studies" on mobility and immobility. During this work, however, another unit has come more and more into focus—the school. And luckily our interviews allow us to build up a picture, certainly not complete but often quite detailed, of the social structure and dynamics of each of the twelve schools we worked in. "Luckily"—because we would now argue that the school has an independent importance in the class/education equation that we didn't see at the start.

The educational fate of individual kids is affected by the way their school is working, its general educational relationships and social dynamics; these in turn are profoundly affected by the social composition of the school's "catchment" and by the history of the relations that catchment has with the state, with academic knowledge, and with the teaching trade. For instance, one of the working-class comprehensives in our sample, Greenway High, is having noticeably more trouble in teaching the conventional syllabus and maintaining order than is another school of apparently similar social composition. To understand this, it is vital to know that Greenway used to be a selective school whose internal order was overwhelmed when comprehensivization brought in suddenly a mass of kids who didn't accept the academic curriculum and teacher authority and who were too many to be marginalized. The school simply didn't have time to evolve the kinds of responses that are working in schools with different histories.

Before launching into our account of a ruling-class school and the forces at play in and around it, a note about the evidence. To protect the anonymity of interviews, we have constructed a composite picture out of evidence from three real schools. This is possible only because these schools are in fact quite similar; the same could not be done with any combination of schools. The "Jamieson College" of this paper, then, is a portrait of a type of school. We would still stress that it is a portrait grounded in fact. Every incident and process comes from our interviews; there is nothing fictitious in what follows.

SCHOOL AND CATCHMENT

Jamieson College is an old-established private secondary school for girls, with an enrolment a little upwards of 500. The first impression gained by a visitor, particularly one from the state school system, is of effortless good order. The buildings are respectable rather than elegant. The grounds—characteristically—are handsome and spacious and very clean. All girls wear uniforms, and all uniforms are neat. There are no raised voices; and there is very little running in the playground at breaks.

This is one of the handful of schools which cater to the daughters of the city's Establishment. Some names on its books could be found among the pastoral and mercantile elite of the nineteenth-century colony; and among present fathers are some of the richest and most powerful men in the state. One of the girls we interviewed drives to school in a family Mercedes. But that *is* exceptional; a school of this size must draw from a rather wider base. So one finds the daughters of insurance brokers, middle-ranking civil servants, dentists, corporate executives on the way up, pastoralists on the way down, and even professors, rubbing shoulders with the daughters of the very rich and very powerful. There is still a definite lower bound. The Principal notes that the school's scholarships are not given to working-class girls: they would not fit in, and it would simply be "cruelty" to sponsor their entry to such a school. She is undoubtedly right.

In what sense is this a "ruling class" school? By that we do not mean that its clientele is homogenous and confined to the very top. No class is homogeneous; nor is a school simply defined by the groups it draws from. Indeed, we would suggest, the fact of incoherence and heterogeneity is one of the things that defines its task; and the class character of a school is also a matter of what it does for its clientele, as well as who they are. More of this later. For the moment, we may define Jamieson's "catchment" as families who come exclusively from the upper half of the total distributions of income, occupational status and the like, with a marked concentration in the upper levels of that half; mostly resident in a group of expensive and prestigious suburbs in a particular sector of the city; with a high concentration of university degrees (among the fathers) and private-school backgrounds (mothers as well); and including owners of large family capital as well as the affluent salariat. The Principal finds herself talking to the fathers "as one executive to another"; they understand each others' problems.

Jamieson delivers, and is carefully organized to deliver, what those parents ask for. Though each puts things differently, we can tease out three main themes that run through most of their statements. First, a desire for moral order—which some phrase in terms of a Christian education (the school is a Protestant foundation) and others in terms of sexual protection or control over the girls. Second, a demand for academic performance. The school offers an "academic emphasis," and currently 80 per cent or more of its girls matriculate. (This may be compared to 20 per cent or less in our working-class schools.) Third, an "all-round education": school-based cultural, social, and sporting activities that together enclose much more of the girls' lives than a state school is able to do.

The school also delivers some things which the parents want, but are less likely to acknowledge as explicit demands. The school offers exclusiveness (*vide* the Principal's remark on scholarships) and a sense of social superiority. Closely related, it offers to teach, or reinforce, a particular cultural style. (One quite important sign of this is a style of speech, almost an accent, which most girls at the school learn quickly and never lose.) And it offers very significant assistance with two of the three main ways ruling-class families have of transmitting their class location from generation to generation. To the direct inheritance of capital, of course, the school is largely irrelevant. But it is highly relevant to the reproduction of class position by access to meritocratic careers. And it is also very relevant to the construction of social networks. Jamieson is plugged into a circuit of social relations that embraces the city's leading boys' private schools, a fact that is a major determinant of the girls' present peer groups and future marriages.

To say that the school "delivers" certain goods to the parents implies something that should be made explicit. The parents literally buy an educational service from one of a number of organizations that are in business to provide it. Many put the matter in just these terms, and they are very much concerned to see that their money has been well spent. The staff are well aware that "the parents shop around," as one Jamieson teacher puts it. We may say more generally that whereas the relation between the working class and its schools is mediated by a state bureaucracy (the Department provides a set teaching service for a particular district according to its general regulations and compels the children's attendance), the relation between the ruling class and its schools is mediated *by a market*.

Of course this is not a clinically-pure free market *à la* Milton Friedman. Religion, geography, family tradition may all direct a particular family to a particular school. Yet all real markets are "imperfect" in various ways; and given these constraints, it is still impressive how effectively market pressures operate. In the ruling-class school, the teachers are the paid agents of the families, and they are made to feel it:

> The kids sort you out. If you're no good you'll get kicked out. The kids will see to that. (That does happen then?) Very much. It's controlled by—the school's run by—the kids. I mean, the level at which the teachers work—and they work very hard here—is controlled by the kids, their expectations. If you don't match up, you're out. My colleague, an English teacher here, wasn't very good. And the parents, a deputation of parents came to the school, and at the end of second term, he was out. (And that's not unusual?) No. That's how it operates. (Alan Milson, science teacher)

The present Principal of Jamieson admits that she does not like to sack staff but is sometimes obliged to by pressure from parents. (Her formula is to ask unsatisfactory teachers to move on, rather than actually dismiss them.) The staff have no job security and no protection in a confrontation with the Principal except what support they can mobilize personally. There is a union—but it was set up mainly to prevent the government teachers' union getting coverage of private school staff, and it has no industrial muscle. There has never been a strike in these schools.

The market, then, structures relationships within the school in definite ways. Equally important, it is a mechanism of change. Some notes on the recent history of Jamieson College will suggest how.

For a couple of generations the school's main rationale had been to furnish a general education for young ladies whose future was centered on a suitable marriage. A particular style of femininity was an important part of the school's product. Academic work was by no means neglected; indeed the school had at times something of a blue-stocking air in comparison with the more "social" girls' schools. But its *forte* was culture rather than science, and academic excellence was cultivated more as part of a general fitting-out, and as an index of the school's suitability, than as an entree to a high-flying career. Jamieson's graduates reproduced their families' positions in the ruling class by marrying executives and professionals rather than becoming them.

By the late 1960s, this service was not as marketable as it had been. The reasons are complex: changes in the composition of the ruling class that are familiar in late capitalism, changes in the labor market, the development of feminism, and rising competition from the state secondary schools; and the end of the postwar boom, all played a part. While the girls thought more and more in terms of careers, their parents watched their dollars more closely. Private school staff noted a sharp increase in *fathers'* interventions in the conduct of their daughters' education, a sure sign of an economic crunch.

In these choppy seas, Jamieson under its previous Principal, Mrs. Smith, wallowed. "Discipline" was becoming a problem. Many teachers felt that the Principal was giving them little help in the difficulties they had with the girls. Parents felt that teachers were failing to keep the students in line, or were even getting out of hand themselves. The old "house" system which had enlisted the students in the enforcement of the school's authority was losing its moral force. Academically the school was still successful, but no longer pre-eminent, among girls' schools, and its success was tied to now-declining humanities. Mrs. Smith's style of running the school depended heavily on personal authority; and the charisma wasn't working any more. Enrolments tailed off. Teachers became disheartened, slacked off, or left.

The upshot was a new Principal. The details of the crisis that led to Mrs. Smith's premature retirement need not concern us; the basic fact was that having lost the support of parents and seen the school slide in the market, she was unable to resist the pressures put on her to go. Mrs. Johansen, the new incumbent, set to work with a will. A "smarten up" policy (a teacher's phrase)—a blitz on the details of dress, etiquette and order—signalled to students and teachers that a new regime had begun. The privileges of the older girls were cut back; but in exchange they were given a new pedagogy. More tests and exams underwrote a renewed stress on academic excellence, especially in the sciences where some new staff were recruited and the way was cleared for a heavier emphasis on science in the school's offerings. Parents were given a more careful hearing while, at the same time, teachers were protected—as long as they measured up. Those that didn't were asked to go. (Heavy staff "turnover" is a common feature of changes of regime at such schools. As the principal of another school, who had pushed through an even more drastic renovation, observed at an end-of-year dinner for retiring staff: "Some are born redundant, some achieve redundancy, and some have redundancy thrust upon them".)

In the eyes of parents, teachers, and students, Mrs. Johansen has wrought a transformation. The changes haven't pleased everybody: those who were sacked, obviously; some of the girls who find the new tautness oppressive; some teachers who are in subjects marginal to Mrs. Johansen's reforms and who get no resources for new curricula they have been developing. But such opposition has been swept aside, at least for the time being, by the tangible success of the overall policy. It is not just expressed opinions that tell the tale. Enrolments have risen steeply and continue upwards.

We can see a number of ways in which the market shaped this renovation. It put the parents in circumstances where they had to formulate their needs and wishes, and it gave them the means of transmitting their wishes as individual consumers and the means by which their actions cumulated to affect the school's viability. The market mechanism forced the school to change, to reconstruct itself in response to a new pattern of ruling-class demand. And once changes were under way, the market mechanism set the seal on the authority of the new principal and the new policies.

Yet it would be quite wrong to suppose that the market (or any combination of the market and other means of control) constitutes a simple belt for the transmission of parental wishes into educational practice. There are many reasons why the market does *not* give fingertip control to the parents—or why, as one observant teacher noted, parents' relations with the new Principal remain often "very abrasive." The "imperfections" already noted—religion, geography, family pride—act as a brake on parents taking their business elsewhere. The school's council can resist, as well as articulate, market pressures; and the principal may not prove easy to dislodge. The ship of many a private school has gone down with its Head. Nor are the pressures from the market always consistent among themselves. There is, for instance, tension between the effort to reproduce both femininity *and* class position; the dilemma experienced by the girls as "marriage or a career" is experienced by the school as a dilemma of educational policy, demanding constant trade-offs and compromises. There are conflicting educational ideologies among the parents, usually related to their own class biographies. The renovation at Jamieson was linked to changes in the composition of the ruling class, and the school continues to be subject to different pressures from the aspiring bureaucrats, old capital, new-rich entrepreneurs, and elite professionals. Above all, these conflicting demands are made upon a most peculiar institution which has its own needs for autonomy.

INSIDE THE SCHOOL

Schools are peculiar in a number of ways. They are socially, and often physically, separated from other institutions. They have an extremely unfocussed task (or set of tasks, focussed in very different directions), and the business of shaping people admits of no easily agreed-upon measures of output that could be equated with other kinds of production. In the pursuit of this task, schools are organized internally around two principles of differentiation—age and knowledge—which indeed occur in other institutions but whose combination practically defines a school. Neither of these differentiations is as simple as it may seem. "Age," for instance, is not just a matter of chronological age; there is also some sort of "educational age," corresponding to promotion through grade levels; and some sort of "emotional age," constantly appealed to by teachers in their descriptions of particular kids as "immature," "mature," etc. Knowledge is more complex again. And both of them interact in complicated ways with the structure of class and gender that impinge on, and penetrate, the school.

Jamieson College shares these features with other schools. What is distinctive about it, and other ruling-class schools, is not different principles of internal structure but the way these common structures interact, how they are made to work, and the internal order that is constructed out of them. "Made to work" is important. There is a constant danger in discussions of the social structure of education that the "structures" will seem to work by themselves, independent of the people toiling within them. On the contrary, we would insist, structures exist only in social practices; and the "structural constraints" on education exist in and work through practices *constructed mainly within the school.* Most important of these is the classroom practice worked out in the endless negotiation between teachers and students.

We stress this point because the process of construction *can* go in different directions; and which direction it goes in has a lot to do with the educational fate of a particular child and the way the school as a whole works. In Jamieson, as in any school, there are variations from classroom to classroom; but we can say firmly that the dominant pattern is a teacher/student practice constructed around individual competition in appropriating a hierarchically-ordered academic syllabus. Where teachers in working-class schools have to labor to attach their charges to an academic syllabus (the result usually being that several different syllabuses appear, *de facto*, within the same school), the teachers at Jamieson can normally presuppose that attachment. Their problem is not *whether* but *how*—perhaps, more exactly, *how best.*

For the girls they teach in the upper classes are fierce competitors. They work hard. They (and their parents) are skilful examinees. And one of the things they demand from the school is exact knowledge of their competitive situation. There are, of course, girls whose school lives are not dominated to this degree by schoolwork—because their focus of interest is more "social" or for some other reason. (A few are even school resisters, though such are rare in this milieu.) One of the girls at Jamieson produced a charming three-fold classification:

> They're always wearing make-up and you associate them with, a sort of, rather a down group or something like that, a cheap group. I mean, they go out with rockers or something like that. . . . Also there's another group, kids that—the snobbish group, they

always wear makeup. In every year, you always get the sort of snobby groups who just
think they're "It". . . . (Which group are you in?) I'm in an in-between group! (How
would you describe that?) I think—more intellectual. I mean you get kids who want
to work, come to work, and you know, want to work and do well. . . . They can mix
with both groups; you won't usually see the rowdy group mixing that much with the
other group. (Julia Keating, Year 10)

We'll come back to another implication of Julia's ethnography later; here the point
to be noted is that the third of her groups is unquestionably the one which holds
the hegemonic position among Jamieson's girls; and their characteristic pattern of
interaction with the teachers is central to the way the school works.

One consequence of this we have already seen: an unremitting pressure *on the
teachers* for academic performance. The happier side of this is a tremendous boost
to teacher professionalism. The sense of professional identity, traditionally centered
on the possession of specialized knowledge, can hardly fail to flourish in a milieu
where that knowledge is greatly sought after. The contrast with working-class
schools is stark. Here is one Jamieson teacher, who (like many others) had begun
teaching in the state system, explaining why she was willing to work for a socially-
privileged school:

> Because I enjoy the work, and I feel that as a professional I *enjoy* teaching. I found
> that in the state schools, *some* of the state schools I was in, I wasn't teaching. I was
> just trying to discipline apathetic students who didn't want to go, whose parents didn't
> care, and so I was—I looked after them. I almost baby-sat some classes, some of the
> lower streams. . . . But here the response is *superb*, and as a teacher I thoroughly en-
> joy it. And it encourages me to even work harder, and so I thoroughly enjoy my teach-
> ing in this school. (Janet Bagshaw, science teacher)

In the consonance of three things—teacher professionalism, the parents' demands
for an academic syllabus, and the dominant position of academically-oriented girls—
we see much of the basis of the very impressive internal order that Jamieson under
Mrs. Johansen has achieved. The first impression that this order is "effortless" is
plainly wrong—it is taut, it is constantly being recreated; but the degree of hegemony, the subordination of the girls to the school's program, is high. "Everyone,"
declares one of Julia's classmates, "would like to be head [girl] . . . but some girls are
just so much ahead, they've just got so much school spirit and so much leadership. . . ." The school hums.

The school also, at times, grinds; some of the forces at work in the school's integration also produce contradictions. The professionalism that leads Janet Bagshaw
and others like her to savor the girls' responsiveness and to support the parents'
academic goals also leads them to resist attempts to "tell us how to do our jobs." It
leads them to criticize the instrumentalism of many families (especially the
upwardly-mobile) in the name of a broader conception of education and sometimes
to make a point of giving the girls "the other point of view on current events, such

as the strikers' side in industrial disputes which the girls' parents universally con-
demn. The younger teachers at least are well to the left of the parents in politics.
Given the blue-ribbon conservatism of the school's clientele that would not be very
hard; but it is still significant that it is so and that the Principal approves a degree
of radicalism among her staff as a sign of the school's intellectual vigor.

It also, of course, makes life a little harder for her, because the resulting clashes
sometimes land on her desk. The private-school principal is not like the principal
of a public school doing a tour of duty in a particular suburb as the Department's
representative—to the parents, no more than a face that emerges from the gloom,
acts as a law unto itself, and in due course disappears back into the mists. For one
thing, the private-school principal is absorbed into the social network that surrounds
the school. Mrs. Johansen bewails the fact that she gets so many invitations to dinner from her families that she can't accept them all. Another principal in our sample
is so familiar a figure that even parents who are bitterly critical of him still call him
by his schoolboy nickname.

On the other hand, the principal is an *entrepreneur*, with these same people as
her customers. She has to market her product, and to do that she has to know her
market. She also has to raise funds for the school in other ways, with the result that
private-school principals are often excellent sociologists and economists. Another
in our sample produced, at the drop of a hat, an astonishing (until we had thought
about it) run-down of the leading financial and industrial corporations in his city,
their principal executives and degree of prosperity, the social geography of the city,
the changing class composition of different suburbs (with predictions for the next
ten years that could doubtless have been sold for good money to a real-estate firm),
and the impact of multinational corporations on local capital. It is, literally, his
business to know that kind of thing—while still maintaining the persona of an
educator.

On the principal, then, are focussed many of the pressures in this system. The
charisma of old style Headship is failing, as Jamieson discovered under Mrs. Smith;
new forms of authority have to be constructed, more technocratic, more
professionalized. Given also the rising competition from state high schools, the rising
pressure from parents for academic performance and their increased willingness to
intervene in school affairs (not to mention their belief in "going to the top" to get
something done), plus the need to reconstruct curricula and teaching practices
within the school, as well as its routine management—given these pressures, it is
not hard to see increasing personal strain on the principal. Mrs. Johansen delegates
far more than her predecessor, but even so she is overloaded. She works a 7-day
week, 9 a.m. to midnight. In her own phrase, the strain is "incredible," and though
she sees the obvious need to change this, she can't see how. But it is important that
she should, for her preoccupation has the danger of estrangement from the girls:

> She's good with the school and everything but I sometimes think that she doesn't re-
> ally care about the girls. I suppose she does; but I just get the impression sometimes

that she doesn't care as much about the girls as she does about the name of the school. I suppose she puts that attitude over so that we will do the right thing. (Marianne Gracie, Year 10)

We suspect that before very long this is going to force further changes in the pattern of management of these schools.

THE SCHOOL AS CONSTRUCTOR

Let us consider more closely the changes going on in the class from which Jamieson draws. The last generation has seen a significant weakening in its control over the local economy, with the deepening penetration of multinational companies and increasing integration of Australian capital and commodity markets into a world market. What we may call the ruling-class labor process (the actual business of managing, administering, and conducting professions) has altered. Management has had to become more knowledge-based and more technocratic in the new conditions; and that has significant implications for training—as a director of one of Australia's major manufacturing firms said to us, his firm now won't look at a management recruit without a degree, whereas in his youth it was enough to have gone to the right school. There have also been changes in the techniques of maintaining hegemony over the working class, a broad shift toward integrative social management (including the massive expansion of meritocratic secondary education), modulated since 1975 by a move back toward labor-market discipline through unemployment.

There have also been changes in the means of transmitting capital, the significance of the private family fortune declining and that of access to an elite career increasing. And with these changes are coming changes in the ruling-class family. The parents we interviewed have a rigid and traditional division of labor, the husband absorbed in his career, the wife (even when university-educated) in the supporting role of running the home and bringing up the children. There is often a lot of tension about this, but the pattern remains almost universal among our ruling-class sample. A good many of Jamieson's girls are now projecting for themselves a future which is very different from their mothers' present, with careers that will not be subordinated to their husbands'. Their older sisters are already moving along such paths.

How do these changes relate to the internal renovation of Jamieson? We may suggest a sequence something like this. The increasing importance of meritocratic means of reproducing a family's class position, especially for women, leads to a reorganization of school knowledge: a heavier emphasis on competition and assessment in general, and a heavier emphasis on scientific and technical knowledge in particular. One of the consequences of this change is greater exclusion and differentiation within the school through the curriculum, producing in turn some new problems of social control while shifting the patterns of hegemony among the girls.

Such a change is plainly associated with shift in the pattern of authority within the school, a decline in traditional charisma and increased dependence on mores internalized by the girls—hence the heavy pressure on the girls to be "good citizens." It also requires greater technical skills on the part of the staff, who are becoming (as a group) much more highly qualified, and a pattern of management that responds to teacher professionalism by a much greater delegation in the realms of curriculum and method, without however changing the entrepreneurial role of the principal.

Yet if we saw the changes only in this way, we would understand the school only as responding to pressures from its environment. While this would be compatible with a whole pseudo-ecological tradition in the sociology of education, it would also seriously misrepresent what is going on here. Education is more than a dependent variable.

For instance, the school is not entirely innocent in the current changes occurring in the ruling-class family. It may at first have been a matter of outside pressures impinging on the school; but some of the energy now flows in the other direction. Most of the teachers at Jamieson are women, and they are in the class milieu (the professional intelligentsia) in which feminism has been strongest over the last decade. Those who reject feminism of any stripe still take their professionalism seriously and provide the girls with models of the engaged career woman. More, their professionalism involves a highly charged endorsement of a competitive academic curriculum which plugs their students into a competitive career structure; and some are quite explicit that this is a way of changing the subordination of women. To put it in a nutshell, the changed functioning of schools like Jamieson is providing the conditions of a small feminist insurgency within the ruling class.

Nor do such schools simply register or reflect the state of class relations. We have stressed the diversity in Jamieson's "catchment," the degree of incoherence in the class on which it depends—a pattern of difference which, as Julia Keating's little ethnography illustrates, is to some degree reproduced within the school. It is a major part of the school's task to overcome these differences. One familiar way it does so is by institutionalizing the lower boundary, focussing attention on difference from the masses outside:

(Do you think you get a better education here than you would at a state school?) I do. I've only been to a state school for one year which I hardly remember; but I just like a private school. Everyone says "Oh, you're a snob, you're a snob", and you say "Why?" But just little things: like you hear a person from a state school talk, and a lot of the time they just don't sort of speak properly; and just little things that you notice. (Marianne Gracie)

That gate-keeping is familiar; but it's only one expression of something much more general. The customs and procedures of the ruling-class school are systematically organized to overcome differences of wealth, background, and outlook; to synthesize, to subordinate particular interests in a common educational practice and a shared space. It isn't completely achieved, of course; different groups of parents remain at odds, and some (notably the big capitalists) are less dependent on the school for their children's future than others (such as the professionals), so the leverage is unequal. But leverage there is, and the effective principals and teachers use it.

We can now see the market relation between the ruling class and its school in a very different light. It is not only the mechanism by which parents' demands are transmitted to the school. Equally important, it is the mechanism which provides the space, the room for manoeuvre, for the school to play an active role in the construction of the class. The school generates practices by which the class is renewed, integrated, and re-constituted in the face of changes in its own composition and in the general social circumstances in which it tries to survive and prosper. (This is an embracing practice, ranging from the school fete, Saturday sport and weeknight dinners with parents, to the organization of a marriage market—e.g., inter-school dances—and informal networks in business and the professions, to the regulation of class membership, updating of ideology, and subordination of particular interests to those of the class as a whole.) The ruling-class school is no mere *agent* of the class; it is an important and active *part* of it. In short, it is organic to its class. Bourdieu (1966) wrote a famous essay about "the school as conserver"; we would suggest an equal stress should be laid on the school as constructor.

We may therefore propose a further point about the school principal. She is not just an entrepreneur stitched up with a pedagogue: the combination defines a precise position. She is, in Gramsci's phrase, an organic intellectual of her class. And, we would add, among the most significant—quite on a par with bishops and marketing managers. It is no accident that the leading private-school principals' annual "Speech Day" addresses are reported with some prominence in the capitalist press.

If the market is the mechanism of change (as we have suggested), it follows that change cannot be fully understood by looking at a single school. Strictly, it has to be analyzed in terms of the group of schools which are (in however muted a way) in competition with each other. We don't have space to explore the character of such markets here, except to register their impact: for instance, the close scrutiny of innovations in neighboring private schools (such as coeducation or changing curricular emphases); and the way some entrepreneurs can succeed by market segmentation (a notable case being a new school in Sydney with a militantly conservative principal who has successfully marketed military discipline, caning, talk-and-chalk pedagogy, and the like to a group of parents worried about progressivism among teachers elsewhere). But it is necessary, even in thinking about single schools, to note the limits to the reconstruction they can achieve.

The changes to the model of marriage and family life which we have noted among Jamieson girls, for instance, are emphatically not happening in the *boys'* private schools which we interviewed at the same time. And the interviews with the fathers of both boys and girls, the kind of people who will be their employers in a few years' time, show a massive reluctance to contemplate the entry of women into management—basically on the grounds that they would not be able to dominate male workers. (As one Jamieson father bluntly put it, "The men wouldn't wear it".) This may be more rationalization than reason, but it still stands for a significant male resistance to ruling-class feminism, which is operating to divert the girls' paths toward professions rather than management. And that is a familiar way in which a two-career family can be converted into a one-career-and-one-part-time-job family on the arrival of the first child.

Another dilemma is implicit in the second quotation from Marianne Gracie. Ruling-class schools can attract hostility on grounds of privilege and exclusiveness; and the more effective they are in cohering and integrating the class, the more likely they are to create antagonism outside it. It is only a few years since a Labor government introduced a "needs" scheme for federal grants to schools, a scheme in which the wealthiest private schools were to get nothing. A ruling-class outcry pulled the government back into line, and the environment has been balmier under a Liberal cabinet, most of whom went to private schools themselves. But the potential for hostility is still there, indeed is institutionalized in the academic rivalry with the state high schools. In short, the ruling class's need for class organization is in contradiction with its need to preserve hegemony, and its schools have to evolve some sort of solution.

Finally, as much of this will have suggested, the educational ideology of the ruling class is far from cohesive, and there are parts of it that are highly resistant to change. Teacher professionalism is an effective defence of educational modernization up to a point, but that point can be passed; and when it is, teachers find they are dealing with people who have a lot of power and are accustomed to getting their own way.

REFLECTIONS

The "reproduction" of class relations and class positions is no automatic outcome of the functioning of a system. It is not a process, it is an *achievement*—in fact a political achievement. The practices by which it is attempted can, and often do, go wrong (downward mobility of the family, crises in class relations, etc.); to succeed requires energy and organization. The ruling-class school is the scene of a significant group of those practices; its successful functioning may be regarded as a *collective achievement* on the part of the class and its organic intellectuals. And the measure of the energy and organization that has to go into that collective achievement is the burden of work Mrs. Johansen and her colleagues carry.

The ability to change is crucial to that achievement; yet change doesn't come to these schools freely. If we look closely at the points where reforms in schools like Jamieson have gained purchase, we see they are not random; rather they involve the intersection and contradiction of different structures (such as the marriage/career knot) or of incompatible demands which have been generated within the same structure (such as academic differentiation and class integration). We can recognize the force of structural determination without presupposing an endless cycle of reproduction. Not that structural contradiction mechanically produces change. What it does is open the space within which new practices can be developed—such as the reforms at Jamieson—which in turn reconstitute structures in new forms.

These general points apply to working-class schools as well. The educational subordination of working-class children is not automatic; it is a consequence of organized practices. There are contradictions and incoherencies here too, which can make space for different practices. Some of the most important, we would suggest, surround the meritocratic curriculum which working-class schools share with schools like Jamieson. In ruling-class schools, this curriculum is highly compatible with the class interests of the school's clientele; in working-class schools it is not. And that is a principal reason why those schools at present do more to disorganize the working class than to organize and empower it. Struggles to change the curriculum will be vital in deciding whether working-class schools can become organic to *their* class in something like the way Jamieson and its like are to theirs.

Too often in recent years, radical critiques of education have implied there is little that teachers can do; they are the servants of forces beyond their control. It's true that teachers by themselves can't build a new social order. But the implication of this study is that they do have a significant role in shaping the groups that will, in constituting social forces. How this is done, and with what effects, is not predetermined. So the politics of teachers is a question that counts in social struggle on the largest scale—whether teachers like it or not.

NOTES

This chapter is the product of close collaboration on the "School, Home and Work" project by the four authors over several years; our names are rotated in successive publications to make clear that no order of seniority or responsibility is implied. The project has been funded principally by the Education Research and Development Committee, and also by Sturt College of Advanced Education, Macquarie University, Kuring-gai College of Advanced Education, and the Society for the Production of Really Useful Knowledge. The authors wish to express their thanks to the school principals, officers of education departments in New South Wales and South Australia, and other teachers who gave permission for the project and helped it in countless ways; and above all to the students, parents, and teachers who gave their time and energy for interviews that were often long and not always easy.

1. For example, Bourdieu and Passeron (1964), Coleman (1966), and for a review of the English debate, Halsey (1972). We would include here not only large-scale surveys but also studies such as Ford (1969) which began to show how the broad patterns were reproduced within particular schools.

2. For rather more formal critiques of the stratificationist approach to class, see Connell (1977) and Blaikie (1977).

3. While the initial impulse here was theoretical reflection on stratificationist informa-

tion—notably Althusser (1971) and Bourdieu and Passeron (1970)—this line of thought has produced some interesting research too, notably Bowles and Gintis (1976), Willis (1977), and Bourdieu (1979).

4. Willis's troubled advice to careers advisers (1977:187 ff.) is an honorable attempt to be practical and a very clear indication of how hard it is with this paradigm. We have set out our critique of reproduction theory at much greater length elsewhere—see Ashenden (1979) and Connell (1980).

REFERENCES

Althusser, L., *Lenin and philosophy*. London: New Left Books, 1971.

Ashenden, D. J. Australian education: Problems of a marxist practice. *Arena*, 1979, 54, 43–58.

Ashenden, D. J., Connell, R.W., Dowsett, G., & Kessler, S. Class and secondary education: Some proposals for an approach stressing situations and practices. *Discourse*, 1980, 1, 1–19.

Bernstein, B. *Class, codes and control*, Vol. 1. London: Routledge and Kegan Paul, 1971.

Blaikie, N. W. H. The meaning and measurement of occupational prestige. *Australian and New Zealand Journal of Sociology*, 1977, 13, 102–115.

Bourdieu, P. L'école conservatrice. *Revue francaise de sociologie*, 1966, 7, 325–347.

Bourdieu, P. *La distinction*. Paris: Minuit, 1979.

Bourdieu, P., & Passeron, J.-C. *Les héritiers*. Paris: Minuit, 1964.

Bourdieu, P., & Passeron, J.-C. *Reproduction*. London: Sage, 1977 (1970).

Bowles, H., & Gintis, S. *Schooling in Capitalist America*. London: Routledge & Kegan Paul, 1976.

Coleman, J. S. *Equality of educational opportunity*. Washington: HEW, 1966.

Connell, R.W. Logic and politics in theories of class. *Australian and New Zealand Journal of Sociology*, 1977, 13, 203–211.

Connell, R.W. On the wings of history: A critique of reproduction theory. *Arena*, 1980, 55, 32–55.

Connell, R. W., & Irving, T. H. *Class structure in Australian history*. Melbourne: Cheshire, 1980.

Ford, J. *Social class and the comprehensive school*. London: Routledge & Kegan Paul, 1969.

Giddens, A. *New rules of sociological method*. London: Hutchinson, 1976.

Habermas, J. *Theory and practice*. London: Heinemann, 1974.

Halsey, A. H. *Educational priority*, Vol. 1. London: HMSO, 1972.

Lefebvre, H. *The survival of capitalism*. London: Allison & Busby, 1976.

Robins, D., & Cohen, P. *Knuckle sandwich*. Harmondsworth: Penguin, 1978.

Sartre, J.-P. *Critique of dialectical reason*. London: NLB, 1976.

Sennett, R., & Cobb, J. *The hidden injuries of class*. N.Y.: Vintage, 1973.

Thompson, E. P. *The making of the English working class*, 2nd edn. Harmondsworth: Penguin, 1968.

Willis, P. *Learning to labour*. Farnborough: Saxon House, 1977.

Section V

New Directions in the Study of Culture, Learning, and Education

New Directions in the Study of Culture, Learning, and Education

Margaret Eisenhart

This book was designed to introduce you to some of the best thinking and research in the cultural and social foundations of education. With this final framing essay and the chapters in this section, I invite you to consider some recent work and the new directions it provokes and inspires. Although the term "foundations" may suggest a focus on a dusty past, I hope this section, along with the preceding ones, will convince you that these foundations have the capacity to support exciting new ways of thinking about the cultural forces that affect educational opportunities and outcomes in the twenty-first century.

"Things cultural" have received the lion's share of attention in this book. As should be clear by now, interest in how to think about cultures or cultural forms, investigate their aspects, and pursue their influences on education has been central to the work of many educational scholars for most of the twentieth century. Yet during this time, the meaning of "culture" has always been problematic (see also the introduction to this book and to section I).[1] In the early part of the century, culture was often (though not always[2]) defined as patterns in a way of life characteristic of a specific social group and passed down from one generation to the next. Whether scholars' specific interests were in language, communities, families, beliefs, values, school achievement, or classroom climate, they have investigated and written about culture as evidenced by patterns in the collective behaviors and central orientations of socially distinguishable groups. Differences in cultural characteristics (such as language, family life, and so on) are thought to produce "cultural differences" between and among groups, and these cultural differences make it hard for members of one social group to understand the actions and values of those in other groups. Social groups identified from the outset by country, region, place (setting), ethnicity, religion, skin color, social position, or first language have been the most likely subjects of culturally oriented studies in education and beyond.

This approach to culture and cultural differences (also referred to as "cultural discontinuities" in Michèle Foster's framing essay for section III) has been and continues to be theoretically, practically, and politically powerful. It has effectively accounted for the difficulties of many nonwhite, nonclass-privileged children in mainstream U.S. schools (Miller 1995). It has provided direction for the development of instructional and curricular changes (including those associated with multicultural education) that, at least in the short run, improved these children's success in schools (e.g., Heath 1983; Jordan 1984, 1985; González, Moll, Floyd-Tenery, Rivera, Rendón, Gonzales, and Amanti 1993; Vogt, Jordan, and Tharp 1993, and section III of this volume). For many years, it has been a compelling argument in the struggle to gain more equal educational opportunities for students from nondominant groups.

Despite its political significance, there have been numerous challenges to this approach. John Ogbu (1978) was one of the first to point out that not all culturally different children do poorly in mainstream schools. Recently immigrated groups, for example, often do well in U.S. schools, while long-standing minority groups often do not. The success of some culturally different students is not accounted for by cultural difference (or discontinuity) theory.

Other critics of cultural difference theory have demonstrated that group differences in orientations toward school are not always or only linked to differences in home communities. Ideas about such things as readiness for school, popularity, romance, or plans for the future are sometimes shared by groups composed of individuals who do not share a social history or home community (Eckert 1989; Eisenhart and Graue 1993; Foley 1990; Holland and Eisenhart 1990; and Willis 1977). These views seem to develop as small groups or individuals work out their relationships and identities in relation to the school. Meanings brought to school can be reconfigured as students and parents respond to what they find there. Drawing on meanings available in various settings, but actively appropriated and modified to fit an unfolding context at school, groups of parents, students, and teachers from diverse backgrounds may come to share an orientation to school.

This approach to culture, in which the focus shifts toward meanings actively appropriated, constructed, and manipulated in specific contexts, and away from ideas about culture as a given "way of life," gained momentum as part of cultural anthropology's shift toward interpretivism in the 1970s (Erickson 1986; Geertz 1973). At the time, quite a few anthropologists began to focus on culture as "webs of significance," or meanings partially shared and manipulated by those who experience them.

At about the same time, a group of researchers inspired by social reproduction theory (see especially Willis 1977) drew attention to some of the disabling (as well as the enabling) features of culture. In Willis's ethnography of English working-class school boys (the "lads"), he demonstrated how the countercultural ways of thinking about self and identity that the lads produced for themselves led them to oppose values of the school—values that might have enabled them to improve their job prospects and social standing.

Ray McDermott and Hervé Varenne's work on culture and disability (1995; Varenne and McDermott 1999; cf. Hugh Mehan, section IV) is another, more contemporary example of the disabling effects of culture. They analyze how "disabilities" are culturally constructed in the United States; that is, how cultural forms identify some people—with certain characteristics—as atypical or disabled. Thus, although a designation of "disabled" in school can, for example, allow for the provision of valuable services, it also can denigrate individuals and groups by marking them as odd.

During the 1980s and 1990s, new perspectives have focused attention on still other ways of thinking about culture. From within anthropology as well as from literary criticism, feminist studies, ethnic studies, and cultural studies, increasing numbers of scholars are pointing to contemporary phenomena that seem to defy explanation in conventional cultural terms.

Recent challenges to old ideas about culture have their origins in empirical evidence from contemporary global events, new social movements, and changing demographics. New modes of transportation, communication, and migration have created mixed or mixed-up social relationships by traditional anthropological standards. The spaces, times, relationships, tasks, and tools that seemed to constitute collectively organized society in the past, took their meanings from culture, and served as the focal points of anthropological research, have been transformed with the changing conditions of contemporary life. Today, for example, it is not surprising to hear of a researcher traveling half way around the world to visit a key informant—say, a Hindu priest in India—only to find that he has moved to serve parishioners in Houston (Appadurai 1991). Similarly we hear about "a medicine man who at one time feels a deep respect for Mother Earth and at another plans a radical real estate subdivision" (Clifford 1988, 338). It is not uncommon to listen to political or educational debates in which members of the same ethnic or racial group take different sides. It is not unusual to find children and adults spending hours a day communicating via computer technologies, video games, or popular music that connect them to people, values, and economic networks far removed from home or school. Paul Willis, discussing the increasing allure of popular culture among young people, writes:

> Many of the traditional resources of, and inherited bases for, social meaning, membership, security and psychic certainty have lost their legitimacy for a good proportion of young people. There is no longer a sense of a "whole culture" with allocated places and a shared, universal value system. . . . [There is no longer a supply of] ready values and models of duty and meaning to help structure the passage into settled adulthood. (1990, 13)

Today, varied social settings—for childcare, education, leisure, and work—and new forms of media—mass media and communications and computer technologies—take the place of, or function together with, homes and communities to socialize large numbers of children and young people.

For reasons like these, it is no longer straightforward for anthropologists to plan to study "cultural groups," that is, designated groups of people with coherent, shared value systems, households or communities with clearly defined boundaries, or shared funds of knowledge transmitted primarily from adults to their children. Conventional assumptions about culture as being coherent and coterminous with social background, language use, region, religion, or ethnicity, have become impossible to sustain. Certainly, societal changes that challenge conventional ideas about culture have been occurring for some time, but recent critics from feminist, ethnic, and cultural studies have been the ones to drive the point home. One consequence of their critique has been a turn toward "identity" in studies of "culture."

Signithia Fordham's article in this section, " 'Those Loud Black Girls': (Black) Women, Silence, and Gender 'Passing' in the Academy," illustrates how one group of black high school girls struggled to develop meaningful and empowering identities for themselves in school. In the abridged version of Fordham's article included here, she reveals how black girls learn to define themselves *within* and *against* the images of, and around, them (see also Davidson 1996, for a related discussion of students' identity formation in school). In Fordham's conception, culture is the total complex of available images, some of which are contradictory and contested, all of which make sense in part because of their *relationship* to others (e.g., "black" is at least in part "not white," and "woman" is in part "not man"). Individual girls fashion their identities, positive or negative, out of these images. The identities they form have serious implications for academic performance and routes to womanhood. Fordham uses the metaphor of "loudness" to represent the black girls' efforts to establish their own positive identity, as well as to represent the school's (negative) reaction to it.[3]

Jan Nespor's chapter, "Tying Things Together (and Stretching Them Out) with Popular Culture," takes up identities as well, but in a different way. His focus is popular culture—things like television shows and commercials, music, and computer programs—and the ways young people use elements of popular cultural forms to represent, shape, and extend their own identities. He illustrates the improvisations of, and constraints upon, elementary school students as they express elements of popular culture in their interactions with each other (see also Fisherkeller 1997; Mankekar 1993; and Shaw 1996, for other recent examples). Nespor suggests that the unit of analysis for studies of young people's socialization may no longer be their experiences in a community, family, household, or cultural group, "but the emergent associations of kids producing selves and identities through the [relatively stable] infrastructures of popular culture" (see also Willis 1990, for a similar argument).

Another recent turn in studies of culture is reflected in Sherry's Ortner's "Fieldwork in the Postcommunity." Ortner's main topic is ethnographic fieldwork and how it might be used to understand contemporary "communities"—such as a high school graduating class—whose identity and significance are maintained over time even though participants are widely dispersed in space and circumstances. In this sense, her article, like Nespor's, illustrates one way to grapple with the methodological difficulty of studying group and personal identities that are stretched out beyond face-to-face interactions and geographic proximity. These identities are made possible by audio-visual technologies, computer-based networks, and high-speed transportation and communication systems that link together people, and enable ongoing relationships among them, across long periods of time and vast distances (see also Nespor 1994).

But Ortner's piece reveals something else: that powerful memories of past shared experiences—whether face-to-face or not, whether positive or negative—constitute "communities of the mind" that continue to organize people's networks of affiliation (who's in and who's out) and patterns of behavior (e.g., attendance at class reunions, or reestablished phone contact with former classmates). These mind-communities also evoke intense feelings and contribute to the stories of self and past told to others, including children. In these patterns of organization and story telling, Ortner argues, "forms of social difference, asymmetry, and solidarity practiced in the high school community persist" as meaningful categories of adulthood and socialization. A "once-local community" may continue to exist long past the local phase—through reunions, long-distance phone calls, e-mail and Internet, holiday letters, exchanges of favors, visits to "home," and so forth. Such once-local communities may continue to have social consequences for members, their children, and their friends even when they are far removed in time and space from the original local experience.

As the twenty-first century begins, ideas like these about the emerging social conditions that characterize lives, the new and interesting forms culture takes, and how to study and understand these conditions and forms are moving studies of education in new directions. One exciting area of application for these emergent ideas is in studies of "learning." Until recently, few educational scholars have given serious consideration to conceptualizing how individuals actively and inventively contribute to cultural continuity or change (but see Erickson 1982; and Wolcott 1982). Yet, as conceptions of culture are changed or updated, ideas about what it means to "develop," "learn," "change," or "continue" culture within and across generations are also undergoing revision. In my chapter, "The Fax, the Jazz Player, and the Self-storyteller," I take up this issue directly. In the portion of the article abridged here, I discuss the link between anthropologists' views of culture and their studies of how culture is passed from one generation to the next, that is, how culture is transmitted and acquired or learned. In addition, I suggest that "building or claiming an identity for self in a given context is what motivates an individual to become more expert; that developing a sense of oneself as an actor in a context is what compels [people] to desire and pursue increasing mastery of . . . skills, knowledge, and emotions" (after Holland 1992). In this way of thinking, to study learning means to study how individuals actively develop their personal skills, styles, and beliefs—their identities as persons—over time and out of whatever is around to be used. In the full text of my article, I suggest that the "stories of self" people tell about themselves in new situations are one clue to how individuals "interpret the past, construct the present, and launch the future" in socially and culturally meaningful idioms; that is, how they learn and continue culture. Other anthropologists have recently suggested their own approaches to this new direction in anthropological studies of learning (e.g., see Chaiklin and Lave 1993; Lave and Wenger 1991; and Wolcott 1991).

Cultural studies of learning have also received a boost from current research that relies on Lev Vygotsky's writings about the "cultural tools"—historically produced ways of thinking, remembering, and using language, artifacts, and beliefs—that people learn growing up and depend on to make sense of their world and act in it. Vygotsky was a Russian psychologist whose writings of the 1920s and 1930s have had a major influence on contemporary scholars of culture and learning. Vygotsky's primary interest was in developing a comprehensive approach to human intellectual functioning—an approach that could describe and explain both elementary and complex mental processes (Cole and Scribner 1978). Unlike most psychologists of his day (who stressed behavioral origins), Vygotsky stressed the social and historical origins of language and thinking, thereby becoming "the first modern psychologist to suggest the mechanisms by which culture becomes a part of each person's nature" (1978, 6). Tools and sign systems (language, writing, and number systems), which are created and changed by societies over the course of human history, were these mechanisms. Vygotsky believed that as tools and sign systems were picked up, used, and internalized by individuals, the tools and signs formed the bridge, or "mediator," between the social and the psychological (as when using a computer becomes a way of thinking about one's life), and between elementary and higher forms of intellectual development (as when producing text becomes a way of writing a novel). (See also Eisenhart, Finkel, and Marion [1996], Emihovich and Lima [1995], and Moll [1990] for recent overviews of Vygotsky's contribution to research on learning and culture.) Although Vygotsky's ideas were very provocative, he did not succeed in developing the comprehensive theory he sought.

Since Vygotsky's death in 1934 and the translation of his writings into English in the 1970s, scholars of culture and human development have continued to work with Vygotsky's ideas. One direction that this work has taken are attempts to bridge the gap between anthropological theories of learning (that focus on what people know and do with what they know) and cognitive psychological theories of learning (that focus on how people think and develop their thinking).[4]

In conclusion, all the chapters included in this section hint that social and cultural worlds, and scholars' ways of conceiving of them, are changing. Today, varied social settings—for childcare, education, leisure, and work—take the place of, or function together with, homes, schools, and communities to socialize large numbers of children and young people. Widespread access to transportation, the mass media, and computer technology opens avenues of communication far wider and more diverse than in previous generations (Holland, Lachicotte, Skinner, and Cain

1998; Nespor 1994). In her 1996 epilogue to *Ways with Words* (1983), Shirley Brice Heath nicely captures some of these changes and their consequences for anthropological studies of young people:

> Fieldwork such as that behind *Ways with Words* [1983] has [become] impossible. Present day households and communities of children and youths lack the easily described boundaries of their parents. . . . In many of these households [in 1996], weeks go by when no two members of a household eat at the same time, share any chore, or plan work together. Hours go by when no one is anywhere near home. Over a decade ago, I could generally find the children of Roadville and Trackton at home or at school. Today, with no one at home to organize chores or to watch over play in the community, children and young people scatter and disappear. Youngest children are in daycare centers. School-age children go inside friends' houses to watch television or play video games; they crowd into the vans of community youth athletic leagues and move from sport to sport by season. . . . Older youths either race to their cars when the schoolbell rings and head for fast-food restaurants or malls, or ride the bus to one another's houses and then scatter to favorite gathering places with their friends. On the go, they listen to car radios or wear headphones and throb to the muffled beat of their compact discs or cassettes. Older and younger children segregate themselves by gender, activity, space, and sounds. . . . If the movement of adults and children in and out of households and their uses of space, time, work and leisure [have changed] so much, then ethnographers must develop new methods of seeing and understanding. . . . Now ethnographers must learn patterns of affiliation in numerous networks of different spaces and times, follow modes of physical transport and learn where [people] meet, and delineate technological means and sources of communication. (1996, 370–372)

These are cultural phenomena to which scholars of education and learning must turn their attention.

To meet challenges like these, we will need new concepts, tools, and strategies for better capturing these phenomena as we are coming to understand them. In particular, we will need ways of thinking about and studying culture and learning that can travel across, while also remaining sensitive to, times and spaces (historical and social contexts), and category labels in everyday use (e.g., racial minorities, immigrants, and women). We will need strategies to explore friendships and other relationships that stretch out across time and space, to identify relatively brief encounters that have special or longer-term significance, and to analyze activities, discourses, and entertainment taken up locally but formed and controlled elsewhere.

Some of these interests and commitments have been long-standing in anthropologically oriented studies of education, but they must be expanded and updated to more closely correspond to the world we are presently trying to understand and the educational improvements we want to effect. Other interests are relatively new and will require correspondingly new ideas and approaches. In other words, there are a lot of exciting possibilities for important, new thinking and research by new and diverse students of cultural and social foundations.

NOTES

1. See Eisenhart (forthcoming) for an extended discussion of changing patterns in conceptions of culture during the past half-century. Portions of my summary here are taken from that article.

2. See, for example, Jacob (1999), who discusses the long tradition of associating "culture" with a particular setting or context, such as a school or classroom, as well as with social groups.

3. Fordham's arguments are more fully developed in her book *Blacked Out* (1996).

4. A good example of this new work is the article by Dorothy Holland and Michael Cole (1995), in which the authors' use of "discourse theory" represents an anthropological approach, while their use of "schema" theory represents a psychological approach. They discuss one kind of tool, a "cultural artifact" which, they suggest, bridges the two approaches. They define a cultural artifact as an aspect of the material world (i.e., of the "real" world)—such as a hammer, a computer, or (in Holland and Cole's case) a scrap of paper—that has a historically derived, collectively agreed-upon use in some human action (to pound a nail, in the case of the hammer). As Holland and Cole put it, "a theory of the task" and "a theory of the person" who performs the task are captured when an individual picks up a tool/mediator and uses it in real time. For example, when a child picks up a hammer for the first time, or sits down at a computer, "learning" entails figuring out how to use the tool for present purposes, but what is possible to do with the tool in the present will be constrained by its historically developed parameters. Because of the parameters of past use, a child is unlikely (for example) to be able to use *either* the hammer or the computer to pound nails successfully. Hammers have developed as cultural artifacts for pounding nails; computers have not. Studies of learning via cultural artifacts—how individuals and groups develop uses, modifications, and extensions of them—promise to be another exciting new direction.

REFERENCES AND READINGS

Appadurai, A. 1991. Global Ethnoscapes: Notes and Queries for a Transnational Anthropology. In *Recapturing Anthropology: Working in the Present*, edited by R. Fox. Santa Fe, N.M.: School of American Research Press.

Chaiklin, S., and Lave, J., eds. 1993. *Understanding Practice: Perspectives on Activity and Context*. Cambridge: Cambridge University Press.

Clifford, J. 1988. *The Predicament of Culture: Twentieth-century Ethnography, Literature, and Art*. Cambridge, Mass.: Harvard University Press.

Cole, M., and Scribner, S. 1978. Introduction. In *L. S. Vygotsky Mind in Society: The Development of Higher Psychological Processes*, edited by M. Cole, V. John-Steiner, S. Scribner, and E. Souberman. Cambridge, Mass.: Harvard University Press.

Davidson, A. 1996. *Making and Molding Identity in Schools: Student Narratives on Race, Gender, and Academic Engagement*. Albany: SUNY Press.

Eckert, P. 1989. *Jocks and Burnouts: Social Categories and Identity in the High School*. New York: Teachers College Press.

Eisenhart, M. Forthcoming. Changing Conceptions of Culture and Ethnographic Methodology: Recent Thematic Shifts and the Implications for Research on Teaching. In *The*

Handbook of Research on Teaching. 4th ed. Edited by V. Richardson. Washington, D.C.: American Educational Research Association.

Eisenhart, M., Finkel, E., and Marion, S. 1996. Creating the Conditions for Scientific Literacy: A Reexamination. *American Educational Research Journal* 33 (2): 261–295.

Eisenhart, M., and Graue, M. E. 1993. Constructing Cultural Differences and Educational Achievement. In *Minority Education: Anthropological Perspectives*, edited by E. Jacob and C. Jordan. Norwood, N.J.: Ablex.

Emihovich, C., and Lima, E. S. 1995. The Many Facets of Vygotsky: A Cultural Historical Voice for the Future. *Anthropology and Education Quarterly* 26 (4): 375–383.

Erickson, F. 1982. Taught Cognitive Learning in Its Immediate Environments: A Neglected Topic in the Anthropology of Education. *Anthropology and Education Quarterly* 13 (2): 149–180.

———. 1986. Qualitative Methods in Research on Teaching. In *The Handbook of Research on Teaching.* 3rd ed. Edited by M. Wittrock. New York: Macmillan.

Fisherkeller, J. 1997. Everyday Learning about Identities among Young Adolescents in Television Culture. *Anthropology and Education Quarterly* 28 (4): 467–492.

Foley, D. 1990. *Learning Capitalist Culture: Deep in the Heart of Tejas.* Philadelphia: University of Pennsylvania Press.

Fordham, S. 1996. *Blacked Out: Dilemmas of Race, Identity, and Success in Capital High.* Chicago: University of Chicago Press.

Geertz, C. 1973. Thick Description: Toward an Interpretive Theory of Culture. In *The Interpretation of Cultures: Selected Essays*, edited by C. Geertz. New York: Basic.

González, N., Moll, L., Floyd-Tenery, M., Rivera, A., Rendón, P., Gonzales, R., and Amanti, C. 1993. *Teacher Research on Funds of Knowledge: Learning from Households.* Report of the National Center for Research on Cultural Diversity and Second Language Learning. Tucson: University of Arizona.

Heath, S. B., ed. 1983. *Ways with Words: Language, Life, and Work in Communities and Classrooms.* Cambridge: Cambridge University Press.

———. 1996. Reprint. Epilogue. In *Ways with Words: Language, Life, and Work in Communities and Classrooms*, edited by S. B. Heath. Cambridge: Cambridge University Press. (Original edition, Cambridge: Cambridge University Press, 1983.)

Holland, D. 1992. How Cultural Systems Become Desire: A Case Study of American Romance. In *Human Motives and Cultural Models*, edited by R. D'Andrade and C. Strauss. Cambridge: Cambridge University Press.

Holland, D., and Cole, M. 1995. Between Discourse and Schema: Reformulating a Cultural-historical Approach to Culture and Mind. *Anthropology and Education Quarterly* 26 (4): 475–490.

Holland, D., and Eisenhart, M. 1990. *Educated in Romance: Women, Achievement, and College Culture.* Chicago: University of Chicago Press.

Holland, D., Lachicotte, W., Skinner, D., and Cain, C. 1998. *Identity and Agency in Cultural Worlds.* Cambridge, Mass.: Harvard University Press.

Jacob, E. 1999. *Cooperative Learning in Context: An Educational Innovation in Everyday Classrooms.* Albany: SUNY Press.

Jordan, C. 1984. Cultural Compatibility and the Education of Ethnic Minority Children. *Educational Research Quarterly* 8 (4): 59–71.

———. 1985. Translating Culture: From Ethnographic Information to Educational Program. *Anthropology and Education Quarterly* 16 (2): 105–123.

Lave, J., and Wenger, E. 1991. *Situated Learning: Legitimate Peripheral Participation*. Cambridge: Cambridge University Press.

Levinson, B., Foley, D., and Holland, D., eds. 1996. *The Cultural Production of the Educated Person: Critical Ethnographies of Schooling and Local Practice*. Albany: SUNY Press.

Mankekar, P. 1993. National Texts and Gendered Lives: An Ethnography of Television Viewers in a North Indian City. *American Ethnologist* 20 (3): 543–563.

McDermott, R., and Varenne, H. 1995. Culture as Disability. *Anthropology and Education Quarterly* 26 (3): 324–348.

Miller, L. S. 1995. *An American Imperative: Accelerating Minority Educational Achievement*. New Haven, Conn.: Yale University Press.

Moll, L., ed. 1990. *Vygotsky and Education*. Cambridge: Cambridge University Press.

Nespor, J. 1994. *Knowledge in Motion: Space, Time and Curriculum in Undergraduate Physics and Management*. London: Falmer.

Ogbu, J. 1978. *Minority Education and Caste: The American System in Cross-cultural Perspective*. New York: Academic.

Shaw, T. 1996. Taiwanese Schools against Themselves: School Culture versus the Subjectivity of Youth. In *The Cultural Production of the Educated Person: Critical Ethnographies of Schooling and Local Practices*, edited by B. Levinson, D. Foley, and D. Holland. Albany: SUNY Press.

Varenne, H., and McDermott, R. 1999. *Successful Failure: The School America Builds*. Boulder, Colo.: Westview.

Vogt, L., Jordan, C., and Tharp, R. 1993. Explaining School Failure, Producing School Success: Two Cases. In *Minority Education: Anthropological Perspectives*, edited by E. Jacob and C. Jordan. Norwood, N.J.: Ablex.

Willis, P. 1977. *Learning to Labor: How Working Class Kids Get Working Class Jobs*. New York: Columbia University Press.

———. 1990. *Common Culture: Symbolic Work at Play in the Everyday Cultures of the Young*. Boulder, Colo.: Westview.

Wolcott, H. 1982. The Anthropology of Learning. *Anthropology and Education Quarterly* 13 (2): 83–108.

———. 1991. Propriospect and the Acquisition of Culture. *Anthropology and Education Quarterly* 22 (3): 251–273.

21

"Those Loud Black Girls": (Black) Women, Silence, and Gender "Passing" in the Academy

Signithia Fordham

In the academy women are compelled to "pass" as the male dominant "Other" if they desire to achieve a modicum of academic success (Pagano 1990:13, K. Scott 1991:150; White 1985:36). "Passing" implies impersonation, acting as if one is someone or something one is not. Hence, gender "passing," or impersonation—the coexistence of a prescription and proscription to imitate white American males and females—suggests masquerading or presenting a persona or some personae that contradict the literal image of the marginalized or doubly refracted "Other." For example, Patricia Williams (1988), an African-American who is also a Harvard Law School graduate, describes the seemingly contradictory strategies her mother encouraged her to use to succeed in the academy. These strategies were intended to negate her identification with her mother—a dubious role model for success in the academy and the larger society. These same strategies were also supposed to motivate her to reclaim the disinherited white components of her identity.[1]

> My Mother was [constantly] asking me not to look to her as a role model. She was devaluing that part of herself that was not Harvard and refocusing my vision to that part of herself that was hard-edged, proficient, and Western. She hid the lonely, black, defiled-female part of herself and pushed me forward as the projection of a competent self, a cool rather than despairing self, *a masculine rather than a feminine self.* [P. Williams 1988:20, emphasis added]

Likewise, Pagano describes how the academy compels female teachers to hide their femaleness to obtain the desired academic approval of their male peers and superiors. She notes that female teachers often

> present [themselves] as the genderless "author," "artist," or "scientist" . . . [in order] to quell any doubts [they] may have about [their] right to so present [themselves], to speak

in the voice of authority—the tradition—and to compete with [their] male colleagues for scarce academic resources . . . hunch [their] bodies in shameful secrecy as [they] walked the corridors of [their] departments for fear that someone would notice [they] were in drag. [Pagano 1990:13]

Gender "passing" is thus a reality for both African-American women and white women. Indeed, it could be debated that the first—and some would argue the only—commandment for women in the academy is "Thou must be taken seriously." "Thou must be taken seriously" is a euphemism for "thou must not appear as woman." Therefore, for women to be taken seriously in the academy, they must not only receive a form of schooling the contents of which prepares them to survive and prosper in a world organized by and for men (not women) (Rich 1979:238), but in addition they must transform their identity in such a way that the resulting persona makes the female appear not to be female. This evolving persona reflects and highlights socially defined maleness. "Being taken seriously," then, implies discarding or at least minimizing a female identity in a self-conscious effort to consume, or at least present the appearance of being, the male dominant "Other." It also suggests avoiding the traditional dichotomous definition of womanhood: good girl–bad girl, virgin–seductress, angel–whore. The problem, however, is much larger than a common or universal definition of womanhood; it is also the larger society's "acceptance of and complicity in a hierarchy of female goodness that imputes moral superiority to some women's lives and immorality to others" (Palmer 1989:151).

In America, white womanhood is often defined as a cultural universal.[2] Yet, the moral superiority of white womanhood is rarely explicitly verbalized in the academy. Indeed, it is most often labeled "femaleness" minus the white referent. Nonetheless, *white* and middle class are the "hidden transcript[s]" (J. Scott 1990) of femaleness, the womanhood invariably and historically celebrated in academe. In striking contrast, black womanhood is often presented as the antithesis of white women's lives, the slur or "the nothingness" (see Christian 1990; Walker 1982) that men and other women use to perpetuate and control the image of the "good girl" and by extension the good woman. Hence, the academy's penchant for universalizing and normalizing white middle-class women's lives compels black women and other women of color to seek to appropriate the image and attempt to consume the lives of the female "Other."[3]

Ironically, gender "passing" is rarely identified as a factor in the differentiated academic performance of African American and white American students. It is also seldom identified as a factor producing asymmetrical outcomes in African-American males' and African-American females' school performance. This response persists despite widespread acknowledgment that (1) African-American students' school performance is gender-differentiated at all levels of the academy; (2) America's patriarchal system is stratified, with some males having more power and privileges than other males in the patriarchy; and (3) African-American females are doubly victimized by the existence of a two tiered patriarchy.

A central goal of the analysis presented in this article is to identify and describe how the existence of a subversive, diverse womanhood among African-American women, juxtaposed with a two-tiered dominating patriarchy, influences and often adversely affects academic achievement. An ancillary goal is to document how the absence of "official" recognition of gender diversity in a predominantly African-American high school [Capital High] in Washington, D.C., mutilates the academic achievement of large numbers of female African-American students.

I also include . . . documentation of African-American females' resistance to this silence and imitation mandate. Although acknowledging the common features of the high-achieving female students—they work hard, they are silent; when they vocalize, they speak "in a different voice" (Gilligan 1982)—I focus my analysis on Rita, a high-achieving female who symbolizes this composite image. Rita, I argue, epitomizes black women's struggle to commingle or fuse two divergent lives concurrently. I postulate that she is both unwilling and unable to be silent. She is also irrevocably committed to the retention of her female, African-American gendered "Self." Moreover, I argue, her speech is masked and disguised in ways that nullify and negate the perception of her femaleness. I try to show how her speech, thinking, voice, and writing styles emulate the dominant male "Other" while embracing her largely unconscious perceptions of African-American womanhood. I also cite several examples of how the child-rearing practices of the parents and teachers of the high-achieving females unwittingly cremate these young African-American women's efforts to flee the African-American community and, in the process, paradoxically enhance their affiliation with the large American society. The concluding section of the article focuses on some of the possible implications of constructing an African-American female for success in the academy and the excessive price she pays for transforming her gendered "Self."

THE SOCIAL CONTEXT OF THE SCHOOL

Capital High School (a pseudonym) is located in a predominantly African-American section of the city of Washington, D.C. Essentially, it is a school within a school. As a school within a school, Capital attracts students from all socioeconomic segments of the city of Washington. Indeed, its recruitment efforts are very successful. More than a fourth of the students are noncommunity residents who travel from various parts of the city to participate in the school's advanced placement and humanities programs.[4] Hence, Capital High is not a school that can be accurately labeled low-income or inner-city, euphemisms for slums and the "underclass." The school's complex student body and diverse, rudimentary class structure[5] do not lend themselves readily to such uncomplicated labeling. It is far more accurate to label Capital a "magnet school," because through its multilevel, multirigorous curriculum it accurately reflects the diverse population of the entire city.

The first two years of the study were the most intense. During the first year, 33 11th grade students whose parents had consented to their participation in the study served as key informants. As key informants, these students' were self-consciously interrogated. They were interviewed, observed, and analyzed for more than a year. These students formed a varied group, representing both high-achieving and underachieving students—male and female—and the diverse population described above.

Constructing and Nullifying Cultural-Specific Femaleness

In a socially, culturally, and racially stratified society like the United States, cultural-specific routes to womanhood are inevitable. Indeed, the stratified nature of state systems suggests the following: (1) gender construction is not universal and (2) status inequity vis-à-vis gender is a sine qua non in such contexts. Hence, femaleness in such contexts is not the same for all women, just as maleness is not the same for all men. Gender diversity (i.e., what it means to be male or female in different social classes and social groups) is rarely officially acknowledged in the academies of contemporary nation-states. Therefore, like most other women of color, African-American women are compelled to consume the universalized images of white American women, including body image, linguistic patterns, styles of interacting, and so forth. Because womanhood or femaleness is norm referenced to one group—white middle-class Americans—women from social groups who do not share this racial, ethnic, or cultural legacy are compelled to silence or gender "passing." Although all women born and reared in America are "educated in romance," in Holland and Eisenhart's (1990) term, and victimized by sexism, not all American women take the same train to a common sexist station. Therefore, as Evans suggests:

> [Anthropologists] need to examine the ways by which the Women's Movement has perpetrated a type of cultural imperialism that takes the oppression of white women as its norm and develops its theory from the experience of a small minority of women in global terms. [1988:189]

"Those loud Black girls" is an example of both the diversity of gender construction in Euro-American contexts and the efforts to suppress that diversity. It is also a quintessential example of African-American women's commitment to being visible as culturally specific women. Curiously, these young women appear to be motivated to highlight the practices of gender-specific constructions in contexts that compel male impersonation or, at the very least, the adoption of a male voice.[6] "Those loud Black girls" is also an example of how a people's history is reflected in their daily lives. As Davis (1971) argues so convincingly, African-American women bring to the academy—broadly defined—a history of womanhood that differs from that of white or any other American women. African-American women's history stands in striking contrast to that generally associated with white womanhood and includes (1) more than 200 years in which their status as women was annulled, compelling them to function in ways that were virtually indistinguishable from their male slave counterparts; (2) systemic absence of protection by African-American and all other American men; (3) construction of a new definition of what it means to be female out of the stigma associated with the black experience and the virtue and purity affiliated with white womanhood; and (4) hard work[7] (including slave and domestic labor), perseverance, assertiveness, and self-reliance. In other words, the history of African-American males and females includes an extended period when gender differences were minimized, resulting in a kind of "deformed equality" (Davis 1971), or, as Cary (1991) describes it, a period when African-American females were "officially" classified as the "neutered 'Other.'"

These images flooded my psyche the day I discovered Grace Evans's (1980) article entitled "Those Loud Black Girls." At long last, I thought, someone has accurately captured what I learned about black womanhood at Capital High and what I personally experienced growing up African and American. Since the word *anecdotal* is almost always preceded by the word *merely*, prior to reading Evans's essay, I never quite trusted the validity of my personal experiences. Growing up female and African-American in American society, I learned early on to discount the validity of my experiences. Evans, an African-American social studies teacher in the public school system in several inner-city schools in London, locates "those loud Black girls" in the following setting:

> In staffrooms [of the schools] a common cry to be heard from white teachers—usually women, for male teachers seldom revealed that everything for them was not firmly under control—was, "Oh, those loud Black girls!" This exclamation was usually followed by the slamming of a pile of folders on to a table and the speaker collapsing into a chair or storming off to get a cup of coffee. The words were usually uttered in response to a confrontation in which the teacher's sense of authority had been threatened by an attitude of defiance on the part of a group of Black girls in a classroom or corridor. The girls' use of patois and their stubborn refusal to conform to standards of "good behavior," without actually entering the realm of "bad behavior" by breaking any school rules, was exasperating for many teachers. The behavior of the girls could be located in the outer limits of tolerable behavior, and they patrolled this territory without much skill, sending a distinct message of being in and for themselves. (Evans 1988:183]

Elsewhere I described the black girls who were academically successful at Capital High as "phantoms in the opera" (Fordham 1990). I made this assertion because the academically successful black girls achieved academic success in the following ways: (1) becoming and remaining voiceless or silent or, alternatively, (2) impersonating a male image—symbolically—in self-presentation, including voice, thinking, speech pattern, and writing style, in the formal school context when formally interacting with their teachers in classrooms, assemblies, club meetings, and so forth. At the same time, however, I noted that silence for the African-American female is not to be interpreted as acquiescence. Rather, I argued that silence among the high-achieving females at the school is an act of defiance, a refusal on the part of the high-achieving females to consume the image of "nothingness" (see Christian 1990) so essential to the conception of African-American women. This intentional silence is also critical to the rejection and deflection of the attendant downward expectations so pervasive among school officials.

Pagano acknowledges and describes women's forced emigration toward silence and maleness in the academy. She declares:

> The more successful [women] have been as students, scholars, and teachers, the greater has been [their] active participation in [their] own exclusion. [Pagano 1990:12]

She goes on to document how women pawn their collective voice in exchange for success in the existing patriarchic structure. By engaging in such practices, she argues, women ensure the continued existence of authority in the male image and their (women's) complicity in the lie that asserts that they are naturally silent. She concludes by asserting that women who either remain or become silent are instrumental in maintaining female dependency and invisibility in the academy. Hence, "those loud Black girls" are doomed not necessarily because they cannot handle the academy's subject matter, but because they resist "active participation in [their] own exclusion" (Pagano 1990:12).

In analyzing a small portion of the Capital High ethnographic data, Pagano's claim is verified in a predominantly African-American context. The following general patterns emerge among the high-achieving females: (1) resistance as a tenuous, ghostlike existence and status at the school; (2) the coexistence of excellent grades and the appearance of an erasable persona; (3) parenting, teaching, and child-rearing practices that reward their silence and obedience with good grades, as well as the assertive suppression and denial of physicality and sexuality; (4) alienation and isolation from the black fictive kinship system's ad hoc orientation; and (5) the assiduous commingling and maintaining of an academically successful persona *and* a "nice girl" persona with very little external reward or remuneration from parents or guardians, especially mothers. Such parental child-rearing practices suggest that nurturing a black female for success—as defined by the larger society—is far more disruptive of indigenous cultural conventions and practices than previously thought. Evans acknowledges some of the costs involved:

> The prize of a good education [is often] attained at the cost of great sacrifice on the part of one's parents, sometimes the entire family. Aside from this cost, another price is paid by the recipient of an education, and this is the personal cost of the process of deculturisation, or de-Africanization, whereby all personal expressions of one's original Africa culture are eliminated and [Euro-American] codes established instead. The mastery of standard English to replace West Indian patois is only one aspect of this transformation. It includes training the body to adopt European body language and gesture, and the voice to adopt European tones of speech and non-verbal expression. . . . The price of a good education, a [Euro-American] education, in short, was, and still

is, the denial of one's Black cultural identity. This is the price of entry to the middle-class. It is this legacy of education as a double-edged sword that creates a similar suspicion towards Black teachers on the part of Black students as exists on the part of the Black community towards Black members of the police force. The presence of Black faces does not change the essential nature of an institution, nor does it alter its ethos. [Evans 1988:185]

In stark contrast, the following salient patterns are common among the under-achieving females in the study: (1) striking visibility and presence—(these young women were known by everyone at the school and did not try to minimize the disruption that their visibility implied); (2) lack of congruency between grades and standardized test scores, with standardized test scores frequently dwarfing Grade Point Average (GPA); (3) parenting and child-rearing practices that suggest unconditional support for their daughters' self-defined academic plans and other espoused goals; (4) encapsulation and immersion in the black egalitarian (i.e., fictive kinship) system (see Fordham 1987, 1988, 1991a, 1991b; Fordham and Ogbu 1986); and (5) obtaining and maintaining support and nurturing from peers and the significant adults in their lives.

Gender "Passing": The Female High Achievers

As Rich (1979) and Pagano (1990) suggest, gender "passing" in the academy is unavoidable. Also, as I have already indicated, during the schooling process women receive a form of schooling the contents of which prepare them to survive and prosper in a world organized by and for men, not women (Rich 1979:238). Consequently, "being taken seriously," that is, becoming a good student, implies certifying male knowledge, conferring the names of the father and contradicting (women's) own biology (Pagano 1990:37–38).

The high-achieving female students at Capital High are living by the first academic commandment for women: "thou must be taken seriously." At the same time, each of them is guilty of seeking a "safe cultural space"[8] to retain their varied perceptions of the gendered African-American "Self." Virtually all of them—Alice, Sia, Lisa, Katrina, and Maggie—are thought of as serious young women, headed for the fast track and a life away from the ghetto. Each of these women is somehow able to walk the tightrope that living two divergent lives mandates. In striking contrast, Rita presents a less balanced persona. Like the other high-achieving female members of the sample, she is compelled to commingle two divergent lives. The important distinction, however, is that she is far less willing than her high-achieving female counterparts to camouflage, in the school context, her perceptions of the gendered African-American female "Self."

Rita is acknowledged to be a brilliant student, but all her teachers and many of her peers worry about her because she presents a "polyrhythmic, nonsymmetrical, nonlinear" persona. She is bold and sassy, creative, complex, and indeflatable. She frequently challenges the values and rules of the school with conviction, vacillating between demanding total adherence to the dominant ideology of the larger society on the part of her teachers and other school administrators and discounting and disparaging these same values and rules in her personal life. Her actions suggest a "contradictory unity"—an attempt to suture that which is socially defined as incompatible, both in terms of her perceptions of what it means to be black and female and in masking the mastering aspects of the school curriculum. For example, Rita identifies math as her weakest subject in the core curriculum. At the same time, however, she is quite knowledgeable of how computers function and is able to decipher and manipulate computer hardware and a bevy of software quite well.

It was the possession of these computer skills that inspired her math teacher, Ms. Costen, to pay her $40.00 to develop a program for one of her friends who was failing a computer course. Partly as a sick joke, and partly because Rita is convinced that Ms. Costen was acting inappropriately when she asked her to perform what she perceived to be an intellectually dishonest task, she deliberately sabotaged the computer program. She also did not return the $40.00. Her reasoning was that Ms. Costen is a teacher and teachers are supposed to be paragons of virtue, modeling behaviors and attitudes sanctioned by the larger society. In general, although Rita expects teachers to rigorously adhere to the norms, values, and rules of the educational establishment, she feels that it is acceptable and even admirable for her and her peers to blatantly flaunt these same ideals by resisting and outsmarting the teachers at their own game. As she perceives it, her efforts and those of her peers are to be labeled subtle, ongoing resistance to the celebration of the dominant "Other" endemic at Capital High. As students, she and her peers are free to subvert the existing dominating system. On the other hand, as a teacher, Ms. Costen—despite her blackness—does not have the same options available to her. As Rita perceives it, Ms. Costen's role as teacher takes precedence over her connectedness to the black community. Also, according to Rita's perception, her teacher's desire to create a "safe cultural space" is a contested concept.

Hence, like those "loud Black girls" discussed in Evans's essay (1988), Rita refuses to "conform to standards of 'good behavior' . . . without actually entering the realm of 'bad behavior' by breaking any school rules." Rather, she lives on the edge, self-consciously stretching legitimate school rules to help her retrieve a safe cultural space.

As I have already indicated, all 33 key informants were 11th graders. During the spring of the academic year, those students who had performed well on the PSAT were strongly encouraged by their teachers and other school officials to apply for admission to the colleges that they were interested in or that had indicated an interest in them. Since Rita had the highest score on the verbal component of the exam, she had received letters from numerous colleges inviting her to apply. Responding to these letters was no problem. Her dilemma emerged when her English teacher, Ms. Apropos, asked all the students in her English class to share their essays so that she could help them make a good impression on the various admissions committees. She advised them to write strong, upbeat essays that reflected a positive outlook on life. The other students followed her advice unequivocally. They created positive, upbeat essays.

Rita was the only exception. She decided not to write an essay in this genre. She chose, instead, to write about the value of death and dying. Ms. Apropos was speechless. She could not believe that a teenager whose life is on the uptake would even be capable of thinking such morbid, melancholy thoughts. Ms. Apropos had secretly harbored doubts about Rita's sanity for a long time.[9] These fears grew by leaps and bounds when she assigned the class *The Crucible* and Rita refused to read it, claiming that it violated her religious beliefs. When she later asserted that she was going to write about death and dying in her college admission essay, all doubts regarding her mental stability were removed. Ms. Apropos was absolutely sure that "girlfriend" was crazy. This initial impression was reinforced when she tried and failed to get Rita to change her mind.

Rita's willingness to display these dialectic characteristics at school appear to make her an unfeeling and thoughtless person. She is not. Admittedly, she has learned the ideology of the society well. And, at some level, she believes that American society is truly democratic and that the individual makes it or fails based solely on ability. In the school context she is committed to the meritocratic ideals promulgated there and does not want to have any information around her that might suggest that what she has learned, and perhaps is learning, in school is misleading or even untrue. She is definitely a child of the post–civil rights era, in that, like many nonblack persons, she wants to believe that African-Americans have achieved socioeconomic parity with the dominating group: white Americans.

> Some—a lot of times I have people ask me "Do you think you are a white person?" But I don't know, maybe it's me. Maybe I don't carry myself like a black person. I don't know. But I'm black. And I can't go painting myself white or some other color, it's something that I have to live with. So it's the way it is, and it's not like having herpes or something—it's not bad. It's—I think it's just the same as being white, as far as I'm concerned—everybody's equal. [Interview with author, 4 May 1983]

At the same time, Rita's consistent practice of breaching the cultural assumptions so valued in the school context often leads her teachers to erase their perception of her as a bright, intelligent person. Also, the "slam dunking" part of her persona that propels her to the margins of good behavior, without actually forcing her into the realm of "bad behavior," makes "shrinking lilies" out of most adults who interact with her or, alternatively, motivates them to avoid contact with her, if that is an option. Needless to say, Rita submitted her essay on the value of death and dying. She was also accepted at her chosen institution.

As noted above, the most salient characteristic of the academically successful females at Capital High is a deliberate silence, a controlled response to their evolving, ambiguous status as academically successful students. Consequently, silence as a strategy for academic success at Capital is largely unconscious. Developing and using this strategy at the high school level enables high-achieving African-American females to deflect the latent and not too latent hostility and anger that might be directed at them were they to be both highly visible and academically successful. Invisibility is a highly valued prerequisite for academic success. This is particularly true for these young teenage girls whose evolving sexuality and reproductive capabilities actually undermine their chances of success in the public domain. Learning silence, then, is an obligatory component of Capital's high-achieving females' academic success. They are taught to be silent by their parents, teachers and other school officials, and male peers—both explicitly and implicitly—in order to allay the perception that they are just women, that is, that they will behave in ways typically associated with women and femaleness. Gilligan (1982) has described women as being preoccupied with "relationships." Further, she asserts that this "way of knowing" (relating) is not loudly applauded in the academy. With only a couple of exceptions, the high-achieving females at Capital High are invisible in the highly visible arenas at the school (e.g., classrooms, assemblies in the auditorium, and so forth). Females are encouraged to be "seen rather than heard," to be passive rather than assertive.

Most of the academically successful girls acknowledge that this newfound silence represents a change from the way they once behaved in school. Each of them can recall when her female voice was not a deterrent to academic success. Some of them attribute their growing, evolving silence to parental controls that are increasingly directed toward limiting both their extrafamilial activities and the fulfillment of their female sexuality. Others are unable to articulate why they have come to be silent. They only know that, for some reason, they are learning or have learned not to speak, not to be visible.

It is important to acknowledge that a common, relentless theme in the child-rearing practices of virtually all of the mothers of the high achieving females is an absolute insistence that their daughters be "taken seriously." In addition, these mothers demand control of their daughters' lives and even the options they seriously consider for their futures. The mothers' conditional support for their daughters' voiced academic aspirations confuses them, making their enormous efforts in school appear less valuable. For example, Rita's mother was ambivalent about her daughter's desire to go to college. Indeed, it is probably more accurate to say that she was fearful of Rita's school achievement and what it meant in terms of options for her.

I'm going to tell you like this, Ms. Fordham: I am really happy that Rita's doing what she's doing [in school], and I'm not going to be hypocritical about it. But if Rita didn't go to college, it would not make me a bit of difference. . . . No, it would not. Because, like I said, you know, education is good. And I think that Rita—she says that she wants to go into neurology or something to that effect. And from studying the Bible and looking at the events the way that they are today, the Bible shows that this system is not going to be here that long. Whenever it is that it's going to come to an end—well, not the system, it is not going to end, but the end of wickedness, we don't know. See, the Bible says there's going to be people that's going to survive the destruction of the system of things. But from looking at the way that things are going on the world scene, and looking at your colleges and things today, I mean, they have—the individual, when they're going to college and things, they go there for the right purpose—because there's a lot of kids that go there and—for the right purpose, but a lot of things happen in college. See? And . . . I mean kids that get hung up with drugs, and these sororities and things now, the things that they—r [I] was reading some article in the paper about these sororities [fraternities] initiating these young guys, and they died from drinking all this—over-drinking and stuff like that, the things they make them do. And, basically, I just—you know, I'm just not that enthused. [Interview with author, 5 May 1983]

The sources of this mother's ambivalence were quite varied. There was the religious principle mandating that unmarried women remain in their parents' home until marriage. There was also the verbalized fear of crime and drugs and other unacceptable social problems.

At this point in their young lives, the high-achieving females read their parents' insistence on silence and invisibility in the school context and strict extrafamilial limitations—no dating, no after-school activities, and so forth—as well as uncertainty and/or ambivalence about their academic goals, as a lack of support for what they dream of doing: going to college immediately after high school and living their lives in ways that parallel their white American peers.

The silence attendant to female academic excellence is exacerbated in the school context where, again, the high-achieving females are given episodic, rather than continuous, unlimited support for their academic achievement and their voiced future dreams. This is the reality, despite the fact that the teaching staff and other adult members of the school are primarily African-American and female.

CONCLUSIONS AND IMPLICATIONS

I began this analysis by asserting that gender "passing" is a sine qua non for women in the academy if they desire to achieve a modicum of academic success (Pagano 1990:13). I followed this observation by emphasizing that the first commandment for women in the academy is "Thou must be taken seriously." Further, I argued, for women to be seen as being serious about the work of the academy, they must receive (as opposed to claim) a form of schooling the contents of which prepares them to survive and prosper in a world organized by and for men, not women (Rich 1979:238). 1 went on to point out that, for African-American women in the academy, being taken seriously also means dissociating oneself from the image of "those loud Black girls," whose "refusal to conform to standards of 'good behavior,' without actually entering the realm of 'bad behavior' by breaking . . . school rules," severely undermines their limited possibilities for academic success. Moreover, I documented, with data from the Capital High research site, how "those loud Black girls" are doomed, how their reluctance to engage in "active participation in [their] own exclusion" (Pagano 1990:12) from the academy strips them of a sense of power. J. Scott (1985) has described responses of this nature on the part of those who have been historically excluded as the "weapons of the weak." Audre Lorde asserts that responses in this genre on the part of African-Americans and other peoples of color indicate that they know they cannot use "the master's tools . . . to dismantle the master's house" (1990:287).

The distinctive history of people of African ancestry and their current social conditions, I argue, are implicated in the structure and configuration of their gender roles. African-Americans' continuous, on-going lack of dominance and power in the Euro-American patriarchic structure has had, and continues to have, severe implications for African-American women (and men). Still further, I indicate that, in the case of the academically successful females at Capital High, silence and invisibility are the strategies they feel compelled to use to gain entry into the dominating patriarchy.

The findings presented here certify that at Capital High black females are the more successful students. Ironically, they are also the least visible. They are the people "passing" for someone they are not: the white American female and, ultimately, the white American male. Silence is implicated in their greater school success because it conceals their female voice and the resulting gender expectations.

For African-American women, socialization to silence and invisibility is not without pain. It is painful because, as I documented in the above analysis, black females pay an inordinate price for academic success: it leads to an "ignorance of connections," an uncertain "fork in the road." Although I have talked about black girls' school achievement in one particular context (Capital High), it is important to acknowledge that parental ambivalence about the value of academic learning is not limited to the parents of the students at Capital High. The disheartening, unintended consequences associated with the uncertainty of academic excellence are frequently recorded in the research literature. For example, in her book *Talking Black* (1989), bell hooks describes how her parents' ambivalence about her preoccupation with school-related learning robbed her of her confidence, threatening her pursuit of academic excellence. At the same time, she acknowledges that it was her parents' ambivalence about the value of school and schooling that forever welded her to the African-American community.

> My parents' ambivalence about my love for reading led to intense conflict. They (especially my mother) would work to ensure that I had access to books, but would threaten to burn the books or throw them away if I did not conform to her other expectations. Or they would insist that reading too much would drive me insane. Their ambivalence nurtured in me a like certainty about the value and significance of intellectual endeavor which took years for me to unlearn. While this aspect of our [race]

reality was one that wounded and diminished, their vigilant insistence that being smart did not make me a "better" or "superior" person (which often got on my nerves because I think I wanted to have that sense that it did indeed set me apart, make me better) made a profound impression. From them I learned to value and respect various skills and talents folk might have, not just to value people who read books and talk about ideas. They and my grandparents might say about somebody, "Now he don't read nor write a lick, but he can tell a story," or as my grandmother would say, [he can] "call out the hell in words." [hooks 1989:79]

Socialization to silence and invisibility is also distressing because it isolates and alienates black girls from their more communal and popular underachieving female cohorts. Still further; learning to be silent can be so distressful that it sometimes results in a decision to abandon the effort to succeed in school because, in part at least, it evokes "ignorance of connections." This occurs because many of the high-achieving girls do not understand why their parents—particularly their mothers—and many of their female teachers do not appear to be supportive of their academic achievements.

However, lack of adult female support is a misperception. As hooks's analysis suggests, the seeming lack of support solders the African-American female to the black community forever. It is also a misperception to see parental support as universally constructed. As this analysis suggests, parental support is not a universal construction. Indeed, this analysis documents that the existence of gender diversity and what it means to nurture are pervasive. Hence, for the African-American female to achieve school success, all of the usual symbols of nurturing are turned upside down and/or inside out. These data clearly suggest that what can be labeled nurturing is cultural-specific. The academically successful females at Capital High are using a Euro-American definition of power and nurture in concluding that the significant adults in their lives are not supportive of their academic goals. They come to this enormous conclusion because they view their underachieving friends' parents' drastically different interactional patterns as the more appropriate model. The academically successful girls also study the Euro-American model via television and other media sources, including their textbooks. These sources strongly influence what they come to value and define as nurturing and supportive.

Regrettably, the high-achieving females at Capital High do not discern that their mothers and their seemingly unsupportive teachers are often unconsciously preparing them for a life away from the black community, a life in which they are the "doubly-refracted 'Other.'" As the "doubly-refracted 'Other,'" the African-American female's survival "out there" is largely dependent upon her ability to live a life saturated with conflict, confusion, estrangement, isolation, and a plethora of unmarked beginnings and endings, jump starts, and failures. It is also likely to be a life in which a family of pro-creation and connections takes a back seat to "makin' it."

Therefore, the central questions haunting this entire analysis and smoldering in the lives of all African-American females are the following: Is gender diversity something to celebrate? Should we seek its fragmentation? If so, how? Should our goal be to transform "those loud Black girls"? Should success for African-American women be so expensive? Finally, should the African-American female seek to reconstruct her life to become successful, pawning her identity as a "loud Black girl" for an identity in which she is the "doubly-refracted [African-American] Other"?

ACKNOWLEDGMENTS

The research on which this analysis is based was funded initially by grants from the National Institutes of Education (NIE-G-82-0037), the Spencer Foundation, and a dissertation fellowship from the American University in Washington, D.C. More recently, a National Science Foundation training grant has afforded me time away from the classroom and the opportunity to consider and develop the analysis presented here. An earlier version of this chapter was presented at the Anthropology Bag Lunch Symposium in the Department of Anthropology, Rutgers University, New Brunswick, New Jersey, 20 February 1991. I wish to thank my colleagues in the Department of Anthropology at Rutgers for helpful comments and suggestions. I would especially like to thank the faculty, staff, and students at Capital High, their parents, and all other adults in Capital Community for allowing me to intrude in their lives. In addition, I wish to express a special note of thanks to Linda Chalfant and Professors Gerald Davis and Brett Williams for helpful comments and suggestions on successive drafts of this manuscript. I am solely responsible for this final version.

NOTES

Loudness, as I am using it here, is not meant to convey the usual meanings, including noisiness, shrillness, flashiness, ostentatiousness, and so on. Rather, it is meant as one of the ways by which African-American women seek to deny the society's efforts to assign them to a stigmatized status that Christian (1990) has described as "nothingness." Therefore, "those loud Black girls" is here used as a metaphor proclaiming African-American women's existence, their collective denial of, and resistance to, their socially proclaimed powerlessness, or "nothingness."

1. P. Williams's (1988) maternal grandfather is racially identified as white.

2. I am sensitive to the possibility that I will be accused of making essentialist claims (Fuss 1989) regarding race as well as white and black womanhood. It is currently fashionable to argue that much of what is written related to these issues can be dismissed because the writer is likely to be accused of making claims regarding some "true essence—that which is most irreducible, unchanging, and therefore constitutive of a given person or thing" (Fuss 1989:2). This is not my intention. What I hope to show in this analysis is how African-American women are compelled to construct an ad hoc identity in a context where, for much of their history in this country, they have not only been barred from its "hallowed halls,"

but have also, at the same time, been defined and represented by those who repeatedly defined them as "nothingness." I am not positing that there is some "pure or original [race or] femininity, a [race or] female essence, outside the boundaries of the social and thereby untainted . . . by a [racist or] patriarchal order" (Fuss 1989:2). Indeed, I realize that there is more than one of each of these, including white womanhood within the dominant community. Nevertheless, I am positing that when the issue is black and white womanhood, white womanhood in all its various forms is usually elevated.

3. It is important to point out that both black and white women "are objectified, albeit in different ways, . . . [in order to] dehumanize and control both groups" (Collins, 1991:106).

4. This is the fictitious name I gave the flagship academic program at Capital High.

5. As many researchers have suggested (see, for example, Cox 1948; Dollard 1957; Frazier 1969; Landry 1987; Ogbu 1978), race undercuts class in the African-American community. Hence, class phenomena do not have the same meaning in the black and white communities. For example, Ogbu (1978) argues quite convincingly that there is a lack of congruency among the various classes in the African-American and white communities. As he describes it, middle class in the white community is not analogous to middle class in the black community. The same is true of the designations: working class, lower class, upper-middle class, and so forth. Furthermore, as I am beginning to analyze the quantitative data collected during the Capital High study, I am overwhelmed by the unanimity of the response to the following question: "Would you say that socially your family belongs to the upper class? middle class? the lower class?" "Would you describe your neighborhood as mainly upper class? middle middle class? lower class?" Almost invariably, the students chose "middle class" as the appropriate response.

6. Payne (1988) supports Evans's (1988) analysis of gender diversity by noting that the school context is impregnated with male norms and values. These features are so pervasive, she argues, that for some women existence is tantamount to "suffocat[ing] in comfort" (see Emerson, cited in Hendrickson 1991). Payne highlights resistance as a primary female response to this construction of the academic context, even postulating that for some young women in the academy pregnancy is an attempt to validate and affirm their female "Self" in this male-dominated institution.

7. Hard work is probably best described as work outside the home (i.e., paid labor). It is also accurate to describe hard work as laborious and intense. As enslaved females, African-American women received no, or virtually no, remuneration for their labor outside the home. Once manumission occurred, they were further victimized in that they were not adequately compensated for their labor.

8. Following Collins (1991), I am defining a "safe cultural space" as a site where African-American women are able to celebrate and applaud their varied sense of "Self." Elsewhere (Fordham 1993b) I have indicated that the academy neither encourages nor promotes gender diversity. Further, I argue, because the African-American female "Self" is seen primarily as an illegitimate form, these women's quest for a safe cultural space is often pursued surreptitiously. Hence, finding a "safe cultural space" is a challenge for all African-American females at Capital, regardless of level of achievement or academic effort.

9. I am able to make this assertion because I was at the school for more than two years. During that time, I had numerous conversations with Ms. Apropos about Rita (she was only one of several students in the sample that Ms. Apropos taught) and many other students. I was able to observe many of these students in Ms. Apropos's English classes. She was one of several teachers who was willing to share with me information that went beyond the

rudimentary, about the students, their parents, and the administrators. Ms. Apropos was frequently baffled and buoyed by Rita's contradictory behaviors, her concurrent acceptance and rejection of school norms and values.

REFERENCES

Cary, Lorene. 1991. *Black Ice*. New York: Knopf.

Christian, Barbara. 1990. What Celie Knows That You Should Know. In *Anatomy of Racism*. David T. Goldberg, ed. Minneapolis: University of Minnesota Press.

Collins, Patricia Hill. 1991. *Black Feminist Thought: Knowledge, Consciousness, and the Politics of Empowerment*. New York: Routledge.

Cox, Oliver C. 1948. *Caste, Class and Race: A Study in Social Dynamics*. New York: Modern Reader.

Davis, Angela. 1971. Reflections on the Black Woman's Role in the Community of Slaves. *The Black Scholar*.

Dollard, John. 1957 [1937]. *Caste and Class in a Southern Town*. Garden City, NY: Doubleday.

Evans, Grace. 1980. Those Loud Black Girls. In *Learning to Lose: Sexism and Education*. London: The Women's Press.

Fordham, Signithia. 1987. *Black Students' School Success as Related to Fictive Kinship: An Ethnographic Study in the District of Columbia Public School System*, 2 vols. Washington, D.C.: American University Press.

———. 1988. Racelessness as a Factor in Black Students' School Success: Pragmatic Strategy or Pyrrhic Victory? *Harvard Educational Review* 58(1): 54–84.

———. 1990. *Phantoms in the Opera: Black Girls' Academic Achievement at Capital High*. Symposium: New American Women. Paper presented at the Annual Meeting of the American Anthropological Association, November, New Orleans.

———. 1991a. Peer-Proofing Academic Competition Among Black Adolescents: "Acting White" Black American Style. In *Empowerment Through Multicultural Education*. Christine Sleeter, ed. Pp. 69–90. New York: SUNY.

———. 1991b. Racelessness in Private Schools: Should We Deconstruct the Racial and Cultural Identity of African-American Adolescents? *Teachers College Record* 92: 470–484.

———. 1993. *Acting White and Book-Black Blacks: An Ethnography of Academic Success at Capital High* (working title) (in press).

Fordham, Signithia, and John U. Ogbu. 1986. Black Students' School Success: Coping with the "Burden of 'Acting White.'" *The Urban Review* 18(3):176–206.

Frazier, E. Franklin. 1969 [1957]. *The Black Bourgeoisie*. New York: The Free Press.

Fuss, Diane. 1989. *Essentially Speaking: Feminism, Nature and Difference*. New York: Routledge.

Gilligan, Carol. 1982. *In a Different Voice: Psychological Theory and Women's Development*. Cambridge, Mass.: Harvard University Press.

Hendrickson, Paul. 1991. *Reporter Out of No Man's Land: Gloria Emerson, Taking Sides from Vietnam to Gaza*. *Washington Post*, June 5: B1, B8, B9.

Holland, Dorothy C., and Margaret A. Eisenhart. 1990. *Educated in Romance: Women, Achievement, and College Culture*. Chicago: University of Chicago Press.

hooks, bell. 1989. *Talking Black*. Boston, Mass.: South End Pres.

Landry, Bart. 1987. *The New Black Middle Class*. Berkeley: University of California Press.

Lorde, Audre. 1990. Age, Race, Class, and Sex: Women Redefining Difference. In *Out There: Marginalization and Contemporary Cultures*. Russell Ferguson, Martha Gever, Trinh T. Minh-Ha, and Cornel West, eds. Pp. 281–288. Cambridge, Mass.: MIT Press.

Ogbu, John U. 1978. *Minority Education and Caste: The American System in Cross-Cultural Perspective*. New York: Academic Press.

Pagano, Jo Anne. 1990. *Exiles and Communities: Teaching in the Patriarchal Wilderness*. Albany: State University of New York Press.

Palmer, Phyllis. 1989. *Domesticity and Dirt: Housewives and Domestic Servants in the United States, 1920–1945*. Philadelphia, Penn.: Temple University Press.

Payne, Irene. 1988. A Working-Class Girl in a Grammar School. In *Learning to Lose: Sexism and Education*. London: The Women's Press.

Rich, Adrienne. 1979. *On Lies, Secrets, and Silence: Selected Prose 1966–1978*. New York: W. W. Norton.

Scott, James. 1985. *Weapons of the Weak: Everyday Forms of Peasant Resistance*. New Haven, Conn.: Yale University Press.

———. 1990. *Domination and the Arts of Resistance*. New Haven, Conn.: Yale University Press.

Scott, Kesho Y. 1991. *The Habit of Surviving: Black Women's Strategies for Life*. New Brunswick, N.J.: Rutgers University Press.

Walker, Alice. 1982. *The Color Purple*. New York: Harcourt Brace Jovanich.

White, Dorothy Gray. 1985. *Ar'n't I a Woman? Female Slaves in the Plantation South*. New York: Norton.

Williams, Patricia J. 1988 On Being the Object of Property. In *Black Women in America. Social Science Perspectives*. Micheline R. Malson, Elizabeth Mudimbe-Boyi, Jean F. O'Barr, and Mary Wyer, eds. Chicago: University of Chicago Press.

22

Tying Things Together (and Stretching Them Out) with Popular Culture

Jan Nespor

Late in the school year, on a fifth-grade fieldtrip to the Booker T. Washington National Monument, we were eating lunch at some picnic tables near the parking lot after having walked the grounds. The park ranger had warned us as we set out from the visitors' center to stay on the path and to watch out for snakes and ticks in the grass. We found no snakes, but those of us at the tables nearest the woods found ticks all around. While most of us ate quickly and went elsewhere, Earl used a plastic sandwich bag as a kind of glove to pick up some ticks and take them over to the table where his "girlfriend" was eating. There, he revealed himself, ostensibly to his friend Duane and another boy who had tagged along, but also to the audience of girls, to be the "tickinator." He proceeded to play with the ticks and try to crush them.

Six days later, back at the school, Earl and some of his friends were talking and the topic of "pets" came up:

Earl: I have one dog, four cats, two hermit crabs, and one fish now.
Helen: I got you beat.
Neal: [to Helen] What have you got, a shark?[1]
Jan: [to Earl] Hermit crabs?
Earl: Probably got roaches! [laughter] That counts up.
Duane: [to Earl] You got termites!
Earl: No, we killed them. Orkin man.
Helen: At least you didn't walk into my house, saw a bunch of cockroaches sitting on the couch going "we are family!"
Earl: I don't think so. Orkin man just came around and drilled about 400 holes in my house.
Neal: 400 holes.

344

Earl: [Earl mimes the Orkin man killing bugs] Terminator. "Goodbye bug, I am the roachinator."
Duane: [in a Schwartzenegger accent] "I am the terminator."
Earl: This is my roachmobile.
Duane: Remember, remember when we were at Booker T. Washington.
Earl: I remember, it was a *tick*mobile.
Duane: Oh, yeah, the tickmobile. . . .

In this kind of competitive improvisation (one of many such episodes among these kids), popular culture is not the object of contemplation but a thread used to weave identities and perform social distinctions. Such *uses* are at the center of popular cultural practices. "The question is not what does it mean," as Frith argues in his analysis of popular music, "but what can I do with it; and what I can do with it is what it means" (1996, 12–13).

What did the kids do with it? Earl boasted of how many pets he had. Helen claimed to have more. Earl countered by suggesting that Helen's pets were cockroaches. Duane used this comment as a bridge to recall Earl's termites. Helen responded to Earl's gibe (her phrase "we are family" was either a variant on the "we're a great big happy family" line from the *Barney* theme song or a reference to the phrase commonly used in newspaper and other announcements of the birth of a child), but Earl and Duane ignored her and went down a path that allowed them improvisational possibilities and excluded Helen and Neal from the discussion: They layered representations from movies and a television commercial onto Earl's termite experience, and from there were able to shift the discussion to the fieldtrip.

Nowhere in this exchange did the boys talk about the content of the films or commercials, or deal with them in their entirety. Instead, they sectioned out and combined *elements* of disparate cultural artifacts. In the language of actor network theory, the boys "translated" this imagery, assembling "the bits and pieces needed to build a coherent actor" (Law 1994, 101), in large part by aligning and coordinating their actions with events and characters mobilized in the artifacts (Latour 1987). Earl and Duane created "a link that did not exist before and that to some degree modifies two elements or agents" (Latour 1994, 32; Latour 1987; Callon 1986): They bent the meaning of the film and commercial imagery to serve their interactional ends, and at the same time the imagery refracted the boys' interests.

None of this would have been possible if there hadn't been relatively stabilized and widely distributed material and representational infrastructures available. An "infrastructure," according to Star and Ruhleder, "occurs when local practices are afforded by a larger-scale technology, which can then be used in a natural, ready-to-hand fashion" (1996, 114). In this case, Earl and Duane didn't have to create the unlikely link between termites and movie characters because it already existed in the form of a television commercial in which the "Orkin man" appears as a cyborg exterminator (owing as much to *Robocop*, I think, as *The Terminator*) and wipes out an inconvenient insect population. They didn't have to build the connection between the fieldtrip and the later discussion because schooling itself combined them through an infrastructural effect: spatially collecting the kids, providing them opportunities for relatively unregulated interactions, and keeping them in each others' company.

Such infrastructures made it possible for Earl and Duane to use the "terminator" imagery to fold the events at the Booker T. Washington Monument into what was happening at the moment in the room. The result was a kind of spatio-temporal bubble connecting the boys to (and through) the movies, the commercial, the fieldtrip, and their shared interactional pasts.

POPULAR CULTURE AS PRODUCT AND PRACTICE

The contingent and improvisational *work* of popular culture illustrated in this example is obscured when popular culture is treated as a text defined by some static constellation of meanings or meaning potentials (e.g., Giroux and McLaren 1994; Steinberg and Kincheloe 1997; cf. Radway 1996; Press 1996). Consider the claim that: "For a generation of home-aloners Culkin's Kevin [from the film *Home Alone*] is a character with whom they can identify, for he negotiates the cultural obstacles they also have had to confront. He offers them a sense of hope, a feeling that there is something heroic in their daily struggle" (Kincheloe 1997, 50).

By attributing a uniform response to a broadly defined class of participants, approaches that produce such claims deflect attention from questions of how kids differentially positioned by language, gender, race, or age use media not only to make meanings, but to articulate interactions among themselves and across those dimensions of difference. By foregrounding the whole product, such accounts fail to address the mixing and chaining of representations across media and genres. By asserting that particular ideas will be transmitted, they presume a theory of learning in which "meanings" pass intact and unmediated from public representations to internalized psychological representations. Above all, they decontextualize practice. They ignore the networks of home, family, peer, school, media, and markets that coordinate kids' engagements with popular culture. Popular culture in such accounts takes place outside place, nowhere in particular, a stance that makes it impossible to look at media culture as produced by and producing space.

To make sense of the tickinator, we have to abandon such positions. We have to study popular culture from multiple "standpoints," including most importantly the kids',[2] foreground everyday practices instead of whole products, and focus on popular culture's uses as media of performative affiliation and on the spatializing and power effects that produce and follow from such uses. As Radway suggests, research must: "take the fluid *process* of articulation as its topic, that is, the process whereby the historical human subject is constructed through the linkage, clash, and confluence of many different discourses, practices, and activities. Such an ethnography would have to begin with the everyday, not with texts" (1996, 245).

HOW I CAME TO WITNESS THE TICKINATOR

My efforts to study these "everyday" uses of popular culture were part of a two-year ethnography of a multiethnic[3] urban elementary school in Roanoke, Virginia (Nespor 1997). In addition to participant observation in fourth- and fifth-grade classrooms, I interviewed teachers, parents, and the principal; and observed and recorded parents' meetings, teacher meetings, and inservices. I talked informally with kids, interviewed them in groups and individually, ate lunch with them, and helped some of them do research of their own (Nespor 1997; 1998).

How I worked with the kids shaped my understanding of popular culture. Most researchers who look at uses rely on interviews to focus participants' attention on the whole product or performance (e.g., Buckingham 1996). Interviews, however, can privilege referential meanings, suppress playful, ironic, emotive, and artistic speech (Briggs 1986), and obscure precisely the uses of popular culture as media of participation, association, sociability, and dominance that should be of primary interest.[4] Although some of my data come from one-on-one interviews with kids in which I asked them to draw and talk about maps of their neighborhoods, most do not. The tickinator exchange occurred in one of a series of group discussions with fifth graders. Other exchanges were recorded when I passed around a microphone and recorder on bus rides to and from fieldtrips or during impromptu interactions on school grounds. On occasion I raised films, television, comics, and sports as topics, but most of my data come from instances where the kids raised such topics themselves or used popular culture in interactions.

Although these fieldwork strategies avoided some of the pitfalls of standard interviewing practices, my very presence undoubtedly suppressed certain kinds of uses, and the spacetime arrangements of the school settings shaped the range of uses I observed. The quick shifting appropriations of imagery illustrated in the tickinator story, for example, may be peculiar to the situations in which I observed them: momentary spaces of play or freedom seized in the interstices of the school's control practices.

FORMS OF POPULAR CULTURE USE[5]

Representative or not, the tickinator example suggests some critical differences between "popular culture" and the standard curriculum. For one thing, popular culture comes in forms that allow it to be transported and disseminated through circuits of exchange much more extensive than the networks defined by school systems. Unlike school-based representations that circulate through interactional systems dominated by adults, kids can use popular culture to define spaces in which adults are absent or peripheral. Popular forms can also be more easily combined in creative ways (as in the tickinator example), while school-based artifacts have more restricted uses and are thus generally limited to classroom-, school-, or disciplinary scales. Popular culture, by contrast, allows variable linkages through which users can "jump scale" (Smith 1993) across great physical and social distances to connect themselves to core concerns of childhood traditionally absent from the curriculum: gender, sexuality, race, violence, and power (Nespor 1997).

The labels I use to characterize some of these uses—*exchange, invocation, inhabitation*, and *appropriation*—are only loose markers for pointing to the varied performances in which people use popular culture to link, align, or coordinate distributed activities. The networks produced through these practices function as "funds of knowledge," a term Moll, Tapia, and Whitmore (1993) use to refer to: "The diverse social networks that interconnect households with their social environments and facilitate the sharing or exchange of resources, including knowledge, skills, and labor essential for the household's functioning, if not their well-being."

If we extend the "fund" notion to include consumption and leisure practices as well as productive activities, drop the assumption that social networks are defined solely by associations among *adults*, and allow funds of knowledge to include inanimate or nonhuman elements (e.g., media characters and popular culture commodities), we can use the concept to talk about the role popular culture plays in extending the practices of youth across space and time in relatively durable configurations. The unit of analysis is no longer the "household," but the emergent associations of kids producing selves and identities through the infrastructures of popular culture. Adults remain participants in these networks—indeed, one of the networks' main effects may be to coordinate certain kinds of adult-child relations—but they are not the dominant participants. To paraphrase Moll, Tapia, and Whitmore (1993), kid-centered funds of knowledge connect kids (who may never meet face-to-face) in ways that facilitate the exchange of information and shape lines of association and identity.

In "exchange," the giving, taking, buying, and selling of popular culture *objects* define relations among people and position them within social networks.

"Invocation" designates the practice of referring to popular culture products, performers, or performances to generate meanings or interpretive frames for the immediate situation. The references align kids' identities with (and help instantiate) the cultural meanings of the invoked forms. Such references constitute public claims on identities, presume shared knowledge among participants in the event, and thus play a role in collective definitions of identity.

"Inhabitation" involves longer-term uses in which kids insert themselves into popular culture narratives as participants or invest some understanding of themselves in the actions of the characters (e.g., rewriting stories taken from television shows, movies, or comics, with themselves as protagonists). Alignment or coordination of identities is accomplished by borrowing plots from particular products.

Finally, by "appropriation" I refer to events where people mix elements drawn from multiple sources of popular imagery into their unfolding interactions. As I've already discussed one example of this use, the "tickinator" discussion, I treat the category only briefly in what follows.

EXCHANGING POP CULTURE

Popular culture comes in forms that can be physically possessed, controlled, and displayed. Kids are entwined in systems of objects through market transactions or networks of giving or exchange that define the objects' value and meaning. As Appadurai puts it, to understand "things" we have to examine the conditions under which they "circulate in different *regimes of value* in space and time" (1986, 4, original emphasis). The meanings of things "are inscribed in their forms, their uses, their trajectories" (5).

In some situations, exchange takes the form of a market transaction: the monetary value of the object is paramount and no lasting relations are forged through the act of exchange. Trading cards, for example, were often discussed in terms of dollar values, and I saw kids in one fifth-grade class carefully examining a pricing catalog for baseball cards. In fact, some kids seemed to know little about their cards *except* that they were worth something:

> *Jan:* You said you had some collectors items, what are those?
> *Doug:* Two of them.
> *Jan:* Who are they?
> *Doug:* I don't know.
> *Jan:* How do you know they're collectors items then?
> *Doug:* My grandad bought them for me. And one of them's the Sox, and another one is, I think, New York Yankees.

Even this kind of blind acquisition, however, may entail more than a simple accumulation of property meaningful only for its market value. Doug, like many of the kids, obtained artifacts like cards as gifts from parents or relatives. Such gifts situated him in an extended family network organized by this circulation of formally exchangable objects that, in practice, were not likely to be exchanged outside his tightly circumscribed family or friendship groups. Thus, commodity-based networks of pop culture could operate as "gift economies" in which the circulating objects were (1) "heritable within a closed descent group," and (2) tied to "cosmological forces—the dead, the ancestors, the gods, or sacred places" or, in the case of the kids I knew, to sports heros, Power Rangers, or Elvis (Frow 1997, 129). Acts of giving and receiving could in this way define cross-generational lines of association and identification, especially when the gifts belonged to thematically linked constellations of objects and events (e.g., gloves, bats, baseballs, televised baseball games, baseball cards, and so on) that included both adult- and child-oriented objects or objects both could possess. Alf, a fifth grader, claimed to have started collecting baseball cards when he was five years old and boasted of having upwards of two thousand cards. This gave him a link to his father that he could literally possess and manipulate: His father was a collector too, and like Alf played baseball ("My dad's got a Mickey Mantle rookie worth $3,000,"[6] "My dad taught me how to play it [sports], I mean, watch it."). Alf and his dad could thus align themselves through a popular culture constellation that coordinated both family relations and a particular performance of masculinity.

By contrast, nine-year-old Carol's collection of Elvis paraphernalia, supplied by parents and aunts, reflected an assymetrical enrollment in an adult-focused network of interests and cultural investments (including a certain construction of femininity):

> Well, my hobby is, I got Elvis all over the place. . . . I got his book—and he signed it! I guess, I guess he signed it. I know *all* about Elvis actually. I got tapes, I got pictures of him. My aunt, she went to that Salem fair, and she got two real pictures of Elvis, someone took of him. And I've got them in my room. And I got two other pictures of him, but they are like, like people painted them. And I got one of them oven mits that has him on it. And I have a towel, and one of them little wash rags of him, his face. I got a shirt of him on it. I got a baton, whatever them little things are called, of him. I got cards of him. I got something else but I forgot.

The adult-centric fund of knowledge outlined here paralleled the spatial organization of Carol's life: She wasn't allowed out of her yard without adult accompaniment, had few friends, and spent most of her time playing in her fenced backyard. In contrast to the boys, among whom possession of baseball cards could serve as a pretext for interaction, knowing about Elvis probably helped Carol little with her peers. Moreover, although Carol's icons were probably "inalienable objects," the boys could wheel and deal with at least some of their cards:

> *Jan:* What do you do with the cards?
> *Duane:* Trade 'em, sell 'em.
> *Alf:* Trade 'em, sell 'em, buy 'em, book 'em up, keep 'em.

These kinds of transactions, however, were only one moment in the trajectories of the cards. Duane, at least, admitted to also having an emotional investment in them—"whenever I get mad at home," he explained, "I look at baseball cards."

Popular culture artifacts, then, can move in and out of commodity status (Appadurai 1986). Kids' decisions about what to buy, what to sell, what to read, and what to store away in plastic trace different networks of association (Law 1994, 15). Different actors (e.g., comic book authors, distributors, and the kids) work on these networks, operating with materials of different durability and transportability, moving across different spatio-temporal scales. Exchange is not about transactions in which cleanly bounded and well-defined objects possessed by individuated actors pass back and forth through a market medium. Rather, popular culture artifacts that are given, taken, or exchanged, function as "boundary objects"—"both plastic enough to adapt to local needs and the constraints of the several parties employing them, yet robust enough to maintain a common identity across sites" (Star and Griesemer 1989, 393)—that can be used to coordinate, for example, global marketing and production strategies and kids' local performances of self. The actual work of making affiliations and linkages persuasive, however, depends on how people can invoke, inhabit, appropriate, or otherwise perform with them.

INVOCATIONS OF POP CULTURE

Kids *invoke* elements of particular popular culture products (rather than mixes of products) to "problematize" (Callon 1986) or define their identities by linking themselves to distant people, images, or events. The meanings of these linkages are specific to their performative contexts. Invocations thus presume active, participating audiences and spaces for performance that allow kids proximity to chosen others but separate them from adult supervision. For example, during the bus ride on one field trip, several kids grabbed my microphone and recorder and, without anyone explicitly defining the frame, began to produce a kind of music/radio show:

> *Lauren:* I'm gonna sing, "My boyfriend's back." [sings the entire song] [pause] Ch, ch, ch, ch—I'm changing the channels: [sings] "It's my party, I'll cry if I want to"—Oh I hate that. I'll change the channel. Ch, ch, ch, ch, ch, ch, ch, ch, ch—Oh! Here goes something "You are my sunshine, my only sunshine . . ." [Sings more of that song, then sings "It's my party" again, and follows this with a weather forecast, then:] Now back to Effie, with her song, "Jesus's Will."
> *Effie:* [sings the gospel song, then sings "I'm not a superwoman, I'm not that kind of girl," and hands the microphone to Felix.]
> *Felix:* Okay, this is Snoop Doggy Dog. This is when I was really little. [sings a little, then speaks in character] . . . Hey girl in the pink dress [Effie], what do you want to be when you grow up?
> *Effie:* A nurse!
> *Felix:* That's a good thing. Hey girl in the blue dress, what do you want to be when you grow up?
> *Desiree:* A tap dancer! I don't know.
> *Felix:* Hey you, in the braids, what's your name? My name is Snoop. What do you want to be when you grow up? I want to be a mother hustler. You better axe some! I want to be a mother-fuckin' hustler!! You better ask somebody!! Nurr Nurr Nurr Uh! Ah! . . . —[Responding to Desiree's gesture of shock]—That was in the song![7]

The alignments produced in this particular performance defined roles and identities in counterpoint to the kids' usual classroom personae. Effie, the gospel singer, was an African American girl who constantly managed to get herself in the teacher's doghouse by talking out of turn or showing an excess of enthusiasm. Lauren was a perky, middle-class European American, all sweetness and obedience (until the teacher's back was turned), and Felix, performing the kind of hyper-masculinized (and wildly misogynistic) rap of Snoop Doggy Dog, complete with profanity, was one of two boys in the fourth grade who openly expressed his attraction to girls, which got him labelled as "queer" by other fourth-grade boys.

INHABITING POP CULTURE

In addition to invoking cultural forms, kids also actively *inhabited* roles or characters drawn from the media. That is, they enrolled themselves in ready-made narratives:

> *Jan:* What are you writing?
> *Earl:* It's just a, about, kind of like a movie I watched. I'm kinda writin' a book about
> it. It's different.
> *Duane:* You should put, "Duane, Earl."
> *Jan:* [Reading the title] "Operation Kill Earl"—is that something you saw on TV?
> *Earl:* No, it was really the movie *Toy Soldiers*, but I changed it.
> . . .
> *Duane:* —When me and Earl were thinking about that story about the school, getting
> invaded? We just let our imagination run wild didn't we?
> *Lucy:* Oh, where's that story?
> *Earl:* I used to make myself dream of the school being invaded and then I'd save it.
> [laughs]
> *Duane:* I know.
> *Jan:* Did you show anybody that story?
> *Duane:* We couldn't print it. The printer was broken.

Media artifacts like *Toy Soldiers* (a film in which adolescent boys at a military
school become heroes by defeating invading terrorists) can be seen as parts of larger
"mediascapes," a kind of infrastructure that provides "elements (such as characters,
plots, and textual forms) out of which scripts can be formed of imagined lives"
(Appadurai 1996, 35). The uses of such artifacts, however, are shaped by the articulations of multiple processes. In this case, they depended not only on the movie
(and the general similarities between the movie content—boys in a school they
don't like, and with Earl and Duane's own everyday lives), but on the availability
of a computer (allowing joint composition), Earl's house (as a playspace), and the
school infrastructure itself (which brought the boys together). The "scripts" produced in such articulations are similarly contingent. The boys didn't passively assume the roles and personae presented in the film (Earl insists his story is "different"), but instead strategically adopted parts of the ready-made, disposable identities
it provided to generate a "border zone" (Heath and McLaughlin 1994, 475) where
they could look both at their everyday lives and the alternative lives formulated in
the film (cf. Dyson 1997).

APPROPRIATIONS OF POP CULTURE

Certeau reminds us that the meaning of a representation comes from "its manipulation by users who are not its makers" (1984, xiii). But as the tickinator story I

discussed at the outset suggests, use and "manipulation" don't require that interactions be focused on one particular representation or series of representations. The tickinator exchange was *not* a commentary on the movies and commercial imagery it deployed. Rather, the boys appropriated *elements* of popular culture products and moved those elements across genre and product boundaries to create tools for fashioning situated meanings for particular purposes.

The difference between the tickinator and "Operation Kill Earl" is that instead of borrowing a narrative from a popular culture product, the kids in the tickinator pulled popular culture elements from several sources to situationally enact widely distributed meanings (about masculinity, among other things). The boys' brief collaboration with the imagery developed fluidly and entailed no lasting alignment with the commercials or the movies they appropriated. I never heard them mentioned again.

POPULAR CULTURE AS INFRASTRUCTURE

People are always doing things "locally," but some people do things through media and artifacts that, because of their material properties of durability and transportability, can be distributed across great physical distances and function as boundary objects linking widely dispersed practices. People who can't congeal their efforts in such forms (or in forms of their own creation, at any rate) nonetheless find that it's easier to get on with everday life if they put such objects to "use." Sometimes there's little choice. Either way, in using popular culture we intertwine ourselves in the expansive projects of others: Sometimes we can mobilize alternative infrastructures to instantiate locally determined meanings in opposition to those projects, and sometimes we find ourselves just blending into them.

The scales at which popular culture operates, and the meanings and uses possible with it, can thus never be read from a text. When kids use popular culture in the ways I've described, they "translate" or create performative links with practices, interests, and agendas originating far outside their immediate range of face-to-face experience: in a sense, they localize distant practices by bringing them to bear in their everyday affairs (that much should be obvious from the examples I've quoted), but at the same time they redistribute themselves as actors across the much larger scales defined by the networks. Social interactions articulated through popular culture have this character of being simultaneously global and local. Indeed, concepts such as "global," "local," and many of our notions about "scale," are viable only if we treat them as contingent effects of practice rather than inherent qualities of things. As Massey suggests:

> A so-called "local" youth culture [is] . . . not a closed system of social relations but a particular articulation of contacts and influences drawn from a variety of places scattered, according to power-relations, fashion, and habit, across many different parts of

the globe. Social spaces are best thought of in terms of complicated nets of interrelations in which each particular culture is differently located . . . the social relations which constitute space are not organised into scales so much as into *constellations of temporary coherence* (and among such constellations we can identify local cultures) set within a social space which is the product of relations and interconnections from the very local to the intercontinental. (1998, 124–125)

If the imagination, as Appadurai puts it, has become "a social practice" (1996, 31) situated within transnational flows of technology, finance, imagery, and ideology, such flows are not placeless. They move along channels or networks that both reflect and constitute relations of power and dominance (Castells 1996, 413). They presuppose spaces—shopping malls with stores like Toys 'R' Us—tying together global networks of consumption organized around the act of looking. More importantly, and this is the point I'll close on, they cannot be separated from the structures and organizations of children's embodied spaces. We cannot make sense of popular culture without situating its uses in the lived geographies of its users.

Consider this rapturous description given by a fourth-grader, Tina, as she drew a map for me of the Detroit neighborhood she'd lived in before moving to Roanoke:

All my cousins would go over, my grandma would be there, she would entertain me with church songs. My mom would be there. And then my dad would pick me up. I usually spent every single day outside over by my dad, because they had a boys' and girls' club over there—which I *can't* hardly find over here. I had a card to get in, I could go swimming. I could go eating there. In the summer they had lunch for free there. Then, uh, some days like for Halloween they gave you candy. And there was an art room, you could make anything you want. You just had to ask. And then there was— everywhere you go there was a corner store. And I'd walk there. I miss that! . . . I loved it over there because . . . my sister's dad had a *taqueria*, that's a little small place that just sells tacos. . . . My aunt had a beauty shop. My uncle had a restaurant, a bakery, and a bar. On all the same street, I could get food, free tacos, free hamburgers, free drinks. I could get half-price on haircuts. I could get free bread. . . . That's the way it used to go. . . . There was a big market over here called, not Market Place, but they had like a shopping store right here, a clothes store. Dunkin Donuts. A big store right here. A tire store right here. Toys 'R' Us right over here. A *big* plaza over there.

Tina said she rarely watched television in Detroit and followed only one series. By contrast, when I asked if there were places she liked in Roanoke, she replied only: "my room." And when I asked what she did away from school she first told me "nothing," then added that she *did* watch TV, and quickly named sixteen shows (from *Animaniacs* to *Melrose Place*) that she watched regularly.

This kind of radical shift in the use of popular culture suggests that it's worth asking how kids' engagements with genres and products vary with their access to other kinds of infrastructures (cf. Dimaggio 1990, 118). Lash and Urry argue that "for true mass culture, more traditional social, and especially class and family, structures must partly subside, and atomizing, niche marketing and lifestyle creating communication networks must take their place" (1994, 134). By this reasoning, popular culture's role as an infrastructure of young people's everyday world may be increasingly important as modern cities immobilize kids in apartments and neighborhoods devoid of the kind of city life Tina described (not just the density of her relatives, but more importantly the businesses, clubs, and public spaces she had easy access to) (Katz 1998; Valentine 1996; Ward 1978). When kids lack access to safe outdoor spaces and their houses and apartments are surrounded by busy streets, they become dependent on their parents and on institutions like the school and television for access to the world at large. It's as kids become "prisoners of their homes" (Katz 1998, 135) that popular culture assumes paramount importance.

It follows that the uses and effects of popular culture change as kids gain or lose access to other infrastructures: as they move from elementary to secondary school to the workforce, learn to drive, get poorer or richer, as new parks are built (or existing parks are privatized), as stores close, malls open, mass transit constricts or expands, and neighborhoods get safer or more dangerous. Popular culture and the media do not replace everyday life, they are technologies for extending, organizing, aligning, and subordinating it in more durable and extensive organizations of power and meaning.

NOTES

1. This was apparently a reference to a long argument about the nature of sharks (prompted by a television special on the Discovery Channel) that Neal and Helen had two weeks earlier.

2. Smith's (1987) arguments about the suppression of women's standpoints work equally well for kids.

3. Kids from the working-class European American neighborhood around the school accounted for about 55 percent of its enrollment, while 40 percent of the students were African American and the remaining 5 percent were Asian American or Mexican American.

4. The reliance on interviews also misses our specifically embodied engagements with popular culture. Words can point at such meanings, but not fully explicate them. (James, Jenks, and Prout 1998, 188; see also Nespor 1997, chapter 4).

5. This section reworks material in Nespor (1997, 168–192).

6. I have no idea if this was true. Hyperbolic claims about such things weren't uncommon. One boy asserted that his grandad had a "Babe Ruth rookie card," a suggestion that even his generally obliging friends laughed at.

7. The song here is "Gz and Hustlas" from Snoop Doggy Dog's *Doggystyle* album (Death Row/Interscope Records 1993). The lyrics can be found at <http://www.ohhla.com/anonymous/snoopdog/>. Felix had access to this song, which wouldn't have played on any local radio station, through neighborhood-based friendship networks: "I listen at my friend's house. . . . My mom won't buy me the CDs."

REFERENCES AND READINGS

Appadurai, A. 1986. Commodities and the Politics of Value. In *The Social Life of Things*, edited by A. Appadurai. Cambridge: Cambridge University Press.

———. 1996. *Modernity at Large*. Minneapolis: University of Minnesota Press.

Briggs, C. 1986. *Learning How to Ask*. Cambridge: Cambridge University Press.

Buckingham, D. 1996. *Moving Images*. Manchester: Manchester University Press.

Callon, M. 1986. Some Elements of a Sociology of Translation: Domestication of the Scallops and the Fishermen. In *Power, Action and Belief*, edited by J. Law. Sociological Review Monograph No. 32. London: Routledge and Kegan Paul.

Castells, M. 1996. *The Rise of Network Society*. Oxford: Blackwell.

Certeau, M. de. 1984. *The Practice of Everyday Life*. Berkeley: University of California Press.

Dimaggio, P. 1990. Cultural Aspects of Economic Action and Organization. In *Beyond the Marketplace*, edited by R. Friedland and A. Robertson. New York: Aline de Gruyter.

Dyson, A. 1997. *Writing Superheroes*. New York: Teachers College Press.

Frith, S. 1996. *Performing Rites*. Cambridge, Mass.: Harvard University Press.

Frow, J. 1997. *Time and Commodity Culture*. Oxford: Oxford University Press.

Giroux, H., and McLaren, P., eds. 1994. *Between Borders*. New York: Routledge.

Heath, S. B., and McLaughlin, M. 1994. Learning for Anything Everyday. *Journal of Curriculum Studies* 26:471–489.

James, A., Jenks, C., and Prout, A. 1998. *Theorizing Childhood*. New York: Teachers College Press.

Katz, C. 1993. Growing Girls/Closing Circles. In *Full Circles*, edited by C. Katz and J. Monk. London and New York: Routledge.

———. 1998. Disintegrating Developments: Global Economic Restructuring and the Eroding of Ecologies of Youth. In *Cool Places*, edited by T. Skelton and G. Valentine. New York: Routledge.

Kincheloe, J. 1997. "Home Alone" and "Bad to the Bone": The Advent of a Postmodern Childhood. In *Kinderculture*, edited by S. Steinberg and J. Kinchloe. Boulder, Colo.: Westview.

Lash, S., and Urry, J. 1994. *Economies of Signs and Space*. Newbury Park, Calif.: Sage.

Latour, B. 1987. *Science in Action*. Cambridge, Mass.: Harvard University Press.

———. 1994. On Technical Mediation—Philosophy, Sociology, Genealogy. *Common Knowledge* 3 (2): 29–64.

Law, J. 1994. *Organizing Modernity*. Oxford: Blackwell.

Lefebvre, H. 1991. *The Production of Space*. Cambridge, Mass.: Blackwell.

Massey, D. 1998. The Spatial Construction of Youth Cultures. In *Cool Places*, edited by T. Skelton and G. Valentine. London and New York: Routledge.

Moll, L., Tapia, J., and Whitmore, K. 1993. Living Knowledge: The Social Distribution of Cultural Resources for Thinking. In *Distributed Cognitions*, edited by G. Salomon. Cambridge: Cambridge University Press.

Nespor, J. 1997. *Tangled up in School*. Mahwah, N.J.: Lawrence Erlbaum.

———. 1998. The Meanings of Research: Kids as Subjects and Kids as Inquirers. *Qualitative Inquiry* 4:369–388.

Press, A. 1996. Toward a Qualitative Methodology of Audience Study: Using Ethnography to Study the Popular Culture Audience. In *The Audience and Its Landscape*, edited by J. Hay, L. Grossberg, and E. Wartella. Boulder, Colo.: Westview.

Radway, J. 1996. The Hegemony of "Specificity" and the Impasse in Audience Research: Cultural Studies and the Problem of Ethnography. In *The Audience and Its Landscape*, edited by J. Hay, L. Grossberg, and E. Wartella. Boulder, Colo.: Westview.

Smith, D. 1987. *The Everyday World as Problematic*. Boston: Northeastern University Press.

Smith, N. 1993. Homeless/Global: Scaling Places. In *Mapping the Futures*, edited by J. Bird, B. Curtis, T. Putnam, G. Rovertson, and L. Tucker. London and New York: Routledge.

Star, S., and Griesemer, J. 1989. Institutional Ecology, "Translations," and Coherence: Amateurs and Professionals in Berkeley's Museum of Vertebrate Zoology, 1907–1939. *Social Studies of Science* 19:387–420.

Star, S. L., and Ruhleder, K. 1996. Steps Toward an Ecology of Infrastructure: Design and Access for Large Information Spaces. *Information Systems Research* 7 (1): 111–134.

Steinberg, S., and Kincheloe, J., eds. 1997. *Kinderculture*. Boulder, Colo.: Westview.

Valentine, G. 1996. Children Should Be Seen and Not Heard: The Production and Transgression of Adults' Public Space. *Urban Geography* 17 (3): 205–220.

Ward, C. 1978. *The Child in the City*. New York: Pantheon.

23

Fieldwork in the Postcommunity

Sherry B. Ortner

This article considers the place of fieldwork in the contemporary United States. "Place" here is meant to invoke the question of both the *relationship* between local ethnographic studies and mass society/culture, and the question of actual geographic location, the *sites* of ethnography. I use ethnography here in a strict sense—that is to say, in the sense of long-term participant observation with a particular group. Whatever else an ethnographic study may include—archival research, questionnaires, interviews, textual investigations (from comic books to sacred books), and more—long-term participant observation is its irreducible minimum. Or so we have thought, taught, and (for the most part) practiced until recently.

My interest in the problem of doing ethnography in America derives from attempting to start a research project on the cultural construction of "class" in this society. Where should one go to participate in/observe this process? Where does class "happen," as it were—where is it enacted, reproduced, and possibly changed? The answer of course is everywhere, yet that does not solve the practical problem of constructing an ethnographic research design. One obvious solution would be to study some sort of workplace, yet workplace ethnographies seem to beg one of the central questions in the study of American culture—the split between home and work, public and private.

Another solution would be to do an ethnography of a relatively small community, in which something like the totality of relations of the society—of class and family and work and play and all the rest—are enacted within a single place. The early great ethnographies in America, *Middletown* (Lynd and Lynd 1929) and the Yankee City series (starting with Warner and Lunt 1941), were organized around issues of class relations. The idea of doing a restudy in one or the other of these communities was very tempting, in part because of the length of the ethnographic and now ethnohistorical record. In many ways I still think these would be interesting and valuable studies. At the same time, the fate of "communities" is precisely one of the issues at stake in contemporary American society. Most Americans live in a condition in which the totality of their relations is precisely not played out within a single geographic location and a single universe of known others, both at a given point in time and across time.

As I continued casting about for a fieldwork form for the project, I received an invitation to the 30th reunion of my high school graduating class, the Class of '58 of Weequahic (pronounced Week-wake or Wee-quay-ic) High School in Newark, New Jersey. The proverbial light bulb lit up in my head. I had a strong retrospective sense of unrecognized class dynamics in the high school, deriving from my own experience as a middle-class girl ("girl" being the correct native term for my age and gender at the time) dating a working-class boy, and hanging out with both crowds, middle-class and working-class, throughout most of my high school career. I went to the reunion—the first I ever attended—with the idea of the project in the back of my head.

The reunion turned out to be more interesting (and less terrifying) than I had expected, and I tentatively decided to make the Class of '58 the ethnographic population for the project. Purely at a practical level, there seemed to be a number of good reasons to start in this place, with these people. For one thing, Newark, our collective point of origin, is a reasonably representative American city (if anything can be said to be representative). For another, my research access to this group would presumably be good. And of course I would have a peculiar kind of ethnohistorical depth, having been a long-term participant in the community in the early part of my life.

In addition, I was both excited and challenged by the time/space trajectory of the group—that is, the fact that the group had been part of an actual on-the-ground community in the past, and was spread all over the United States in the present. This formation seemed more true to the shape of the contemporary world, as represented in earlier discussions of modernity and more recent discussions of postmodernity. The breakdown of communities and increasing geographical mobility were virtual hallmarks of modernity (Friedland and Boden 1994; Pred and Watts 1992); the increasing fragmentation of lives and identities, and the even more radical delocalization of economy and culture under globalization, are central to the idea of the postmodern (Hannerz 1992; Harvey 1989). Recent arguments for changes in fieldwork practices, from highly localized studies (in villages, on islands, and in "communities") to delocalized, "multisited" work, have been built on the point that anthropology was excessively localistic in the past; given the changes in the real world just mentioned, such localism in the present is even more problematic (Appadurai 1991; Clifford 1992; Gupta and Ferguson n.d. a and b; Marcus 1995).

This project took the form of tracking down the members of the Class of '58 (and later, their grown children) wherever they happened to be in the United States, and interviewing them. This article will document the ethnographic tracking of this community, including the variety of forms it takes, its underlying "structure of feeling," and its possible roots. The larger point of the article is to contribute to a rethinking of the ways in which anthropology and other forms of cultural and interpretive studies can remain (or become) ethnographically grounded, even while acknowledging the radical delocalization of life in the late 20th century, and even while recognizing the theoretical complexity of the idea of "the local."

For purposes of this project, the Class of '58 of Weequahic High School consisted of the 304 people whose pictures appeared in the yearbook. Of the 304 people pictured in the yearbook, 14 were known to be deceased at the beginning of the project. Of the 290 living, we had addresses for approximately 250 of them, or 86 percent. The 40 or so lost people seem to represent an irreducible number, plus or minus one or two. It is almost certain that some of them are deceased as well, but none have been confirmed. Occasionally we did find one of the unknowns, but then someone else would disappear—the letter would come back, the phone would be disconnected, and they would be gone.

The fieldwork consisted of traveling all over the country and interviewing people wherever they happened to be, at any site of their choosing. Although the interviews were the dominant form of "data" for the project—and I will say more about that in a moment—I want first to note the variety of forms of participant-observation, however truncated, that constituted at least a part of this project, not even counting the fact that I have lived in this culture all my life, and grew up, from age 10 to 16, in the original community of the study in the first place. I will simply list here the sites of interviewing and other fieldwork encounters, in no particular order: homes, with and without other family members around; restaurants (from the very expensive to the very cheap, including many of those great East Coast institutions, "diners"); bars; shopping malls; brokerage houses; law offices; medical offices; business offices; a schoolteachers' lounge; a principal's office; a country club; a nightclub where a classmate was performing; an examining room in a hospital; a law library; a social worker's office; the Newark Police Department; reunions (2) in catering establishments; synagogues; hotel lobbies; and a Hollywood television studio. . . . I interviewed altogether in about 80 cities and towns of the United States, and drove over several thousand miles of American freeways. The project was conducted intermittently over a four-year period (roughly, 1990–1994), with the most intensive work done in the period 1992–94, when I did a trip for about a week every month. While none of this adds up to classic participant observation—living in a village for a year or two and participating in all its rhythms—nonetheless one can learn a good deal about "America" with this sort of exposure, particularly if one keeps one's eyes, ears, and brain tuned to the ethnography frequency.[1]

Yet again, the core of the project was the interviews themselves, about two hours of talk, plus or minus, into a tape recorder. As I first developed this project, I experienced one of the "methodological anxieties" so well noted by George Marcus (1995) for people engaged in multisited fieldwork: I was very uncomfortable with the fact that the project was so heavily dependent on interviewing, and involved so little participant observation. Not only does one lose much of the deep context participant observation provides—the multiple forms of background that allow one to understand and interpret what is represented to the anthropologist over a tape recorder—one loses, or so I feared, a sense of people's social embeddedness, causing them to appear in one's study as those classic American subjects/objects, decontextualized individuals. Yet as it turned out, one of the things people love to talk about, especially to someone who shares or has shared a social universe with them, is *other people,* past and present, far and near. It was precisely this fact that allowed me to discover, rather than presume, the (transformed) persistence of various kinds of "community" among the dispersed Class of '58, and also to see with particular vividness the practices of inclusion and exclusion that make and remake them. Had I been sitting in one local "community," the local ties would have seemed a lot more "natural" to me than they came to appear through this project, while the more dispersed and delocalized forms of relationship might have been ignored altogether.

FOUR TYPES OF POSTCOMMUNITY

Neocommunity: Circum-Newark

At one level it is important to note that *every person in the Class of '58* has moved away from the address she or he lived at during high school; in this sense there is 100 percent geographic mobility. This of course conforms to images of modernity and postmodernity—the end of "community," the "fragmentation" of relationships.

But other statistics tell a different story . . . [for starters] over half of the class still resides in New Jersey, and if one adds New York to New Jersey, one gets 60 percent of the class.

Further, one could take a compass, put the point down at Weequahic High School in the southwest corner of Newark, and draw a circle with a radius of about 16 miles. This would then include places like Montclair to the north; the popular Millburn, Short Hills, and Livingston areas to the northwest; Edison (which has a large number of classmates, and was used to define the 16-mile limit) to the southwest; and a good part of Manhattan to the east; and parts of Brooklyn and Queens, east of Manhattan. This area contains perhaps two-thirds of the New Jersey–New York classmates; in other words, about 40 percent of the Class of '58 still lives within a 16-mile radius of Weequahic High School.

Many of the Class of '58 members in this region form a "community," in a sense close to one of its original meanings: while people do not all live in a single localized neighborhood, there are nonetheless multiple connections among many of them. There is a density of contact, and a relatively up-to-date maintenance of awareness of each other's lives, that are characteristic of people in a relationship of community with one another.

More generally and routinely, people in this area have each other to dinner and parties, or go out to dinner together. They run into each other at restaurants, in malls, and in movies. Classmates work for and employ other classmates. Classmates are in business together. Several classmates in this area are particularly close friends, and showed up together for their interviews with me. All of this is the classic stuff of community: multiple kinds of face-to-face contact, mutual awareness of relatively intimate aspects of each other's lives, mutual caring, and of course its flip side, mutual judgment.

Invented Community: Florida

The other location where some of the members of the Class of '58 maintain a community somewhat like circum-Newark is in Florida. Only about 20 classmates live down there, and they are much more spread out across the state, but many of them maintain some form of contact with one another, both intentionally, and by way of turning up from time to time in the same restaurants, movies, shopping malls, and so forth. In addition, the elderly parents and some siblings of these people have moved to Florida, reinforcing a sense of naturalness about the community. In some cases, there are several Weequahic people in a single development of homes or condos.

In addition, there is an intentional maintenance of a sort of greater post-Weequahic community. Thus although there are only 20 or so members of the Class of '58 in Florida, there are actually a large number of Weequahic graduates from other years scattered across the state, and aware of one another's existence. One person told me that there is a reunion in South Florida every February for all people from Weequahic High School, "from Year One."

Translocal Community: Networks of Contact

Even among widely dispersed members of the Class of '58, many people have maintained or reactivated contacts with one another. Many people who have moved away still have relatives in New Jersey and return to see them; for example:

> [Richard Morris's wife] was a real Newark booster, missed being there. She and Richard go out [to New Jersey] at least once a year because they still have lots of family there.

Often the New Jersey relatives have contact with former classmates, keeping the moved-away people up-to-date on the activities of those who have stayed, and vice versa. But networks of relations among the Class of '58 also persist in other parts of the country, and across long distances.

> Hot news on the lost-classmate front—I got a letter from Zack Weissman in California. Actually, it's a copy of a letter to another classmate in California, Leonard Riesberg, with whom he keeps in touch. . . .

There is an almost kinship-like sense to many of these contacts, a sense that one can ask old Weequahic classmates for favors, even if one rarely sees them. In addition, Weequahic people may wind up in the same fraternities or sororities:

> Harriet Nunberg called yesterday [from Florida]. . . . The message said that her husband went to a fraternity reunion [in Virginia] recently and met Paul Gold, who was in the same fraternity.

Children of Weequahic graduates may also wind up in the same fraternities and sororities: At one point, three daughters of Weequahic parents (two from the Class of '58, one from the Class of '56) belonged to the same sorority at the University of Michigan. One came from Indiana, one from South Jersey, and one from a different part of New Jersey. None of them knew each other before they came.

One of the factors at work in clustering people accidentally like this is obviously common Jewishness. But class is also at work; both temple congregations and, even more so, fraternities and sororities, are stratified by both material and cultural capital.

Beyond the kind of factors that regroup people accidentally, people may intentionally seek out other Weequahic graduates in distant places expecting, and usually finding, a warm welcome and common interests.

> [One of the doctors in the class] said that when he travels to new places, he looks for three things: a temple, other doctors in his specialty, and Weequahic graduates. He went to Texas and looked up David Grossman from our class. David had married someone from another Weequahic class—he's a doctor and she's a lawyer.

Community of the Mind: Memory

Underlying all the forms of relationship, including hostility, persisting among the members of the Class of '58, are sets of quite powerful memories about the high school experience and about individual people and relationships in high school. I have been impressed and fascinated by the intensity of many people's retrospective feelings including, I confess, my own.

Negative memories are often the basis of continuing distance and disconnection from the class-as-community; for example:

> We looked at the yearbook and there were Roberta Rosenberg and Joan Edelman, and Harriet said they were really "ditzy broads" and she couldn't stand them—and that was one reason she didn't go to the reunion.

Negative memories are often memories of social exclusion:

> I called Daniel Parker this morning and left a message and he was kind enough to call me back, but said he emphatically does not want to participate in the project, he feels no connection to Weequahic, he went to a reunion and it was "all the same bullshit,"

all the cliques making him feel uncomfortable, he doesn't want to have anything to do with it.

Indeed, many of the "lost" classmates were presumed to have hated Weequahic and as it was usually put, did not want to be found.

But many more people had intensely positive memories of this period of their lives. These memories often focus on individuals, on good friendships that had waned with time and distance:

> She was thrilled when I said I had found Tina Nandy, she said they were friends in grammar school. She asked how Tina had felt about Weequahic and I said that she said she had a very good experience. She said, "That's Tina! No matter how hard life was for her, everything was wonderful. . . . She was just so wonderful!"

Positive memories also encompass the Weequahic experience as a whole—the school, the neighborhood, the era:

> Peter Tannenbaum went on and on about how great it was to grow up in the Weequahic section of Newark at that time: "We grew up in the best time in the best place." He said he's been telling his 14-year-old son about our life in Newark and his son is fascinated with it.

Passing on these positive memories to one's children is not at all unusual. Here is another example, from an interview with one of the children of the Class of '58:

> He was another Weequahic High School freak, like [another child of the Class '58]. His mother talked about it all the time. He grew up looking through the *Legend* [yearbook] as a picture book on the table in the living room. Wow.

The positive memories are the obvious basis of a continuing community even in diaspora. These are the sorts of feeling reunions build upon and, at a less organized level, they are the basis for individuals maintaining or reestablishing contact with one another. Yet even people with negative memories often find themselves drawn back into contact with the community, wondering what happened to particular individuals, and experiencing an unexpected nostalgia later in life for the larger experience.

In sum, the fieldwork has revealed the Class of '58 to exist as a kind of postcommunity in at least four distinguishable forms: (1) the neocommunity of circum-Newark; (2) the invented post-all-Weequahic community of Florida; (3) the translocal community of periodically maintained, reactivated, and reworked networks; and (4) the mind-community of memory, drawn upon by the other three forms, as well as by the rituals that briefly pull them all together—reunions.

Again, not every individual is a part of the postcommunity in any of these forms. Where it exists, however, it is quite powerful. It is questionable whether even kinship has the power to provoke such intense memories, or such large numbers of social ties, in contemporary late- or postmodern American society. How can we think about this process?

HIGH SCHOOL AS HABITUS

The answer must be sought largely in the nature of the American high school experience. It is in high schools that many Americans have their first, most fully realized experience of "community," in the specific sense of a dense, intense, and often highly charged set of face-to-face social relations that persist over a long period of time. At the same time, it is in high schools, unlike almost anyplace else one can think of, that most of the structures of difference in American society—class, gender, race, ethnicity, generational conflict—are enacted and reenacted on a daily basis.

It may be suggested in turn that the forms of social difference, asymmetry, and solidarity practiced in the high school community persist as habitus, in Bourdieu's (1990) sense. This is another dimension of what I called the community of the mind. That is, it is likely that the forms of community established in high school, when people were forced to work out their categories and practices with respect to the opposite sex, other "races," other classes, establish much of the basis of the ways in which these categories are thought, and these practices are lived, in adult life.

But these points in themselves would not be enough to account for the intensity of memory/feelings and the durability of multiple forms of community in the group, without—I suggest—one additional factor: the degree to which the high school experience is eroticized. Although I have not emphasized this in the choice of quotations in this article, questions of sexual attractiveness, availability, dangers (the big issue in the fifties was pregnancy), and last but not least, (some level of) actual sexual activity, were high on the list of what the high school experience was (and is) all about for most informants. And like everything else in high school, sexual life is structured by a variety of forms of cultural capital and social "distinction," including, of course, the class/race/ethnic categories discussed throughout this article. But the point must also be turned around: class, race, and ethnic differences are themselves heavily eroticized (or counter-eroticized) in this context, both in the general sense that everything in high school is to some degree saturated with sex, and in the more specific sense that every form of sameness or difference is evaluated with respect to its charge of sexuality.[2]

The endurance of this erotic saturation may be seen at reunions, where the level of flirting among several hundred middle-aged people is noteworthy. Among other things, people confess to one another about high school crushes and desires, thereby playfully invoking sex in the present in the guise of describing the past. The 30th reunion of the Class of '58 excluded spouses, something that annoyed some people but was enjoyed by many others. As far as I know, little if any in the way of actual

sex took place among classmates as a result of reunion flirtation. My point is rather
to suggest, following an old lead of Victor Turner's (1969), that one of the functions of reunions as rituals is precisely to renew the erotic charge as well as the social form of the "community," in all its solidarities and divisions.

OPENING UP SPACE AND TIME IN FIELDWORK

Let me briefly summarize what I take to be some of the key points of this article. I
have argued for the continuing importance of the study of "communities." At a time
when scholars in many fields are latching onto "culture" as a kind of ungrounded
set of images, it is essential to keep those images attached to real lives, practices,
and systems of relations; I have used the idea of "communities" in this article as a
shorthand for this point. But I have argued as well that we can no longer take communities to be localized, on-the-ground entities, or at least that their local, on-the-
ground form is only one moment and site of their existence. I have thus tried to
chart the rather significant variety of forms in which a once-local community continues to exist.

ACKNOWLEDGMENTS

I would like to thank Judy Rothbard for all her help in finding members of the Class
of '58; Lynn Fisher for all her help with mailings and database organization at the
University of Michigan; and Rafael Reyes for his new field data text-management
program, "InterView," and his patient support as I got into it. For financial support
of this project, I thank the John D. and Catherine T. MacArthur Foundation, the
Wenner-Gren Foundation for Anthropological Research, and several offices at the
University of Michigan. For wonderful hospitality, without which I could not have
afforded to do the project, I thank all the people with whom I stayed during the
fieldwork: George and Judy Rothbard in New Jersey and Florida, Julian and Ethel
Decter in New Jersey, Neal and Karin Goldman in Brooklyn, John and Betsy
Canaday in Boston, Margie and Howard Drubner in Connecticut, and all my cousins: Sheila and Frank Tretter on Long Island, Norman and JoAnn Panitch in Los
Angeles, and Anita Auerbach in the Washington, D.C., area. Parts of this chapter
were drafted when I first began to think about this project, and were presented at
the 1989 AAA meetings with the title, "Categories of Un-Modernity: Community."

NOTES

1. I say this with much hedging, as I have deep reservations about Jean Baudrillard's road
book, *America* (1988). But it would be interesting to think about both my own project and
Baudrillard's book in relation to the broader genre of "on-the-road" takes on America.

2. The hidden sexuality of high school social categories, and the hidden class factors in sexual attraction, are precisely what Philip Roth exploited in *Goodbye, Columbus* (1959) and *Portnoy's Complaint* (1969), both of which are set in the Weequahic neighborhood (where Roth grew up) and Weequahic High School (which Roth attended and graduated from about 7 years before I did). See Ortner 1991.

REFERENCES

Appadurai, Arjun. 1991. Global Ethnoscapes: Notes and Queries for a Transnational Anthropology. In *Recapturing Anthropology: Working in the Present*. Richard G. Fox, ed. Pp. 191–210. Santa Fe, NM: School of American Research Press.

Baudrillard, Jean. 1988. *America*. Christopher Turner, trans. London: Verso.

Bell, Colin, and Howard Newby, eds. 1974. *The Sociology of Community*. Portland, OR: Cass.

Bellah, Robert N., Richard Madsen, William M. Sullivan, Ann Swidler, and Steven M. Tipton. 1985. Habits of the Heart: Individualism and Commitment in American Life. Berkeley: University of California Press.

Bender, Thomas. 1978. *Community and Social Change in America*. New Brunswick, NJ: Rutgers University Press.

Bourdieu, Pierre. 1984. *Distinction: A Social Critique of the Judgment of Taste*. Richard Nice, trans. Cambridge, MA: Harvard University Press.

———. 1990. *The Logic of Practice*. Richard Nice, trans. Stanford, CA: Stanford University Press.

Brettell, Caroline B., ed. 1993. *When They Read What We Write: The Politics of Ethnography*. Westport, CT: Bergin and Garvey.

Clifford, James. 1992. Traveling Cultures. In *Cultural Studies*. Lawrence Grossberg, Cary Nelson, and Paula Treichler, eds. Pp. 97–111. New York and London: Routledge.

Davis, Mike. 1990. *City of Quartz: Excavating the Future in Los Angeles*. London and New York: Verso.

Doyle, Roger. 1993. At Last Count: House to House. *Atlantic Monthly*, March: 95.

Eckert, Penelope. 1989. *Jocks and Burnouts: Social Categories and Identity in the High School*. New York: Teachers College Press.

Friedland, Roger, and Boden, Deirdre. 1994. *NowHere: Space, Time, and Modernity*. Berkeley: University of California Press.

Geertz, Clifford. 1983. *Local Knowledge*. New York: Basic Books.

Gupta, Akhil, and James Ferguson. n.d.a. *Anthropological Locations: Boundaries and Grounds of a Field Science*. Berkeley and Los Angeles: University of California Press, forthcoming.

———. n.d.b. *Culture, Power, Place: Explorations in Critical Anthropology*. Durham, NC: Duke University Press, forthcoming.

Halle, David. 1984. *America's Working Man: Work, Home, and Politics among Blue-Collar Property Owners*. Chicago: University of Chicago Press.

Hannerz, Ulf. 1992. *Cultural Complexity: Studies in the Social Organization of Meaning*. New York: Columbia University Press.

Harvey, David. 1989. *The Condition of Post-Modernity*. Oxford and New York: Blackwell.

Howell, Nancy, ed. 1990. *Surviving Fieldwork: A Report of the Advisory Panel on Health and Safety in Fieldwork*. American Anthropological Association Special Publication, 26. Washington, DC: American Anthropological Association.

Jameson, Fredric R. 1988. On Habits of the Heart. In *Community in America: The Challenge of Habits of the Heart*. Charles H. Reynolds and Ralph V. Norman, eds. Pp. 97–112. Berkeley: University of California Press.

Kroeber, Alfred L., and Clyde Kluckhohn. 1952. *Culture: A Critical Review of Concepts and Definitions*. New York: Vintage Books.

Lewis, Oscar. 1951. *Life in a Mexican Village: Tepotzlán Restudied*. Urbana: University of Illinois Press.

Lynd, Robert S., and Helen Merrell Lynd. 1929. *Middletown: A Study in Modern American Culture*. New York: Harcourt Brace Jovanovich.

McDonald, Terrence. 1996. *The Historic Turn in the Human Sciences*. Ann Arbor: University of Michigan Press.

Marcus, George E. 1995. Ethnography in/of the World System: The Emergence of Multi-Sited Ethnography. *Annual Review of Anthropology* 24:95–117.

Ortner, Sherry B. 1991. Reading America: Preliminary Notes on Class and Culture. In *Recapturing Anthropology: Working in the Present*. Richard G. Fox, ed. Pp. 163–190. Santa Fe, NM: School of American Research Press.

———. 1994. Ethnography among the Newark: The Class of '58 of Weequahic High School. In *Naturalizing Power: Kinship, Nation, Religion, Gender, Sexuality*. Sylvia Yanagisako and Carol Delaney, eds. Pp. 257–274. Stanford, CA: Stanford University Press.

———. 1996. *Class and the Jewish Question*. Paper presented at American Anthropological Association Annual Meetings, San Francisco.

———. n.d. Representing Generation X. In *Critical Anthropology Now: Unexpected Contexts, Shifting Constituencies, New Agendas*. George Marcus, ed. Santa Fe, NM: School of American Research Press, forthcoming.

Pred, Allan, and Michael Watts. 1992. *Reworking Modernity: Capitalisms and Symbolic Discontent*. New Brunswick, NJ: Rutgers University Press.

Redfield, Robert. 1941. *The Folk Culture of Yucatan*. Chicago: University of Chicago Press.

———. 1955. *The Little Community: Viewpoints for the Study of a Human Whole*. Chicago: University of Chicago Press.

Roth, Philip. 1959. *Goodbye, Columbus, and Five Short Stories*. Boston: Houghton Mifflin.

———. 1969. *Portnoy's Complaint*. New York: Random House.

Rouse, Roger. 1991. Mexican Migration and the Social Space of Postmodernism. *Diaspora* 1(1):8–23.

Turner, Victor. 1969. *The Ritual Process: Structure and Anti-Structure*. Chicago: Aldine.

Warner, W. Lloyd, and Paul S. Lunt. 1941. *The Social Life of a Modern Community*. New Haven, CT: Yale University Press.

Willis, Paul. 1977. *Learning to Labor: How Working Class Kids Get Working Class Jobs*. New York: Columbia University Press.

Yanagisako, Sylvia. 1979. Family and Household: The Analysis of Domestic Groups. *Annual Review of Anthropology* 8:161–205.

24

The Fax, the Jazz Player, and the Self-storyteller: How *Do* People Organize Culture?

Margaret Eisenhart

Since the early writings of Margaret Mead (1928), Raymond Firth (1936), and Meyer Fortes (1938), anthropologists have been interested in how culture is transmitted, reproduced, and changed. Years ago, Fred Gearing described the special province of anthropology and education as "an array of research and intervention-research interests bearing on . . . the ways schools daily recreate themselves and change, on the patterning of behaviors that occur in and around them, and on the parts played by those behaviors in the transmission of culture to oncoming generations" (1974:1224).

As the quote from Gearing suggests, most of this previous work has focused on the means by which culture is *presented* to children or newcomers, and not on how culture is *learned or affected* by them. In the body of "transmission" research, attention has been directed to the images of personhood in the cultural code and to the ways these images are "brought home" to children and engaged by them in child-rearing practices, rituals, and schooling (see, for example, Fortes 1938, Spindler 1974, Whiting and Whiting 1975). This array of research examines "how culture organizes individuals" and tends to disregard "how individuals organize culture" (Eisenhart 1988).

Transmission theories are crucial if we are ever to produce a cultural theory of education. However, transmission theories alone cannot fully account for cultural continuity and change. Anthropologists of education also must look squarely at how culture is learned and used, and this means conceptualizing a place for an active and inventive individual in the processes of cultural reenactment and change. In 1982, Harry Wolcott wrote, "Our efforts on behalf of an anthropology of learning now invite careful attention to what it is that learners learn of their culture and to how and why learners attend to some things rather than others" (1982:90). In 1994, we still have few conceptual tools for this project.

TOWARD AN UNDERSTANDING OF THE INDIVIDUAL IN CULTURE

A broadening of the anthropological view to incorporate the individual learner is important for several reasons. First, as the quote from Wolcott suggests, individuals do not acquire all the features of culture presented to them. Nor does everyone in the same social environment learn the same things or learn things in the same order (Spindler and Spindler 1991; Wolcott 1982, 1991). We need some way of understanding what aspects of culture individuals take on, how they do it, and why. Transmission models tend to overlook these individual variations. They assume a kind of "fax model" of learning (Strauss 1992:9) in which cultural "facts" are simply copied into internal structures, a model in which culture is learned as a fax is received.

We also have ample evidence that individuals do not passively accept the cultural categories that are presented to them. In Paul Willis's study of working-class boys in a British secondary school (1977), a small group of boys, the "lads," rejected the school's categorization of them and produced a counterculture to it. In my study with Dorothy Holland of college women, we found several women who rejected major pieces of the culture of romance that pervaded the social system of their peers on campus (Holland and Eisenhart 1990). These women formed personal and social identities based in part on a renunciation of the cultural model that was prominent on campus. (For other examples of individuals fashioning identities from parts of the cultural models that surround them, see diLeonardo 1984, Fordham and Ogbu 1986, Kondo 1990, Plath 1980, and the articles in D'Andrade and Strauss 1992.) One of the signal contributions of this body of work is the suggestion that building or claiming an identity for self in a given context is what motivates an individual to become more expert; that developing a sense of oneself as an actor in a context is what compels a person to desire and pursue increasing mastery of the skills, knowledge, and emotions associated with a particular social practice (Holland 1992; Lave and Wenger 1991). An important corollary is that cultural models (e.g., of romance, marriage, success) supply individuals with understandings of possible selves—of what is "right" or "natural"—to guide the construction of their identities both within and across the contexts of their lives (Quinn 1992). But in spite of the pattern, these researchers have found dramatic differences in identity and expertise among persons participating in the same social practice informed by the same cultural model (see also Strauss 1992). Apparently identities can be claimed, modified, rejected, or ignored; they can be developed to a high level of expertise or left unrealized and undeveloped, even within one specific context and with regard to one set of cultural resources. Thus an updated version of Wolcott's question remains: What leads an individual to pursue some identities and abandon or ignore others? It seems that we must find some way of understanding how individuals actively construct their personal goals, beliefs about themselves, and images of self *out of* the cultural models and socialization processes to which they are exposed.   .

Anthropologists also cannot simply accept theories that locate learning in individuals' heads. Most psychological theories of learning focus on the internal accumulation and structuring of cognitive information and on strategies for accessing it (see Lave 1993 for a recent critique of this tradition). In these theories, individuals know, act, and learn in accord with the organization of their brains. Accommodations, expertise, and innovations depend on the complexity of cognitive structures and pathways. This view of the individual learner might be called the "jazz player" model. Roger Sanjek captured this image when he suggested the jazz player as a metaphor for doing ethnography:

> Jazz innovator Miles Davis is known to have told band members: "You need to know your horn, know the chords, know all the tunes. Then you forget about all that, and just play." . . . Like jazz, ethnography [learning] requires the person who improvises the performance, who not only knows how to do it but does it. [Sanjek 1990:411]

Although the image of the jazz player captures individuals as active and inventive, it does not give adequate attention to the social or cultural context of learning. It does not recognize how individuals act or learn *in response to* cultural models and in the context of ongoing social interactional processes (D'Andrade and Strauss 1992; Eisenhart 1990; Erickson 1982).

Finally, anthropologists can no longer ignore the possibility that individual constructions (in response to culture and context) can affect and change culture. Holland and Skinner (1995) have recently drawn attention to the way women's songs, produced by individuals for the Tij festival in Nepal, serve as vehicles of individual identity, collective protest, and change in a patriarchal society. These songs are structured and presented in conventional ways, yet they can have novel elements, stemming from the individual writer's creativity with existing cultural forms, her unique personal experience, or changing social/historical conditions. When the women produce and publicly perform their songs, they add to personal and collective ways of thinking and acting in the world, some of which are new and radical.

If we intend to develop theories of how culture is continued and changed, we must understand how culture is remade and affected by individuals over time. That is, we must understand how individuals organize culture for themselves and others. I will suggest that one means by which individuals organize culture is through the "stories of self" that they express or enact in joining new social settings. I found these stories to be key to understanding how newcomers learned in the nonprofit conservation workplace where I recently completed an ethnographic study.

Telling stories of self is here conceived as a device that mediates changing forms of individual participation and understanding in context, that is, a device that mediates learning (Lave 1993:5–6). The stories are schemas that connect individuals to the social and cultural order, and once performed they launch or "subjunctivize" (to borrow Jerome Bruner's 1986 term) an individual's identity in a specific context. As individuals express or enact these stories in a new setting, the stories guide individuals' emerging sense of who they are and how they relate to other people and objects in the world. Others use individuals' stories of self to anticipate what an individual is likely to do, need, and want. In the educational relationship between old-timers and newcomers (at least among adults), stories of self mediate what is of special interest to newcomers to learn and what is made important for old-timers to teach. Thus, telling stories of self affects how individuals learn and what they know. Stories also can affect the cultural worlds of those who tell them and those who hear them. Telling stories of self in context, then, seems one apt metaphor for an active inventive individual in an anthropological conception of the learner.

DISCUSSION

Stories have attracted the attention of a few anthropologists interested in learning.[1] Dorothy Holland and Debra Skinner (1987), for example, found (counter to their expectation based on cognitive-structure analysis) that attribute lists of gender types elicited from men and women about the world of romantic relationships were insufficient to summarize how their respondents were speaking or thinking about the cultural world of romance. To explain gender types to the researchers, respondents put the gender types into stories, thereby revealing characteristic behaviors, intentions, beliefs, and disruptions. Holland and Skinner realized that "the respondents were thinking of the types in terms of social dramas rather than single attributes" (1987:87). Their findings suggest that knowledge of social types is not learned or remembered in terms of attributes but in terms of stories.

In a 1991 report of a study of Alcoholics Anonymous, Carole Cain argues that becoming a full-fledged member of the group means losing one's old identity and acquiring a new one. Fundamental to the new identity is learning to tell one's personal story in terms of a specific AA story structure. Cain writes:

> As [the drinker] learns the AA story structure, he [learns] to see the events and experiences of his own life as evidence for alcoholism. He learns to put his own events and experiences into an AA story, and thus learns to tell, and to understand, his own life as an AA story. He reinterprets his own past, from the understanding he once had of himself as a normal drinker, to the understanding he now has of himself as an alcoholic. [Cain 1991:233]

Sara Harkness and her colleagues (Harkness et al. 1992) reveal these processes in more detail. Harkness, Super, and Keefer studied first-time parents, propelled into a new context in which they must work to fashion an identity. The parents in the study initiated this identity formation process by telling stories about their children to others. The stories referenced three domains: recollections of the parents' upbringing (positive and negative elements); concerns derived from their informal conversations with other parents; and the information they gained from reading or listening to child-rearing experts. Using elements from the three domains, new parents projected models of appropriate parent behavior and relationship with the child. A model gave the parents a way to think about themselves and to organize their child-rearing behavior for awhile, until some perceived change in the child, themselves, or what they were hearing from others created the need for a new model. In this sense, Harkness et al. described individuals actively and productively "organizing culture" for themselves and those around them. From the particulars of individuals' interpretations of their previous and present experiences, in conjunction with their interpretation of the received wisdom of others, new mothers and fathers formulated stories of parenthood. As parents expressed their stories, they established a conceptual frame that was in turn embodied materially in their interactions with their child and other caregivers.

In a similar way, newcomers [to the nonprofit conservative corporation that Eisenhart calls "CC"] contributed to forming themselves into possible selves within the organization as they interpreted their past and present personal experiences for the CC audience. The claims that they publicly made about themselves had consequences for how they learned (e.g., from whom, for what reasons) and what they came to know (e.g., to demonstrate, to be recognized for).

In complex societies, entering new situations or statuses often requires that individuals identify themselves anew, both to themselves and for others. In the Cain example, the process of identification entailed the gradual reformulation of the story of one's past self into a new story of self consistent with the organization's "party line." For new parents in the Harkness et al. study, identification was an ongoing process of telling "appropriate" stories of self and child by deft use of existing cultural categories, social norms, and personal experiences. For Marty and Dave [two new CC employees whose stories are the subject of Eisenhart's analysis], identification occurred as the stories they told propelled them into specific trajectories of learning.

Thus, telling stories about self is not only a way to demonstrate membership in a group or to claim an identity within it. Telling stories about self is also a means of becoming; a means by which an individual helps to shape and project identities in social and cultural spaces, and a way of thinking about learning that requires the individual to be active, as well as socially and culturally responsive.

Marty and Dave tell their own stories and respond to the effects of their telling. They are neither simply soaking up, like a fax, what is presented to them, nor are they simply playing whatever tune comes to mind for the pure enjoyment of it, like the jazz player. The stories they tell are mediational devices that enable certain kinds of newcomer experiences and disable others; they affect how the newcomers are treated by others, and they anticipate the kind of identities available to them in the organization. Although social and cultural patterns set parameters, there is considerable "space" within the organization for individuals, even within the same program area (as Dave and Marty were), to make different connections, anticipate different identities, and to learn different things. Further, although such spaces are constrained, individuals' actions within them are formative for them as individuals and consequential for culture change.

IMPLICATIONS

It has not been customary in anthropological or educational research to think of individual learners as actively constructing social or cultural categories—that is, as engaged in a social, cognitive, and emotional process in which one works to interpret the past, construct the present, and launch the future. To do so is to expand the traditional subject matter of educational anthropology. This view of the learner also alters conventional thinking about education. Rarely, for example, are students in school given opportunities to express, as Marty and Dave did, how they are thinking about themselves with respect to new activities or categories in the school or beyond. Even more rare is any attempt on the part of school adults to act on the basis of such expressions. This omission is especially striking when one considers findings such as those of Holland (1992), who demonstrates that resistance, avoidance, and lack of interest—when newcomers do not "have their hearts in it" or, in other words, when they do not identify themselves as agents or actors in a cultural or social system—are associated with strikingly less expertise. In education circles, we focus on making logical presentations, increasing students' self-esteem, and even encouraging them to construct their own explanations. We rarely make storytelling about self or joining an activity or institution even an option.

It also has not been customary to think that newcomers, for example, students, could or do exert any pressure on the system to change. Yet, as new kinds of students enter U.S. schools and old solutions no longer seem to work with new problems, it seems patently obvious that changes are occurring. They may eventually be formalized in policy or given catchy category labels by the media, but to begin with, they are being negotiated every day among teachers, students, and parents.

These insights suggest that anthropologically informed studies of adult learning and learning outside of schools have something important to offer educational research. In particular, we can begin to see the outline of an alternative to developmental theories that take children's learning as the standard. In psychology, attempts to conceptualize adult learning suffer by comparison to child development. Child development is usually viewed in terms of advances stemming from physical and cognitive changes of increasing complexity and sophistication. While adults also change, the changes are not ordinarily thought of as "advances" (Cole and Cole 1993). If, however, learning is conceived as changing forms of participation in context, or changes that transform newcomers into old-timers, outsiders into insiders, or amateurs into experts, then it becomes possible to apply the same conceptual tools to children and adults. Regardless of age, the focus of development research would be the mediational devices used by people in various contexts, and the personal, social, and cultural consequences of engaging these devices over time (Cole 1992). Developmental theories could then be directed at understanding the processes of re-creating and changing culture, including but not limited to the contributions of individuals (Bruner 1986). In such a project, adolescents and adults could well become the center, rather than the periphery, of developmental research.

Telling stories of self in new contexts is one mediational device that warrants more attention by researchers interested in both development and culture. Harrison White recently has written, "Stories come to frame choices, from among those innumerable distinctions and nuances that could be imposed upon relationships in hindsight or from the outside" (1992:87). Stories and storytelling provide clues to an understanding of the individual learner in culture.

ACKNOWLEDGMENTS

Portions of this chapter were originally presented at the 1993 Annual Meeting of the American Anthropological Association, In Washington, DC. I would like to express special thanks to Joe Harding, Alex Harding, Maurene Flory, Liza Finkel, Marki LeCompte, and the AEQ reviewers for their comments on earlier versions of the chapter. I also want to thank the people of CC who welcomed me and helped me with this study.

NOTE

1. In educational research, see also Bruner (1986) and Connelly and Clandinin's (1990) use of teacher narratives as metaphors for teaching-learning relationships.

REFERENCES

Atkinson, Paul. 1991. *Urban Confessions: The Morphology of Ethnographer's Tales.* Paper presented to the Gregory Stone Symposium, San Francisco, CA, February.
Bruner, Jerome. 1986 . *Actual Minds, Possible Worlds.* Cambridge, MA: Harvard University Press.
Cain, Carole. 1991. Personal Stories: Identity Acquisition and Self-Understanding in Alcoholics Anonymous. *Ethos* 19(2):210–253.
Cole, Michael. 1992. Culture in Development. In *Developmental Psychology: An Advanced Textbook.* Marc Bornstein and Michael Lamb, eds. Pp.731–789. Hillsdale, NJ: Lawrence Erlbaum.
Cole, Michael, and Sheila Cole. 1993. *The Development of Children.* Second edition. New York: Scientific American Books.
Connelly, F. Michael, and D. Jean Clandinin. 1990. Stories of Experience and Narrative Inquiry. *Educational Researcher* 19(4):2–14.

D'Andrade, Roy, and Claudia Strauss, eds. 1992. *Human Motives and Cultural Models*. Cambridge: Cambridge University Press.

diLeonardo, Micaela. 1984. *The Varieties of Ethnic Experience: Kinship, Class and Gender among California Italian-Americans*. Ithaca, NY: Cornell University Press.

Eisenhart, Margaret. 1988. *Ideas for the Study of Cultural Acquisition*. Paper presented at the annual meeting of the American Anthropological Association, Phoenix, AZ.

———. 1990. Learning to Romance: Cultural Acquisition in College. *Anthropology and Education Quarterly* 21(1):19-40.

Engel, Barbara. 1993. Sister of their Sisters: Russian Women, The Revolutionary Legacy, and the Denial of Personal Life. Talk given at the First Annual Elizabeth Gee Outstanding Scholarship Award Recipient Presentation, University of Colorado, Boulder, CO.

Engeström, Yrjö. 1993. Work as a Testbench of Activity Theory. In *Understanding Practice: Perspectives on Activity and Context*. Seth Chaiklin and Jean Lave, eds. Pp. 64–103. Cambridge: Cambridge University Press.

Erickson, Frederick. 1982.Taught Cognitive Learning in Its Immediate Environments: A Neglected Topic in the Anthropology of Education. *Anthropology and Education Quarterly* 13(2):149–180.

Firth, Raymond. 1936. *We, the Tikopia*. London: Allen & Unwin.

Fordham, Signithia, and John Ogbu. 1986. Black Students' School Success: Coping with the "Burden of 'Acting White'." *Urban Review* 18(3):176–206.

Fortes, Meyer. 1938. Social and Psychological Aspects of Education in Taleland. *Africa* 11(4):supplement.

Gearing, Frederick. 1974. Anthropology and Education. In *Handbook of Social and Cultural Anthropology*. J. Honigmann, ed. Pp. 1223–1249. New York: Rand McNally.

Harkness, Sara, Charles Super, and Constance Keefer. 1992. Learning to Be an American Parent: How Cultural Models Gain Directive Force. In *Human Motives and Cultural Models*. Roy D'Andrade and Claudia Strauss, eds. Pp. 163–178. Cambridge: Cambridge University Press.

Holland, Dorothy. 1992. How Cultural Systems Become Desire: A Case Study of American Romance. In *Human Motives and Cultural Models*. Roy D'Andrade and Claudia Strauss, eds. Pp. 61–89. Cambridge: Cambridge University Press.

Holland, Dorothy, and Margaret Eisenhart. 1990. *Educated in Romance: Women, Achievement, and College Culture*. Chicago: University of Chicago Press.

Holland, Dorothy, and Debra Skinner. 1987. Prestige and Intimacy: The Cultural Models behind Americans' Talk about Gender Types. In *Cultural Models in Language and Thought*. Dorothy Holland and Naomi Quinn, eds. Pp. 78–111. Cambridge: Cambridge University Press.

———. 1995. Contested Ritual, Contested Femininities: (Re)forming Self and Society in a Nepali Women's Festival. *American Ethnologist* 22(2).

Kondo, Dorinne. 1990. *Crafting Selves: Power, Gender, and Discourses of Identity in a Japanese Workplace*. Chicago: University of Chicago Press.

Lave, Jean. 1993. The Practice of Learning. In *Understanding Practice: Perspectives on Activity and Context*. Seth Chaiklin and Jean Lave, eds. Pp. 3–32. Cambridge: Cambridge University Press.

Lave, Jean, and Etienne Wenger. 1991. *Situated Learning: Legitimate Peripheral Participation*. Cambridge: Cambridge University Press.

Linde, Charlotte. 1990. *Narrative as a Resource for the Social Constitution of Self.* Technical Report No. IRL 90-0020. Palo Alto, CA: Institute for Research on Learning.

Markus, Hazel, and Paula Nurius. 1987. Possible Selves: The Interface between Motivation and the Self-concept. In *Identity and Self: Psychosocial Perspectives.* Krysia Yardley and Terry Honess, eds. Pp. 157-172. Chicester: John Wiley and Sons.

Mead, Margaret. 1928. *Coming of Age in Samoa.* New York: Morrow.

Plath, David. 1980. *Long Engagements: Maturity in Modern Japan.* Stanford: Stanford University Press.

Quinn, Naomi. 1992. The Motivational Force of Self-Understanding: Evidence from Wives' Inner Conflicts. In *Human Motives and Cultural Models.* Roy D'Andrade and Claudia Strauss, eds. Pp. 90–126. Cambridge: Cambridge University Press.

Sanjek, Roger. 1990. On Ethnographic Validity. In *Fieldnotes: The Makings of Anthropology.* Roger Sanjek, ed. Pp. 385–418. Ithaca, NY: Cornell University Press.

Spindler, George. 1974. The Transmission of Culture. In *Education and Cultural Process.* George Spindler, ed. Pp. 279–310. New York: Holt, Rinehart, and Winston.

Spindler, George, and Louise Spindler. 1991. Reactions and Worries. *Anthropology and Education Quarterly* 22(3):274–278.

Strauss, Claudia. 1992. Models and Motives. In *Human Motives and Cultural Models.* Roy D'Andrade and Claudia Strauss, eds. Pp. 1–20. Cambridge: Cambridge University Press.

Traweek, Sharon. 1988. *Beamtimes and Lifetimes: The World of High Energy Physicists.* Cambridge, MA: Harvard University Press.

Walkerdine, Valerie. 1988. *The Mastery of Reason: Cognitive Development and the Production of Rationality.* New York: Routledge.

Wertsch, James. 1991. *Voices of the Mind: A Sociocultural Approach to Mediated Action.* Cambridge, MA: Harvard University Press.

White, Harrison. 1992. *Identity and Control: A Structural Theory of Social Action.* Princeton, NJ: Princeton University Press.

Whiting, Beatrice, and John W. M. Whiting. 1975. *Children of Six Cultures: A Psychocultural Analysis.* Cambridge, MA: Harvard University Press.

Willis, Paul. 1977. *Learning to Labor: How Working Class Kids Get Working Class Jobs.* New York: Columbia University Press.

Wolcott, Harry. 1982. The Anthropology of Learning. *Anthropology and Education Quarterly* 13(2):83–108.

———. 1991. Propriospect and the Acquisition of Culture. *Anthropology and Education Quarterly* 22(3):251–273.

Afterword

Implications for Educational Policy and Practice

Bradley A. U. Levinson and Margaret Sutton

This book provides rich resources for teaching and learning about broad social and cultural issues in education. At the same time, it raises a question often heard by instructors in educational foundations courses, and that is, "What is the practical relevance of this material?"—to policy formation, curriculum design, school administration, classroom pedagogy, and so on. This is a fair question, but not an easy one to answer. Social and cultural analysis in education is often more akin to "basic" than "applied" research, to use a distinction common in the natural sciences. The primary purpose of this work is to clarify and expand existing insights, illuminate new concepts, raise new questions, and to reframe perspectives on longstanding issues. To be sure, a few of the authors in this book—notably several in section III—do offer specific ideas for improving educational policy and practice that flow from their research. Most, however, leave the reader to draw out such ideas in the context of his or her own specific experiences and understandings. This kind of contingent "application" is compatible with the interpretive enterprise in which the authors are engaged.

Although social and cultural analyses of education rarely yield immediate applications, they are rich in broad *implications* for policies and practices in education.[1] We prefer the term "implications" rather than "applications" here because of its more flexible and variable meaning. There is, of course, good reason not to insist on immediately identifiable "applications" of this work to improving educational policy or practice. This is because, typically, an "application" is thought to be a relatively uncomplicated procedure or innovation that flows naturally from the findings of a research project. More than any other theme, however, this book illustrates the importance of *context* to educational processes, and therefore indicates the dangers of prescribing specific educational practices that are thought to work well across all contexts. The collective message of this work is to attend to the

378

particularities of each educational context.[2] Thus, the kinds of implications emerging from foundations work must be pointedly specific for certain educational contexts, or, alternatively, sufficiently general to "travel" well, and be adaptable to a variety of possible contexts. For instance, Shirley Brice Heath's findings (section III) about differences in narrative styles between children's homes and their schools has implications for teacher training. She discovers that the narrative styles deeply embedded in two working-class communities conflict with the narrative style prevailing at the local school. Such conflict spells potential trouble for these working-class students' school achievement. Heath's insights might encourage teacher educators to develop inquiry procedures through which teachers regularly investigate the home literacy practices of students, so as to build upon such narrative styles in classroom instruction. This kind of effort to transform cultural discontinuity between homes and schools into cultural congruence could take similar, but certainly not identical, form in other schools and communities.

Together the readings in this book provide a mandate for devoting societal resources to the development of what we might call increased multicultural and intercultural awareness. Such awareness is important because, even as we might identify common implications across the readings, we must be wary of suggesting common solutions. The work collected here does not decree specific actions but rather the cultivation of multicultural perspectives and concepts that will inform thinking about educational policies and practices. This is another way of suggesting the implications of such work. The often-stated purpose of the field of anthropology—"to make the strange familiar, and the familiar, strange"—speaks to this cultivation of multicultural and intercultural awareness.

The readings in section II most clearly realize the first half of this purpose, making the strange familiar. Learning about the recent introduction of schools into societies that previously did not have them serves to alert readers to the universal qualities of formal schooling, as well as to the diversity of practices that underlie surface similarities. In a similar vein, cultural congruence or conflict studies like those presented in section III can illuminate to outsiders the meaning of what may previously have seemed like alien behaviors. For the teachers of Trackton and Roadville students, Heath's study clearly made their "strange" narrative styles more comfortably familiar (see Heath 1983). Such a comparative perspective opens up new depths of understanding.

The book as a whole speaks powerfully to the second purpose, of making the familiar strange. For all who have learned to become part of the formal schooling system, nothing could seem more natural than the features of this system as it now exists. By definition, college students and university-based scholars are people who have already spent many successful years mastering the forms of schooling. It is thus imperative that we learn to make these familiar educational forms into something strange again. Only then can we learn to see schools as young or culturally unfamiliar students might see them. Only then can we stop taking for granted the education occurring in homes and other nonschool sites (think of how Jan Nespor, in section V, shows the educational importance of popular culture outside school). The authors in this book typically develop sharp and sensitive ethnographic portraits of educational exchanges, and thereby expose some of the underlying practices and assumptions operating in and out of schools.

It is perhaps best to understand some of the foundations work represented in this book as a form of social or cultural critique (cf. Marcus and Fischer 1986). By "seeing" more clearly, through ethnographic detail and cultural interpretation (Wolcott 1999), these authors show us how some educational practices damage children, limit their potential, or contradict our cultural ideals. The larger study from which Jules Henry's selection is taken (section I), a book called *Culture against Man*, could be located in this tradition of critique. Among other things, Henry tried to show how U.S. schools of the 1950s overwhelmingly emphasized student docility, and brainwashed children to hate a society (the Soviet Union) they had barely begun to understand. Studies in section IV by Donna Eder and Hugh Mehan also demonstrate such elements of critique, as does the piece by Signithia Fordham in section V. Each of these authors identifies school-based practices that label students and thereby limit their ability to envision themselves as fully capable and empowered learners. Eder critiques ability grouping, Mehan critiques the representation of a "learning disabled" student, and Fordham critiques the prevailing perceptions of "loud" black girls. Though not made explicit, the reader is invited to imagine the implications that flow from such critique—the modification or abolition of ability grouping, the reform of special education assessment techniques, or a more forthright dialogue on race and gender in the high school. By making the familiar strange, this work encourages a critical perspective that is invaluable for constructing effective educational policy and practice in specific contexts. It also undermines forever the assumption, indeed the false confidence, that the effects of a policy or practice will necessarily reflect its overtly stated purpose. Such loss of innocence may be mourned in a small child, but it should be celebrated in educational practitioners![3]

In addition to fostering a critical perspective that emphasizes the importance of context to effective educational practice, the readings in this book, especially those in the last section, emphasize the meaning and importance to education of cultural change. So deep are the recent changes documented by Sherry Ortner, Jan Nespor, and Margaret Eisenhart (section V), among others, that we must ask what it means in the twenty-first century to speak of a community, let alone how specific communities might be identified and their symbolic systems understood. This creates an at-times daunting challenge for educational practitioners. If an educator wishes to design an activity that is "culturally appropriate," where would she begin to gain a grasp of the culture(s) in which her students live? To some extent, this is an old question that is magnified by the rapid communications and mobility of this epoch. As Levinson (introduction) and Eisenhart (section V) have already pointed out, the idea that common group membership implies identical values and beliefs has always been mistaken. What is different now is the increased difficulty of ascribing group membership to any person. Individuals are increasingly likely to de-velop multiple and shifting cultural identities, and therefore a complex repertoire of cultural membership.

Thus, the studies in this book undermine simple beliefs about stable group mem-bership and shared values and beliefs among presumed "members" of a cultural group. We submit that in so doing, these studies ultimately imply a set of funda-mental value premises for educational policy and practice. Such premises speak to the deliberative processes underlying the construction of policy and practice. A cumulative reading of the articles in this book suggests that the more we know about diversity and cultural change, the less we can assume that we know *a priori* about any one person or group or community. Therefore, constructing curriculum and pedagogy that speaks to students and draws out their desire to learn, or formulat-ing policy that addresses diverse educational needs, requires a constant process of inquiry on the part of the educator. And in order to result in effective policy and practice, that inquiry will need to be grounded in democratic ideals. Ultimately, the greatest implication of social and cultural foundations work for educational policy and practice is to foster a robust democratic dialogue, and the full participa-tion of all communities, in the definition of schooling processes.

NOTES

1. In the title to this brief afterword, we reproduce a familiar distinction between "policy" and "practice." Following convention, "policy" is considered the guidelines and binding rules governing the conduct of education, and "practice" is the actual conduct, typically the ac-tions of teachers and students in schools. Yet the making of official educational policy it-self can be seen as a kind of social practice, even as educational practice in schools may constitute very local kinds of "policies" (Levinson and Sutton 2000). In thereby exploding the conventional distinction between policy and practice, we open up further space for think-ing about the implications of the foundations work in this volume.

2. This is a point that Evelyn Jacob (1999), in her recent work on cooperative learning reforms in U.S. elementary schools, drives home particularly well.

3. Fortunately, the potential loss of innocence fostered by these readings is compensated by an increase in analytic resources for coming to terms with a variety of contexts and prac-tices. The wide range of specific social contexts of education that are collected herein lay a solid groundwork for cumulative understanding of educational policy and practice. Though one can never assume, for example, that literacy practices in one community will be the same as in another, the more examples with which an educator is familiar, the more com-petent she is to understand each subsequent context that she encounters. Knowing how Huaorani mark the distinctive space of the school through dress and manner (Laura Rival, section II) alerts the educator to other nonverbal expressions of alienation from the insti-tution of schooling. Seeing exactly how ability grouping creates a dysfunctional learning environment (Eder, section IV) can lead to a more alert and nuanced approach to construct-ing groups of students for collaborative learning processes.

REFERENCES AND READINGS

Heath, Shirley Brice. 1983. *Ways with Words: Language, Life, and Work in Schools and Communities.* Cambridge: Cambridge University Press.

Jacob, Evelyn. 1999. *Cooperative Learning in Context: An Educational Innovation in Everyday Classrooms.* Albany: SUNY Press.

Levinson, Bradley, and Margaret Sutton. 2000. Policy as/in Practice: Developing a Sociocultural Approach to the Study of Educational Policy. In *Policy as Practice: Toward a Comparative Sociocultural Analysis of Educational Policy*, edited by Margaret Sutton and Bradley A. Levinson. Stamford, Conn.: Ablex.

Marcus, George, and Michael Fischer. 1986. *Anthropology as Cultural Critique.* Chicago: University of Chicago Press.

Wolcott, Harry. 1999. *Ethnography: A Way of Seeing.* Thousand Oaks, Calif.: Sage.

Index

ability grouping, 242–43, 248–57; assignment
criteria, 249, 251
academic success: in ability-grouped classrooms,
249, 255; blessings required for, 137; correlated
to learning styles, 173; demanded in ruling
class schools, 301; discouraged by peer groups,
200; East Asians and, 191; and gender
"passing," 328–29, 337–38; of minorities, 164,
191–92, 196, 200, 318; strategies to enhance,
199–200, 202–3, 336–37
academic syllabuses, 305
accommodation: without assimilation, 195–96,
201; and resistance, 290
acculturation, 83, 138
"acting White," 198–99, 201, 226
actor network theory, 345
adaptation to the environment, 84, 211
administrative practices, inadequate, 239
admission essays, college, 334–35
adulthood, 227
adult learning, 374
affective commentaries, 173, 178, 187
African American English, 162, 332
African Americans, 193, 195
African-American women: as the doubly refracted
Other, 339–40; high-achievement, patterns
for, 332–33; as loud, 331; as nothingness, 328,
331–32, 339–40; passing as the male Other,
330–31, 333–38; passing as the white female
Other, 328; Rita (composite), 329, 333–37,
342n9

agency, theory of, 139
'ágodzaahí (historical tales), 45–51
agreements reached without debate, 265
agriculture, 114
Alcoholics Anonymous story structure, 372
Alexander, K. L., 248, 257
allegiance, oaths of, 100
"all-round education," 301–2
Althusser, Louis, 240–41, 246
altruism of teachers, 145
Alwin, D. F., 248, 257
American communities, contemporary, 359, 361–
66
American Indians, 193, 198–99
analogical questions, 182–83, 186
Anglo early life experiences, 214–15
anthropological conception of the learner, 369–75
anthropological theories of learning, 322, 369–70,
374
anthropology, 3, 162, 318, 380–81; apprenticeship
of fieldwork in a tribal society, 20; of
education, 19
Anyon, J., 291, 293
Apaches, Cibecue Western, 20, 41–52
Appadurai, A., 349, 356
apprenticeships, 20, 116; as slavery, 143
Arnold, Matthew, 17
arrogance as a cultural transgression, 132
arrows "shooting" social delinquents, 45, 49–52
articulation as a fluid process, 346
arts, provisions for, 35

383